Adult Children of Dysfunctional Families

Prevention, Intervention, and Treatment for Community Mental Health Promotion

BARBARA C. WALLACE

Westport, Connecticut
London

Library of Congress Cataloging-in-Publication Data

Wallace, Barbara C.
    Adult children of dysfunctional families : prevention,
intervention, and treatment for community mental health promotion /
Barbara C. Wallace.
        p.   cm.
    Includes bibliographical references and index.
    ISBN 0–275–94475–1 (alk. paper)
    1. Adult children of dysfunctional families.   2. Problem families.
3. Family counseling.   4. Parenting—Study and teaching.   I. Title.
RC455.4.F3W335   1996
616.89—dc20   95–45415

British Library Cataloguing in Publication Data is available.

Library of Congress Catalog Card Number: 95–45415
ISBN: 0–275–94475–1

First published in 1996

Praeger Publishers, 88 Post Road West, Westport, CT 06881
An imprint of Greenwood Publishing Group, Inc.

Printed in the United States of America

The paper used in this book complies with the
Permanent Paper Standard issued by the National
Information Standards Organization (Z39.48–1984).

10 9 8 7 6 5 4 3 2

For my beloved brother, Uriel Hamilton Wallace, III (Tertio), or "Tersh," with whom I share more genes than anyone else on the planet. May our love transcend time and space.

For my dearly departed Uncle, Dr. Samuel Carey Bullock, one of the first Black psychoanalysts in the nation, who role-modeled what I wanted to pursue as my life's work.

To the memory of my deceased colleague, clinical psychologist, Lorna McIntyre, Ph.D., and the vital work to be continued in her honor involving assisting immigrant families, their descendants, contemporary dysfunctional families, and, especially, children in realizing their highest potential.

In memory of the outstanding work performed by my deceased colleague, Dr. George Drake, addictionologist and physician, on behalf of crack cocaine addicted patients.

For all the dearly departed and living clients from Terence Cardinal Cooke Health Care Center who taught me about courage, love, death, dying, and the reality of overlapping epidemics of crack and other drugs, violence, and HIV/AIDS.

To all the women of Damon House New York, Inc. who intimately expanded my knowledge of addiction, recovery, parenthood, sisterhood, surviving multiple trauma, and myself—all while I sat and learned a clinical technique for trauma resolution in our weekly, Friday afternoon Women's Group for three years, within a residential therapeutic community (January 1990 to December 1992).

For my own Involuntary Immigrant African Ancestors who adapted to the conditions of slavery in Jamaica and the United States, the Jim Crow South, and the Promised Land of the North to the best of their ability—despite numerous stressors. A dedication also goes to the millions of African slaves who died and drowned at sea during the middle passage. A special dedication goes to the Ancestors whom we thank for guidance and the miracle of survival. I AM THAT I AM; I AM, BECAUSE WE ARE!

Finally, this book is dedicated to all those workers in the trenches fighting for healing of personal and cultural trauma.

Contents

Illustrations

FIGURES

TABLES

Preface

Clinical work with crack cocaine-dependent clients at a time of the overlapping epidemics of violence, Human Immunodeficiency Virus/Acquired Immuno-deficiency Syndrome (HIV/AIDS), and various chemical dependencies exposed me to adult children of dysfunctional families who had survived childhood, adolescent, and adult trauma. The concept of a book on adult children from dysfunctional families who needed a practical approach to resolving their trauma followed from this work. However, the reality that their children vitally need prevention, intervention, and treatment as well could not be escaped. This book utilizes a war metaphor to describe our contemporary societal conditions as the backdrop for service delivery to young children, adolescents, and adults from dysfunctional families. Part I of this book provides introduction, background, and basic training materials in Chapters 1, 2, and 3, respectively.

Chapter 1 presents a broad introduction to the problem of young children, adolescents, and adults from dysfunctional families needing forms of prevention, intervention, and treatment in a variety of school and community-based settings at this time of overlapping epidemics. As this first chapter suggests, it is time to reckon with past societal failure to meet the needs of at-risk children and youth. The three central theses of the book are introduced and community mental health promotion is discussed as representing convergence of the fields of clinical psychology, chemical dependency, and health education. The objectives of the book are spelled out, underscoring how psychoeducational and therapeutic groups can be deployed as the primary tools in promoting community mental health in short-term work emphasizing brief interventions.

This consideration of brief interventions includes motivational enhancement techniques. Discussion suggests that we need to engage in community outreach to those in need of services, following an empowerment model and fostering self-determination in our clients. The book also seeks to serve as a manual for facilitating cultural competence and cultural sensitivity in practitioners, while also demystifying the behavioral change process. Principles to guide the practice of community mental health promotion are offered, while the intended audience for the book is described.

Chapter 2 provides background on the adult children of dysfunctional families movement. The origins and impact of the adult children of alcoholics grassroots movement and the role of professionals are emphasized. Discussion covers the evolutionary progression and scope of the adult child literature, as well as the contribution that this book makes.

Chapter 3 takes a historical perspective, focusing on stressors that may have played a role in promoting the evolution of dysfunctional families. The concept of both unique and common stressors that impacted diverse migrant and immigrant groups permits a focus on nativism and xenophobia—even as they may continue to be manifested up to the present day. Figure 3.1 facilitates discussion of the dynamics of how stressors contribute to family dysfunction. Basic training facilitating the achievement of cultural competence and sensitivity includes an emphasis on family strengths and using knowledge of these attributes to empower families. Training is also delivered on how to deploy the clinical technique of a culturally sensitive empathy. This chapter may be regarded as a psychoeducational curriculum providing a brief multiculural education to counselors and community members. This curriculum serves as preparation to work with a diverse client population in community outreach and counseling.

Part II comprises Chapters 4, 5, and 6. Chapter 4 presents a psychoeducational curriculum that serves as counselor training and may also be delivered by counselors or community members to parents. This psychoeducation defines healthy parenting behavior and discusses ways to avoid engaging in child neglect and abuse. The central elements of healthy parenting behavior are discussed as analogous to a kind of counseling style and guide for healthy interpersonal behavior in general.

The violence epidemic and the resulting crisis in schools and communities have created a need for primary, secondary, and tertiary violence prevention models. Chapter 5 introduces a group model of psychoeducation for primary violence prevention that may be delivered in school and other community-based settings as a nine week one session per week curriculum. Group discussion within this model is fostered via a review of media and research evidence contained within the curriculum. Definitions also serve to increase knowledge of the root causes of violence, moving group members toward changing health beliefs on violence as well as changing violent behavior. A brief multicultural education is also provided to group members.

To facilitate enduring cognitive and behavioral change, it is recommended that a group continue across weeks 10 to 15 and participate in secondary violence prevention, as described in Chapter 6. Group members gain exposure to a psychoeducational curriculum that provides more definitions and stimulates more personal group discussion, while opportunities for role play are also made available. Chapter 6 prepares group members for the work of trauma resolution in groups, taking the time to provide a comprehensive education in ego psychology by covering definitions of defenses.

The extensive use of metaphor in training makes the process of trauma resolution in groups accessible and understandable to a wide audience, permitting implementation in diverse settings. Chapter 6 also serves as a foundation chapter for counselors who benefit from the psychoeducation provided on the process of trauma resolution and the nature of defensive functioning. Many community members exposed to media, interpersonal, family, school, gang, and community violence have sustained trauma and need access to trauma resolution. Hence, Chapter 6 serves as a vital handbook for this work. We cannot ignore the fact that many students and community members have perpetrated acts of violence and require something more intensive to ensure enduring cognitive and behavioral change. Therefore, a second part of Chapter 6 delivers a relapse prevention model against violence, or tertiary prevention. Ideally, all group members continue across weeks 16 to 30 and participate in the tertiary prevention model, incorporating continuation of the task of working through and integrating memories of either being a victim of, witness to, or perpetrator of violence. Meanwhile, in sessions 16 to 30, group members learn to engage in a microanalysis of their past relapse episodes and rehearse and role play how to actively cope in high-risk situations for relapse to violence.

Together, Chapters 5 and 6 provide an academic-year-long curriculum for violence prevention that can be delivered in school or other community-based settings. The curriculum may be adapted to a variety of settings, as it is designed to be flexible and tailored to a community's characteristics and needs. These two chapters also constitute a training manual for teachers and peer educators who may deliver the curriculum. The basic prevention model could also be tailored for other problem behaviors such as compulsive overeating, gambling, or inconsistent condom use.

Part III provides even more in-depth training for the task of trauma resolution by grounding the rationale for the deployment of counseling techniques in integrated theory. Chapters 7, 8, 9, and 10 prepare counselors for the task of trauma resolution in individual and group settings, beginning with Chapter 7's presentation of a graphic and visual method of capturing moments of original trauma and predicting possible alterations or permutations of that trauma.

Utilizing the case of Nancy, Chapter 7 advances two tenets of psychotherapy: (1) If we know the trauma, we can figure out the client's problematic interpersonal behavioral dramas, as well as anticipate them before they manifest, and ultimately transform them via replacement with healthy patterns of interpersonal relating; (2) if clients possess poor self-regulation of affects, impulses, self-esteem, and interpersonal behavior, the risk of regression, relapse, and symptom substitution remains high unless underlying problems in self-regulation are addressed. Following these two tenets of counseling work for trauma resolution, Chapter 7 proceeds to deliver an integration of drive, ego, object relations, and self-psychology, as well as cognitive-behavioral theory. This chapter lays the theoretical foundation and presents the rationale for the deployment of counseling techniques. These recommended techniques include interpretation, affect labeling, empathic mirroring, and cognitive restructuring—including a heavy reliance on the same metaphors utilized in training.

Chapter 8 prepares clients to engage in a group counseling model that seeks to resolve trauma and improve client self-regulation. This chapter presents a client workbook as the tool which prepares clients for group work. As introduction to the workbook and task of trauma resolution to be accomplished in group counseling, the case of Ms. E. is presented. The workbook begins with basic psychological principles that will be evoked in group sessions at moments when psychoeducation needs to be delivered to clarify the group process or a member's experience in the group.

Chapter 9 describes a four-phase model of group work for which clients have been prepared via Chapter 8 and counselors have been trained in Chapters 3 through 7. Chapter 9 explains the manner in which group work may proceed on a level involving psychoeducation, articulation of trauma, "here and now" analysis of problematic interpersonal behavioral dramas, or working through and integrating of traumatic memories—as the four phases of the model. A graphic model of the mind is introduced, which is based in the integrated theory presented in Chapter 7. The graphic model further trains counselors in how to facilitate a therapeutic regression in the service of a client's self-observing ego to fixation points for resolution of trauma. Consistent with the overall thrust of the book, complex theory and psychoanalytic concepts find clear explication with the extensive use of metaphor. This follows from the intent to make treatment accessible to a large population in need of trauma resolution.

Responding to a mental health and physical crisis facing women, Part III ends with Chapter 10, a model of trauma resolution for the battered, the couple, and the batterer. The stages of change model, empathic mirroring as a form of motivational counseling, and relapse prevention are integrated in a practical approach to domestic violence. Case examples that preserve client confidentiality and extensive metaphors are used to train counselors. Counselors may pursue work with either the battered partner who seeks to secretly prepare to leave the batterer, with the couple, or with the batterer alone who desires to change violent behavior. This chapter also offer a novel approach to relapse prevention against a return to domestic violence.

The conclusion presents two compelling case histories that capture the nature of our overlapping epidemics and the resulting societal challenges for which this book was written. A description of the group process of an alcohol and drug recovery group for end-stage AIDS patients illustrates deployment of counseling techniques taught in the book. A discussion of future directions in research concludes the book. The book serves as a training manual for counselors, school psychologists, teachers, volunteers, and peer educators in a spectrum of future grant-funded research that seeks to evaluate the models offered in the book.

I

INTRODUCTION, BACKGROUND,
AND BASIC TRAINING

1

Introduction

As the twenty-first century approaches, we face the devastating societal impact of three overlapping epidemics—the crack cocaine and other drug use epidemic, a violence epidemic, and the HIV/AIDS epidemic. Battle and war metaphors abounded during the height of the cocaine and crack cocaine epidemic in the late 1980s. President George Bush declared our nation's war on drugs, as he displayed a bag of crack cocaine on national television. However, the crack cocaine epidemic was accompanied by a corresponding increase in the availability of handguns and a subsequent rise in violent murders and drive-by shootings (Blumenthal, 1992; Blumstein, 1994; Klein, Maxson, & Cunningham, 1991; Tabor, 1992). Adding to our sense of war raging across this nation, a public health crisis involving violence has been declared (Centers For Disease Control, 1994a, 1994b; Hawkins, 1990a, 1990b; Wood, 1990). Well into its second decade, the HIV/AIDS epidemic ravages injection drug users and their sexual partners now in the 1990s (Des Jarlais, 1992; Moss & Vranizan, 1992). The year 1995 marks a full decade that we have been working with the crack cocaine dependent (Wallace, 1991). Sexually promiscuous crack cocaine users and their sexual partners also succumb to HIV/AIDS, creating a "new wave" of the AIDS epidemic (Carlson & Siegal, 1991; Inciardi, Lockwood, & Pottieger, 1993; Ratner, 1993).

The white homosexual male community has long been decimated by AIDS. However, this trail of tears and deaths from AIDS is now occurring in other communities as well. Male homosexuals and bisexuals of color are now dying in high numbers, along with drug users and their heterosexual partners, while entire social networks are impacted by this disease (Mandell et al., 1994; Perez-

Stable, 1994; Pivnick et al., 1994; Winiarski, 1995). Infants and children with AIDS (Kuhn et al., 1994) battle and either outlive parents, or die before their parents (Goedert & Cote, 1994; Shelov, 1994; Weiner et al., 1994). Even as we utilize a war metaphor, the reality of the high numbers of deaths from HIV/AIDS and homicide suggests that we are losing young lives at a rate that surpasses past actual wars, and that we are engaged in a particularly treacherous and protracted war.

For those of us willing to battle in the trenches against this war, some vital, shorthand directives seem urgently needed for training and preparation. This book serves as both a training manual for preparation and a "handbook" for actual use while working in the trenches of our contemporary war. We seek to assist a population scarred not only from the trauma of violence-ridden childhoods, but also from the violence of the crack and other drug cultures. A prior silent epidemic of violence plagued many of the childhood and adolescent lives of our current front line soldiers, as they coped with parental alcoholism, parental heroin addiction, domestic violence, physical abuse, sexual abuse, verbal abuse, and neglect (Wallace, 1991). Given a decade of experience addressing the violence and trauma associated with a history of suffering child abuse within dysfunctional families, as well as the trauma of addiction and hitting rock bottom in a violent drug culture, a body of knowledge may be codified at this time in a handbook. We are now able to offer valuable training, directives, and instructions for use in battle. The "basic training" in Part I, intermediate training in Part II, and advanced training in Part III are presented in this "handbook" with the hope that a volunteer army corps will find practical utility in this tool.

The conditions of the past decade served as the context for learning about the contemporary adult children of dysfunctional families. We only came to know of the dimensions of their past abuse in dysfunctional families and present suffering because they had become caught up in the crack cocaine or other drug epidemic. The body of knowledge compiled in the 1970s and 1980s about the adult children of dysfunctional families who became alcoholic or presented other traits needs to be augmented with information applicable to working with our more diverse contemporary population of adult children of dysfunctional families. Contemporary times also demand a new level of cultural awareness in working with people of color who occupy the ranks of adult children of dysfunctional families (Harris-Offutt, 1992). Adult children of color have desperate needs at this time, particularly in urban communities.

A TIME FOR RECKONING WITH PAST SOCIETAL FAILURES

The current overlapping epidemics of drugs, violence, and HIV/AIDS require the kind of response that forces us to reckon with past societal failures. Our failures as a society not only include neglecting the needs of children, adolescents, adults, and entire communities in the 1980s to 1990s, but also hearken back to the 1950s, 1960s and 1970s when children, adolescents, and families also possessed pressing needs. As suggested below, several areas may be identified in which we have failed as a society to make adequate provisions for these groups. Society failed to provide adequate

1. HIV/AIDS prevention education—to comuunities of color in particular.
2. Gun control in an era when the crack epidemic spawned spiraling homicide rates and community violence.
3. Treatment and relapse prevention for a large segment of the injection drug use and crack cocaine population.
4. Outreach to those who never entered treatment facilities, or had been rejected for admission/retention because of strict criteria, weeding out those with psychiatric, medical, or behavioral problems leading to violation of treatment program rules.
5. Prevention, intervention and treatment to those who suffered violence, abuse, and neglect when growing up as children and adolescents in dysfunctional families.

Because of our multiple failures, in terms of an inadequate societal response in these five areas, a number of questions now haunt us as we examine the lives of our contemporary adult children. What happened to those who were rejected by therapeutic communities for psychiatric histories and possession of dual diagnoses? What happened to those who first attempted treatment before the creation of specially designed MICA (mentally ill chemical abuser) programs and were rejected by traditional therapeutic communities? What happened to the hordes of crack users who left therapeutic communities—originally designed for injection heroin users—before just one, or three, six, or twelve months had passed? What happened to those crack users who responded poorly to confrontational techniques designed for heroin users, or who were expelled for violation of program rules? More specifically, what happened to those who were thrown out of programs because of a relapse to drug use, or because of sexual or violent acting-out behavior? What happened to those whom we intuitively knew lacked the coping skills to maintain a clean and sober state, and for whom past prostitution had been a survivor skill? Given isolated attempts at outreach, what happened to those who relapsed and shared injection equipment, had sex without condoms, and may have acquired or transmitted HIV? To what extent did inadequate gun control permit the drug distribution trade to introduce carnage into communities overrun with desperate chemically dependent clients not in treatment?

As much as some of us talked about and longed for client access to treatment on demand, it did not exist and society now reaps what was sown via that harsh reality. As we wonder what happened, too many clients walk through the doors of an endstage AIDS unit where I consult and tell me what happened—if they possess the energy and cognitive clarity to answer questions within an assessment interview. Nonetheless, their lives embody the facts of overlapping crack and other drug use, violence, and HIV/AIDS epidemics, and of our societal failure. As we trace their life paths back spanning prior decades, we face the ramifications of other societal failures. Their lives provide answers to yet another question: What happened to those children who experienced forms of abandonment, neglect, violence, abuse, and trauma, but received neither early prevention, intervention, nor treatment in the 1950s, 1960s, and 1970s? In this manner, we speak of the vulnerabilities of our contemporary adult children that go back to their survival and negotiation of dysfunctional families. We speak of a prior silent epidemic that occurred within dysfunctional families, involving forms of child abuse and neglect. This question also forces us to consider the diverse types of dysfunctional families that include phenomena of more recent decades such as the increase of families headed by single parents, impacted by divorce, and having to cope with merged families upon remarriage. We face a crisis wherein as many as three generations within a family have been fatherless, as contemporary adult children search for models of how to successfully engage in parenting (Lewin, 1995). Other contemporary dysfunctional families similarly involve generation after generation being stuck in patterns of family violence involving battering and physical abuse among family members. Sexual abuse, as our most silent crime committed against children, remains another cause of family dysfunction to be found among our contemporary adult children (Blume, 1990; Haugaard & Repucci, 1989; Hunter, 1990; Shengold, 1989).

We also face children and adolescents of the 1980s and 1990s who are from our more contemporary dysfunctional families for whom we may still inquire regarding the current and likely future ramifications of their not receiving adequate prevention, intervention, and treatment. These children and adolescents have grown up in war zones with parents preoccupied with their personal battles of addiction, encounters with violence, and HIV/AIDS. Contemporary life in the war zone and in our diverse contemporary dysfunctional families has exposed youth to interpersonal, family, school, gang, and community violence (Durant et al., 1994). Never before in our history have youth in the United States grown up and lived an extended number of years in war zones of the kind created by our three overlapping epidemics. Far too many youth have been raised by grandparents, aunts, single parents, and foster parents (Chamberlain, Moreland & Reid, 1992; Cimmarusti, 1992; Minkler et al., 1994; Pecora, Fraser, & Haapala, 1992) with many destined to be orphans of deceased soldiers in the twenty-first century. Recognition of the widespread existence of offspring from dysfunctional families creates the need for prevention, intervention, and treatment for community mental health promotion. Engagement in primary, secondary, and tertiary prevention represents a way to begin to deal with our past and present societal failure to adequately meet the needs of families and communities.

THE THREE CENTRAL THESES OF THE BOOK

This book maintains that our nation has always been characterized by conditions that could foster the creation of dysfunctional families. By virtue of the unique and multiple stressors attendant to involuntary and voluntary immigration from a distant shore, as well as from migration within this nation (Takaki, 1987, 1990), dysfunctional family structures readily came into existence. This thesis gives rise to a culturally sensitive approach that embraces those of Italian, Irish, African, Polish, German, and Puerto Rican descent, as well as each and every migrant, immigrant, ethnic, religious, and cultural group. Adult children are urged to obtain a multicultural education that at the very least sensitizes them to the experiences of their own ancestors and relatives during immigration and migration—as they had to negotiate multiple stressors. Cultural competence is fostered by discussion of this thesis, as readers come to appreciate the historical, cultural, and social experiences of diverse ethnic, religious, and cultural groups. Psychoeducation is also provided which assists us in empowering families as we learn to identify family strengths that were historically, and tend to be generally, produced to help cope with multiple stressors.

As this introduction seeks to underscore, however, the overlapping epidemics of drugs, violence, and HIV/AIDS have combined in an unprecedented manner to create unique conditions toward the end of the twenty-first century. These unique conditions involve unprecedented numbers of children, adolescents, and adults struggling within dysfunctional families. These conditions call for the preparation of professionals, paraprofessionals, the recovering chemically dependent, the HIV positive, community volunteers, former gang members, and peer educators for outreach to those in the trenches in need of prevention, intervention, and treatment. In retrospect, the adult children of alcoholics who perhaps became alcoholic for a time themselves, before joining alcoholics anonymous and an adult children of alcoholics group, may have had an easier time than many of our contemporary adult children of a range of dysfunctional families who also got caught up in the overlapping epidemics. Even within the context of a protracted war, we still offer hope and a model suited for our contemporary times.

A second central thesis of this book is that through a handbook or training manual it is possible to prepare a diverse cohort of workers who can facilitate their communities' empowerment and determination of their communities' mental health. Our current level of knowledge in the three fields of chemical dependency, clinical psychology, and health education may also be combined in a unique fashion to accomplish this goal.

This suggests a third core thesis. A body of knowledge and experience in these three fields exists that may support our effort to train workers willing to go into the trenches and engage in community outreach to those impacted by the epidemics, as well as work with the host of diverse members of contemporary dysfunctional families. The integration of these three fields and the selective use of tools and techniques taken from each may permit us to present an effective means of prevention, intervention, and treatment to these individuals.

BENEFITING FROM DEVELOPMENTS IN THE FIELD OF CHEMICAL DEPENDENCY

The field of chemical dependency evolved rapidly in response to the cocaine and crack cocaine epidemic of the 1980s and the urgent need for new, more appropriate treatment modalities. Treatment providers deployed much more integrated approaches, combining active education, psychoanalytic, and cognitive-behavioral theory. Workers in the field of chemical dependency have also attempted to reconcile some of the divisions within the field, fostering, for example, the combined use of twelve-step groups with other treatment modalities, such as individual, group, and residential therapeutic community treatment. The goal is to match clients to interventions that are appropriate in intensity and to time the delivery of interventions for a particular phase of recovery and treatment. Practitioners recognize the need to move the field rapidly beyond treating all clients as though they are the same. As treatment became tailored to individual needs, it was discovered that a large portion of the chemically dependent population were adult children of dysfunctional families who had suffered child abuse. The course of recovery was compounded by the need to resolve trauma or manage the lingering symptoms of trauma. While clients have benefited from this evolution in the field of chemical dependency, more gains need to be made (Wallace, 1992).

At this point, the field of chemical dependency may also hail the twelve step tradition, founded in 1935, and benefit from the over six decades of experience embodied in Alcoholics Anonymous (McGrady & Delaney, 1995). Within Alcoholics Anonymous and it's affiliated twelve-step groups is a long tradition of community self-help, empowerment, and outreach to others. There is also a need to create support mechanisms for the adult children, spouses, and adolescents and children of alcoholics. Following this lead, the field of chemical dependency has acknowledged a role for treating the family and recognizing their needs for prevention, intervention, and treatment. This book seeks to advance this tradition by recognizing that our contemporary adult children from diverse dysfunctional families need special mechanisms created especially for them and the conditions of war in which they live. In addition, their spouses, extended family members, children, and adolescents possess special needs. In the tradition of Alcoholics Anonymous and its affiliated groups, it is necessary to promote self-help and to engage in the tradition of outreach to our contemporary dysfunctional families. This represents a logical next step that follows from evolutionary developments in the field of chemical dependency.

BENEFITING FROM CHANGES IN THE FIELD OF
CLINICAL PSYCHOLOGY

Developments within the field of chemical dependency have also benefited the field of clinical psychology. The knowledge we have gained in clinical work with some of the most difficult clients, especially those presenting dual diagnoses and varied psychopathology, has enhanced the overall practice of psychology. Clinical psychology provides no systematic training in the treatment of chemical dependency. However, clinical psychologists working in this area have created a feedback loop, disseminating knowledge of intervention techniques designed for the clinical population that is prone to relapse and treatment failure.

As was discovered by different practitioners and researchers, motivational enhancement techniques emphasizing empathy and creation of cognitive dissonance, as well as offering clients a menu of options, serves to move ambivalent clients toward engaging in behavioral change (Hester & Miller, 1995; Miller & Rollnick, 1991; Wallace, 1991). It is also critical to improve clients' ego functioning, coping abilities, and self-regulation mechanisms in order to avoid relapse (Wallace, 1992). A focus on the urgency of preventing relapse led to the development of integrated approaches, following a biopsychosocial model (Marlat & Gordon, 1985). The relapse prevention model has been applied to some of the other most difficult mental disorders facing psychologists. Relapse prevention models have been utilized with schizophrenia, depression, obsessive-compulsive disorders, sexual deviance, gambling, anorexia nervosa, and bulimia, for example (Gossop, 1989; Wilson, 1992). Quite often these approaches are seen as "new" when they actually reflect only the application of relapse prevention techniques pioneered in the field of chemical dependency, but now applied by clinical psychologists to other behaviors. The integration of motivational enhancement techniques and relapse prevention is currently driving a quiet revolution in the field of chemical dependency that holds the promise of producing enduring behavioral change for a range of problem behaviors. Moreover, both approaches empower clients.

A biopsychosocial approach that values contributions from neurobiological, psychoanalytic, and cognitive-behavioral fields is the hallmark of the contemporary field of chemical dependency. This integrated, more comprehensive biopsychosocial approach fosters a natural integration of psychological schools of thought that might otherwise remain in competition with each other. Psychoanalysis has provided four clearly articulated psychological theories over a 100-year period—drive psychology, ego psychology, object relations theory, and self-psychology. The integration and refinement of cognitive-behavioral theory and technique has also occurred. This rich knowledge base represents over a century of systematic, progressive, and evolutionary thought among many diverse clinicians and researchers in the field of psychology. As we select and integrate elements from this psychological treasure chest, we may also be in a unique position to integrate theory and schools of thought—following the imperative of the biopsychosocial approach that influenced clinical psychology in the 1980s as a result of rapid developments in the field of chemical dependency.

BENEFITING FROM CHANGES IN THE FIELD OF HEALTH EDUCATION

Health education is the primary tool utilized in disease prevention and health promotion (Glanz, Lewis & Rimer, 1990; Guinta & Allegrante, 1992). The tool of health education may be deployed to promote mental health and prevent disease—whether mental disorders, substance abuse, and conduct disorders. Health education is also the main tool for preventing HIV disease. In this time of overlapping epidemics, delivering health education, or, more appropriately, psychoeducation, is a vital function performed in community-based settings such as the school, worksite, church, and diverse community facilities.

Frequently however, community members and paraprofessionals have taken the lead in conducting community outreach. Whether involving the distribution of bleach, needles, condoms, or pamphlets, the HIV/AIDS epidemic, in particular, has necessitated this kind of aggressive community-based health education (Abdul-Quadar et al., 1992). As a result, health educators joined in partnership with community-based health educators and paraprofessionals in outreach to communities in diverse settings, ranging from the shooting gallery, crack house, street corner, neighborhood launderette, school, church, and housing project. Professionals assist community agencies and paraprofessionals in evaluating their programs to deliver prevention through health education, assisting in the process of receiving additional funding, and disseminating information in the literature on "what works" (Lashof, 1994).

Health educators have sought to increase knowledge among students, workers, and community members, in addition to changing attitudes and beliefs and behavior. The HIV/AIDS epidemic has highlighted the role of sexual behavior and substance abuse as an obstacle to health education goals. Greater immersion in psychological theory and utilization of prevention, intervention, and treatment techniques taken from the fields of chemical dependency and clinical psychology may extend the capabilities and reach of health educators. Deeply ingrained patterns of behavior that also include violence require greater preparation by the health educator in the area of facilitating behavior change.

CONVERGENCE OF THREE FIELDS: PROMOTING COMMUNITY MENTAL HEALTH

The work of clinical psychologists with the chemically dependent may help health educators add to their arsenal for use in community outreach. We may benefit from evolutionary developments occurring on three parallel tracks, involving these three fields. Parallel tracks converge as this book seeks to forge a practical handbook for the training of community mental health workers.

Members of dysfunctional families whose lives and communities have been negatively impacted by our protracted war may find a source of relief and hope in this handbook. This book may serve as a training manual and guide for a dedicated army corps trained in community outreach and for the unique conditions encountered in the trenches of our contemporary war. Contemporary children and adults from dysfunctional families are at risk; by recognizing their needs, we may be able to identify the best methods for meeting those needs.

GOALS AND OBJECTIVES

Psychoeducational and Therapeutic Groups As Our Primary Tool

Psychoeducational and therapeutic groups are our primary tool for delivering prevention, intervention, and treatment. In brief, group modalities present a number of advantages: they are cost-effective, they provide role models and opportunities for identifying with others, and they facilitate more rapid behavioral change. Behaviors that occur outside of psychotherapy over years of individual treatment are demonstrated in groups. Clients metaphorically mount a theatrical stage in a group and reenact their common interpersonal behavioral dramas again and again. Both group leaders and peers may quickly ascertain "what the problem is," in terms of personally feeling and observing the impact of a problematic behavioral pattern. The availability of diverse group members and co-leaders of the group allows them to trigger in clients different feelings, dispositions, and behavioral patterns in a short period of time. The multiple dimensions of an individual's problems rapidly become apparent within a group. The rapidity with which an individual's affective, cognitive, and behavioral problems emerge in a group distinguishes this setting as a superior context for facilitating change.

Groups provide an important means of increasing knowledge, changing attitudes/beliefs, and influencing behavior. Psychoeducational groups represent a powerful tool for delivering a curriculum on specific topics. A natural progression may take place from discussing psychoeducational curriculum in a group and moving on to increasingly personal examples of exposure to violence, for example. Beyond learning definitions within a curriculum and increasing knowledge on a topic related to mental health promotion, groups may become therapeutic when members openly share feelings and painful memories of growing up within a dysfunctional family. Therapeutic groups distinguish themselves as unique environments in which members share parts of themselves that have never been revealed before, and receive the kind of empathy, understanding, and feedback that is typically foreign to the dysfunctional family group experience. Powerful moments of healing occur, and members who gain in trust may tentatively attempt new behaviors for the first time within the group context. The systematic receipt of positive reinforcement permits the shaping of more adaptive and constructive patterns of behavior. Feedback from group members and leaders provides spontaneous positive input that may also be foreign to members who grew up within rigid dysfunctional families, where neglect and insufficient parental feedback and guidance were the rule. Moments of repair, correction, healing, and new growth characterize therapeutic groups and make them uniquely powerful tools for facilitating behavioral change.

Actual resolution of trauma may occur through therapeutic groups. In many ways, consistent with our war metaphor, this handbook prepares us to resolve war trauma. As we prepare for outreach to families and communities, we can recognize war trauma as sustained by community members experiencing interpersonal, family, school, gang, and community violence, as well as from the trauma of watching individuals die from drug overdoses, violence, and HIV/AIDS. The goal is to train a volunteer army corps in how to maintain such groups in community-based settings.

A main objective is to teach workers how to deliver interventions within psychoeducational and therapeutic groups. Whereas Alcoholics Anonymous groups have a group moderator who is in recovery from alcoholism, we seek to provide training to a diverse group comprising our specialized volunteer army corps. For example, a professional and a community volunteer might together conduct a church-based pychoeducational group, following this book as a guide. A teacher and a peer-educator might run a group together in a school, as might a school psychologist and a retired police officer. The potential combinations are infinite and are encouraged.

Beyond trauma resolution, and training diverse group leaders from varied backgrounds, methods of prevention are also found in psychoeducational and therapeutic groups. As prevention, psychoeducational and therapeutic groups seek to resolve the vulnerabilities of individuals at risk for violent, destructive, addictive, and compulsive behavior. We may even employ these techniques and other tools wielded within psychoeducational and therapeutic groups in our own healing and transformation. In this manner, we continue in that tradition of self-help embodied successfully in Alcoholics Anonymous and other twelve-step groups. In benefiting from the tools and techniques offered in this handbook, and in following this manual in delivering prevention, intervention, and treatment to others, we embody the dual principles of self-help and outreach.

Our outreach to the children of crack cocaine users, injection drug users, the HIV positive and diverse families torn by family and community violence is also consistent with the creation of specialized groups for spouses, children, and adolescents from alcoholic families. However, our reach must extend far beyond alcoholic families, given our overlapping crack cocaine and other drug use, violence, and HIV/AIDS epidemics—and our diverse types of contemporary dysfunctional families. Using cost-effective, short-term group modalities in community-based settings, workers conducting psychoeducational and therapeutic groups can assist the currently chemically dependent, those who may relapse, individuals who may resort to other destructive and compulsive behaviors, and at-risk children and adolescents.

As this book suggests, specialized psychoeducational and therapeutic group modalities can be adapted to meet the special needs of specific subpopulations. Given our violence epidemic, at-risk children and adolescents need prevention to avoid engaging in violence. This book therefore presents a recommended psychoeducational violence prevention curriculum for use with the specific subpopulation of school students, but it may also be adapted to diverse community settings. Alternatively, if students and community members have been exposed to violence and physical abuse, or a gang attack, they may need treatment that resolves that trauma and reduces the risk of their engaging in a role reversal. In a role reversal they would place another new victim in the role of one being assaulted and would themselves assume the role behavior of an assaulter. Beyond adolescence, many young adults and diverse community members could benefit from the same kind of psychoeducational violence prevention curriculum, or from a therapeutic group experience involving resolution of trauma from violence. A number of people have also witnessed drive-by shootings, murders, and violent assaults and need trauma resolution in therapeutic groups. In all cases, we recommend psychoeducational groups or therapeutic groups for delivery in school, church, or community-based settings. In sum, this book intends to provide an adequate description of how to conduct the group process in such psychoeducational and therapeutic groups.

A Manual for Cultural Competence and Cultural Sensitivity

A second objective is to provide a training manual, or guide, that is culturally sensitive to people of color, and also produces culturally competent workers. Given the war raging most intensely in communities of color, but also in rural and suburban hamlets across this nation, there is a need for a book on adult children of dysfunctional families that is sensitive to issues of ethnicity and race. An additional goal involves the presence of more culturally competent workers translating into more people of color seeking not only community-based group treatment, but also more individual, group, and family treatment for themselves and their families.

This book's discussion of how dysfunctional family dynamics emerge in response to multiple stressors attendant to immigration and migration is novel. This discussion seeks to enhance appreciation among all societal members regarding how their ancestors and relatives coped with multiple stressors in order to pursue the American dream; to foster greater sensitivity to our own ethnic and cultural group experiences; and to promote the concept of an ethnic, religious, or cultural group's unique and idiosyncratic experiences of trauma.

Demystification of the Behavioral Change Process

The behavioral change process is demystified when we share with workers in the trenches, as well as with community members, the tools and techniques for fostering behavioral change. At the same time, we convey in clear and simple language—understandable to all—the essence of diverse theory which provides the guiding rationale behind what we actually say and do to promote a behavioral change process. Thus, in addition to showing readers how to start, conduct, and maintain psychoeducational and therapeutic groups, we seek to spell out what they may actually say and do within groups to enhance behavioral change in group members. The goal of fostering behavioral change—whether in at-risk children and adolescents, or in adults already possessing deeply entrenched behavioral patterns involving drug use, sexuality, and violence—is of paramount importance. By demystifying the behavioral change process and giving community members access to integrated theory and effective counseling techniques, we may facilitate the process of empowerment and self-determination of behavioral standards and community mental health.

Principles To Guide Community Mental Health Promotion

The new area of community mental health promotion represents an intersection of the fields of chemical dependency, health education, and clinical psychology and necessitates a grounding in several key principles:

1. **Training.** *Provide training that is practical and easy to understand to professionals, paraprofessionals, recovering individuals, the HIV positive, peer educators, and community volunteers which prepares them to engage in prevention, intervention, and treatment. Such training should validate participants for their possession of strengths, while empowering them to deploy new tools, techniques, and terminology.*

2. **Outreach.** *Go to where the people in need are to be found in their very own communities and engage in community outreach—whether a school, worksite, church, or any other community setting.*

3. **Acceptance.** *Accept individuals in the condition, state of readiness to change, or stage of the change process (Prochaska, DiClemente & Norcross, 1992), in which you find them, always provide respect, empathy, hope, and a positive outlook, as you offer assistance and motivate others (Miller & Rollnick 1991; Miller, 1995; Rollnick & Morgan, 1995; Wallace, 1991) to take whatever steps they decide to make toward change and transformation.*

4. **Self-Efficacy.** *Facilitate practical and personal experiential learning (via a workbook, exercises, role play, rehearsal) that increases the self-efficacy (Marlatt & Gordon, 1985) of all participants in psychoeducational and therapeutic groups; and that facilitates their delivery of prevention, intervention, and treatment to others, in turn.*

5. **Empowerment.** *Empower workers in the trenches and community members to engage in the self-determination of their own and their community members' mental health through an empowerment model.*

6. **Cultural Competence.** *Provide culturally sensitive training that produces workers in the trenches who possess cultural competence.*

7. **Self-Determination.** *Adapt interventions to diverse cultures and communities and encourage self-determination of mental health and standards of behavior in that particular setting.*

As we go to where the people are, accept them as they are, and disseminate tools to facilitate behavioral change and increased self-efficacy, we also empower community members to engage in self-determination of their mental health and behavioral standards, while appreciating cultural dynamics in each setting in which we do outreach.

Brief Training and Brief Interventions in Short-Term Work

War conditions are ideal settings for the discovery and refinement of short-term assessment and crisis intervention techniques. However, what is discovered in war may find broader practical application. In the trenches we learn by necessity how to engage in: (I) rapid assessment; (2) rapid triage with matching to the best intervention under the worst circumstances; and, (3) short-term work with trauma clients that produces the most rapid stabilization and return to functioning, since they must soon reenter battle. What has been learned under conditions of war with the most severely traumatized may find application to a wider range of community members needing prevention, intervention, or treatment. When I use the same techniques with my diverse upper, middle, and low-income patients in private practice, the application of the techniques makes for a swifter and more effective healing and recovery. Dependency is not fostered, and a form of short-term psychotherapy results.

What was discovered in the trenches during wartime may be a generic model of short-term work using brief assessment and intervention strategies that effectively stabilize the most traumatized and injured of clients. In this manner, a brief intervention model is described in this handbook, consistent with trends in the treatment field (Hester & Bien, 1995; Hester & Miller, 1989, 1995; Miller & Rollnick, 1991; Rollnick & Bell, 1991). In many cases, we may speak of a six-month to one-year course of participation in psychoeducational and therapeutic groups. Given the magnitude of trauma that many of our contemporary children, adolescents, and adults from dysfunctional families may possess, this represents an extremely rapid course of recovery and healing. The open-ended nature of psychoeducational and therapeutic group participation, following Alcoholics Anonymous, may also permit varied and more extended periods of group participation, as members meet their individual needs.

Discovering "What Works"

Whether we are professionals, paraprofessionals, community members, or adolescents who have talked by telephone to a depressed and distressed peer, we have all discovered "what works." No matter what degrees we possess, our clients and peers reinforce us by either looking at us directly, suddenly listening intently, nodding their heads, or seeking us out again and again. We are thereby reinforced and shaped as counselors and peer helpers into being more effective listeners and helpers. When our clients or peers look away, stop coming to sessions, or fail to respond positively, we are not reinforced and our less effective interventions may undergo extinction and not be repeated. Quite simply, we learn that if it works, try it again and again. As human beings, we truly discover "what works" in assisting other human beings with their mental health.

It is this process that we seek to demystify and make accessible to anyone who seeks this knowledge, as we also validate and empower workers in the field. Instead of coming to an intensive training workshop and receiving this validation and empowerment, this handbook may serve that purpose, while also teaching the novice what to say and do in psychoeducational and therapeutic groups. Or we may begin with self-help, as a first step, with this handbook, first discovering how to transform our own behavior, before deciding to do outreach to others. It seems critical at this time to make this information accessible beyond the private consultation room, graduate school, and postgraduate classroom, because there is a need for workers willing to go out into the trenches and engage in community outreach to our contemporary children, adolescents, and adults from dysfunctional families

INTENDED AUDIENCE FOR THE BOOK

On the one hand, this book is designed for individuals who are already members of the grassroots self-help movement and are recovering from their own dysfunctional family past and related destructive behaviors, perhaps including chemical dependency. Some may be HIV positive, or community volunteers, or peer educators still in school. Yet, all may seek training through this "handbook" in how to help their peers and community members. Others may be formally working as counselors and therapists with adult children who are in chemical dependency treatment or attending varied treatment programs in the community. This book is also intended for certified counselors and those seeking certification. The intended audience includes those psychologists, psychiatrists, and social workers who seek a clinical technique specifically designed for adult children from dysfunctional families.

We also seek to help health educators and community outreach workers to promote mental health and engage in primary, secondary, and tertiary prevention. The potential audience for this book is quite broad, including community church pastors and leaders, or even prison-based support groups, diverse medical personnel, policymakers and school administrators and other school staff; graduate students and those seeking predoctoral and postdoctoral training, such as those at Teachers College, Columbia University; undergraduates planning to become teachers, counselors, or work in community-based agencies involved in grassroots efforts to empower community members; teachers who recognize the urgency of students possessing knowledge of the violence prevention curriculum and honing survival skills for life; and religious leaders who are facilitating their members' survival, empowerment, and healing. In sum, a broad audience is delivered a handbook to guide their work in the trenches—as a specialized volunteer army corps.

CONCLUSION

This chapter introduces us to the problem of children, adolescents, and adults living in communities under siege from three overlapping epidemics, and the subsequent need to train a cadre of professionals and paraprofessionals for community outreach to these groups. We stand at a unique period in our nation's history when overlapping epidemics threaten our communities and literally determine who will survive into the next century. All of our lives, including those in rural, suburban, and hamlets distant from the urban epicenters, are touched by the harsh realities of these three epidemics.

As the legacy of the dead and the stark reality of the dying envelops those of us willing to work in the trenches, we must not forget the diverse needs of those who will likely survive into the twenty-first century. We seek to meet the needs of diverse community members who have been scarred from struggling with any kind of dysfunctional family dynamic. At the same time, we want to provide a practical handbook that is uniquely suited to our times. But even as we deliver a practical handbook, it remains important to answer several sets of questions: Given where we are as a society, how did we arrive here? Where do we need to go? And how do we get there? The remainder of this book attempts to provide practical and timely answers to these questions.

2

Background: The Adult Children
of Dysfunctional Families Movement

The adult children of alcoholics movement stimulated developments that make this book a logical extension of the movement. We would not be able to speak of the needs of contemporary members of dysfunctional families if it had not been for this movement. Consistent with that movement, we may find a role today for professionals who seek to disseminate information regarding how to assist this population. This chapter provides background on the adult children of alcoholics grassroots movement, critical developments in this area, and a summary of the historical role played by professionals in the movement. It gives a partial answer to the question, "How did we arrive here, and where do we need to go?"

THE ORIGINS AND IMPACT OF THE GRASS-ROOTS MOVEMENT

The adult children of alcoholics movement began as a grassroots self-help effort in the 1970s which grew out of Alcoholics Anonymous, Alanon, and Alateen. Quite simply, the pain and suffering of family members of alcoholics began to drive a grass-roots movement. Of particular importance were the efforts of counselors in the field of addiction to whom they turned for help. Counselors sought to understand how the alcoholic or addict affected the family, as they tried to assist the children and spouse of the alcoholic attending Alateen and Alanon who were seeking their support (Kitchens, 1991, p. 3). The written work of numerous writers and therapists helped to establish a process whereby growing numbers of individuals became aware of the impact of diverse traits, family roles, and symptoms rooted in dysfunctional family dynamics and the experience of parental alcoholism (Ackerman, 1986, 1987; Black, 1981, 1985; Brown, 1988; Cermak, 1988; Wegscheider-Cruse, 1986; Woititz, 1983, 1985). A literature on the adult children of alcoholics became available in the 1980s and met the needs of an audience who desperately wanted to understand their own personal experience and the impact of growing up in an alcoholic family.

Different types of shaming experiences, trauma, and events within a range of dysfunctional families have also received a great deal of attention, expanding the focus beyond just families plagued by parental alcoholism (Black, 1990; Bradshaw, 1988, 1990, 1995; Kitchens, 1991). A grassroots movement among recovering adult children from a range of dysfunctional families was born with a blossoming literature guiding this process. It became increasingly acceptable to find an outlet for discussing the varied forms of abuse that adults from diverse types of dysfunctional families experienced in childhood and adolescence. The availability of literature stimulated this gradually more open discussion of troubled family life.

As a result of this grass-roots movement and a popular literature directed toward adult children, we now live in an era in which knowledge about adult children and dysfunctional families is common in our society. It is widely known that President Bill Clinton grew up in a dysfunctional family; he is perceived as a classic "hero" or "responsible child" within an alcoholic family system torn by domestic violence (Ifill, 1992). In our society, roughly 28 million people spent critical childhood and adolescent developmental periods within an alcoholic household, just as did President Clinton. Moreover, some 7 million of these individuals are still under the age of eighteen. Or, to put it another way, one out of every eight Americans has witnessed the impact of parental alcoholism (Rivinus, 1991). The impact of the grassroots movement is reflected in increased societal awareness of dysfunctional families.

The Difficulty of Estimating Contemporary Prevalence Rates

Survivors of dysfunctional families are plagued by incidents of incest, sexual abuse, physical abuse, verbal abuse, domestic violence, parental death, severe poverty, parental separation, divorce, neglect, parental abandonment, and even excessive spoiling of children. In areas plagued by underreporting by parents and families who feel too much shame to report abuses, we can only estimate the prevalence of some kinds of dysfunctional family dynamics. Blume (1990), for example, asserts that more than three quarters of her clients had been molested as children by someone they knew, yet no one identified this as a reason for entering treatment. A growing body of data suggests that boys are sexually abused as frequently as females; authorities generally agree that one out of five girls will be sexually abused before age eighteen (Hunter, 1990).

As we consider this painful reality, we can only begin to speculate on the actual rates and prevalence of the other kinds of family dysfunction that haunt our society today. Landry (1994) maintains that since 1980 over 30 million Americans have used cocaine and nearly 2 million have become compulsive users. How many qualify as parents of children, and how many introduced dysfunction into family life because of cocaine use? If we add users of heroin, marijuana, and other drugs, how many parents with children are our contemporary chemical abusers and chemically dependent who are analogous to alcoholic parents in their destructive impact on family life? The prevalence of dysfunctional families and of the children who have survived these kinds of dysfunctional family settings is difficult to estimate. However, their prevalence is widespread and suggests the continued need for what has emerged as a grassroots movement. A contemporary grassroots movement is needed to address the damage done to survivors of such families, as well as to provide assistance to the children and families. Many contemporary chemical abusers and the chemically dependent sadly recognize that, using a different chemical, they repeat their parents' pattern of alcoholism in broad design. Generational cycles keep repeating themselves, as dysfunctional families keep manifesting themselves in new and varied forms, as well as with exact replication of some dysfunctional family dynamics.

Historical Developments in the Adult Child and Dysfunctional Family Field

Pioneering professionals established some of the first specialty groups for adult children of alcoholics and children of alcoholics (Ackerman, 1986). For example, Stephanie Brown and Timothy Cermak started their first long-term therapy group for adult children of alcoholics in the fall of 1978 at the Stanford Alcohol Clinic, while others such as Claudia Black were also beginning their pioneering efforts (Brown, 1988). Professionals conceptualized and described this work (Ackerman, 1986; Black, 1981, 1985; Wegscheider-Cruse, 1986; Woititz, 1983, 1985), permitting other therapists to follow in their footsteps and start yet other adult children groups. Ackerman (1987) contributed important research findings on adult children; he identified factors such as sex and age of the child, sex of the alcoholic parent, the existence of two alcoholic parents, or, in addition to verbal abuse, the experience of physical abuse and domestic violence.

Blume (1991) cites the origin of the professionals' role in focusing societal attention on children who grow up within alcoholic families in the work of Cork (1969), who studied a relatively large group of these children. Indeed, Blume (1991) cites two falacious assumptions that held sway in the 1960s prior to Cork's (1969) vital contribution: (1) children could only be helped if their parents sought treatment, and (2) children would automatically recover once their parents had stopped drinking or using drugs (p. ix).

Blume (1991) also recognizes the founding of the Children of Alcoholics Foundation in 1982, as well as her own early work with this foundation as critical events that stimulated research into prevention for this at risk population (Children of Alcoholics Foundation, 1986). It was also in 1982 that a group of professionals, including Claudia Black, formed the National Association for Children of Alcoholics. Early studies that made professional contributions to the literature focused upon the defensive adaptation and resulting role behavior assumed by children within alcoholic families. Black's (1981) description of the family role behavior commonly adopted by children in alcoholic families (the responsible chlld, the adjuster, the placater, and the acting out child) established Black as a leader in this field. The family roles adopted by children in alcoholic families proposed by Wegscheider (1981) included the hero, mascot, scapegoat, and lost child; these roles gained popularity through the work of Bradshaw (1990) and his public broadcast television series.

Black (1985) was one of the first writers to recognize that many different dysfunctional family dynamics are involved in growing up with a depressed parent, or a parent suffering from a mental illness, or experiencing some kind of abuse. Black (1990) also coined the term double duty to refer to those adult children who contended with multiple negative stressors within their family of origin, such as alcoholism and incest. Her work is on the cutting edge in its consideration of how a "dual identity" may also be at issue for those adult childen who are people of color, only children, gay and lesbian, and physically disabled—establishing some of the first discussion in this field on such issues. Black (1990) notes that some of these dual identity issues have barred many from actively participating in twelve-step groups and professionally led specialty groups for adult children. Black also observes that some recognition of these issues is necessary and can lead to increased participation in these groups. Her work is a point of departure for this book, which seeks to consider multiple experiences of trauma within and across developmental eras in the lives of contemporary adult children. This book also seeks to deliver training in cultural competency, perhaps going further than any other book in this area heretofore in considering the lives of adult children of color and the unique stressors they and their families have experienced.

Bradshaw (1990) has presented a resource and plan of action that is based on the integration of developmental and other theory. However, this resource is largely of value to the self-identified "adult child" who is encouraged to engage in some exercises and seek out the services of a professional therapist. But what of the availability of resources to counselors and clinicians who want to feel competent in working with these self-identifed and self-referred adult children who want to change specific problem behaviors? This book seeks to fill that void by serving as a training manual in techniques for use in counseling work with contemporary adult children.

Bradshaw has also personally served as a vehicle for the wide dissemination of knowledge of dysfunctional family life and its consequences through his public broadcast series. Bradshaw's most recent book and public broadcast series (1995) is on family secrets and their disclosure. His public broadcast series provides an intensive education on dysfunctional family dynamics, adding to widespread societal knowledge of these issues.

Yet another contemporary writer and counselor, Kitchens (1991), focuses on the broad range of family patterns of dysfunction that wound children and help to produce codependence. We are also reminded of the significant impact of the grassroots movement, as the term codependent has also entered into our common language. Many acknowledge their historical development in a dysfunctional family by self-identifying as codependent, often with humor and open confession of personal shortcomings that need to be understood by others.

According to Kitchens (1991), while a growing amount of scientific research is focusing upon adult children of dysfunctional families, the malady from which the adult child is suffering can be called codependence. Taking a novel approach, Kitchens sees codependence as involving the enactment of learned role behavior; internal emotional problems; shame; conformity to unhealthy rules; rejection and chaos; an addiction; and as involving adaptation to a family culture. He also provides basic guidelines for counseling the adult child suffering from codependence, describes how to organize and structure a model of time-limited group psychotherapy that is both psychoeducational and experiential, and makes recommendations in regards to conducting individual and family therapy. The power of group modalities will also be recognized in the present book's emphasis on the use of psychoeducational and therapeutic groups, as well as short-term or brief interventions.

Tuchfeld (1986) similarly emphasizes the power of the short-term psychoeducational group with adult children. This kind of cognitive intervention gets people moving on the problem once they cognitively understand the problem—with the goal of increasing their use of therapy and twelve-step groups. Clark and Jette (1991) also endorse the value of the short-term psychoeducational group for it serves as a catalyst for change.

In addition, Brown (1988, 1991) and Vannicelli (1989) support the special utility of group modalities with this population, offering detailed guidance on how to implement and conduct such groups. Given an apparent consensus regarding the importance of group modalities, and of conveying how to implement and conduct groups, the present book is consistent with a tradition established within the adult child field and literature.

The Proliferation of Diverse Twelve-Step Groups

After the birth of Alanon and Alateen, we have seen the creation of twelve-step groups designed specifically for adult children of alcoholics (ACOA Groups), as well as the more recent Incest Survivors Anonymous, Sex Addicts Anonymous, Sex and Love Addicts Anonymous, Sexual Compulsives Anonymous, Sexaholics Anonymous, Narcotics Anonymous, Cocaine Anonymous, Gamblers Anonymous, Overeaters Anonymous, and Positive Anonymous (HIV positive). These additional self-help groups that are spinoffs of the original twelve-step group, Alcoholics Anonymous, have also formed a part of the grassroots movement that has additionally been impacted by professional involvement. For example, among professional contributions to this area, the work of Carnes (1991) provides a practical guide for the recovering sexually compulsive individual, as well as for the clinician working with this population, or for anyone seeking to structure a treatment program.

Breaking the Silence on Sexual Abuse

The public disclosures of talk show host Oprah Winfrey, the comedienne Roseanne, and a former Miss America regarding their own histories of sexual abuse and incest, have encouraged more survivors to acknowledge their trauma and to seek out appropriate treatment. Media celebrities therefore contribute to the momentum of a grassroots movement, particularly in the area of sexual abuse and incest.

Hunter (1990) takes a novel approach by focusing on the plight and subsequent needs of the estimated 50,000 boys who are sexually abused each year, while admitting that a clear assertion of the number of men sexually abused in childhood is not possible, even though varying prevalence rates are reported in the literature.

Levine (1990) shows that classic psychoanalysis, too, has been touched by a grassroots movement that has drawn our attention anew to childhood sexual abuse. Masson (1984) accuses Freud of turning his back on the facts of actual traumatic childhood sexual experience, abandoning his original seduction theory citing the role of childhood seduction in the development of neurosis, and instead emphasizing childhood sexual fantasy life and infantile sexuality. Levine (1990) admits that Freud may have inadvertently contributed to the tendency in psychoanalysis to downplay or minimize the impact of actual traumatic events on the etiology of neurosis (p. 5). Levine also recognizes, however, that Freud worked with simplistic theory in comparison to what we have available today, may have felt some pressure in the face of a skeptical and resistant audience, and always did recognize the impact of genuine traumatic events, including childhood sexual abuse. In any event, psychoanalysis acknowledges that significant portion of the patient population who are victims of childhood sexual abuse and present tremendous clinical challenges in terms of eroticized transferences, sexual acting out, difficulty trusting, and long and difficult treatments (Levine, 1990). The present book takes advantage of the availability of more complex theory, integrates theory, and seeks to extend current efforts to address the special needs of sexually abused adult children.

A Focus upon the Experiences of Trauma

Several writers have focused upon trauma as a way to conceptualize the experiences of children negotiating dysfunctional family life. Shengold (1989) defines trauma in terms of chronic overstimulation, with the concomitant systematic brainwashing of children. Shengold discusses the "soul murder" of victims of childhood abuse and deprivation. Through compelling cases of sexual abuse involving mothers and sons and patients from wealthy dysfunctional families, Shengold lays out the clinical issues and challenges to be confronted and clinically managed in such cases. In this way, he contributes to the study of trauma, and the psychoanalytic view and approach to significant trauma in childhood sustained from sexual abuse and incest.

Other writers (Johnson, 1989) focus on children's experiences of trauma produced by mass shootings, homicides, drug-distribution violence, and other violence in their families and communities. Johnson's data show that the experience of such trauma can lead to a higher incidence of problems in adolescence, and he provides a resource for teachers and therapists regarding the use of interventions that can be school-based. Prothrow-Stith and Weissman (1991) provide a model for school and community-based violence prevention through a curriculum that addresses the problem of black-on-black homicide and other community violence. Other writers offer radical approaches to the resolution of trauma (Grove & Panzer, 1991; Herman, 1992).

This book extends this trend in the literature by focusing on trauma and considering it as encompassing diverse events—ranging from sexual abuse to school, gang, and community violence. Hence, the problem of the experience of some childhood trauma, and the task of trauma resolution (whatever the source of that trauma) are seen as centrally related to the plight of our target population. Moreover, prevention and early intervention are needed to assist vulnerable children and adolescents. This book offers a psychoeducational violence prevention curriculum and proposes a therapeutic group model for schools and other community-based settings that actually seeks to resolve trauma.

Other Contemporary Trends in the Adult Child Literature

The literature on the adult children of dysfunctional families discusses a range of other compulsive and destructive behaviors observed in this population. Yates (1991) focuses upon compulsive exercise, or activity disorders, and on eating disorders—covering important cultural factors, treatment, and theory. Staying within the realm of the eating disorders—anorexia, bulimia, and compulsive overeating—is the work of Zraly and Swift (1990) who describe a hospital-based treatment model for this subset of our adult child population. As we will see, an array of compulsive behaviors must be discussed and understood as problems and symptoms of adult children. These problem behaviors and symptoms suggest the kind of disorders that must be prevented for a large at-risk population of children and adolescents of dysfunctional families. In this book, we continue this trend in the literature and discuss how a rigid and compulsive religious involvement may even come to characterize members of dysfunctional families (Chapter 3).

Other writers examine the experiences of children who grow up in families impacted by divorce, discussing the issues characterizing this subset of our adult child population (Berman, 1991). Since there is such a broad, and specialty-focused literature, we may ask, "Why is there a need for yet another book on dysfunctional families?

A NEW APPROACH FOR USE WITH CONTEMPORARY DYSFUNCTIONAL FAMILIES

This book continues in the tradition of literature in the adult child and dysfunctional family field with a focus on psychoeducational and therapeutic groups as main tools, as well as on the need to resolve experiences of trauma. This book also extends the literature and adult child field by taking a new direction.

No other book in this field currently addresses in so substantial a manner the relevant history, background, and experiences of adult children of color, or persons who self-identify as belonging to a particular racial, ethnic, or religious group. Nor does the prior literature address the implications of these factors for cross-cultural counseling. A stated goal that makes this book unique is that of producing cultural competence in practitioners.

Only culturally competent counselors may be able to effectively empower clients to engage in the self-determination of their own behavior and mental health. Empowerment of community members may follow when outreach workers convey genuine respect, empathy, and hope—perceiving the inherent strengths possessed by family and community members. This book is unique in offering an empowerment model.

Public health crises, or epidemics, involving crack cocaine, heroin, and other drugs as well as violence and HIV/AIDS demand recognition. These conditions call for novel approaches to promoting the public's mental health. In this work, we promote a new standard of "wellness" and national childcare. Psychoeducation describes exactly what healthy parenting encompasses, helping to bring about a new standard of child-care and fostering functional family life. This is part of an effort to meet the needs of at-risk children and youth. By using psychoeducational curricula designed for parents and students, this book may help create a school environment conducive to the affective, cognitive, moral, interpersonal, and social development of children from dysfunctional families, following the recommendations of Comer (1980). However, regardless of the setting in which at-risk youth may be found, we seek to engage in outreach to them and provide early prevention, intervention, and treatment to avoid some of the symptoms and problem behaviors characteristic of adult children of dysfunctional families.

This book also seeks to teach counselors how to prevent symptom substitution. In symptom substitution, after one compulsive behavior, such as addiction, is surrendered, another emerges such as compulsive overeating. This book assists clients in integrating and working through memories of trauma in short-term groups as a means of removing the tendency toward symptom substitution. This work may also help mental health professionals improve treatment efficacy and long-term treatment outcome.

Both principles of behaviorism are embraced, as well as psychoanalytic notions of remediating underlying psychopathology and unconscious dynamics toward the goal of avoiding symptom substitution. This book resolves tensions between psychoanalysis and behaviorism by demonstrating that both theories can be used to understand the aftermath of trauma. The delivery of psychoeducation constitutes a cognitive approach. By taking an integrated approach, this book selectively utilizes psychoanalytic drive theory, ego psychology, object relations theory, and self-psychology, as well as cognitive-behavioral psychology. Even while we integrate what appears to be complex abstract theory, the use of graphic models and metaphors facilitates understanding and visualization in trainees of "what to do and why to do it." Moreover, this book is distinct in directing this training to a diverse group of paraprofessionals, community members, volunteers, former gang members, peer-educators, and professionals, while asserting that they can engage in counseling and community outreach.

CONCLUSION

This chapter provides important background information on how a grassroots movement was born out of the desperation and hope of alcoholics, their spouses, and family members. Our contemporary public health crises involving crack cocaine, heroin, and other drug use, in addition to violence, and HIV/AIDS, necessitate that we further stimulate growth in the grassroots movement and the role played by professionals and paraprofessionals. By reviewing the past contributions of professionals in research and writings, historical development in the field of adult children of dysfunctional families is conveyed. This background provides a partial answer to the question, "How did we arrive here?" By specifying what distinguishes this book within the adult child literature, we have also begun to provide a partial answer to the question, "Where do we need to go, and how do we get there?"

There is justification and need for a handbook to train a new specialized volunteer army corps that can build on the use of psychoeducational and therapeutic groups, and the use of short-term or brief interventions, and that can work as teams of professionals and paraprofessionals, for example. Responding to public health needs, we seek to engage in community outreach and to conduct these groups in a variety of community-based settings, using an empowerment model and fostering self-determination.

The next chapter considers how societal and cultural forces have helped to create dysfunctional families. This discussion necessitates that we learn our history of immigration, migration, and the stressors on families that helped to produce the millions of adult children children from dysfunctional families.

3

Stressors Promoting the Evolution of Dysfunctional Families

As we continue to explore the questions "How did we arrive here, and where do we need to go?," it is important to understand historical background on immigration and migration in the United States. Immigration and migration may be either forced and involuntary, or voluntary. Forced or involuntary immigration and migration experiences typically produce trauma for members of that cultural group. Within the forced immigration and migration experience, cultural trauma typically involves members of a cultural or societal group experiencing forms of violence (physical blows, displays of power, the target of misinformation/myths) collectively by virtue of cultural group membership. The cultural trauma sustained by African slaves and Native Americans constitutes a peculiar part of our history as a nation that engaged in the forced involuntary immigration and migration of these two groups, respectively. This history also involved open displays of hate, the spreading of misinformation and myths, hateful stereotyping, and the condoned unleashing of violence against the "different" disdained group members of African and Native American heritage.

This chapter reviews this history of African and Native American cultural group trauma and the virulent forms of nativism and xenophobia which greeted a variety of immigrants and migrants. Nativism involves native citizens feeling superior to new arrivals, and xenophobia is a fear of strangers. Nativism and xenophobia created considerable stress for new immigrant and migrant arrivals, who subsequently lived in fear of violence, discrimination, and prejudice. Strong pressures to assimilate resulted from these stressors. To become more like natives might permit escaping hatred, violence, prejudice, and discrimination. It is in light of this historical background on immigration and migration that we explore a central question in this chapter: Could the unique and multiple stressors attendant to involuntary and voluntary immigration, as well as migration, facilitate the formation and perpetuation of dysfunctional family structures? Historically, as stressors were endured for periods of time, eventually signs of strain emerged and a negative impact on family members manifested itself as families crossed a thin line into dysfunction.

This chapter's brief multicultural education curriculum may also enable counselors to attain to a greater level of cultural competence and to emerge capable of empowering families. Counselors may identify and celebrate with profound respect valid family strengths; it becomes easier, while recognizing valid family strengths, to then acknowledge or point out to clients that because of the continued impact of certain stressors families often fall into dysfunction.

We can empower families only if we do not replicate subtle interpersonal dynamics that involve counselors and outreach workers feeling superior to clients, while clients are perceived as inferior and are secretly feared. Relevant guidelines are presented in order to prevent the perpetuation of harmful interpersonal dynamics between client and counselor that reflect this nation's centuries-old history perpetuating nativist and xenophobic practices.

THE UNIQUE STRESSORS IMPACTING INVOLUNTARY IMMIGRANTS AND MIGRANTS

Unique and incomparable experiences are associated with forced or involuntary immigration and migration. Two examples of cultural group trauma within the history of this nation involve the forced involuntary immigration experiences of Africans and the invountary migration of Native Americans.

The Cultural Group Trauma Perpetrated against Africans

Little approaches the horror of being enslaved, packed like sardines in the belly of slave ships, and watching the millions who could not survive these harsh conditions systematically thrown overboard into the Atlantic Ocean. It is also difficult to imagine the horror of observing others getting raped on board these ships—wondering who might be next when and if the one being brutally and repeatedly raped died. And, what of the experience of being an involuntary immigrant arriving on a foreign shore for forced lifetime servitude and being separated from family in Africa for life? Still, little compares to being placed on a slave ship for a second time and being transported from the West Indies to the shores of the United States to enter the southern plantation economy as a slave. The experience of violent whippings, rapes, the loss of African culture, and close daily contact with a master is unique to African-Americans, who in this manner had a distinct experience as involuntary immigrants—twice transported long distance on slave ships (Light, 1987).

What of the pain of separation from children and family who could be sold away to another plantation as slaves, and what of the lack of recognition by masters of marriages and family bonds? Slaves were cut off from their African culture and forced to assimilate to the master's culture—including a new language and religious beliefs. Africans were also the focus of religious, pseudoscientific, and other propaganda campaigns that sought to justify the enslavement of Africans, effectively brainwashing citizens to the legitimacy and supposed advantages of enslavement for the African.

Multiple and Chronic Cultural Group Trauma Perpetrated against African Descendants

The legalized disenfranchisement suffered after the end of slavery, the horrid conditions in the Jim Crow South, and the lynchings and mob attacks perpetrated by the Ku Klux Klan and others created an incomparable historical experience for African-Americans. In many respects, it is appropriate to conceptualize this history as involving multiple experiences of trauma, as well as chronic trauma—as certain events were repeated century after century and decade after decade. Imagine: 1952 was the first year in which a lynching did not occur in the United States (Corbin, 1986). Meanwhile, mob attacks, beatings, and police brutality continued as the legacy of living in a society in which violence had always been condoned against Africans, since their arrival on this country's shores as debased slaves. The possession of a black skin color continued to serve as a powerful stimulus for conditioned beliefs about African descendants and violent practices that fueled attacks against African-Americans—long after slavery had been abolished and civil rights obtained (Wallace, 1993, 1995). Thus, a powerful legacy was born that lingers to the present day as a result of a violence-ridden, forced, involuntary immigration history involving African slaves and White masters.

The Cultural Group Trauma Perpetrated against Native Americans

The experiences of other groups also emerge as unique historically. Native American tribes had the most spectacular land taken from them. They were forced to pursue a trail of tears, involuntarily walking at gunpoint for miles and miles to barren reservations. This involuntary migration experience destroyed tribal life and culture as the Native Americans and their ancestors had known and experienced it (Dinnerstein et al., 1990). Native Americans were also the focus of propaganda campaigns (Takaki, 1987, 1990).

The intentional spread of disease as well as the concerted and systematic efforts made to destroy Native American civilization characterize this sad chapter in our nation's history. As their way of life began to collapse, Native American children were legally kidnapped and forced to attend boarding schools far removed from their families. Family and culture were denigrated as male children were compelled to have their hair cut. Children were punished if they spoke their native languages and their clothing and all the symbols from their culture were removed and replaced with symbols of assimilation. Living in fear, children commonly went hungry when unable to tolerate inadequate meals. Children who tried to run away were severely punished and beaten (Dinnerstein et al., 1990).

The Continuing Impact of Cultural Group Trauma

Africans and Native Americans in this country suffered not only from violence, but also from the spread of misinformation and myths. Stereotypes and negative beliefs about African and Native American descendants may persist up to the present day, as a result of propaganda campaigns that effectively spread misinformation and myths within this nation. This history also illustrates how these two groups were cut off from their cultural group practices, values, and traditions. Other groups, such as war and political refugees, may be examined for their experiences of surviving unique stressors and for sustaining cultural group trauma. Meanwhile, it is important to consider the impact of cultural group trauma suffered by Africans and Native Americans who were cut off from their culture as they once knew it.

COMMON STRESSORS IMPACTING IMMIGRANT AND MIGRANT GROUPS

German, Italian, Irish, Jewish, Chinese, Japanese, Mexican, Puerto Rican, Cuban, West Indian, African, Asian, Haitian, Catholics and many other immigrants and migrants encountered xenophobia, nativism, racism, discrimination, abuse, and prejudice upon their arrival (Bonacich, 1987; Dinnerstein et, al, 1990; Garcia, 1987; Higham, 1987; Jordan, 1987; Light, 1987; Loo & Ong, 1987; Rodriguez, 1987). Each group may have had unique conditions back home which set the stage for voluntary immigration, and may also have experienced unique stressors once they entered the United States. However, we search here for common themes and stressors within the voluntary immigration and migration experience—identifying factors that also impact the descendants of involuntary immigrants and migrants. Within the context of the seventeenth, eighteenth, nineteenth, and twentieth centuries, what common stressors impacted these diverse groups?

Nativism, Xenophobia, and the U.S. Culture of Violence

Common stressors that are part and parcel of the immigration and migration experience involve the classic encounter with those already present and assimilated American citizens who were ripe with nativism and xenophobia. Immigrant arrivals underwent socialization in a country in which the enslavement of Africans and the displacement of Native Americans had established this country as one in which nativism, xenophobia, and socially condoned violence against specific groups thrived. The historical treatment of Africans and Native Americans provided social conditioning in the affects of hate that were readily directed toward any new and different immigrant arrival.

In many respects, this nativism, xenophobia, and the practice of directing violence toward the new and different immigrant or migrant arrival to an area justifies referring to the United States as a culture of violence. U.S. culture has always practiced forms of violence, going back to the treatment of Africans, Native Americans, and new voluntary immigrant arrivals. This culture of violence involves practices, traditions, and beliefs that have been passed from group member to group member and from generation to generation. Traditional practices also involve the spreading of stereotypes and the denigrating of immigrant groups (Wallace, 1993).

A precedent was set by the U.S. government in spreading misinformation and myths about slaves and Indians (Jordan, 1987; Takaki, 1987). Society conditions us with cognitions, or thoughts, and members of the society spread these "conditioned cognitions" or stereotypes from member to member and from generation to generation. Each new immigrant arrival, as a new member of the larger culture of the United States, may acquire new knowledge and beliefs regarding the practices of unleashing violence (Wallace, 1993).

Opportunities for social learning often occur at the family dinner table wherein parents provide role models for attitudes of disdain toward yet another immigrant, migrant, or racial or ethnic group—for at least some brief period during family mealtime. For many of us our parents have been "Archie Bunkers," or have engaged in a negative discourse about a "different" group in a bigoted and spirited fashion at a time when minds are the most impressionable and parents are children's primary role models for what to think, feel, as well as how to behave.

For example, typically, at the Irish dinner table denigration of Italians occurred. Meanwhile, the Italians denigrated Irish, Protestants denigrated Catholics, and Catholics denigrated Protestants. In a similar fashion, American Blacks belittled and criticized Jamaicans and West Indians, while Jamaicans and

West Indians talked about American Blacks disparagingly. Puerto Ricans spoke negatively about Dominicans, while Dominicans derided Puerto Ricans, as Cubans disparaged both Puerto Ricans and Dominicans. The list of ethnic groups engaging in negative discourse regarding some "different" group continues ad infinitum. This reflects the way in which American socialization includes the learning of affects of hate, stereotypes, myths, a host of misinformation, and discriminatory and violent behavioral practices in regard to many "different" ethnic, religious, and cultural groups (Wallace, 1993). Dinnerstein et al. (1990) discuss how, historically, different ethnic, religious, and cultural group members expressed hate and disdain toward each other.

Societal propaganda, newspapers, and, more recently, the mass media, have played a vital role in spreading misinformation and myths about specific racial and ethnic groups. The mass media permit widespread conditioning of both cognitions and violent behavioral practices. For example, in 1991, television viewers witnessed for over a year the videotaped beating of the African-American male Rodney King by White Los Angeles police officers. Quite a powerful opportunity for nationwide social learning and systematic conditioning existed when national and local television repeatedly presented the images of this horrific beating. Any new immigrant arrival to this nation may have received systematic conditioning regarding a seemingly condoned practice of unleashing violence against a person with dark skin color (Wallace, 1993).

A television viewer might be conditioned to believe that they and the police officers were superior to this base, dark criminal being beaten like an animal, arriving at a nativist assumption, or racism. Just as the police officers seemingly feared this dark criminal, whom they had to so subdue thoroughly, a television viewer might learn a xenophobic response to a person with dark skin color. How many new immigrant arrivals are conditioned into nativist beliefs and xenophobic attitudes and practices? How many of us, as U.S. citizens, reflect the nativist and xenophobic tradition of this country?

A process of social conditioning regarding violent traditions, practices, and beliefs began with the nativism and xenophobia that greeted new immigrant and migrant arrivals in earlier centuries in the United States and continues in this country up to the present day. A legacy of this social conditioning process may be seen in contemporary times with nativism and xenophobia being learned anew by the latest immigrant arrival. The mass media can effectively condition beliefs and practices that in their essence still constitute forms of nativism and xenophobia. Historically, nativism, xenophobia, and the resulting culture of violence perpetuated by negative stereotypes, myths, and misinformation created considerable stress in the lives of new immigrants and migrants. The threat and possibility of violence, mob attacks, and rioting followed from nativism and xenophobia.

The Stressor of Fierce Competition for Jobs

Fierce competition among new immigrant group arrivals and U.S. citizens for jobs and wages (Bonacich, 1987) led those who were climbing the ladder to the American dream to utilize the next immigrant's neck and back as a footstep for the upward climb. The latest immigrant had to endure the worst job, the worst pay, and the worst work schedule. Although jobs were often readily available, they were largely contingent on accepting the lowest pay and the least desirable work schedule.

Frequently, violence erupted (Higham, 1987), as strikes were broken with some new and exceedingly desperate immigrant or migrant arrival to the area. The use of new immigrant arrivals for strike-breaking illustrates the fierce competition for jobs. Immigrants and their families were routinely left frightened by the possibility of some xenophobic or economic-based hostility and violence that might erupt. Anger over the use of new immigrant or migrant arrivals to break a strike could easily lead to the unleashing of violence against the desperate new workers, or to rioting.

This competition extended beyond the acquisition of jobs to include competition for housing and real estate (Light, 1987). Success in competing for jobs affected one's subsequent ability to compete for housing and real estate. Obtaining the worst job with the worst pay often translated into living in the worst available housing. Again, many of these themes continue to the present day as common stressors in the lives of the latest immigrant and migrant arrivals to an area in the United States.

The Stressors of Poverty, Prejudice, and Discrimination

Among the stressors impacting immigrants and migrants, poverty, prejudice, and discrimination head the list. These stressors frequently led people to work under horrendous conditions. Poor Italian women worked in factories for pennies in the early part of this century, and in an era before child labor laws, children worked under inhumane conditions for next to nothing in order for their families to survive. Negro domestics and other migrants from the South worked for the lowest wages and had to live in the very worst northern, urban tenement housing or in boarding homes. Typically, living in cramped apartments within tenements, Negro migrants often lived doubled and tripled up in rooms and even beds—with virtual strangers—in order to survive. Cutting across the experience of diverse immigrant and migrant groups is the impact of stark poverty, prejudice, and discrimination, as significant stressors (Dinnerstein et al., 1990).

Stressors of Separation from Children and Family and Loss of Social Supports

Trying to escape poverty and a lack of jobs in the South, Negro migrants arrived in the North only to encounter new forms of prejudice and discrimination. Separation from children left behind had to be endured, especially as the reality of a new level of northern poverty meant delays in their dream to send for the children. Prejudice and discrimination also meant that Chinese men from an earlier wave of immigration had to endure without children and wives, as outright racist immigration policy barred these arrivals, while favoring the entrance of other European immigrant groups (Dinnerstein et al., 1990). These and numerous other groups suffered the stressors of separation from children, family, as well as loss of the social support systems back home.

LINKS BETWEEN PAST CULTURAL TRAUMA AND FAMILY DYSFUNCTION

Light (1987) argues that a group forced to survive specific sets of stressors may have a unique experience that seems linked to subsequent levels of functioning among that group's descendants. He suggests that the impact of slavery in the south was so great that many African cultural practices were destroyed, placing newer West Indian immigrants at a distinct advantage as they came to the United States and competed for jobs, housing, and real estate.

We can also ask, what was the impact of multiple cultural trauma or several eras of cultural trauma? The extent and degree to which a people are placed at a distinct disadvantage by virtue of having experienced a major societal trauma emerges as worthy of consideration. So why not consider the impact of multiple trauma?

A distinguishing historical feature for African-Americans may be the experience of multiple eras of cultural trauma. Just as a woman may experience one developmental period of physical child abuse, another adolescent and young adult period of domestic violence by a lover, and a violent rape in the crack culture as an older adult woman (Wallace, 1994), we may speak of multiple eras of trauma for a cultural group across several generations. If a woman shows symptoms and problem behaviors because of the cumulative impact of three developmental experiences of trauma, might an ethnic group show more symptoms and problem behaviors because of cultural trauma sustained across several generations?

**Pluralism: Opportunity for Recovery of What Was Lost under
Pressure to Assimilate**

In our efforts to become a pluralistic society, new immigrant arrivals are being permitted to retain their cultural practices and distinctiveness. In the past, when the pressure to assimilate prevailed, children sat in classrooms where only English was spoken and many families changed their last name to facilitate assimilation and avoid prejudice, discrimination, and violence. Under pluralism, however, for diverse immigrant groups increasingly language is retained, ethnic or religious group holidays are publicly celebrated, and various clothing and behavioral practices remain valued and displayed. But what about those whose relatives immigrated when assimiliation was the prevailing rule and imperative? Perhaps we need to grieve with a Welch grandmother who at age 95 can recall giving up a treasured culture for the sake of assimilation. We may also grieve for the subsequent generations because she was not able to pass on to her grandchildren or great-grandchildren one full sentence from the language back home, or the date of one Welch holiday. We may all need to take advantage of the prevailing conditions of pluralism and seek greater knowledge of what was given up in the process of assimilation by our ancestors and relatives, as they adapted upon immigration or migration to a host of stressors.

THE DYNAMICS OF STRESSORS CONTRIBUTING TO
FAMILY DYSFUNCTION

Stressors impacting families in any era contribute to the emergence of family dysfunction. Either in the past or today the stressors of nativism, xenophobia, poverty, prejudice, and discrimination affect families. These stressors may lead families to cross a thin line and enter into dysfunction. Discussion of how these common stressors in past and present eras may lead families to fall into dysfunction follows, in order to augment our multicultural education and increase cultural competence.

A Thin Line Separating Family Strengths and Dysfunctional Dynamics

In examining Table 3.1, it helps to imagine a thin line separating the information on the left from that on the right. This reinforces the notion that a "thin line" separates what we consider a family strength and the ever so subtle emergence of a dysfunctional family dynamic. As counselors and diverse community members who seek to engage in outreach, we may impart good news that empowers, as well as the sombering news that may provoke change in familes.

Table 3.1
Family Strengths, Enduring Multiple Stressors, and Crossing a Thin Line into Family Dysfunction.

Family Strengths Permitting Survival	Dysfunctional Family Dynamics
• *The extended family and reliance on caretakers.* Informal adoption, alternative childcare arrangements.	• Poor judgment in entrusting children to unreliable caretakers; insufficient protection of children; more opportunities for molestation, abuse, and neglect.
• *Courage and the endurance of trials and tribulation.* Confidence to immigrate/migrate and separate from family. "Temporary" separations of children from parents to pursue dreams in U.S.	• Pain from loss of support network. Temporary absence turning into an abandonment experience for children left behind. Anger and pain felt by children upon reunion. After reunion and time spent in U.S., children feel shame over their culture, ethnicity, race, accents, and illiteracy of parents/themselves.
• *Endurance of low wages, the worst work schedule, poverty.* Long hours away from home.	• Children receive little time and attention due to parents' work schedule. Poverty, living in dilapidated, cramped housing causes shame.
• *Flexible family roles and the responsible child.* Husband and wife share roles; responsible child takes on parental behavior. Both parents working or single parent households struggling to "make it."	• Children fill adult roles in home (age 31 at 13) and experience the burden of having to translate, write, pay bills, fill out job applications. Overworked parents come home tired; the responsible child is overwhelmed or rebels. Role behavior breaks down and no adult or child cleans, cooks, supervises, or nurtures children. Stress may lead to abuse and family violence.
• *Religious and spiritual faith as sustainer and nurturer.* Family members benefit from spiritual faith, as well as support network and structure associated with religious involvement.	• Rigid and defensive religious activities to ward disillusionment that the "dream" is not becoming reality. Religion as escape from pain. God's unconditional love replacing lack of acceptance in U.S.. Religious rules are too rigid; children are overcontrolled.
• *Communal social activities with members of one's community.* Share news, relax, celebrate.	• Adults role model hedonistic pursuit of pleasure, and excessive alcohol/substance abuse, gambling, compulsive sex, overeating. Intoxicated, disinhibited adults become violent.
• *Exposure to divergent role models in the home and community.* Observe variety of role models adapting and surviving through coping skills, strengths, and endurance.	• Exposure to contradictory and contrasting role models through observation of rigid, defensive religious involvement, as well as hedonistic pursuit of pleasure. This confuses children, creating potential for adult children alternating between the two types of behavior.

Families, through psychoeducation, may receive the good news regarding family strengths that permitted survival in the face of massive stressors. In addition, with sufficient empathy, we may point out some of the dynamics that emerged, which were dysfunctional and harmful to the development of children. We explain how the foundation was laid for children to grow up and exhibit codependence or maladies and problems associated with being adult children from dysfunctional families.

This section covers families of all socioeconomic levels, religions, and ethnic backgrounds. We frequently utilize the classic first family of the United States, the Kennedy clan, as an illustrative example, alongside cases of poor immigrants and migrants. This discussion also benefits substantially from a literature on the strengths of Black families.

Extending a Literature on Black Family Strengths As Universal

A literature on Black family strengths emerged partly in response to critiques of the Black family as pathological, advanced by Moynihan's (1965) classic report for the United States Department of Labor and a prevailing deficit view of Black families among White social scientists. Moynihan's controversial work provoked wide-ranging discussion of the rampant pathological Black family with its poor female-headed households from deficit and "blame the victim" perspectives. Focusing on strengths, African-American families have been described as extended families with specific adaptive features (Billingsley, 1968; Boyd-Franklin, 1989; Hill, 1972; White, 1972; McAdoo, 1981).

The classic Black family strengths discussed in this literature include informal adoption and the absorption of other's children and the elderly into family systems. Other strengths involve the adaptability and flexibility of family roles, as well as a strong religious or spiritual orientation.

Boyd-Franklin (1989) explains the manner in which Black extended family structures and roles interplay when they are functional, in addition to how they may become problematic and dysfunctional (p. 51). Within this discussion, we take the base of knowledge on Black family strengths and transform it into a universal prescription for survival for any poor family facing multiple stressors. We identify common strategies that are critical to survival in the face of multiple stressors. We may identify survival strategies that are universal, or simply characteristic of any family trying to adapt in the face of common stressors attendant to immigration and migration.

Family Strengths and the Emergence of Dysfunctional Dynamics

The seven family strengths that permit survival are listed in Table 3.1. We attain a greater level of cultural competence as counselors who come to understand how to view family strengths and empower families with our identification of these strengths. Within an empowerment model, we may utilize Table 3.1 to ever so gently point out how stressors may have led families to cross a thin line and enter into dysfunction. In this manner, the table is a practical tool that may find a role in the training of counselors, in the process of community members' self-reflection and analysis of their own family experiences, in the assessment of families, and in the course of providing feedback and psychoeducation to families. Discussion covers the point at which families may cross a thin line with the appearance of dysfunctional family dynamics, some trauma, or harm to family members beginning to manifest itself.

The Extended Family and Reliance on Caretakers

A family's ability to survive multiple stressors involves utilizing an extended family network for resources and caretakers. To create such a network emerges as adaptive when parents must work to survive. Also relevant is the use of informal adoption arrangements; a woman with four children has a fifth and "gives" this newborn daughter to an older aunt or sister to raise who has fewer or no children. This has been common in African-American extended families struggling to survive. The need to work in order to survive economically leads to alternative child care arrangements. Extended family networks may also include nonbiological neighbors, following immigration/migration to a new area. This process involves a struggling mother or working couple somehow managing to get to know one's elderly neighbor, accepting her offer of babysitting for infants/children, occasionally inviting her over to share meals or special holidays, and having one's children address her as "Miss" or "Aunt," showing respect. Survival practices of creating extended family networks in new immigrant/migrant communities have been critical at a time when new arrivals have lost old domestic, familial, and other social supports. These practices have been key to Black family survival.

In this discussion, we may also speak of upwardly mobile and rich families, such as the Kennedy clan, who have utilized many a "Nanny" or caretaker within their families. Our two-career families of the 1980s and 1990s are also to be included, for many hire an "au pair" or foreign live-in or daytime caretaker for their children. Urban playgrounds contain a rainbow of caretakers who usher White children from swings to sliding boards. The close bonds that often develop between the nanny and the children they care for suggests that many nannies in effect become extended family for children.

An African-American male Princeton University graduate who had been a freshman in the early 1970s at a time when there were few African-Americans in attendance, revealed that, to his surprise, some White males approached him with a great deal of warmth. Their attitude was born out of their affection for their Black nannies who were like extended family to them.

Despite such positive experiences among the rich with Black nannies, and countless other diverse experiences with alternative childcare arrangements, these kinds of arrangements sometimes contain the roots of trauma. Crossing a thin line into dysfunction, often parents use poor judgment in entrusting their infants and children to unreliable caretakers, and insufficient protection of children prevails. The very alternative childcare arrangements that one seeks as a means of family survival may present more opportunities for sexual molestation, abuse, and neglect.

In this regard, Shengold (1989) provides several relevant case histories. For example, a rich family taking a six-week or several month vacation abroad might find that the child or adolescent they left behind was sexually abused by the gardener, or some other caretaker. Wealth and privilege, notwithstanding, use of extended family and alternative caretakers may create opportunities for child abuse and neglect.

Courage and the Endurance of Trials and Tribulations

Many of those who have come to the American shores represent the "cream of the crop" relative to those who remain behind. They showed a great deal of confidence and inner resources in leaving their small village or home town, whether in Italy, Jamaica, or the American south. They have also had to endure many trials in their new environment, such as separating from a social support system of family members one might never see again, especially parents and grandparents. For example, Chinese men had to separate from children and spouses who were barred from immigrating because of the United States racist immigration policy. Perhaps most painful for mothers were separations from children. Unfortunately, "temporary" separations were frequently initiated with immigrants and migrants from places such as the West Indies, Puerto Rico, or the southern United States telling children of the "fine schools, nice apartments, and good jobs" to be found in the United States, or up north in the promised land. Many parents frequently told their children that they would be able to join their parents in their new home in a year or two. But all too frequently, a "temporary" separation turned into a prolonged period of abandonment, for the immigrant/migrant reality was more difficult than the anticipated dream. Some parents enjoyed the meager fruits of their relative upward mobility, while still in relative poverty. Child care options were unavailable or could not be afforded. A Negro live-in domestic might not have been able to figure out who would care for her children on a daily basis if they moved north—while the mother worked and slept elsewhere.

So, many parents endured the trial and tribulation of leaving their children waiting, hoping, and dreaming between packages and occasional visits—a quite painful abandonment experience. Opportunites for the abuse and neglect of those children left back home with relatives were introduced. Typically a five- and seven-year-old set of children is left waiting until the age of twelve and fourteen to finally join their mother in an immigrant or migrant port such as New York City. Typically, too, children and adolescents experience anger and pain upon reunion with their parents. These adolescents and children are often teased at school and in the community because of their different accent and odd clothing. For many of these children, the dream of reunification turns into a painful nightmare. For others, reunification is managed relatively well and is, indeed, a pleasant dream come true. Nonetheless, the lengthy period of separation and waiting for reunification represents a significant abandonment trauma.

Within the context of career and government service, members of the Kennedy family experienced some periods of separation from their children and family. Regardless of the socioeconomic status or rationale for separation from children, one may explore for the possible experience of feelings of abandonment during periods of separation. Most poignant, however, are the trials endured by migrants and immigrants which involved lengthy separation from children, as well as loss of social supports back home. Dysfunction may be introduced into families as a result of these separations.

Endurance of Low Wages, the Worst Work Schedule, Poverty

Immigrants and migrants have historically had to endure the worst jobs, pay, and work schedule, and have had to experience a new level of poverty—even if all this represented an improvement over conditions back home. Whether this meant working for pennies in the factories of the early twentieth century or for minimum wage on the night shift, or being a live-in domestic in the 1940s, these less than ideal work conditions have been tolerated. Frequently, Negro women who migrated north had to delay sending for children precisely because of their low wages, work schedules, and poverty. Even today, immigrant workers persevere in horrendous factories, working for less than minimum wage, often under a contract where they owe thousands of dollars for their illegal passage to the United States. Somehow most survive these conditions.

For families willing to work hard for the worst wage and following the worst work schedule, time spent on the bottom rung of the ladder means enduring poverty and unique stressors; for African-Americans time spent on the bottom rung of the ladder seems perpetual. The stress of poverty pushes many families across a thin line toward dysfunction and trauma. For example, some may feel shame and guilt about their cramped and dilapidated housing. Distant relatives may not be able to imagine the housing conditions endured in poverty; invitations to visit are avoided for shame. Not suprisingly, children who run free in open green spaces down south are not readily sent for to subsist in crowded one-room tenements in filthy, hostile northern neighborhoods overrun with vermin. Even greater shame attaches in having to return south and admit one's inability to make it up north. Therefore, conditions of northern poverty have often been endured in silent shame.

Culture, ethnicity, or race might also be sources of shame. The process of social comparison, wherein one discovers how others are living, can lead to a sense of shame. Shame also may follow when obscenities are shouted, teasing occurs, or one is exposed to the content of stereotypes about one's group. Children and adolescents may also feel this mortification over things such as their accent, their skin color, their parents' or their own illiteracy, or their language problems. The weight of guilt and shame may lead to alcohol abuse and engagement in other destructive and compulsive behaviors, such as overeating or gambling.

Shame and guilt may also be felt when domestics observe the privileged conditions of the White children they care for, compared to the far from ideal conditions under which their own children live. These feelings are especially intense when the domestic's children are abandoned for five or six days a week in a small tenement apartment with little or no adult supervision. Again, these conditions open the door for children to be sexually abused and molested by neighbors and irresponsible caretakers. When parents return to their children on their day(s) off, emotional pain as well as bodily fatigue from their heavy work schedule may plague them. Parents may remain emotionally unavailable for children whom they may barely know after a long separation and who only talk about problems at school or in the neighborhood because of an accent or strange clothing. All too soon, depressed parents have to return to their "worst work schedule" and endure for the worst pay. Shame and guilt may be camouflaged when telephone calls or letters back to the hometown or homeland betray the reality of struggling with the worst pay, worst work schedule, and persisting poverty. But parents and families endure, even as they cross the thin line toward family dysfunction.

Flexible Family Roles and the Responsible Child

The family strength of flexible roles permits survival. Flexible roles entail a father also cooking, cleaning, and actively caring for children while women work. Historically, in most African-American families women by necessity had to work, whether as domestics, factory workers, nurses, or school teachers. Both parents had to work in order to survive. Similarly, many families survive poverty by virtue of flexible family roles. Flexible family roles, which have been typical within the African-American community, found broader application in the 1970s when the women's movement led White women to enter the workforce in unprecedented numbers. With this trend continuing into the 1980s and 1990s, some men now stay at home to care for the children. But African-American men long ago cooked for families and gave children baths after a long day at work—while the wife's work schedule may have taken her away from her children after school and in the evenings as a nurse, nurse's aide, or live-in domestic.

Two parents working the worst work schedules for the worst pay also significantly impacted family life. Babysitters, cooks, and supervisors of younger siblings may have by necessity been other older siblings or a "responsible child" who acted like a parent. The parental child, or responsible child, was called upon to step in for parents when poor, struggling immigrant and migrant families could not afford babysitters. This child, quite flexibly, surrendered some of the comfort of childhood and assumed the extra responsibility of cooking, cleaning, and babysitting for siblings of diverse ages. Whereas in Hispanic families this role is typically taken on by the oldest female child, any child, especially the oldest male or female child, might end up in such a role within other families.

For example, an interracial couple with multiracial children in an era when marriages between the two major race groups in this country were illegal might find their responsible child in the oldest son. Imagine a five year old in the early 1960s standing on a chair cooking breakfast when the fire alarm goes off from excessive smoke and this responsible child follows his mother's instructions and takes each of his two younger siblings out of the apartment to safety. The lack of social supports meant that this responsible child was cook and babysitter in an era in which social supports were absent and society was least sensitive to the plight of a vulnerable family left without proximal social supports from their Black family down south, nor the White family up north who disowned the mother for her marriage choice.

Migration and immigration, as well as prejudice and discrimination, create considerable stress when a society does not give social support to those who have lost contact with their extended family and support network back home. A classic response is for that oldest child to become the responsible child. A child at age 13 must respond to the pressure to act as if he or she is age 31. Hence a short-hand method of recalling the essence of being the responsible child is to imagine being age 13 but behaving as if age 31. The price paid for one's childhood service in the name of family survival often involves growing into an adult who by age 31 feels like behaving like a 13 year old. A responsible child may become a rebellious adolescent or adult. Rebelliousness replaces an old responsibility, as evidence of fatigue from past acts of parenting siblings and bearing the weight of excessive responsibility and pressure. Quite simply, too many responsible children were overworked, overstressed, and paid an exceedingly high price for surrendering their childhood. The reality is that they frequently did not have a choice, as they were thrust into such a role to facilitate family survival. No child nor family member would eat if parents did not leave the home where the responsible child was left in charge.

Because of other common adult problems such as low educational attainment, language barriers, and illiteracy, children across diverse immigrant and migrant groups often had to be responsible children, deploying their knowledge of the English language and literacy. Children had to read and write for parents, pay bills for them, manage all their mail correspondence, translate for them, and even fill out all forms and job applications. Children often missed school to attend various appointments to translate and fill out forms for parents. Sometimes these tasks were also performed for extended family members and neighbors. Many of these responsible children also emerged fatigued and tended toward irresponsibility and rebelliousness as adults. Adult children and adolescents who played the role of the "literate one" or "translator" may harbor unconscious feelings of anger for the role they had to play. Feelings of guilt may prevent them from acknowledging deeper feelings of anger. Guilt involves recognition that the role they played was absolutely critical to family survival; so, why do they resent having played that role? Why do they feel they will explode if they have to write one more letter or translate one more time? Why do they feel tired and depressed, and why do they engage in passive-aggressive behavior?

Responsible children who grow up and turn into rebellious, child-like, depressed, passive-aggressive, fatigued adults illustrate how deployment of children in a responsible and parental role means crossing a thin line toward dysfunction. It involves the delivery of subtle, but significant, trauma to responsible children. Who would think that what constituted family members surviving the best that they could would emerge as a dominant and harmful pattern involving a "responsible child"—often called "hero" within the adult children of alcoholics movement? President Clinton took care of his younger brother and stood up for and protected his mother from domestic violence; as noted earlier, he is a classic example of a hero or responsible child from a dysfunctional family (Ifill, 1992). However, without debating the impact on our president, we must consider if and when a thin line is crossed toward the experience of some trauma and the emergence of family dysfunction.

Many contemporary families of divorce, single-parent households, and other diverse immigrant and migrant families enter into dysfunction, as a thirteen-year-old child begins to perform like a thirty-one year old. Conditions in these families, wherein parents work and responsible children step in to perform varied parental duties, may dictate that little or no attention be given to all of the children in the family. Whereas the children receive too little attention or no empathy, the responsible child is too immature, overextended and stressed by his or her responsible role to adequately meet the emotional needs of siblings.

The frustration inherent in the role may lead to sibling physical abuse and neglect.

Families that depend on a responsible child to take care of children at home, while parents work the worst job with the worst pay, may fall into chaos. In such families sometimes no one steps forward to fill a critical role because of fatigue, stress, and overwork. Perhaps no adult or child cleans, cooks, or supervises younger children. Parents who have been converted into functional workaholics from working for the worst pay on the worst schedule return home tired. Children go hungry and neglected. Laundry is not done. Dishes remain dirty, and vermin proliferate. Homes may become chaotic and filthy. Thus, families move ever so subtly across a thin line toward dysfunction. Hungry children feel frustrated. Tensions rise. Neighbors and schoolchildren begin to tease those who do not wear clean clothes, are hungry and steal or beg for food, smell like urine, and fail to reflect receipt of good and consistent supervised grooming. Tension, shame, guilt, frustration, and anger increase in such families, and violence may ensue. The criteria of a dysfunctional family are met, while parents still march off to work the worst work schedule for low wages, leaving the responsible child in charge.

Religious and Spiritual Faith As Sustainer and Nurturer

Within the Kennedy clan a strong religious faith sustained and nurtured Rose Kennedy and other family members in the face of tragedy. The African slaves may not have survived the Middle Passage, forced servitude, and violent whippings in the southern plantation economy had it not been for their religious or spiritual faith. Similarly, the religious or spiritual faith of Irish, Italians, Latinos, and other groups played a vital role in their coping with a multitude of stressors. Especially under the worse of circumstances, religion or spirituality becomes critical to persevering.

Religious activities may become rigid, however, and may be used defensively to ward off negative feelings. Feelings of ambivalence, disappointment, and disillusionment frequently emerge for new immigrants and migrants when the "dream" conflicts with an unpleasant reality. Both women and men may end up escaping a life of "work, work, work"—in adherence with their worst pay, worst jobs, and worst work schedules—through religious and spiritual pursuits. God's unconditional love, and connecting with it through a collective or individual state of worship, can be compulsively sought to replace the lack of love and acceptance in one's own life. Religious activities may become a preoccupation, since they provide for good feelings and are a source of reinforcement. The children and adolescents in these households may find themselves being rigidly overcontrolled by religious rules and activities.

The dysfunctional family rules of "Don't talk, Don't feel, and Don't tell our family secrets" are quite similar to the biblical injunction "Children are to be seen and not heard." In this way, a rigidity may come to dominate some religious families. Children may be negatively impacted by the subsequent rigidity, the loss of some childhood and adolescent spontaneity, freedom, and joy, as well as the lack of empathy and mirroring of their own internal emotional states. A home free of cigarettes, alcohol, and overt violence may be a setting in which some harm to children occurs by virtue of an excessive rigidity and failure to meet some of the children's needs. In innumerable cases, religious involvement provides structure, social support, and a nurturant environment for parents and children. However, we may need to consider those families where a thin line has been crossed, with religious and spiritual activities leading to dysfunction. At the same time we must still acknowledge and appreciate the critical role of religion and spirituality in fostering survival of the very worst of times.

Whenever religious or spiritual involvement becomes obsessive or harmful, we must at the very least ask what background conditions or stressors may have set the stage for an "escape into God's unconditional love." If we identify those stressors and provide social supports and other appropriate interventions, then we may assist the religious or spiritual individual or family in improving their functioning, without making any judgment as to whether or not religious or spiritual involvement is excessive.

Extreme caution and sensitivity must be exercised in this area, especially since fundamental cultural, ethnic, and religious values may be at issue. It may be more important to avoid being judgmental, than to raise an issue that may alienate or offend someone from a particular cultural, ethnic, or religious group. If we seek to empower community members to engage in the self-determination of their own standards of behavior and mental health, then we may simply respect their decisions regarding family involvement in religious and spiritual activities. However, when families acknowledge their religious or spiritual involvement as having negative consequences, perhaps after having access to this information, then we may assist them in pursuing behavioral change.

Communal Social Activities with Members of One's Community

Creating opportunities for socialization, particularly during one's leisure time, permitts survival in hard times or in a new strange place. Benjamin Franklin, while well known for discovering electricity and for speaking numerous wise words is less well known for maligning the German immigrants of Pennsylvania. Indeed, Franklin angrily criticized the Germans for their excessive affiliation with members of their own community, their social clubs, and their tendency to communicate predominantly with their own community members (Dinnerstein et al., 1990). Franklin's vocal outrage contributed to stereotypes and the very hostility and stress for which socializing with like members of one's community is perfect balm and healing.

Whether we speak of the German social club, the social activities in the Black church basement, the Irish pub on the neighborhood corner, the illegal "speakeasy" in a poor neighborhood selling liquor on Sundays and after bar closing hours, or the contemporary illegal social club that services new Central American immigrants to a neighborhood—all provide survival functions for new arrivals and families. These gathering places give people the chance to socialize, relax, and share news from the old country, meet prospective partners for dating and marriage who are also from one's own ethnic or religious group, or operate as the site for marriage receptions, birthday parties, and celebrations of births.

A thin line is crossed into dysfunction and trauma when these settings turn into sites for excessive alcohol use, substance abuse, or drug dealing—as have many. Gambling, promiscuous sex, and compulsive overeating may occur in these settings, being used to ward off negative affect and painful feelings, boost self-esteem, and create feelings of control. Hedonistic pursuit of pleasure to escape pain, bitterness, and feelings of not being in control of one's destiny may emerge among stressed out, disillusioned, or upwardly mobile American dreamers, regardless of the ladder rung on which they stand.

Perhaps the best example of when this line has been crossed can be seen in the lives of the Kennedy clan who have used Cape Cod, Massachusetts, and Palm Beach, Florida, as traditional locales for socialization with family and community members. However, these have also been the settings for excessive alcohol use, substance abuse, and the hedonistic pursuit of sexual pleasure. Socializing with members of one's own community, whether Irish, Italian, African-American, Latino, Asian, or other, has also created opportunities for families to experience dysfunction.

Exposure to Divergent Role Models in the Home and Community

A grassroots movement for adult children of alcoholics arose because these adults could recall all too well, and even emulate, the behavior of their parents and other community members who were unwitting role models for the hedonistic pursuit of pleasure and other compulsive behavior. There is massive evidence in the grassroots recovery movement that far too many children emulate the hedonistic pursuit of pleasure and engage in excessive alcohol or other drug consumption.

There is also exposure to role models in the home and community who have survived difficult conditions through coping skills and perseverance. However, complexities arise, and here, too, a thin line is crossed, supporting the emergence of family dysfunction and trauma, when young children have divergent role models. Children who observe role modeling by powerful individuals engaged in contrasting and contradicting sets of behavior may alternate between the two types of behavior, perhaps at different points across the lifespan. For example, Ted Kennedy may engage in raucous and wild alcoholic partying and sexual escapades, returning to his role as the humble, faithful, moral, and religious public servant. His son, Patrick Kennedy, may be the cocaine abuser as well as the pristine public servant. At different times, behavior reveals past identification with contradictory sets of role-modeled behavior. Within the Kennedy clan, we see evidence that children effectively gained exposure to role models of service to government with spiritual and religious moral overtones that are embraced and valued, as well as to alcoholism and sexual promiscuity. Even within one individual family member, evidence of both sets of identifications prevailing at different times can be found.

BEYOND NATIVIST AND XENOPHOBIC TRADITIONS CREATING STRESS IN CLIENTS' LIVES

Counselors and outreach workers need to be trained to become culturally competent because modern-day forms of nativism and xenophobia too frequently characterize those who have been socially conditioned in the United States. The traditional training of counselors provides inadequate preparation for cross-cultural counseling; feelings of superiority over and fear of certain clients may serve as an obstacle to effective service delivery. Encountering nativism and xenophobia in counselors creates stress in clients who often feel compelled to disengage from treatment or are disillusioned when subtle forms of prejudice and discrimination become manifest (Wallace, 1995).

The overlapping epidemics may compound feelings of fear held toward clients. Individuals from groups impacted by an epidemic may be in double jeopardy: counselors may look down on and may respond to them phobically. When a new program serving drug users, parolees, or HIV/AIDS clients "threatens" to enter a neighborhood, strong emotion akin to nativism and xenophobia is frequently aroused. Some of us who seek to engage in community outreach may have been members of communities who protested "not in my back yard."

Steps Toward Achieving Cultural Competence

In this part, we pursue the goal of producing cultural competence in trainees, compensating for professional training devoid of adequate preparation to work cross-culturally. We also seek to recondition citizens who because of their U.S. group membership need to remove the socially conditioned responses of nativism and xenophobia. As a first step, the goal is to take responsibility for possession of socially conditioned cognitions that reflect knowledge of myths and stereotypes, as well as for any responses of superiority and fear toward disdained group members.

Second, the way in which certain stimuli possessed by individuals trigger our beliefs and stereotypes must be observed. These triggers are typically suggestive of membership in a "different" or "disdained" group. When we encounter the stimuli of dark skin color, a last name, lower socioeconomic status, or low educational attainment, we may observe our own responses. These responses typically involve the experience of automatically processing common stereotypes and projecting them upon, or attaching them to, the target individual. For example, perhaps a last name suggestive of membership in a certain ethnic or religious group triggers stereotypic assumptions within us. We then project upon, or attach to, the individual stereotypes. Many Jewish, Polish, and members of other ethnic and religious groups changed their last names in order to escape prejudice and discrimination. However, dark skin color and heavy accents are not readily changed. Individuals possessing distinctive traits find that they cannot easily avoid triggering in others socially conditioned responses of superiority, fear, and the projection of stereotypes.

Third, the goal of attaining cultural competence requires a conscious transformation of automatic, socially conditioned responses of nativism and xenophobia into an intent to do no harm to other individuals by no longer making assumptions and judgments about them. Following Jung (1969a), we need to retract our projections. Observing that we have just attached a stereotypic assumption to an individual, we promptly retrieve it. If we consciously stop and suspend our cognitive processes we may no longer respond in an unconscious, automatic, "knee-jerk" fashion—being triggered into cognitively processing stereotypes and projecting them. We strive to interrupt and stop an automatic stream of myths, stereotypes, and misinformation entering consciousness as a reponse to another human being. We strive to be able to gain the ability to self-observe our socially conditioned cognitions, avoid projection of stereotypes, and achieve cultural sensitivity. (The graphic model introduced in Chapter 9 depicts this process, further enhancing our understanding of cross-cultural dynamics; see Figure 9.5.)

An Ethical Standard: Do No Harm and Engage in No Covert Violence

As counselors and community members engage in community outreach, it is imperative that we adhere to an ethical standard that does no harm and not engage in violence during interpersonal interactions with clients. When a counselor sits with a client and reacts to dark skin color, an accent, tattered or dirty clothing, or low educational attainment and projects a stereotype or negative and low expectation upon a client, a moment of covert and invisible violence has occurred.

Could an expectation of a poorer prognosis secretly held by the counselor, consistent with stereotypes and negative and low expectations, in any way contribute to unfavorable treatment outcomes? We strive to avoid the problem of unfavorable client outcomes by adhering to an ethical standard that will consider the projection of stereotypic, negative, and low expectations on a client as constituting a subtle act of invisible and covert violence.

Entering the Clients' Unique World View Versus Solely Following Anthropological Guidelines

One approach to training for cross-cultural counseling might seek to provide anthropological guidelines for social interaction with diverse groups, covering each cultural group's practices, traditions, beliefs, and values. This codification of rules for interpersonal conduct would have to cover a range of diverse groups, such as Chinese, Japanese, Koreans, Vietnamese, Cubans, Puerto Ricans, Dominicans, and Eucadoreans. With each new wave of immigration, we would have to add new chapters to our anthropological guidelines. Moreover, with a consideration of rate, degree, and extent of acculturation, as well as level of education, rural or urban background, socioeconomic level, and employment experiences, we would have to modify our guidelines for interpersonal interaction. The danger of utilizing anthropological guidelines rests in our coming ever so close to promulgating stereotypes or offending those newest immigrant groups that have not yet been added to our guidelines. We may also offend some individuals when we follow the guidelines (Wallace, 1995). For example, to greet a Latino family in Spanish at a bilingual clinic might offend, if we have not adequately assessed level of acculturation and other background factors (Curtis, 1990).

Hence, we seek to enter the world view of individual clients instead of falling victim to the pitfalls and dangers inherent in solely following anthropological guidelines. To engage in an individualized and thorough assessment of clients and family members, while attempting to enter their unique world view, represents a viable alternative that is highly recommended (Wallace, 1995).

A Possible Need for Additional Reading, Psychotherapy, and Supervision

Some people have been so harshly conditioned by family, peers, or the media that they may be solidly locked into the habitual projection of their own disdained parts onto classic societal scapegoats—groups that we feel deserve our expressions of racism, sexism, and homophobia. In such cases, reentrance into professional psychotherapy or participation in other kinds of professional workshops may heighten our awareness of unconsciously projecting onto "different" others (Wallace, 1993). Some of us may need more than what is offered in this chapter. Whether we pursue additional reading, an in-depth multicultural education, personal supervision, or additional psychotherapy, it is critical that we learn to retract our projections and avoid doing harm to clients.

Clients whose lives are ridden with violence and past traumas hardly need to be a secretly hated, disdained, xenophobic object from the counselor's perspective. If we cannot move beyond this level of automatic, knee-jerk projection of stereotypes and negative and low expectations, then we are better off not engaging in cross-cultural counseling and community outreach. Quite simply, it is an ethical imperative that counselors do no harm and engage in no violence.

THE CLINICAL TECHNIQUE OF A CULTURALLY SENSITIVE EMPATHY

The experience of a culturally sensitive empathy being deployed by counselors and genuinely felt by clients is the therapeutic goal when the ethnicity, race, religion, sexuality, or cultural background of client and counselor differ. Although I have never been an Italian immigrant boy who stood with anger and shame as my father was taken advantage of in business transactions, I have sat with such a client and achieved empathy with his inner self still full of these painful feelings. I have no idea what it is like to be an eight year old Yugoslavian immigrant girl and to feel deaf because I understand no English. Once English is leaned, I have no idea what it is like to fill out job applications for my immigrant parents, or what it is like to have made over 10,000 translations for my parents as I grow into an adult. But I have sat with such a young woman and felt empathy with her inner self that still feels overwhelmed with tension, pressure, anger, shame, and guilt (Wallace, 1993).

The deployment of this culturally sensitive empathy requires that I merely sit across from clients, listen ever so keenly to their stories and feel empathy for their inner self experience. The next step is to ever so gently hold up a mirror and reflect back to clients what we have felt and experienced empathically as perhaps their inner feelings, feelings that I may now label, identify and encourage the client to process by talking about their feeling and situation further. To the extent that we do this with some success, our clients who look across from us, seeing us and our overt "differences," feel genuinely understood and validated. Their inner self feels gratified that another self has felt their pain and validated their private inner experience without conveying judgment, criticism, or condemnation (Wallace, 1993).

When we effectively deploy a culturally sensitive empathy, we nurture the establishment of a therapeutic alliance. Regardless of a client's socially conditioned cognitions such as "White people can't be trusted," "Shrinks can't be trusted," or "Treatment does not work," a therapeutic alliance may permit continued work in psychoeducational and therapeutic groups (Wallace, 1993).

The first contact that a community member or client has with a representative of the mental health profession must be positive. If the aim is to promote community mental health, great responsibility rests with the client's first counselor or outreach worker. The counselor needs to greet the client with a genuine culturally sensitive empathy and must convey real concern and appreciation of the reality of another's pain, pride, and strengths, following an empowerment model. After the clients' and community members' therapeutic contact with counselors and outreach workers trained to be culturally competent, an increase in self-efficacy, confidence, and self-esteem should be observed among those assisted (Wallace, 1993).

For clients who have had repeated relapses and many different treatment experiences, our ability to be an exemplary professional/paraprofessional who does not project negative and low expectations or prophesy a poor prognosis can be quite reparative. With a culturally sensitive and empathic counselor or outreach worker, a client may develop a new, more positive attitude toward treatment, holding out hope for their positive transformation and behavioral change (Wallace, 1993). Patterns of underutilization of community mental health services might be reversed if more of us achieve cultural competence as spelled out in this discussion.

THE NEXT STEP OF RESOLVING PERSONAL TRAUMA: THE COAT RACK METAPHOR

Following a coat or hat rack metaphor, when a negative and low expectation is projected onto an individual, the possession of "hooks" permits the projection to land and stay affixed as though the projection were a coat or hat landing firmly upon and resting on a hook. If I possess low self-esteem and have internalized the cognition that "I am nothing" or "I am no good," then I am in possession of a "hook" that will permit another's negative and low expectations, or projections, to land on me and to rest and impact my functioning. It becomes very easy to unconsciously fulfill a prophecy that one is lazy, inferior, criminal, promiscuous, or some other aspect of a projected negative and low expectation when one can readily receive and hold on to such a negative projection. Thus, it follows that preventing the victimization of clients by any form of violence rests in reducing the potential for being placed into and remaining in a victim status (Wallace, 1993). This may occur by helping clients to address and resolve their experiences of personal trauma. Trauma resolution removes "hooks" and a tendency to unconsciously participate in receipt of a projection, enacting the stereotype. A case history describes this process (Wallace, 1993). Clients who receive trauma resolution respond to a projection as though it were water rolling off their back and shoulders. They emerge as resilient and capable of determining their own behavior, despite other's negative and low expectations. The important task of trauma resolution may be cost-effectively carried out in group settings, as described in Chapters 6, 7, 8, and 9.

CONCLUSION

Does our knowledge of the seven basic family strengths, or successful coping strategies with multiple stressors, and how a thin line is crossed as families become dysfunctional resonate with our own experience? Can we better understand protective factors in families that have enabled some siblings or children to emerge with a resiliency (Anthony & Cohler, 1987; Herrenkohl, Herrenkohl, & Egolf, 1994), a capacity to cope, and an ability to create a loving functional family in the next generation? Does an increase in our knowledge of historical factors that helped to create dysfunctional families translate into more empathy and understanding for families that seem to reflect an impact from a prior generation's experience of stressors or trauma? Does our common history as a nation full of immigrants and migrants who had to negotiate typical stressors suggest any solutions? Do we feel challenged by the ethical standard of doing no harm and avoiding covert, invisible violence in interactions with clients and community members?

What may emerge from our analysis of family strengths and the thin line separating family strengths from dysfunctional family dynamics is a clearer picture of how contemporary mental health promotion for our vulnerable families is absolutely essential. This is particulary true when forces of immigration and migration take away social supports and leave families in desperate need of solutions. Some of these problems are purely economic and might justify solutions that go beyond the purview of mental health promotion; we may need to become involved in advocacy. Other solutions may involve the systematic provision of mental health promotion through school- and community-based prevention, intervention, and treatment. In this way, this discussion has not only begun to justify contemporary mental health promotion, but has also provided practitioners with a psychoeducational knowledge base and a multicultural education, and may contribute to possession of cultural competence and the ability to empower families.

Part I effectively answered the question "How did we arrive here?" However, we only partially answered the question "Where do we need to go?" We have seen how three overlapping epidemics of crack and other drugs, violence, and AIDS create unique conditions that call for community mental health promotion involving outreach to children, adolescents, and adults within dysfunctional families. Taking an historical perspective, we have come to appreciate how stressors promote the evolution of dysfunctional families. This introduction and background has begun to provide those willing to engage in community outreach with a psychoeducational base of knowledge.

Part II provides intermediate training for the task of engaging in prevention and intervention when counselors and other community workers do outreach to children, adolescents, and adults. The three psychoeducational models presented in Part II provide training to outreach workers and constitute a curriculum for delivery to children, adolescents, and adults from dysfunctional families. Based on the information provided in Part II, we seek to more explicitly answer the question, "Where do we need to go?" Partial explanation is provided regarding the question, "How do we get there?"

II

PREVENTION AND INTERVENTION: INTERMEDIATE TRAINING FOR CONDUCTING PSYCHOEDUCATIONAL GROUPS

4

Psychoeducation on Healthy Parenting Behavior: Prevention of Child Neglect, Abuse, and Torture

In Chapter 3, we sought to understand how we have become a nation full of dysfunctional families. An historical perspective enabled us to appreciate the impact of stressors attendant to immigration and migration. Family strengths have also permitted a variety of diverse outcomes. While we might presume that the majority of families have ended up dysfunctional, various factors have enabled resilient children (Anthony & Cohler, 1987; Herrenkohl, Herrenkohl & Egolf, 1994) to grow into adults and exhibit healthy parenting behavior with the next generation of children. A healthy involvement with one's place of worship, community, school, special teacher, mentor, or other sources of support may have assisted families and individual children in maximizing their strengths. It may therefore be more appropriate to discuss a continuum of family types. Families ranging from the healthy to the abusive, to actually torturers of children may be identified. In community outreach to families, parents, and children, families are found to fall along this continuum. Growing up in different types of families is associated with varying degrees of problem behavior in children, adolescents, and adults.

Discussion of what constitutes healthy parenting serves as a guide for counselors and community members who desire to engage in outreach to others. What is good, healthy parenting? What is abuse and neglect? Too many parents who have been accused of abuse have defensively exclaimed, "There is no course on how to be a parent!" In this chapter, we make available the content of a psychoeducational curriculum that meets this critical need. This psychoeducational curriculum may be delivered across several sessions. Parents may participate in Part I in which the curriculum material, definitions, and categories are discussed, as parents offer their reactions. Parents may go on in Part II to experience a therapeutic group process for several more weeks. This experience permits parents who begin to learn about different forms of healthy parenting, abuse, neglect, and even severe abuse and torture of children to talk in more depth, and perhaps to recall personal memories of their own traumas in childhood and how they went on to repeat some of the same patterns in the parenting of their own children. Some of this discussion may be quite painful, especially for recovering chemically dependent parents. At the same time, other parents may appreciate how their own resiliency was manifested, since they went on to engage in healthy parenting, despite a past personal history of torture and abuse by a parent. It may be that psychoeducational group participants gain a new appreciation for that one parent, kind godmother, special teacher, mentor, giving neighbor, or best adolescent friend who gave some of what is described as healthy parenting. Group participants may begin to figure out how healthy parenting behaviors, whatever their source, helped them to survive and turn out as well as they did, even though a parent or an adult abused them.

The previous chapter showed how dysfunctional family dynamics may have begun several generations ago because of the stressors on family members who underwent immigration or migration without adequate social support. Patterns of dysfunctional behavior may have been role modeled to children in that generation, creating a propensity for dysfunction to continue in the next generation. Parents today may take advantage of an opportunity to break generational cycles of dysfunction by using this psychoeducational curriculum. They may learn about healthy parenting and how to recognize abusive and neglectful forms of parenting.

Counselors and diverse community members who seek to engage in community outreach and lead psychoeducational and therapeutic groups will also find in this psychoeducational curriculum a training guide in a new kind of counseling style based on the description of healthy parenting behavior. Counselors and outreach workers may also engage in a kind of "re-parenting" of those who were once abused and neglected by their own dysfunctional parents. Counselors, teachers, and community members need to know how certain modes of interacting are fundamentally healthy and beneficial to all human beings, whether we call it healthy parenting, a healthy mode of human interaction, or a preferred counseling style with those from dysfunctional families. This chapter's psychoeducational curriculum conveys critical information on healthy parenting behavior which may find application both in training counselors and in educating parents and other community members as to a healthy mode of human interpersonal interaction. The curriculum may ultimately foster discussion so that communities can engage in the self-determination of their own standards of behavior.

A CONTINUUM OF FAMILY TYPES

The psychoeducational curriculum utilizes Figure 4.1 as the centerpiece for discussion during one or several group sessions, depending on the length of the session and what participants decide to share. The Figure 4.1 presents a continuum of family types. At one end of the continuum is "healthy parenting," while at the other end is a kind of parenting and sets of experiences that constitute "torture." In the broad middle range, varying forms of neglect and abuse are located. On a continuum, any individual family might fall at a particular point, but we can speak of three broad categories or ranges of experiences: (1) healthy parenting, (2) a middle-range of varying forms of child abuse and neglect, and (3) more traumatic experiences with caretakers that qualify as forms of torture.

Analogous Distribution to the Normal Curve in Psychology

Psychology's bell-shaped or normal curve of distribution is suggestively placed above the continuum of family types. This superimposed bell-shaped or normal curve in Figure 4.1 suggests the relative distribution of various family types in our society. The vast majority of families within our nation fall within a broad middle-range of varying forms of child abuse and neglect. This category falls under the main portion of the curve and represents the majority of cases to be found occurring with the highest frequencies. Toward the left and right tails of the curve are cases that occur with much less frequency—families with healthy parenting and families with more traumatic experiences with caretakers, including torture.

HEALTHY PARENTING

Healthy parenting may be defined as the performance of behaviors by caretakers that promote the development of children affectively, cognitively, interpersonally, and behaviorally. Parents or caretakers appropriately interact with, stimulate, supervise, guide, shape, and reward children. Caretakers use empathy in relating with and responding to children in a manner that is consistent over time and becomes expected and predictable by children. Healthy parenting creates an overall home environment that tends to be orderly, consistent, predictable, and relatively calm. Parents may also be spontaneous and use humor, perhaps also playing with children or encouraging play behavior.

Figure 4.1
A Continuum of Family Types Providing Diverse Experiences for Children.

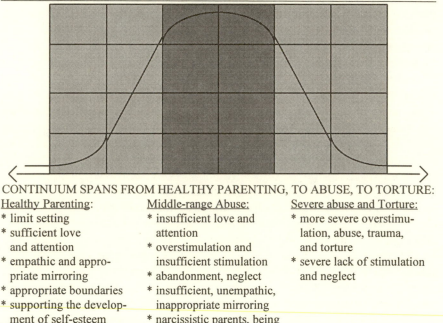

CONTINUUM SPANS FROM HEALTHY PARENTING, TO ABUSE, TO TORTURE:

Healthy Parenting:
* limit setting
* sufficient love
  and attention
* empathic and appro-
  priate mirroring
* appropriate boundaries
* supporting the develop-
  ment of self-esteem
* needs of child met
  above and beyond
  food, clothing, and
  shelter, as a new
  childcare standard

Middle-range Abuse:
* insufficient love and
  attention
* overstimulation and
  insufficient stimulation
* abandonment, neglect
* insufficient, unempathic,
  inappropriate mirroring
* narcissistic parents, being
  a parental self-object,
  codependency
* failure to foster boundaries
* verbal abuse, cognitive conditioning, and brainwashing

Severe abuse and Torture:
* more severe overstimu-
  lation, abuse, trauma,
  and torture
* severe lack of stimulation
  and neglect

EXAMPLES WHICH SPAN THE CONTINUUM:

Healthy Parenting:
* parental behavior is
  consistent and
  predictable and family
  environment is calm
* parents may use humor
  and play occurs in home
* use of verbal correction
  and non-violent punish-
  ment

Middle-range Abuse:
* classic dysfunctional
  family; chaos, inconsis-
  tency, unpredictability
  reign in household
* punishment by whipping
* physical, sexual abuse
* exposure to parental
  alcoholism, substance
  abuse, sex, fighting

Severe abuse and Torture:
* severe, chronic, or multiple
  trauma sustained
  through physical abuse,
  sexual abuse, domestic
  violence
* witness of violence, rapes

The figure uses psychology's bell curve to suggest the relative distribution and frequency of occurrence of diverse family types characterized by healthy parenting, a middle-range of abuse, or more severe trauma and torture of children. The key aspects of each form of parenting are described below the category; examples which span the continuum are provided, describing healthy parenting, middle-range abuse, and severe abuse/torture.

In this way, healthy parenting stands in contrast to a *dysfunctional family*, which may be defined as a family in which parents are unpredictable and inconsistent in their behavior and the overall family environment is at times chaotic, with the abuse and neglect of children also typically occurring.

Identifying Healthy Interpersonal Behaviors for Staff

Within mental health promotion, and specifically while engaging in pre-vention, intervention, and treatment, counselors and outreach workers must remember and embrace this description of healthy parenting behavior.

Counselors and outreach workers need to actively role model healthy parenting behavior as a way of being with others we seek to nurture and assist, and utilize it as a new kind of counseling style. As we work with, deliver services to, and nurture parents, families, adolescents, and children, we need to do so by performing the consistent and predictable behaviors entailed in healthy parenting.

Unfortunately, as a majority of community members and counselors may come from dysfunctional families, we may end up working in agencies that replicate a dsyfunctional family. If we engage in healthy parenting as an interpersonal style with our peers, we may improve community agencies as the context for service delivery. We may elaborate on the specifics of this interpersonal style, or recommended counseling style, by identifying a range of behaviors that are part and parcel of healthy parenting behavior with children—but also with clients, colleagues, and many others with whom we share and cultivate healthy relationships. If we introduce an interpersonal style that enables us to benignly interact with, support or nurture others, then aspects of what is described as healthy parenting behavior may find broad application.

Limit Setting

Among the behaviors that are vital to healthy parenting, limit setting is crucial. *Limit setting* entails establishing and repeatedly reaffirming that certain kinds of behavior are permitted and are subject to positive reinforcement, or the receipt of the reward of praise, for example. However, behaviors that are forbidden will cause the withholding of positive reinforcement and a possible felt experience of punishment upon learning the consequences of violating the set limits. A violation of set limits may mean receiving silence, no comment, a blank facial expression, or being left alone for a period of time, as possible examples. The therapeutic milieu that we aspire to create during a one-on-one interaction, or within a school, clinic, or community setting may only come about if it is a safe and therapeutic environment—made so by virtue of limit setting and the adherence to rules by staff and group members.

Limit setting typically involves clear rules that making threats, engaging in violence, or sexually acting out will not be tolerated. Limits set serve to maintain calm, peace, and order. Limits enforced with consistency and predictability should characterize an overall school or community environment. In effect, we avoid falling into chaos with consistent and predictable limit setting. The reality and facts of unpleasant consequences for violating rules also need to exist. However, an individualized assessment and approach should also be deployed with our vulnerable at-risk clients. Limit setting need not turn into a rigid and inflexible system that is blind to individual extenuating circumstances and the possibilities of relapse. In response to a violation of set limits, we may often match the offender to appropriate, more intensive, or tailored interventions for impulse management, behavioral change, or treatment for resolving the underlying trauma that may be causing poor regulation of sexual and aggressive impulses. We do not want to replicate patterns reminiscent of dysfunctional families, for institutions reflect a rigidity that further abuses and neglects clients. Throwing clients out of institutions and treatment programs in a reflexive, knee-jerk fashion is a sad legacy of the chemical dependence field. We must strive both to maintain and to enforce set limits, keeping environments safe and therapeutic as our top priority, while also meeting individual client needs for special, tailored treatment.

Managing Extreme Instances of Loss of Control of Violent Impulses

Healthy parenting behavior for managing instances of loss of control of violent impulses involves firmly and effectively holding children and preventing them from doing harm to themselves or others. In the case of a tantrum, or a sibling attacking another child, the violent child may be firmly embraced around the arms and body, perhaps sitting with her on the floor in this position until she calms down. Parents may also talk to the child in order to restore a state of control, as well as encourage the child to talk it out instead of acting out aggression and rage. Contemporary psychological approaches to childrearing discourage the use of beating or whipping, for this approach role models the use of violence for communication and for the control of others. Punishments such as "time out" are encouraged whereby individual children sit in a corner and may be excluded from desirable activities for a period of time, lasting anywhere from a couple of minutes to much longer periods, depending on the age of the child. Children may receive punishments that involve being denied access to their favorite activities for violating limits set by parents.

The Power of the Long Talk and Question and Answer Period
Versus Whippings

Parents who laugh and scoff at psychologists' recommendations are encouraged to avoid violence nonetheless and absolutely never to hit in a manner that leaves bruises or scars. In some cases, punishment may be warranted to prevent toddlers from harming themselves, such as by touching or reaching toward an open flame on a stove; a toddler's hand may appropriately be gently hit, while saying "No, don't touch. Hot!; No, don't touch. Hot!" However, with older children we underestimate the power of a long talk on the subject of the proper way to behave, involving asking a child repeatedly what they should have done differently and will do in the future. This lecture and question and answer format may be experienced as worse punishment than being slapped or hit, from the perspective of a child familiar with corporal punishment. The advantage is that we do not role model and teach the use of aggression and violence to solve conflicts. Instead, we teach children how to think, problem solve, anticipate, and plan—critical survival skills.

Masters Whipped Slaves, So Why Whip Your Child?

One approach to convincing African-American parents that healthy parenting behavior excludes beating children involves making an analogy to how masters beat slaves. Moreover, does any parent really want to beat and whip their child in a manner that is highly reminiscent of how a master beat a slave? Horrible parallels involve having children strip and stand naked before us. Parents who urge children to "stand still" during a whipping nearly replicate the way slaves with bare backs were tied down to prevent movement during a whipping. The selection of instruments for the delivery of the whipping is also uncanny. Instruments selected for a whipping strongly resemble the master's whip. The use of switches, leather belts, plastic ironing cords, and extension cords all harken back to the master's long and flexible whip. Parents who receive this psychoeducation may put away their whiplike instruments and resolve never to whip their child again. Creative energies may be put instead into the design of punishments that are suited to each individual child and their needs. So many children are both highly sensitive and extremely intelligent; we can talk to them and explain the error of their ways, almost reducing them to tears and hurting their feelings with verbal correction alone. The inadequacy of whippings for enforcing limits and in meeting our children's unique and individual needs for correction and instruction emerges. Many parents literally make swift and immediate resolutions to never beat their children like slaves again.

Control and Management of Violent Impulses in Groups

Within psychoeducational and therapeutic groups, counselors observe survivors of trauma responding to triggers that may upset them or cause flashbacks. Dysfunctional families may have also role modeled violence as a solution to disagreements or as an acceptable form of communication. We seek to change behavior of this type within psychoeducational and therapeutic groups. However, in extremely rare instances, individuals may verbally or physically threaten violence, or they may appear to be preparing themselves to engage in violence. In such circumstances, we respond actively and use our voice to set limits, such as "Sit down and listen. I said to sit down and listen." We use our voices in a strong, firm, and calm tone. However, at other times, we may actually rise, sit next to the upset group member, and place our hand on a client's wrist and hold the person firmly.

We set limits in psychoeducational and therapeutic groups and make the following principle clear from the very beginning of groups: "Violence is not acceptable behavior. If we become angry, upset, or frustrated, remember violence is not an option." We make this statement repeatedly in groups, offering a powerful suggestion and setting a clear limit. While it is always acceptable to talk about one's feelings and about flashbacks capturing our trauma, violence is never acceptable in the group. It simply must not occur. Thus, we need to develop a counseling style and mode of interpersonal relating in which we consistently set firm limits and enforce them in order to create a safe, therapeutic environment. It is to avoid the rare occurrence of an actual threat of violent behavior that we take the time to consistently set limits. By doing so, our group members and clients, even in the heat of anger, may possess deeply engrained knowledege of what is acceptable and unacceptable behavior. By conveying and enforcing clear limits, we help clients internalize a new standard of behavior.

We also foster in clients the internalization of a new standard of behavior involving group members talking about feelings, impulses, and traumatic memories. Counselors, parents, teachers, and community members encourage, support, and guide individuals in learning how to talk about feelings of anger and other affects.

Sufficient Love and Attention

In healthy parenting, affectionate and appropriate touching, embracing, and warm and calm interaction with children and adolescents occur. Children and adolescents need sufficient love, attention, and physical touch that is nonsexual. It becomes a bit of a challenge to translate this aspect of healthy parenting into an interpersonal mode or counseling style. However, we need to consider how sufficient love and attention also involves delivering to our children, or clients, on a regular, consistent, and predictable basis the positive reinforcement (reward) of our interest. Interest is a powerful emotion and involves our giving active attention to other human beings. We maintain eye contact, actively listen to what they are saying, ask questions, answer their questions, and offer responses in conversation that show we were listening to them. Interest feels good to the one being attended to and receiving it. Even in a counseling relationship, this begins to feel like the expression of love and attention to the one in whom we show interest.

Through genuine interest, high-quality time is spent with someone, and our emotional presence serves important functions. Interest, love, and attention are vital to the growth and development of the child, adolescent, and adult. Especially when we are arrested in development, stuck, or fixated at a certain developmental level because of past trauma, this form of interest, love, and attention serves as a powerful balm that stimulates healing and growth. Metaphorically, it is as though we have a wilted and stunted flower on which we begin to pour water and direct sunshine. Before our eyes the wilted flower begins to grow and is healed from past neglect and abuse. So it is with the display of genuine interest in another human being.

Twelve-step groups reflect the expression of unconditional love and acceptance and a level of affection or physical touch that is based on warm hugs and embraces that are not sexual in nature. Herein may rest one option for the counselor or community outreach worker. Another training standard for clinical psychologists may also be appropriate for consideration; herein any kind of gratification of clients' wishes and needs is not acceptable because hugging is generally avoided—although exceptions are to be found. A middle ground for counselors may involve permitting one's self to respond to a client's gesture indicating that a reciprocal "hug" or touch is appropriate. We do not want to appear insensitive, overly rigid, or reject or damage a client or student. But on this middle ground, we may never initiate or ask for a hug ourselves as counselors. Moreover, when any physical contact occurs, it is the counselor who at such moments is acutely aware of limits and boundaries, delivering a brief reciprocal hug with no sexual undertones.

If we know a client has sexual feelings toward us we may need to set limits and interrupt a hug with conversation, placing our hands on the client's shoulders and maintaining distance. Or we may need to discuss hugging behavior within the context of the client's feelings of sexual attraction toward us as their counselor or teacher. Nonetheless, limits need to be maintained to ensure that damage is not done by permitting a sexual relationship to develop with a client or student. Having once established a counseling or teaching relationship with an individual, it represents an abuse of power for a sexual relationship to develop even after termination of the formal relationship. Being careful to avoid exacerbating feelings of guilt or rejection in the client or student, care is taken in explaining how reactions of love and attraction toward a counselor or teacher are normal, but no possibilities for a sexual relationship exist.

We need to understand how our expression of the affect of genuine interest and active listening may feel like precious drops of water being poured on a wilted flower, or like invaluable love and attention, leading vulnerable clients to harbor feelings of love, gratitude, and attachment toward counselors. Like proud gardeners watching a flower we have watered and nurtured grow, we may even feel reciprocal feelings of pride, admiration, attachment, and love for a client. Ideally, however, this is the kind of love a gardener does feel for his flower collection or that a proud aunt feels for a nephew; it is a nonsexual love that does no harm and does not traumatize.

Because of the risk of sexual feelings between client and counselor, and because histories of sexual abuse may be high in the client population, the safest approach is to avoid physical contact and hugging altogether. Only brief, minimal affirming touches may be offered, such as placing our hand on a person's arm or on the center of the back when someone is crying. Clearly, individual decisions need to be made for individual clients and specific circumstances with an acute awareness that the client's unconscious wishes for sexual closeness should not be gratified. On the other hand, brief hugs that are natural and normal parts of our human relationships are appropriate.

By performing the behaviors of healthy parenting with clients during mental health promotion, we may "re-parent" clients and create the conditions under which a corrective emotional experience can occur. Yet, psychoeducation can empower current parents of children and adolescents to change their behavior "midstream" so that they can begin to initiate "healthy parenting" behaviors. For example, a parent begins to actively listen to an adolescent, hugs him, and tells him how special he is and how he is loved. The adolescent begins to bloom like a flower after a spring rain, while mother and son feel gratified by a healthier relationship.

Empathic and Appropriate Mirroring

Education on how to provide empathic and appropriate mirroring is also empowering for parents and counselors as well as for those who engage in community outreach. We use our inner self and the evidence of our children's and client's facial expression to achieve empathy (Berger, 1987; Hamilton, 1988; Rowe & Mac Isaac, 1989) with what they may be feeling inside. *Empathic mirroring* occurs when counselors and parents metaphorically hold up a mirror to children and reflect back to them their own emotional responses, the content and implications of their facial expressions, and what we have emotionally attuned to as their inner emotional experience. It may also involve creating cognitive dissonance by pointing out the discrepancy between a person's avowed refusal that "There is no problem!" and the facts of their having made some contradictory statements indicating that there is some problem (Wallace, 1991). Empathic mirroring may also involve creating cognitive dissonance by pointing out to children or clients how a discrepancy may exist between their protestations and denials of there being "No problem!" and the facts of their facial expressions and inner emotional experience. An adolescent, child, or adult client may sit with head hung low and eyes averted, perhaps even with tears falling, and protest "There's nothing wrong, nothing happened." We may need to drop our groceries, turn off the television set, or persist in one-on-one or group sessions in holding up a mirror and reflecting to them what we see. At the same time, we try to use our inner self to feel what they feel, also reflecting back to them, as in a mirror, what we sense they feel.

It is important to develop the ability to consistently observe and respond to diverse facial and emotional expressions, and to achieve appropriate empathy by also asking questions out of concern, and mirroring back what we feel and perceive is going on with the client, child, or student. This is a critical skill for counselors, parents, and teachers to cultivate and possess. This training in empathic mirroring may permit much more effective detection and intervention for children's and adolescents' problems. Suicides and school fights may be prevented, for example. This psychoeducational curriculum therefore serves to train counselors, parents, teachers, clergy, and diverse community members in empathic mirroring. Each one may teach one, for counselors may use this curriculum to train parents and other community members in a critical technique to foster healthy emotional growth in children. The skill of empathic mirroring is highly valued because it teaches human beings how to identify, label and process their own inner feelings. This represents a survival and communication skill that permits us to convey to others what we feel inside, as human beings. If we can verbally communicate our feelings, the option of using violence to communicate anger or frustration can be replaced with verbal exchange; or, we may be able to verbalize and process feelings, instead of reflexively self-medicating feelings to cope with the emergence of powerful affect. When human beings take the time to engage in empathic mirroring, they open the door for another person to achieve greater self-knowledge through the ability to identify, label, process, and verbalize affects. Empathic mirroring is discussed further in Chapter 6, along with the related technique of empathic attunement (Rowe & Mac Isaac, 1989).

Appropriate Boundaries

The deployment and maintenance of appropriate boundaries remains of paramount importance. Parents need to understand the importance of developing appropriate boundaries in children and adolescents. Appropriate boundaries serve to protect children, adolescents, and all family members, regardless of age. Maintaining a clear boundary may protect us from states of sexual, or aggressive, or emotional overstimulation that could lead to trauma. A *boundary* is analogous to a door that only we should decide to open or close, helping us to feel safe, calm, protected, and in control. A door protects us from stimuli that may be overwhelming, because we can decide to close the door. Individual preferences for what is too loud or too offensive also prevail when diferent persons make idiosyncratic decisions as to when they want to close their door. Boundaries may prevent the experience of overstimulation of a child or an adult. Overstimulation may occur through exposure to another human being's sexual or aggressive behavior which somehow penetrates or bypasses our door, when we would prefer to close our door, or keep up our boundary. Aggressive and sexual impulses could be expressed verbally or physically toward one who ends up having his or her boundary violated. When a boundary is violated, it is as though someone kicks in our door, enters our private space, upsets us, and destroys our sense of safety and control.

The deployment and maintenance of boundaries prevents children and adolescents from witnessing parental sex, nudity, and fighting, or other sources of overstimulation. To witness these events could cause overstimulation and could constitute a violation of boundaries. In addition, excessive and unwanted physical touching and hugs could also constitute a boundary violation and cause overstimulation. Individual difference in desires for love and affection should be respected. Children should not witness parental sex or be able to experience even covert forms of incest and sexual overstimulation by virtue of overhearing or being able to glimpse parental sex. Parents should similarly not observe, witness, or try to glimpse their adolescent's sexual expressions and practices, or a child's masturbation habits—if boundaries are adequately maintained. Some events are meant to occur when individuals are in private and safe behind their boundary or closed door. A closed door may be respected, as it both concretely and metaphorically may be a symbol of a boundary that is not to be crossed or transgressed.

We must continually evaluate the nature of physical touching and other verbal interactions with clients to ensure that overstimulation does not occur. Even discussion of substantial information on the part of the counselor or teacher about issues that go beyond the tasks of mental health promotion or teaching may suggest some loss of boundaries, or our failure to maintain appropriate boundaries. Why open our door so others can look within us, if it may overstimulate others? Some dimensions of our personal life, such as our sex life, would fall into this category. However, in contrast to a training standard for clinical psychologists who are told of a preferred neutrality and avoidance of talking about one's personal experience, greater flexibility exists on the part of counselors, paraprofessionals, and other community members who within the context of a psychoeducational group might tell a story touching on personal experience. Personal decisions may dictate at what points boundaries need to be maintained by not engaging in too much self-disclosure. Clearly, we all need to avoid verbal, physical, and sexual abuse, all of which would indicate violation of appropriate boundaries. We want to avoid the unwanted and undesirable overstimulation of child, client, or student. Maintaining boundaries enables us to do this.

Supporting the Development of Self-Esteem

Healthy parenting facilitates the development of a healthy, high, and positive self-esteem. We want children, adolescents, adults, and clients to have a sense that they are of value. In developing self-esteem, social conditioning occurs and results in internalized cognitions, or self-statements that individuals can effectively deliver to themselves or share with others. Cognitive conditioning of self-statements occurs when we verbally state aloud and discuss with clients or with others around them in their presence clients' positive attributes and strengths. We hold up a mirror and reflect back to them what we see or observe about them, also utilizing empathic mirroring, but now to build self-knowledge of their positive attributes. This effectively proves that we have carefully observed different things about them when we listened and showed interest.

We can also think of these verbal comments as what is said aloud when the mother has that "gleam in her eye" of pride, fostering a healthy narcissism and self-love in the toddler. The individual receives positive social reinforcement of praise. By simply stating "I'm so proud of you," we create a situation in which we socially condition in our children, students, or clients new cognitions about themselves. These conditioned cognitions may reemerge as positive self-talk, or as a guiding self-concept in regards to how they are, and how they function as a person of value in this world. For children, adolescents, and adults to be told that they are kind, smart, and artistic, or possess some other attribute creates a metaphoric "tape recording" that may be "played back" or delivered in positive "self-talk." This counters any low self-esteem from past verbal abuse (see pages 77 and 78). The individual has the ability to maintain a healthy state of self-esteem. The tool for maintaining healthy self-esteem involves playing back the tape recording or delivering to the self positive "self-talk" and a description of one's positive attributes. Internally, it is as though we have the capacity to deliver messages to ourselves that cover the topic of our self-worth and value.

Little did I think as a counselor that a critical intervention would be simply to state "I am so proud of you," as I seek to "re-parent" individuals who never heard such words fall from the lips of their parents or any other adult. However, the seeds of self-esteem are sown in this simple and vital act appropriate for counselors, parents, teachers, and other community members. In this way, we empower clients and students to regulate their self-esteem because we provide them with the content of self-talk and tape recordings they can deliver to themselves—covering how they are of value. They are empowered to be able to hit a playback button on a taperecording and hear anew a listing of their positive virtues.

A New Standard of Childcare

By providing this psychoeducation on healthy parenting behaviors, we assist in establishing a new standard of childcare. This standard requires that we strive to meet more than the basic needs of food, shelter, and clothing. A depression era standard is captured as we imagine a parent standing over the dinner table and telling a twelve-year-old child, "You've got food on the table, clothes on your back, and a roof over your head. Sit down and shut up." The parent may reinforce the message with a backhand slap aside the youth's head. During the Great Depression, high standards for parenting were being met under such circumstances. However, a new standard is needed toward which parents may strive, even when "midstream" and in the process of raising children and adolescents. Moreover, through this psychoeducation, a variety of members of the community may learn appropriate techniques if they are to step forward and join in raising children in that community. Behavior for use within a counseling style also emerges from this psychoeducation on healthy parenting behaviors.

A MIDDLE-RANGE OF VARYING FORMS OF ABUSE AND NEGLECT

The majority of those who attend psychoeducational groups can identify elements of their own parents' past behavior, or their own parental practices within a broad middle-range of parenting involving forms of abuse and neglect. A number of behaviors can be characterized as constituting this typical style of parenting. Within these "middle-range" families we may observe verbal abuse, fondling, harsh punishment, physical abuse, sexual abuse, parental alcoholism, or chemical abuse and dependence, or open parental sex. Such families may produce a significant and substantial amount of trauma in their dysfunctional family survivors. By necessity, we may compare unhealthy, abusive, and neglectful forms of parenting against the standards of healthy parenting behavior we have just described.

Insufficient Love and Attention, or Inappropriate Attention

Within this middle-range of neglect and abuse, opportunities for feeling loved may become confusing when attention and interest involve the expression of parental or adult sexuality. A parent's interest and attention may be in the form of physical abuse. When parents are preoccupied with their own domestic violence they may not give appropriate attention to children. Because parental behavior is inconsistent and unpredictable, children and adolescents who may have received, or do receive, some love and attention, may only receive it in accord with the family principles of being inconsistent and unpredictable. Children get attention when parents are not fighting, or when Daddy is not drunk. Or a child cannot predict when a parent will beat them, as it may not matter what they do or how they behave.

Overstimulation and Insufficient Stimulation

Shengold (1989) discusses both overstimulation and insufficient stimulation. *Overstimulation* occurs when children, adolecents, or adults experience more fear, anger, confusion, or emotional pain than they were ever meant to experience as human beings—or as human beings at that particular developmental level. An adult may be severely battered physically and a child may witness this beating; both parent and child would suffer overstimulation. Or a child is sexually abused and experiences the arousal of sexual tension that is not meant for that developmental stage; this constitutes overstimulation. A child may be verbally abused and humiliated by a parent in public or in front of siblings and neighbors. This child experiences an intense state of shame, again exemplifying overstimulation. Intoxicated alcoholic parents may engage in uninhibited sex in the living room and children witness this act, being overstimulated. For children experiencing forms of abuse and violence directed against them—whether physical, sexual, or verbal abuse—we may refer to the experience of states of overstimulation. In addition, we can assume that some violation of boundaries has occurred. A metaphoric door, or boundary, has been opened, or kicked in, or ripped off of its hinges, depending on the severity of the overstimulation and trauma.

At yet another extreme, we can discuss instances of *insufficient stimulation*, as in severe neglect (see page 74). This may occur in instances where children are left unattended for hours, days, or weeks. An infant who is left for four to seven hours of waking time to play alone in a playpen represents a possible context for the experience of insufficient stimulation. Those elements of healthy parenting behavior involving the provision of empathic mirroring are absent for long periods in the infant or child's life. We may also define insufficient stimulation as involving the absence of sufficient parental love, interest, and attention. If parents are preoccupied with their own depression, or other mental illness, have an alcoholic blackout, nod for hours on heroin, or leave a child alone without caretakers to go out to get high on crack, insufficient stimulation may damage and traumatize children. Such children are like flowers that begin to wilt and are stunted in growth because of insufficient water and sunshine. An adequate sense of self may not develop, or there may be an interruption in development.

Abandonment and Neglect

Abandonment occurs when infants, children, and adolescents who developmentally still need the guidance, supervision, nurturance, attention, and love from a parental figure do not receive it. Frequently, insufficient stimulation occurs along with abandonment. A lack of interest, attention, and stimulation may be the result of the parent's voluntary or involuntary absence—either physically, geographically, or mentally and emotionally, or because of some disability or impairment. Abandonment may also include being left without sufficient emotional or social support, perhaps as a "responsible" or parental child cares for a younger sibling. Parents show insufficient love and attention when they are absent and the responsible child has to literally fend for herself and her siblings, during stressful periods that may last from several hours to weeks, months, or years. A trauma results that varies in its degree and extent, depending on the child's age and maturity level at the time of the abandonment, the stress of also caring for other abandoned siblings, the conditions and length of the abandonment, and the presence and impact of other stressors and factors. Abandonment may be complicated by poverty, lack of food, and endurance of hunger.

Neglect typically involves periods of physical abandonment by a caretaker who leaves the home so that children do not receive sufficient attention, supervision, nurturance, as well as the basics of food, clean clothing, and a safe environment. Neglect may also involve an abandonment that is emotional; a parent who is physically present is unavailable to perform caretaking behaviors for some period of time—either because of drug addiction, alcoholism, or periods of mental or physical incapacity. The degree of damage sustained by a child as a consequence of neglect depends on the age of the child, his or her ability to engage in self-care activities (make a sandwich or a bowl of cereal), and the frequency and length of the periods of abandonment. The more frequent the abandonment and the longer it lasts, the more severe the damage to children. Insufficient stimulation may also occur as a part of neglect.

Within this middle-range of parental abuse and neglect of varying forms, examples of abandonment experiences include an alcoholic or drug addicted parent on a one day or weekend binge, or a parent with mental illness who is depressed or caught up in hallucinations and delusions. Another example may be a parent who migrates or immigrates and leaves children in the small village or town back home with relatives, or a parent who spends an entire weekend gambling away from home. By virtue of having been abandoned, the experience of neglect typically follows for children in these circumstances.

Insufficient, Unempathic, and Inappropriate Mirroring

Insufficient, unempathic, and inappropriate mirroring involves the discovery that one's interpersonal relationship with key parenting, caretaking, and nurturing figures is such that no one seems to search the child's face for emotional expressions in order to hold up a mirror and reflect back with empathy and concern what the child seems to be feeling. Any interactions that are validating to that child's inner self-experience occur on an insufficient basis. Or the feedback is devoid of empathy for the child's internal emotional state, or at the time is much too unempathic. There may also be a form of mirroring that is inappropriate. When inappropriate, parents might taunt and tease or put their offspring down for their feelings, perhaps telling them they are "soft" or "weak" or a "cry baby." As a consequence, some harm or trauma may occur, particularly when what happens instead is the conditioning of the inhibition of affect, or a socialization process emphasizing the restriction of affect, or a hardening against the appearance of even having inner affects. Parents hit children who are crying and urge them, "Stop crying, I said stop crying," as they hit a lip that is poked out, or slap them against the head. Children conditioned in this manner may grow up not knowing what they feel, or how to process, communicate, and express internal feelings. They lack a critical survival skill and are more vulnerable to the use of violence for communication when angry, frustrated, or upset. They are in double jeopardy for communicating with violence if their parents also role modeled violent behavior.

Narcissistic Parents and Being a Parental Self-Object: Codependency

Another possibility involves finding within this middle-range of abuse and neglect opportunities to interact with an alcoholic, high, or otherwise highly narcissistic parent. A *narcissist* is self-centered, self-absorbed, and temporarily regressed to a developmental stage wherein they are egocentric like a three-year-old. The narcissist expects to be the center of attention and focus of others—not unlike an egocentric toddler. Metaphorically, the narcissist is like the sun and all others are like the planets who revolve around the sun; the planets merely reflect and mirror back the light of the sun. Interaction with the narcissistic parent involves finding that one can easily become a "self-object" or extension of the self of that narcissistic parent. The mother of a little girl named

Nancy may begin to drink heavily when the child is five years old. Ideally, Nancy's self and feelings are the center of her focus and concern. And her parent also mirrors back to Nancy what she is feeling. Instead, the alcoholic or narcissistic parent becomes the center of the household and is the focus of the little girl; the little girl must awaken and ask, "How is mother feeling?" Nancy does not get in touch with how she herself is feeling. Her main concern is how mother is feeling, since a more irritable or frustrated mother may become violently out of control. Instead of continuing to develop as a separate and distinct self-object with the help of an empathic mother who mirrors back to her how she is feeling, Nancy begins to develop as an extension of the mother's self. She begins to function as a self-object of the mother or as a codependent. To be a self-object or an extension of a parent's alcoholic self means that a child may perform vital functions for the alcoholic mother's self, such as some of that "self-care" mother should be exhibiting. Instead of mother being able to calm herself as a form of good self-care, Nancy attempts to calm and soothe mother. Nancy brushes mother's hair, dresses her, puts her to bed, feeds her, and bathes her—especially when mother is drunk and most prone to violence if frustrated.

Other types of narcissistic parents can be seen experiencing any perceived lapses in their child's goodness, perfection, or state of ideal beauty as a moment of catastrophe calling for release of rage or emotionally falling apart. Such a mother may methodically dress a young child to perfection, as before a wedding, and once the child's mother discovers a dirty spot on the child's clothing, goes into a rage and attacks. Mother might scream, "I hate you! You ruin my life! You have spoiled everything! We can't go anywhere looking like this." Such a narcissistic mother is experiencing her son as an extension of her self, reflecting ever so directly and personally on her own inner self-experience and self-concept.

When functioning as a self-object for a narcissistic parent, there is a profound boundary violation that holds sway on a protracted basis. Mother's door is constantly open when she is drunk, high, or overinvolved and overconnected with her child. In addition, the child's door or boundary has been pushed open, and a plank or ramp connects the two doors. However, events occurring inside of the mother spill over, enter the child's door, and dominate the child's experience of life. The child begins to consider and respond to what is happening inside of mother, and not to what happens inside of him or herself, or is transpiring behind his or her own closed door. To be a self-object for a narcissistic parent on a protracted basis may mean that a child does not develop a separate sense of self. How can the child do so if she always attends to and focuses on mother and what is going on inside of mother's self?

As mother or father loses control and fall apart—either emotionally or through alcoholic intoxication—the child learns to perform behaviors to help the parent have the appearance of regaining control. The child learns to think of what to do to calm the parent or take care of the parent, no longer thinking about his or her needs as a separate object. Stiff, fancy clothes are worn as a child struggles to stay clean and be perfect, or mother's vomit is quickly cleaned up and her face washed. This analysis of the impact of states of parental narcissism or intoxication within dysfunctional families suggests a definition of codependency. *Codependency* represents the predominance of a personality style and orientation to interpersonal relationships that have its basis in the early conditioning, or learning of role behavior where one was forced to serve as a self-object for another narcissistic, self-centered individual. As a result of this past history of learning, the individual may manifest rather fixed patterns of action that reflect a tendency to repeat or reenact that pattern of behavior wherein one serves as a self-object for another narcissistic individual. With the metaphoric door wide open, one unconsciously seeks to connect with a self-centered individual who expects others to respond to their internal needs. The codependent extends a plank or ramp to the narcissist's or new adult addict's door who is their new romantic partner; events within the life of the narcissist/addict come to dominate the life of the codependent.

Failure to Foster Boundaries

As already discussed in our analysis of the middle-range of varying forms of abuse and neglect in its many manifestations, failure to foster and maintain boundaries is common. Such a failure is inherent in committing any form of violence against another human being. Following our definition, to do violence in the form of verbal, physical, and sexual abuse is to violate a boundary. Exposing children to parental sex, excessive parental nudity as children get older, or domestic violence, might overstimulate the child. Whenever the child's ego cannot understand, or make sense out of an experience, or when the stimulus barrier (door) is broken, a state of overstimulation is experienced. When parents engage in behaviors that serve to produce a state of overstimulation in their child, the boundary violation causes a level of anxiety, fear, and aggression that has a harmful and traumatic impact on development.

Parents are supposed to shore up and support their infant's and children's barrier (door) to aversive stimuli, not be the cause of that stimulus barrier being overwhelmed and penetrated by unforgettable states of overstimulation, pain, anxiety, and trauma. Of further note, parents within this middle-range of neglect and abuse may also be inconsistent and unpredictable in violating children's boundaries. This may serve to overstimulate children intermittently, just as to be a dysfunctional parent means being inconsistent and unpredictable in parental behavior. To ensure that no harm is done to children, parents should be willing to step in front of, block, and reinforce a child's door, or metaphoric boundary. Instead, many parents have opened, kicked in, and taken the hinges off the doors—failing to preserve boundaries and violating boundaries. In contrast, counselors, educators, and trusted persons are supposed to consistently support and strengthen children, clients, and students—and not be a source of overstimualtion by failing to respect boundaries.

Verbal Abuse, Cognitive Conditioning, and Brainwashing

Children sustain *verbal abuse* when they are severely criticized, called names, and receive feedback about themselves that is negative and demeaning. During verbal abuse, *cognitive conditioning* occurs—as children learn cognitions or thoughts about themselves that are negative and bad. Metaphorically, parents who engage in verbal abuse and systematically teach their children bad thoughts about themselves are recording information on the child's tape machine. Unfortunately, children will be able to hit a playback button and hear again and again negative information about themselves. Verbal abuse typically produces feelings of low self-esteem.

In *brainwashing*, a process of cognitive conditioning occurs that involves children being systematically socialized into a distorted dysfunctional view of reality that contradicts their internal feelings and responses. Children experience forms of brainwashing when a dysfunctional family denies that certain things have happened in the home or to the child. What the child perceives and experiences as real is not suported, validated, or spoken about. The dysfunctional family may act like the event never occurred. In this regard, Shengold (1989) informs us not only regarding a view of overstimulation and degrees of overstimulation and insufficient stimulation, but also regarding brainwashing. The family system's and parent's denial effectively serves to provide a form of brainwashing. When we see mother constantly intoxicated by the time she is cooking dinner and no one ever mentions the vodka bottles that fall empty out of the laundry basket and kitchen cabinets, we are cognitively conditioned into "thinking nothing of it." While a child may feel that there is a major problem, the family socializes the child into taking the classic dysfunctional family stance involving massive denial and no open discussion.

As counselors, parents, and teachers, we perform a critical function by listening with full interest and attention to tales and stories of what children witnessed and experienced; we believe them and validate that what they experienced was overwhelming, shocking, and horrible—even if a part of them got used to it as a common occurrence. In this manner, we assist in breaking through a denial and brainwashing that was part of the dysfunctional family experience. We affirm their reality and assist in giving up denial of painful aspects of that reality. We provide psychoeducation of the kind offered in this chapter explaining forms of parenting that they should have experienced; we distinguish healthy parenting from the forms of abuse and neglect that they suffered. Clients, students, and parents may learn for the first time that what was typical in their home was actually a form of abuse or neglect. They may appreciate for the first time that their symptoms and problem behaviors relate to their past dysfunctional family experiences; and for the first time in their lives, they may come to understand their experiences as constituting trauma.

MORE TRAUMATIC EXPERIENCES AND TORTURE WITH CARETAKERS

At the end of our continuum of family types are cases that occur far less frequently; cases that involve "more traumatic experiences with caretakers" and even "torture." Some caretakers have, in short, been torturers of children, adolescents, and family members. Or children and adolescents had encounters with some caretaker or adult who abused or tortured them. Some adults, siblings, and family members may have led lives where the absolute free and unrestrained release of aggression or sexual impulses by some dominant family member was the rule of the day. Human objects in these social environments have been traumatized, and often severely so, when aggressive and sexual impulses found release upon them.

More Severe Overstimulation, Abuse, Trauma, and Torture

Shengold (1989) discusses how under conditions of severe overstimulation, or where yet greater trauma is occurring, we see even more massive violation and penetration of boundaries. Severe overstimulation involves states of even more intense and heightened anxiety, fear, and pain. Sometimes we marvel at how the experience of these states was endured and how people survived.

Typically, those who experienced severe overstimulation had to wonder about the possibility of death and experienced the anxiety associated with being trapped. When anxious and frightened, an instinct to engage in either "fight or flight" may be activated. Many survivors of severe overstimulation could neither fight nor flee, experiencing overwhelming states of high anxiety as they felt totally dominated, completely helpless, and trapped. "Fight and flight" impulses were triggered by the presence of the aggressor, and both were often blocked as viable options, as victims may only be able to stand frozen in fear, sustaining an assault. There may be a moment when an organism senses that death is imminent, and they may relent, submit, and prepare to die. Some severely tortured adults, adolescents, and children have had this experience. In psychoanalysis, in sensing imminent death and the anxiety and fear associated with this intuition, *thanatos*, or the death instinct, may be said to have been activated. The resulting state of overstimulation would indeed constitute the experience of a considerable degree of trauma.

Within this category of parenting behavior, encompassing traumatic experiences with caretakers, much more severe forms of abuse occur than in our previous middle category. Here, we encounter evidence of some of the most unhealthy, dysfunctional behavior on the part of parents who engage in acts characterized by the release of sexual and aggressive impulses, as well as a powerful rage, during interpersonal behavior with children. Instances of physical and sexual abuse, and witnessing violence against another family member, as well as witnessing sexual scenes and rapes of siblings abound in this category.

The experience of multiple and chronic trauma also justifies a reference to severe overstimulation. For example, in *multiple trauma*, one experiences several overstimulating events—perhaps being both physically and sexually abused, and also a witness to domestic violence or the abuse of one's siblings. In *chronic trauma*, there may be repeated instances of overstimulation (rape and sexual abuse) across several years, or spanning from early childhood to adolescence. Or for many years one may experience physical abuse by a parent which may escalate in severity and not end until young adulthood and a move out of the home. Alternatively, chronic trauma might involve witnessing domestic violence nearly every day and over every weekend lived with alcoholic or crack cocaine-addicted parents—spanning many years and witnessing innumerable bloody battles. Through chronic repetition of the overstimulation, the subsequent overall experience of the victim goes beyond the bounds of what any human being was ever meant to endure or experience.

In this manner, both multiple and chronic trauma represent common combinations for those tortured. An explanation of torture clarifies how in some cases of abuse, trauma, and overstimulation, the individual victim is forced to endure over a long period of time. We *torture* when we press the very limits of what any human being was ever meant to experience or endure. This explains why the death instinct, thanatos, may even be activated in someone physically beaten beyond human recognition, or in a person who is repeatedly raped for hours on end, perhaps being tied down. Suggesting chronic overstimulation, as well as torture, a gang rape may last an entire weekend while the victim is held hostage. This same woman may have already experienced severe childhood physical abuse in several different foster care homes, indicating multiple trauma across developmental stages. A child may be locked in a basement with rats in the dark for many hours or overnight and not be fed that entire day. Or a parent takes a hammer and makes a child keep his hands on the table, while each of ten fingers is systematically broken. These examples of torture constitute profound violations of another's basic and fundamental humanity. Unfortunately, far too many people, from infant to adult stages, have experienced torture. Too many of us, in reading this psychoeducation, now realize that we survived torture, or multiple and chronic trauma. Or perhaps we have tortured others.

As a final note, we may now understand why Shengold (1989) speaks of soul murder in an attempt to capture the devastating impact of severe overstimulation. Following his metaphor, we see parents as rats who viciously attacked their children as though they were mice. Shengold (1989) also explains the enduring loyalty that children may still feel toward parents who have abused them, in an effort to preserve the image and concept of a good parent. The hope of a therapeutic breakthrough that permits access to trauma resolution—by the common citizen not able to pay for years of psychoanalysis—is needed, in light of the profound and painful impact from chronic trauma, multiple trauma, severe abuse, torture, and soul murder.

Severe Lack of Stimulation and Neglect

There are also extreme cases of abandonment and neglect that border upon torture, as children do not receive sufficient stimulation. Being left to manage severe states of anxiety from abandonment, resulting in stunted growth, may be a sign of having survived a severe form of trauma. We must appreciate the importance of human interaction for infant and child development. For the ego to develop and for us to be able to focus on reality, we need a human object to draw, capture, and cultivate our attention. Severe deficits in ego and cognitive functioning may result where the most severe forms of neglect and lack of stimulation prevailed during critical developmental periods.

CONCLUSION

A continuum of family types identifies three broad categories of parenting behaviors that occur with a frequency analogous to the areas under the bell of a normal curve distribution in psychology; healthy parenting behaviors and extreme abuse and torture encompass the two tail ends, and occur with relatively low frequency. A middle-range of families engaging in varying forms of abuse and neglect makes up the majority of our nation's family types, occurring with greatest frequency. The psychoeducation provided in this chapter can train counselors and other community members for outreach to those in need of prevention and intervention. This psychoeducational curriculum may also be delivered to parents, teachers, and others who seek to know what constitutes healthy parenting behavior and what is abuse and neglect. In addition, by mastering healthy parenting behavior we can arrive at a new interpersonal mode or counseling style that effectively nurtures others.

The chapter suggests a new standard of "wellness" for children, or of healthy childcare. This new standard involves receipt of healthy parenting behavior. If these standards influence the overall public health, fewer at-risk children and adolescents will need prevention, intervention, and treatment. Society needs to begin to promote new standards of childcare, perhaps by having counselors and community members deliver this type of psychoeducational curriculum and engaging in outreach.

Although we may reach out to parents and provide them with vital psychoeducation that may begin to break generational cycles of dysfunctional families, their chilren also need a psychoeducational curriculum. The next chapter presents a school- or community-based psychoeducational curriculum for violence prevention which may begin to assist children, adolescents, parents, and community members in ending the epidemic of violence plaguing our society. In this manner, we continue to answer the question, in both this chapter and the next, "Where are we and where do we need to go?" as a society.

5

Group Psychoeducation for Primary Violence Prevention in Schools and Other Community-Based Settings

Violence has had a devastating impact on our entire society and on African-Americans in particular. An argument can be made that there is a vital need for a culturally sensitive psychoeducational violence prevention curriculum that empowers individuals and can be readily adapted to diverse community, religious, and school settings. Kochanek, Maurer, and Rosenberg (1994) note the widespread public attention paid to the reversal in the 1980's of a nearly century-long trend. The historical trend observed since 1900 involved life expectancy at birth generally increasing for males and females of both major race groups—the Black and White populations. The disturbing trend for the period 1984–1989 showed that life expectancy decreased for Black males and females. This "strong and persistent divergence in the mortality patterns" (p. 942) involved improvements among the White population in heart disease, stroke, and accident mortality. Meanwhile, for the Black population, the negative impact of HIV infection, homicide, diabetes, and pneumonia overwhelmed improvements in mortality from other causes (p. 943). In essence, the increasing gap in health between the two major races widened in an unprecedented manner during the late 1980s.

As Thomas et al. (1994) suggest, such growing disparities in life expectancy and health status—when comparing African-Americans to Whites—"threaten the well-being, economic productivity, and social progress of our society as we approach the 21st century" (p. 575). Moreover, health status is profoundly affected by poverty and racism (Thomas et al., 1994). Pappas (1994) reminds us that race "is often used as a proxy for social class" (p. 892). More specifically, factors such as a poorer education and lower occupational standing impact the survival of both adults and children. The "complex ways in which social and economic class and race create disadvantages and produce disparities in health" should be more fully investigated (p. 892). Therefore, among the factors to be explored in understanding the widening gap between the Black and White populations are historical factors such as poverty, racism, and other barriers to economic productivity and social progress which have existed historically for Blacks—and negatively impact society as a whole.

The widening gap in life expectancy reflected in the data presented by Kochanek et al. (1994) is consistent with diverse analyses of events in the late 1980s, coming from various fields and perspectives. The bottom line is that things "simply got worse." The crack cocaine epidemic certainly made things considerably worse for communities, families, and chemically dependent individuals. At the conference, "First Annual Summit on Crack Cocaine," held in Houston, Texas, in September 1991, state-of-the-art treatments were described for chemically dependent clients caught up in an epidemic that began with the availability of crack in 1985. The conference director and organizer, Dr. George Drake, underscored an urgent dimension of the crack epidemic reflected in nightly news reports of violent murders of adolescent Black males, occurring during the very same days of the conference. Drake (1991) offered a prophetic story of a daughter with her mother pointing to a statue in a square in the year 2020. The two-year-old daughter asks, "What is it?" The mother replies, "It's a Black male. They went the way of the dinosaur." Drake aptly characterized the plight of urban Black males living in crack epidemic epicenters as being analogous to that of an endangered species because of the concurrent dramatic rise in violence.

Above and beyond the decrease in life expectancy for Black males and females, for the entire population in the United States the late 1980s was a period in which there was a 25 percent increase in the annual crude homicide rate (CDC, 1994a). For the period from 1985 to 1991, the rate per 100,000 persons increased from 8.4 to 10.5, while for the 15–34 age group, the rate per 100,000 increased from 13.4 to 20.1—a 50 percent increase. Quite dramatic was the 76 percent increase for the group of 20–24 year old males, from 23.4 to 41.2 per 100,000. Focusing specifically on the adolescent group aged 15 to 19, the annual homicide rates increased most dramatically from 13.0 to 33.0 per 100,000—a 154 percent increase. For the adolescent age group 15–19, the annual homicide rate for the 1985–1991 period represents a dramatic change from the pattern for the prior two decades (1963–1984). Graphically, this is depicted as a sharp upward rise that is most alarming. Looking at documented causes of homicide, among this 15–19 age group we find firearms-related homicide accounted for 88 percent of all homicides in 1991. Moreover, firearms-related homicides accounted for 97 percent of the increase in the rate of homicides for 1985–1991 (CDC, 1994a).

Christoffel (1994) states that violence contributes disproportionately to years of potential life lost from injury and poses a considerable current and future burden in terms of public health costs. Moreover, with regard to solutions to violence, we find that there is immaturity in the work on violence, as reflected in lack of unanimity on its definition (Christoffel, 1994, p. 540).

As a snapshot of the magnitude of the problem of adolescent violence for the African-American community, Fulton County, Georgia, which encompasses Atlanta, provides interesting data for a sample of homicide victims (N = 106) from 1988 to1992. Fulton County, through the Board of Commissioners, has declared violence to be a public health emergency. This declaration is justified in light of data showing that homicide is the leading cause of death among adolescents in the county. During 1988–1992, 12 percent (N = 106) of homicides involved adolescents aged 18 or less—with 75 percent of these aged 13 to 18; this is in a county with a population of 648,951 in 1990 (CDC, 1994b). Of the 106 adolescent homicides during 1988–1992, a full 84 percent (N = 89) of the deceased were Black males of U.S. origin. A full 82 percent were born in Georgia and 72 percent were born in Fulton County, while 92 percent were residents of the metropolitan Atlanta area (CDC, 1994a). For this sample of deceased mostly Black males, over two-thirds, or the vast majority (67 percent) were students; another 15 percent were employed, and 18 percent were unemployed or had never worked. Two of the deceased had the same mother, poignantly showing that in this contemporary urban war of community violence, a mother may even lose two sons. Among the murdered adolescents, a third (33 percent) were killed within 1.4 miles of home, while 56 percent were killed within 2.8 miles of home (CDC, 1994a). Most of the perpetrators of these adolescent homicides were Black males, just as their victims were Black males (CDC, 1994b). The reality of students involved in violence, gang violence, and community-based violence plaguing African-Americans emerges from the CDC (1994a, 1994b) data.

This chapter focuses on factors that may have contributed to both the late 1980s crack cocaine epidemic and the dramatic increase in violence that has begun to constitute a public health crisis, especially as it impacts African-American adolescent males. Pappas (1994) suggests that in order to gain "an even more sophisticated understanding of the distribution of health risk, ethnic and cultural patterns of health beliefs must also be considered" (p. 892). Hence, this chapter offers an original approach by considering ethnic and cultural patterns of "health beliefs on violence," as well as their origin in social conditioning factors inherent to U.S. history. The main intent is to go beyond race as a variable in the field of violence and to understand how race may be a proxy not only for socioeconomic factors, but also for historical, psychosocial, and social conditioning factors. This chapter provides a psychoeducational group curriculum that delivers primary prevention against violence across weeks 1 through 9. It serves as an introduction to the psychoeducational group curriculum that delivers secondary prevention against violence in weeks 10 through 15, and a psychoeducational group curriculum for tertiary or relapse prevention against violence in weeks 16 through 30—which are described in Chapter 6. Students and community members who complete the curriculum presented in this chapter are sufficiently prepared to receive secondary and tertiary prevention against violence, as described in the next chapter.

The curriculum may also be adapted to church and community-based settings and delivered by peer-leaders, teachers, health educators, ex-gang members, diverse professionals and paraprofessionals, as well as community volunteers. The objective of the curriculum is to increase knowledge on the root causes of violence and to provide individuals with definitions and a language for discussing the role of violence in their lives. In addition, an objective is to change health beliefs on violence, as well as to change violent behavior. Given the magnitude and scope of the negative impact of violence on our society, there is a vital need for such a comprehensive approach to violence in the form of a culturally sensitive, community-based empowerment model. While part of the curriculum delivers information and stimulates discussion of the material, other parts of the psychoeducational group process afford ample opportunity for group members to self-determine the content and direction of their participation and of the group activity as a whole.

WEEKS 1–9: PRIMARY PREVENTION IN THE PSYCHOEDUCATIONAL GROUP

Primary prevention involves providing an intervention to a group who may not as yet have any problems with violence. Primary prevention constitutes risk reduction for those who may have a potential to engage in violence or become victimized by violence. Even though some students may already have problems with violence, still everyone is exposed to this basic, introductory curriculum, while we recognize that some students definitely need more than what is offered as primary prevention. The curriculum in Chapter 6 seeks to meet this need for something more.

In sessions 1 through 9, group members participate in a psychoeducational group that delivers primary prevention against violence. The *psychoeducational violence prevention group* may be defined as a setting in which primary violence prevention is delivered, typically in a classroom setting with the classic arrangement of seating. Or a circle may be formed, creating a somewhat different kind of group setting. The circle suggests a nonhierarchical structure that may be more conducive to the open sharing of thoughts and feelings, as well as memories of violent experiences. Table 5.1 summarizes the content of the curriculum to be delivered across weeks 1 through 9.

Table 5.1
A Psychoeducational Violence Prevention Group Curriculum.

WEEKS 1–9	PRIMARY PREVENTION CURRICULUM

WEEK:	TOPIC FOR GROUP DISCUSSION:
WEEK 1:	INTRODUCTION TO THE CURRICULUM: THE ROLE OF PSYCHOSOCIAL AND SOCIOECONOMIC VARIABLES The Crack Cocaine Epidemic, Poverty and the Loss of Services, Guns and Violence
WEEKS 2–4	MEDIA AND RESEARCH EVIDENCE—MULTIPLE DOMAINS OF VIOLENCE
Week 2:	Evidence of Family and Media Violence in a Rural Community, Evidence of Violence in a Suburban Community
Week 3:	Research on Child Homicide and Child Maltreatment, Research on Violent Behavior in Schoolchildren
Week 4:	Research on Relationships Between Exposure to Violence and Violent Behavior, Research Supporting Violence As Reversal of Roles Post-Victimization, Analysis of the Body of Media Evidence and Research Data
WEEKS 5–7	KEY DEFINITIONS WITHIN A VIOLENCE PREVENTION CURRICULUM
Week 5:	Definitions of Violence, Personal Trauma, Cultural Trauma, Culture of Violence, Ethnic Group, Conditioning, Social Conditioning, Role Model
Week 6:	Definitions of Health Beliefs on Violence, Violent Behavioral Practices, Role Reversal, Affects, Affects of Hate, Triggers, Racism, Ethnic Group Hatred, Sexism, Homophobia
Week 7:	Definitions of Ego, Self, Self-observing Ego, the A,B,Cs of Violence Prevention (Affects, Behavior, Cognitions/Health Beliefs)
WEEKS 8–9	A MULTICULTURAL EDUCATION AND DEFINITIONS ON A MORE ADVANCED LEVEL
Week 8:	Definitions of Multiculturalism, Pluralistic Society, Dysfunctional Family, Nativism, Xenophobia
Week 9:	Sensitivity to the Culture of the Dysfunctional Family, Sensitivity to the Distinct Ethnic/Religious Culture, Sensitivity to the United States Culture of Violence

WEEK 1: INTRODUCTION TO THE CURRICULUM: THE ROLE OF PSYCHOSOCIAL AND SOCIOECONOMIC VARIABLES

The delivery of the definition of a psychoeducational violence prevention group and the making of a decision regarding seating arrangements occur in week 1. Consistent with a major theme of the book, group members are essentially encouraged to reflect on the question, "Where are we and how have we arrived here, in terms of the prevalence and forms of violence surrounding us?"

The causes of the public health crisis of violence may be found in multiple factors, including the crack epidemic, gang violence, drug distribution, and related psychosocial and socioeconomic variables. Actually, the crack epidemic and public health crisis involving violence may be analyzed as inextricably linked.

Discussion in session 1 focuses on these variables, as students and group members offer their own views on what happened in their communities and to their families in the late 1980s up to the present. The following information may stimulate such discussion.

The Crack Cocaine Epidemic

The crack cocaine epidemic saw the birth of cottage industries in which any gang, family, or group might organize in the successful distribution of a "ready to smoke" crack cocaine product, finding an easy market for an inexpensive $5, $10, or $20 rock of crack. Users who sought to emulate Richard Pryor in freebasing cocaine, following widespread media reports, or merely use cocaine as did the rich and famous, did not have to encounter the risk or acquire the skill of converting powdered cocaine hydrochloride to the smokable cocaine alkaloid. Community-based distributors' preparation, packaging, marketing, and distribution of "ready to smoke" crack solved their dilemma, as new cottage industries boomed (Wallace, 1991).

Poverty and the Loss of Services

Meanwhile, Halfon (1989) reminds us not to neglect an important factor that may explain the motivation to develop a drug economy by the mid-1980s. For Halfon, inextricably linked to the evolution of the booming cottage drug industries is the loss of services and the poverty that characterized the 1980s. The gap between rich and poor in the 1980s, the gutting of programs for the underpriviliged, and the evolution of a drug economy centered on the packaging, marketing and distribution of crack cocaine all fueled what became an epidemic of "rock" on the West Coast and of "crack" on the East Coast. By 1985, media reports and street drug researchers were documenting the appearance of rock and crack (Wallace, 1991).

Guns and Violence

It is therefore not surprising that the availability of crack cocaine in 1985 and the resulting crack epidemic of the late 1980s and early 1990s coincided with the dramatic increase in the annual homicide rate for 15 to 19 year olds by 154 percent and for 20 to 24 year olds by 76 percent for the period 1985–1991. There was an inevitable motivation for gangs, groups of adolescents, and families to protect their booming cottage industries, given the reality that large caches of cash quickly grew and were part and parcel of crack distribution. The purchase, availability, and distribution of guns grew alongside the availability of crack in communities. As multiple media reports have further clarified, discipline of workers in drug distribution networks, protection of drugs and drug distribution turf, and disputes over turf often meant the increasing use of guns. Drive-by shootings, drug-related disputes, and random gunfire have contributed to the increase in homicides within even the 0–5 age group.

Others have also noted as possible causes of the dramatic upturn in annual homicide rates the recruitment of adolescents into the drug trade, the use of guns within the trade, and a subsequent diffusion of guns throughout the community, making guns available for settling disputes (Blumstein, 1994; CDC, 1994). Additional factors recognized as possible immediate precursors to violence include poverty, inadequate educational and economic opportunites, as well as social and family instability. Moreover, some individuals in our society are being frequently exposed to violence as an acceptable or preferred method of resolving disputes and disagreements (CDC, 1994a; Reiss & Roth, 1993; NCIPC, 1989). Socioeconomic and psychosocial variables played a role in the increase of violence/homicide and drug use/distribution, as things got worse in the late 1980s.

This discussion in session 1 should end by underscoring the need for a primary, secondary, and tertiary violence prevention curriculum that may be delivered to those in school settings, as well as to youth, gang, and community members no longer in school—utilizing diverse church and community-based settings for delivery of the curriculum. Ex-gang members, former drug dealers, and diverse group members also emerge as experts, possessing intimate knowledge of what happened in communities as the crack cocaine epidemic reached its height and the proliferation of guns and violence was intimately witnessed by them; many members also emerge as experts on the increasing poverty and the impact of other psychosocial factors in the 1980s. A sense of empowerment may result, for group discussion reveals that community members are eyewitnesses to and experts on the phenomenon of the crack cocaine epidemic and public health crisis involving violence. Ultimately, because group participants may be in training to be peer-leaders, community health educators, and group moderators, this empowerment process and the validation of their possession of expertise are important parts of the preparation for group leadership. Individuals also engage in self-determination, as they decide what experiences to self-disclose and steer the direction of group discussion.

WEEKS 2–4: MEDIA AND RESEARCH EVIDENCE— MULTIPLE DOMAINS OF VIOLENCE

Media events and research findings may be analyzed to determine which multiple factors contribute to the current public health crisis involving violence. This section presents sample evidence, revealing multiple domains of interpersonal, family, school, community, and society-wide media violence. This information on current events or other research data should be discussed in sessions 2, 3, and 4. Students and group members are encouraged to take a new critical attitude toward the media and to learn how to conduct research and seek out for themselves the kind of facts and statistics presented in this section. To develop a critical attitude toward the media also represents an empowerment process, as individuals learn to trust and refine their own sensibilities, and to respond to media information more critically. Critical thinking skills are further developed in the process as well. The group can analyze and discuss the meaning behind and implications of media messages.

Week 2: Evidence of Family and Media Violence in a Rural Community

Events involving family violence provide noteworthy evidence that violence also exists in rural America and impacts children. Susan Smith's murder of her two small children in the fall of 1994 in rural Union, South Carolina, and her initial indictment of a Black male in a ski cap as her children's kidnapper reflect the reality of rural homicide, of homicide involving victims in the 0–4 age group, and the myth of the Black male as the prototypical criminal. This case also illustrates society-wide media violence, which involves perpetuating the myth of the Black man as the prototypical criminal, since newspapers and television showed the image of a side-portrait of a Black male in a ski cap who was the alleged perpetrator of the kidnapping. A few years earlier in Massachusetts, a man named Mr. Stuart originally described a Black man as the murderer of his pregnant wife but eventually admitted his own guilt, just as Mrs. Smith admitted to the murder of her two children. The eventual admission of guilt does not negate the damage done to African-Americans in this nation. This society-wide media violence conditions American minds to perceive the Black man as the prototypical criminal.

The events in Union, South Carolina, suggest dual realities. One is that interpersonal violence in the United States involves White Americans, rural communities, and young children via family violence. Second, a form of violence is done when the image of the African-American male is repeatedly linked falsely to criminality. In this manner, society-wide media violence occurs, involving the spreading of misinformation and myths (Wallace, 1993) as to Black criminality, fostering the perception and expectation of the Black as prototypical criminal.

A legitimate question arises as to the repercussions of this media violence. What is the impact of widespread socialization via a medium that encourages a false perception, a damaging prophecy, and a negative expectation about likely African-American behavior, encased in mythic stereotypes of the Black male as criminal? Is there a possible relationship between this form of society-wide media violence and data on the rising homicide rates for Black adolescents murdered by other Black males, discussed earlier. A possible self-fulfilling prophecy may be at work when Black males become violent. Among the complex of socioeconomic and psychosocial variables implicated in the etiology of different forms of violence, this suggested relationship remains a possibility. Group members are encouraged to discuss their interpretations of and responses to these media events.

Evidence of Violence in a Suburban Community

A second tragedy that occurred in late 1994 received notably less national media attention. It involved an act of youthful savagery that stunned two suburban communities (both that of the victim and the violent perpetrators) outside of Philadelphia. In Abington Township, two dozen youths armed with baseball bats piled into cars and drove to Northeast Philadelphia in search of revenge. These violent youths were responding to a false allegation by a White female who said she had an argument at a McDonalds and was also raped. Armed with baseball bats and looking for trouble, these youths encountered a White sixteen-year-old male who had nothing to do with the original incident involving either the argument or the alleged rape. This sixteen-year-old male was severely beaten; his skull was fractured in seven places, as he was viciously killed. The two White middle-class communities were shocked by this incident of violence, having felt removed from urban violence in their suburban environs. A senior, Stephen Lutz, from Abington High School, offered the following assessment: "Maybe we can learn violence is not a city thing. It's not a suburban thing. It's not an Abington thing. It's a society thing. It can touch you anywhere" (Jones, 1994, pp. A1, A9). In essence, even as national mortality data highlight the crisis of violence as it impacts urban African-American adolescent males, the scope of the crisis is much wider. A violent murder of a White middle-class youth in suburbia by a group of White middle-class youth indicates the need for a violence prevention curriculum in the suburban school setting as well. This need exists despite prevailing stereotypes about urban violence which student Stephen Lutz correctly attempts to debunk. The need for a violence prevention curriculum in the suburbs across the United States is consistent with CDC (1994a) data that for the entire population there has been a dramatic increase in the annual crude homicide rate, and for the adolescent group aged 15 to 19 a 154 percent increase for the 1985 to 1991 period. The 1994 incident in Abington Township, Pennsylvania, suggests the nature, scope, and magnitude of violence in the 1990s. Group members may go on to discuss other myths that need to be debunked about violence, perhaps with their own examples of how myths have been transmitted by the media.

Week 3: Research on Child Homicide and Child Maltreatment

Research data may also foster discussion and increase group members' knowledge of different forms of violence. Suggesting the wider scope of the problem of violence, data indicating a negative contribution to life expectancy for Black males come partly from homicides for ages 1–4 and 10–34 (Kochanek et al., 1994). These data reflect not only gang, street, or community violence, but also interpersonal and family violence, or maltreatment, directed against young children in the 1–4 age group. Motivated by the finding that homicide is the fourth leading cause of death among 1 to 14 year olds, Sorenson and Peterson (1994) use a matched case control design to investigate differences between children who died of unintentional injury and children who died of homicide. They found that both groups of children came from troubled families, but that homicide victims were "3.14 times as likely as unintentional injury victims to have a documented history of social and protective (maltreatment) service before their deaths" (p. 625). Equally important is the finding that the great majority who died of homicide had no prior contact with child protective services. Sorenson and Peterson view documented maltreatment as possibly serving as a proxy for other factors such as socioeconomic status, substance abuse by caretakers, and family disruption and discord to name a few. The authors suggest the need for better detection of children who are victims of maltreatment and for new mechanisms to detect children at risk of homicide, while "existing service delivery agencies may serve a unique preventive function" (p. 627) against homicide.

Research on Violent Behavior in Schoolchildren

In a small study comparing seventeen cases to twenty-seven matched controls, Sheline, Skipper, and Broadhead (1994) investigated risk factors for violent behavior in Hispanic elementary schoolboys with violent behavior problems in Albuquerque, New Mexico. Cases were defined as students in the 530 student elementary school in an inner-city, low-income Hispanic neighborhood who received two or more infraction notices from teachers during the first semester of the school year. Infractions were for fighting, bringing dangerous items to school, or using gangs to intimidate others. Findings indicated that children who exhibited violent misbehavior in school were eleven times as likely not to live with their fathers and six times as likely to have parents who were not married. In addition, the violent children had almost twice as many siblings as the controls. Also, the primary caretakers of violent children (N = 15) were more likely than those of matched controls (N = 20) to indicate that they rarely or never expressed "pride or affection to their child and that they used spanking for discipline when the child misbehaved at home" (p. 663). Findings suggest that these Hispanic second through fifth graders possess background characteristics and familial experiences of violence that increase their risk for violent behavior in the school setting. There may be a learning or conditioning process regarding the use of violence through their intimate experiences with physical spanking delivered as punishment within their homes. Quite simply, when we use violence or aggression with children, we in effect teach them to use violence by virtue of our having role modeled that behavior. It is not a great leap from physical hitting, to use of weaponry, to fatal outcomes. A school-based curriculum for violence prevention also seems to be needed in this Hispanic New Mexico community, suggesting the appropriateness of a violence prevention curriculum adaptable for multicultural school settings. Parents, too, need a psychoeducational curriculum focusing on parenting techniques that address spanking and verbal expression to children, perhaps delivered in a school, church, or community-based setting.

Cotten et al. (1994) indicate that in the last decade the rates of violence-related child and adolescent fatalities have increased in the United States. Physical fights and aggression often precede behavior leading to actual violence-related fatalities. These authors cshow that 37 percent of a low-income, North Carolina African-American adolescent sample (N = 436) had been involved in physical fights in school, 18 percent had been suspended for fighting, and 19 percent reported taking a weapon to school. Cotten et al. recommend that school teachers and public health practitioners work together to address both the immediate and more subtle factors "associated with adolescent violence in order to stem the escalating acts of aggression seen in our schools today" (p. 621).

These findings are not unlike data from state and local surveys showing that between 34 and 56 percent of students (median: 42 percent; national prevalence:

42 percent) had been in at least one physical fight during the twelve months preceding the spring 1991 survey (N = 12,272) conducted by the CDC (1992). Among participating students, 16 percent to 39 percent (median: 26 percent; national prevalence: 26 percent) carried a weapon such as a gun, knife, or club at least one day during the thirty days preceding the survey. Of those who carried a weapon, the most often carried was a gun by some 5 percent to 41 percent (median: 11 percent; national prevalence: 11 percent); and male students were more likely to carry a weapon than were female students (CDC, 1992, pp. 57–58). Collectively, these studies underscore the significance of and need for violence prevention efforts that practically respond to the public health crisis involving violence through a school, church, and community-based psychoeducational curriculum for students and parents.

Week 4: Research on Relationships Between Exposure to Violence and Violent Behavior

Any viable psychoeducational curriculum for violence prevention needs to be sensitive to multiple variables contributing to violence. Data on a sample of urban male and female African-American adolescents living in a Georgia housing project (N = 225) reveals significant associations between self-reported violence and other factors. Specifically, Durant et al. (1994) found that self-reported violence was associated with exposure to victimization and violence in the community, degree of family conflict, and severity of corporal punishment and discipline. A full 84 percent admitted to engaging in at least one form of violent behavior. Durant et al. suggest that these relationships may be covariational in nature; as they state, "viewing violence in the community, personally experiencing violence and crime, and witnessing violence and conflict among family members in the home, being a victim of severe corporal punishment, and actually using violence dynamically" may each interact with one another as these events co-occur (p. 615). According to Durant et al. their data support the cultural transmission theory (Sutherland & Cressey, 1978) that has proposed how adolescents' use of violence is learned within intimate primary groups (families, peer groups, gangs) via modeling.

In addition, Durant et al. believe that their work supports a body of literature (Gladstein & Slater, 1988; Shakoor & Chalmers, 1991; Widom, 1989a, b) which argues that being a victim of violence increases the risk that adolescents will use violence interpersonally toward others. Finally, Durant et al. conclude that a lack of modeling of nonviolent conflict resolution skills in homes and communities, and a reality wherein there are neither incentives nor skills to avoid the use of violence, suggest the need for "both national and personal commitments in initiating prevention programs during childhood and early adolescence" (p. 617). Clearly, parents, community members, and schoolchildren all need exposure to a source of conditioning regarding nonviolent behavior.

On the other hand, the current social context for the conditioning of violent behavior also needs to be considered. The qualitative research of Stevenson and Abdul-Kabir (1995) includes a video-taped interview of a poor single mother who defends her parenting techniques in violent contexts, as the researchers also emphasize her adaptive strengths. As shown in extensive interviews with women living in a poor section of West Philadelphia called the "Bottom," African-American women may use forms of physical discipline that are congruent with the violent reality of their surrounding community and school. The use of parental violence as discipline may serve to foster the survival of children in a violent social environment.

If we are to be culturally sensitive, then we must appreciate the larger cultural and societal context of family violence. In conversation with parents in a similar Philadelphia neighborhood, I have heard verbal instruction and seen actual teaching of children in how to fight physically—also in an attempt to help children survive in a violent context. Therefore, not uncommonly parents urge children to fight and to physically defend themselves in school and in the community, as did a woman in the videotape which is a part of the qualitative research of Stevenson and Abdul-Kabir (1995). In this manner, the actual video-taped comments of a research subject add a realistic dimension to the concurrent home, school, and community violence which Durant et al. (1994) document as being related to youth's violence. However, a valid question raised by Stevenson and Abdul-Kabir's qualitative research is whether or not parents using corporal punishment with their children, even if congruent with the violence surrounding them in their school and community, ever cross the line into physical abuse and warrant intervention by child protective services? Or what is taught by the use of a physical punishment which seems appropriate from a mother's perspective on how to foster the survival of her children in a violent community, but may leave bruises? These difficult and challenging questions should promote group discussion, as group members may be reminded that they can agree to disagree.

More research data can be provided, however, to suggest the possible negative consequences of being exposed to physical abuse which follow individuals for the rest of their lives. Research supports the relationship between childhood victimization, involving validated cases of physical and sexual abuse and neglect ($N = 908$) from 1967 to 1971, and violent offending. Rivera and Widom (1990) compared these documented cases to matched controls ($N = 667$) and showed that "officially recorded abuse and neglect increase the likelihood of having an official criminal record and speed up entrance into officially recorded delinquent activities" (p. 32). These long-term consequences differed dramatically by race. White children who were abused and neglected did not have significantly higher rates of violent arrests than the controls, whereas Blacks who were abused and neglected, compared to their Black controls, had substantially higher juvenile and adult arrest rates for violent offending (p. 30). In analyzing these data, we might follow Pappas (1994) and wonder whether race is serving as a proxy for social class or other factors related to the poorer education and lower occupational standing of Blacks. However, Rivera and Widom conclude that "early childhood victimization does not appear to place one at increased risk of continuing a life of crime" (p. 32); nonabused and neglected children are just as likley as abused and neglected children to continue violent offending once they have begun. Hence, primary, secondary, and tertiary prevention against violence is needed for a range of students.

Research Supporting Violence As a Reversal of Roles Post-Victimization

Several research studies provide evidence of how many instances of violence represent the victim going on—perhaps immediately post-victimization, or later in a subsequent developmental era (adolescence, adulthood)—to reverse roles and assume the role of assaulter, while placing another in the role of victim. Milner, Robertson, and Rogers (1990) found that childhood history of physical abuse (whipping, slapping, kicking, poking, punching, hair pulling, or sexual abuse) in a 93 percent White sample (N = 341) was significantly related to adult physical child abuse potential. The more chronic the childhood abuse the higher the abuse potential as an adult. Moreover, pre-puberty abuse seemed to have a more detrimental impact than abuse after age thirteen. A moderating impact for child abuse potential was found from the childhood experience of a caring adult or a caring friend. Findings supported an intergenerational transmission hypothesis. Milner et al. (1990) conclude that early social learning plays an important role in the development of adult child abuse potential for a White sample of undergraduates from Western Carolina University and Oklahoma State Univerity.

For a sample of males referred as possible sexual abuse victims (N = 77) in Florida between 1985 and 1989, Roane (1992) reports evidence of child abuse by other than the parent (55 percent), while the parent was the most common abuser (32.4 percent), followed by acquaintance of family (20.8 percent) and stepparent (11.7 percent). A primary reason why one-fourth of the sample was referred to the child protective agency was sexual acting-out behavior. "Specific recapitulation of victimization was reported among 14 (18.2 percent) of the abused boys. This recapitulation occurred almost exclusively with younger children as victims" (Roane, p. 236). Apparently, victimization can lead to a potential for victimizing others, even in a sample where the average age of the boys was eight years old. To place someone else in the role in which one has been, victim, seems to occur after the experience of victimization. Recapitulation, or acting out of violence and abuse, seems commonly to transpire—whether soon after the abuse as a child, or later in adolescence during juvenile delinquency, or later in adulthood as parental child abuse. The term *role reversal* can be utilized to capture the act of recapitulation as it may involve sexual abuse of peers, or physically abusing one's child as an adult, after having been abused one's self as a child. Group members may determine the course of the group process, as some members decide to self-disclose their own experiences, or those of their family members, in regard to acts of recapitulation and role reversals; or to provide examples of restraint and individuals successfully refusing to repeat generation-al cycles of violence.

Analysis of the Body of Media Evidence and Research Data

The media evidence and research data reviewed suggest the interplay of interpersonal, family, school, community, and society-wide media violence. As we have seen, in all instances of violence, ubiquitous social learning processes take place, as when a role reversal or recapitulation reveals the impact of some prior role modeling. Having discussed this media evidence and research findings in sessions 2, 3, and 4—and having fostered a critical attitude toward television and other media, as well as a curiosity to seek out facts and research statistics—a final point to make is how an alternative socialization regarding nonviolent alternatives needs to occur. Group members may engage in discussion regarding how they think this should occur.

WEEKS 5–9: KEY DEFINITIONS WITHIN A VIOLENCE PREVENTION CURRICULUM

The fifth session begins with a broad definition of violence which rests at the center of the psychoeducational violence prevention curriculum. Indeed, approximately thirty definitions are delivered across sessions 5 through 9, creating a comprehensive curriculum to be delivered in part of a fall semester, for example, of an academic year. The curriculum focus on definitions is consistent with a health education goal of increasing knowledge, for definitions typically serve to increase knowledge, as a first step. Again, illustrative examples taken from history, current events, the media, and students' and group members' lives are also discussed in groups.

Week 5

Violence is defined as the delivery of physical blows (with or without weaponry), the display and misuse of power, or bombarding a person with destructive misinformation and myths so that in effect an assault or injury occurs either upon a person's physical body or to the self-concept, identity, cognitions, affects, and consciousness of the victim of violence (Wallace, 1993, p. 10). Examples of violence include domestic violence, physical abuse, sexual abuse, verbal abuse, slavery, the historical dispersal of propaganda justifying slavery, the miseducation of schoolchildren, past and present White supremacist activities, institutionalized racism, societywide discrimination, prejudice, and the media's presentation of an illusory and false view of violence—while spreading misinformation, myths, and stereotypes through televison and movies (p. 10).

One consequence of violence, *personal trauma*, can occur at any point in the life cycle and may be defined as involving the witnessing or experiencing of domestic violence, incest, sexual abuse, rape, physical abuse, or being the victim of some street or school violence, or of taunts and verbal abuse. Examples include being battered by a police officer, being assaulted by a partner or acquaintance, witnessing murders and assaults, or experiencing institutionalized racism as an adolescent or an adult (Wallace, 1993).

Another consequence of violence, *cultural trauma*, may be defined as involving members of a cultural or societal group experiencing forms of violence (physical blows, displays and misuse of power, receipt of misinformation or myths) collectively by virtue of cultural group membership (Wallace, 1993). Examples include African enslavement, the Holocaust, the destruction of Native American civilization, the 1994 slaughter of Tutsi by Hutus in Rwanda (and vice versa), and assaults and murders of homosexuals in "gay-bashing." The 1995 murder of a gay man after the taping of a Jennie Jones talk show, in which a man's secret admirer turned out to be another man, suggests the extent of hatred and willful violence toward gays, creating cultural trauma for homosexuals.

A definition of the culture of violence offers an explanation of how the United States sustains a historical and contemporary international reputation for being a particularly violent nation, given the murders of German tourists and Japanese students. *Culture of violence* may be defined as a way of life, behaviors, beliefs, practices, and traditions that are taught and transmitted from group member to member and from generation to generation regarding the use of physical force, displays of power, and the spreading of misinformation and myths. This transmission of practices and traditions occurs in such a way that historically traumatic events profoundly shape and impact what is transmitted to different cultural group members and across generations (Wallace, 1993, p. 10). For example, the historical trauma of African enslavement or the internment of Japanese and the bombing of Pearl Harbor serve to sustain beliefs, traditions, and practices that lead to forms of violence being directed against contemporary African-Americans and Japanese Americans.

Typically, it is an ethnic group that has experienced a cultural trauma. An *ethnic group* may be defined as a collective of people who share common history, experiences, language, values, practices, and religion, and continue to pass on the influence of their history as well as language, values, and practices from generation to generation and from group member to group member.

We also need to understand and define conditioning. *Conditioning* means learning. *Social conditioning* can be defined as learning that occurs because of our interaction with other human beings, or learning that we acquire from observing other human beings. This learning, or social conditioning, occurs while we interact with family members, members of our ethnic and/or religious group, and members of the larger culture of the United States. Social conditioning takes place as we observe strangers perform behaviors, either in person or on television and in the movies.

The people we have observed performing behaviors may be called role models. A *role model* is someone who has demonstrated or performed a behavior that we therefore come to know about and may end up imitating. Some role models have been members of our family, ethnic, or religious group, or members of the larger culture of the United States, and some role models demonstrate and teach us negative and violent behavior. Role models may demonstrate and teach us not only about behavior, but also about beliefs and feelings.

Week 6

We may expand on the notion of beliefs being transmitted from group member to member and across generations by considering the specific transmittal of health beliefs regarding violence. *Health beliefs on violence* may be defined as socially conditioned cognitions or conditioned thoughts and attitudes reflecting what we have been taught or have learned about violence. Health beliefs on violence serve to guide violent behavioral practices. Examples of health beliefs on violence collected in formative evaluation research involving use of focus group interviews and open-ended questionnaire follow: "Spare the rod and spoil the child"; "It was done to me, so it should be done to you"; "You deserve it; you're no good"; "This gives me control over you." A more complete and systematic presentation of this questionnaire and focus group data goes beyond the scope of this discussion. However, these brief examples suggest that subjects can identify health beliefs on violence upon inquiry, as well as identify the sources of these health beliefs—typically identifying the influence of past social conditioning of these cognitions.

Violent behavioral practices—passed on from generation to generation and from member to member—are often driven by possession of health beliefs on violence. For example, a parent who believes "Spare the rod and spoil the child" or "It was done to me, so it should be done to you" will feel justified in delivering physical blows with or without the use of weaponry (a stick, a belt, an ironing cord); their health beliefs on violence guide or direct their violent behavior against a child which may qualify as child abuse. Or an adolescent holding the health belief on violence that "You deserve it, you're no good" may feel justified in assaulting and murdering a gay man, for this health belief directs violent behavior and the committing of a hate crime of "gay bashing." *Violent behavioral practices* may be defined as learned interpersonal patterns of responding which include verbal abuse, sexual abuse, physical abuse, domestic violence, mob attacks, gang violence, public beatings, lynchings, shootings, drive-by shootings, bias crimes, and hate crimes. We often engage in violence because we are survivors of violence and have learned at first hand from our assaulter how to perform violent behavioral practices. A *role reversal* is defined as the performance of violent behavioral practices, as a consequence of having experienced a personal trauma. It involves a person being put in the role of victim in nearly the exact same fashion as the survivor of violence once experienced the role of victim in his or her original personal trauma. In a role reversal, the survivor of violence now becomes an aggresssor/assaulter or perpetrator of violence.

While we engage in a violent behavioral practice, or role reversal, our facial expression often suggests that we are experiencing the affects of anger and hate. An *affect* may be defined as an emotional state, or feelings that arise within us. *Affects of hate* are feelings of anger that often accompany health beliefs on violence and violent behavioral practices, and have also been taught or transmitted from generation to generation and from group member to member. Affects of hate may also be defined as feelings of anger conditioned by personal experiences of violence and frequently directed toward the part of ourselves that was the victim of violence, as well as toward the violent assaulter. Affects of hate may generalize to others who merely remind us of our victim role experiences or of our assaulter. Or people remind us of the part of ourselves victimized, made to feel bad, and that we came to hate, and we now hate the person who so reminds us. (See Chapter 8 and the discussion of "my mirror.")

Triggers for affects of hate may be defined as anything that provokes us to anger, such as someone's behavior, appearance, or remarks; an example of a trigger is a person being tall or having a loud voice. We may be triggered to experience an affect of hate when we encounter someone who shares the traits of our assaulter. We may ask someone, "Why do you hate Uncle John?" A response illustrating how affects of hate may be triggered in us would be, "Because he reminds me of my father and my father beat me."

Affects of hate characterize racism, sexism, and homophobia. *Racism* is defined as hatred of a racial group. *Ethnic group hatred* involves directing affects of hate toward an ethnic group. *Sexism* is defined as hatred and discrimination, typically directed against women. Here we define *homophobia* as an unreasonable fear and hatred of gay and lesbian people. Affects of hate toward racial groups, ethnic groups, women, and gays and lesbians are typically accompanied by health beliefs on violence, such as "It is okay to direct violence toward members of the hated group." Such health beliefs on violence foster violent behavioral practices. Perceiving race, or dark skin color, a female, or behaviors and symbols suggesting sexual orientation may each trigger conditioned affects of hate and violent behaviors, while our health beliefs on violence make us feel justified in unleashing violence.

Even if we have long automatically responded to triggers and felt affects of hate, and could classify ourselves as being racist, sexist, or homophobic, we can learn to change and no longer respond automatically to triggers. We can learn to observe the thoughts and feelings that arise within us, and we can learn how to stop or interrupt our learned or conditioned responses to triggers we encounter in the environment. We can also learn to direct ourselves to perform a new alternative behavior instead of performing our old conditioned responses of affects or hate, thinking old health beliefs on violence, and performing old conditioned behavioral practices of violence. As we repeatedly observe our thoughts and feelings as they arise within us, as we catch ourselves about to respond to a trigger, and as we stop ourselves and pause, we are in the process of developing a self-observing ego.

Week 7

The *ego* may be defined as that part of us that is focused on reality and makes judgments about reality. For example, it is because of our egos that we know what time it is and if we are hungry, for example. The ego may make judgments about reality, such as "This person is gesturing in a violent manner and seems intoxicated; so I think I will walk out of this room." The ego can be distinguished from the *self*, which may be defined as the part of us that represents the core of our being and responds with a range of positive to negative feelings to events that occur in reality, either moving toward or moving away from, behaviorally, objects in reality—based upon the self's felt emotions. The self may want to move toward human objects who are empathic, warm, and nurturing. Conversely, the self may want to move away from human objects who are hostile and violent. When the ego observes the experiences of the inner self and the felt emotion arising inside, the ego might make a judgment about what is happening in reality and decide to walk away, or to engage in an act of self-defense, or become silent and avoidant.

Self-observing ego can be defined as a part of the ego that has developed the capacity to observe our internal thoughts and feelings, as well as our performance of behaviors, often commenting on all of these within an internal dialogue, as judgments are made about our experience. The self-observing ego can affirm our existence and value ("Good, you did not blurt out that racist joke at dinner!"; or, "It was a good decision not to verbally provoke or taunt that intoxicated man carrying the stick on the subway, and to move to a different subway car"). The self-observing ego may also validate our experiences, interrupt and stop automatic conditioned responses (negative affects, cognitions/beliefs, violent behavior), and direct us to perform good self-care and new, more positive behaviors.

The key definitions offered in this section are intended to train group leaders and serve as their curriculum guide when they deliver violence prevention. A main objective of delivering the curriculum that is centered around teaching and discussing these definitions is to increase the learner's level of knowledge about violence and the experiences of themselves and others in response to violence. These key definitions and illustrative examples may be delivered to group members of various ages.

The ABCs of Violence Prevention: Key Definitions for Younger Students

The key definitions and illustrative examples covering affects of hate, violent behavioral practices, and health beliefs/cognitions on violence, when delivered as a psychoeducational violence prevention curriculum in a school setting with younger students, may be entitled *The ABCs of Violence Prevention*. With older students and community members the ABCs represent a convenient summary of key definitions. Repetition, review, and brief summation are therefore provided to reinforce learning within the curriculum. Consider the following definitions or explanations of the *ABCs,* as we provide a more simplified summary, or core curriculum for youth in elementary school:

- "*A*" stands for *Affects* or feelings such as anger and hate that we have been taught to feel toward members of certain groups; or if we are a survivor of violence, we may feel anger or hate toward our assaulter and toward the part of ourselves victimized by violence.
- "*B*" stands for *Behavior that is violent* and imitates what we have been taught about acting aggressively toward individuals or groups of people. Examples of behavior that is violent include verbal abuse, sexual abuse, physical abuse, mob attacks, public beatings, shootings, gay bashing, or bias crimes.
- "*C*" stands for *Cognitions or health beliefs on violence* that are socially learned thoughts and attitudes we hold about violence. These thoughts and attitudes serve to promote and justify violent behavioral practices. For example, if we believe that "it is okay to unleash violence against blacks, women, and gays," then we may feel motivated to engage in violent behavioral acts and feel justified after unleashing violence against members of these groups.

WEEKS 8 AND 9: A MULTICULTURAL EDUCATION AND DEFINITIONS ON A MORE ADVANCED LEVEL

We can also adjust our violence prevention curriculum for various age, grade, and reading levels, covering information on a more advanced level that is appropriate for many children, adolescents, and adults. In sessions 8 and 9, we seek to offer a multicultural education through several key definitions and through the discussion they generate.

Week 8

Multiculturalism can be defined as living or existing in a condition or state where there are many or multiple cultural influences. We both exist as multicultural human beings and live in a nation that is multicultural. For example, if we are multicultural human beings living in the United States, most of us reflect the impact of three cultural influences on us. We have received the transmittal of traditions, practices, and beliefs from generation to generation and from group member to member which has come from three sources: (1) the culture of our family, (2) the culture of our ethnic and/or religious group, and (3) the larger culture of the United States of America. Our existence reflects these three cultural influences at the very least. Others of us may be biracial, may have parents from two different ethnic or religious groups, may even be multiracial, and may have spent several years of our life being raised in another country. Because of the media and technology, we increasingly perceive and feel what it means to live in a world community that is multicultural. When we interact socially with others who are from other types of families, other ethnic and/or religious groups, and also from other countries, this social condition constitutes multiculturalism. In this way, we arrive at another definition of multiculturalism that goes beyond our personal condition or state which reflects multiple cultural influences.

A *pluralistic society* is defined as a society in which we all respectfully learn about each others' experiences, practices, values, traditions, and beliefs, as we interact socially—as members of different ethnic, religious, and cultural groups. Within a pluralistic society, we strive to achieve more than just tolerance of each other's values, traditions, and beliefs. Ideally, we arrive at a level of acceptance and respect for those who freely practice traditions that are different from our own. We have yet to reach this goal in the United States.

In order to further understand violent influences on ourselves as multicultural human beings, we can consider how processes of social conditioning regarding violence occur on three levels. There is a level of learning about affects of hate, violent behavioral practices, and cognitions or health beliefs on violence that occurs by virtue of membership within (1) a dysfunctional family. A *dysfunctional family* may be defined as a family in which the behavior of parents or caretakers is inconsistent, unpredictable, and/or abusive, while overall family life is chaotic. Typically, we gain exposure to role models who engage in verbal abuse, physical abuse, sexual abuse, domestic violence, and demonstrate insufficient nonviolent conflict resolution skills. The victims of violence within a dysfunctional family sustain personal trauma. (2) There is also a level of learning about affects of hate, violent behavioral practices, and cognitions or health beliefs on violence that occurs by virtue of membership within the culture of an ethnic or religious group. (3) Another level involves learning about affects of hate, violent behavioral practices, and cognitions or health beliefs on violence by virtue of membership within the larger culture of violence of the United States. Historically, public discussion, gossip, pamphlets, and tracts spread misinformation, myths, and stereotypes, while in contemporary times, society-wide media violence also facilitates social learning.

For example, historically, native citizens experienced feelings of *nativism*—defined as feelings of superiority over new arrivals and a desire to preserve the indigenous culture of the United States. A common result of nativism was that citizens directed violence against new immigrant/migrant arrivals who brought their own cultural practices from their homeland. Nativism when combined with *xenophobia*—defined as an unreasonable fear of strangers or of the new immigrant/migrant arrival—frequently led to verbal abuse of new immigrant arrivals, the calling of names, and physical abuse, including unleashing violence in mob attacks against new immigrants and rioting. In this manner, from the treatment of literally every new immigrant group—fueled by nativism and xenophobia, and including verbal and often physical violence directed against a new immigrant group—we can characterize the United States of American as having always been a culture of violence. The lynching of Blacks in the Jim Crow South era, the 1991 Los Angeles police beating of Rodney King, the modern-day murders in Florida of German tourists, and the contemporary murder of Japanese students collectively suggest that this characterization of the United States is apropos.

Week 9

Since our goal in the United States is to foster a pluralistic society, teachers, health educators, and volunteer community health educators need to encourage respect of different ethnic and religious groups, ensuring that we provide prevention against students and community members engaging in the kind of nativism and xenophobia that has long characterized the United States. More pointedly, we seek to prevent or transform affects of hate that are associated with the performance of violent behaviors, and the holding of cognitions or health beliefs on violence that also fuel violent behavior. All students and community members should emerge from participation in sessions 8 and 9 possessing three levels of *cultural sensitivity*—which may be defined as possessing (1) *sensitivity to the culture of the dysfunctional family* with its distinct health beliefs, attitudes, behavioral practices, patterns of violence, and values; (2) *sensitivity to the distinct ethnic and/or religious culture* of the individual and the unique historical patterns of violence and trauma which that group has experienced, as well as to the resulting health beliefs, behavioral practices, patterns of violence, and values that result from that history; and (3) *sensitivity to the United States Culture of Violence* and the distinct beliefs, socially conditioned cognitions, behavioral practices, and patterns of violence (media, movies, television, bias crimes) to which individual members have been exposed over generations in this country.

For example, in our classroom or psychoeducational group, we need to remember that a student is struggling with an alcoholic parent and comes from the culture of a dysfunctional family where one has been conditioned to "not tell family secrets, nor talk about feelings." At the same time, this or another student may be from a family that has suffered a particular ethnic or religious trauma such as the Japanese internment, the Jewish Holocaust, the Vietnamese war and refugee trauma, or has a gay relative who has suffered a bias crime within our culture of violence. In sum, sessions 8 and 9 attempt to instill sensitivity to the reality and impact of the culture of the dysfunctional family, ethnic/religious group, and larger Culture of Violence of the United States.

CONCLUSION

This chapter introduces a primary prevention curriculum against violence designed to be delivered across nine sessions. The sharing of background information in sessions 1 through 4 and the delivery and discussion of definitions and illustrative examples in sessions 5 through 9 serve the first step of increasing knowledge, as well as beginning to change health beliefs on violence. However, other steps and additional sessions may be necessary to change deeply conditioned beliefs and behavior—especially for those who have already engaged in violence or been victims of or witnessed violence. Chapter 6 offers secondary and tertiary violence prevention in psychoeducational support groups. It is highly recommended that the delivery of the curriculum described in this chapter be followed with the delivery of the secondary and tertiary violence prevention curriculum offered in the next chapter.

The chapter has taken a novel perspective in seeking to increase knowledge of the root causes of violence as a means of changing not only health beliefs on violence but also behavior. This approach is culturally sensitive and pays particular attention to the variables of race and ethnicity. Recent homicide statistics showing a sharp increase for African-Americans may reflect how race may serve as a proxy for social and economic factors—such as education, occupation, and lifestyle; these factors end up contributing to the widening health gap between the Black and White population. However, race might also be seen as a proxy for historical, psychosocial, and social conditioning factors, as suggested by the definitions put forth in this chapter. The suggested discussion of the root causes of violence that is likely to be fostered in classroom, church, community, and diverse psychoeducational groups may produce important qualitative data that may direct attention to a complex of psychosocial and socioeconomic variables in future quantitative research, perhaps further elucidating possible proxy effects.

This chapter's contribution to understanding the social conditioning of health beliefs on violence and how to change them in psychoeducational groups may be seen as promoting maturation in the field of violence. The definitions proposed suggest the etiology of health beliefs on violence in important cultural and historical factors, also expanding in concrete ways our view of proxy effects in research using race as a variable. The discussion stimulated in psycho-educational groups around the key definitions offered in this chapter may also produce qualitative (focus group) data that bring to light a range of ethnic health beliefs on violence and differences across various ethnic and religious groups in types of health beliefs held by group members. The utility of such data regarding various group's health beliefs on violence will be   discussed in Chapter 6 in regards to relapse prevention against a return to violent behavioral practices.

6

Psychoeducational Support Group: Secondary and Tertiary Violence Prevention

This chapter provides secondary prevention against violence—as the same group members who received the curriculum described in Chapter 5, ideally, continue in a psychoeducational support group. The chapter is divided into two main sections. A first section presents a curriculum for secondary violence prevention, and the second section presents relapse prevention, or tertiary prevention, against a return to violent behavior.

Secondary prevention is designed for individuals who have already had some involvement with the problem behavior of violence, either as perpetrators, victims, or witnesses of violence. Because they already have some degree of involvement, we seek to prevent them from experiencing more severe problems with violence. This is the rationale for providing secondary prevention.

Tertiary prevention is designed for those who have had substantial and serious involvement with violence, typically as perpetrators. Victims are in danger of a role reversal and of themselves becoming violent perpetrators, whereas witnesses of violence have experienced powerful role modeling and may emulate violent behavior. Tertiary prevention seeks to address the needs of this population. Hence, the rationale of tertiary prevention is to prevent a return, or relapse, to violence. The literature is devoid of models of relapse prevention designed for violence; this chapter seeks to fill this gap.

WEEKS 10–15: SECONDARY VIOLENCE PREVENTION

To accomplish more substantive behavioral change in sessions 10 through 15, group members need to form a circle and use a nonhierarchical group structure.

We may think of this structure as a psychoeducational support group. A *psychoeducational support group for violence prevention* may be defined as a group setting in which members share and disclose their personal experiences of violence and learn new nonviolent health beliefs and nonviolent behavioral practices. Information is held in confidence, trust is developed gradually, and individual group members may feel free to practice the expression of new beliefs and enact new behaviors. Group members receive support and encouragement for their first, new, tentative efforts and progressive efforts at behavior change.

A member's behavior comes to approximate a goal over time with continual rehearsal within the group. Formal role play is also used. A *role play* may be defined as a dramatic enactment of a real life situation in which two or more actors try to display effective communication skills, social skills, coping skills, and conflict resolution strategies. One or more actors may try to challenge or provoke the one being urged to display effective coping. After a role play, or the member trying a new coping behavior, group members provide feedback, recommendations for improvements in coping, and suggestions for what could have been said or done differently in the role play. The one who was challenged to display effective coping receives positive reinforcement and encouragement from other group members as well as from the group moderator, convener, or leader. New affective, cognitive, and behavioral coping skills are learned and practiced in the group. In this manner, new skills and coping strategies may come to replace old affects of hate, old tendencies to engage in violent behavior, and old health beliefs on violence.

In terms of new affective coping skills specifically, individuals learn to identify, label, and express feelings. Group members learn to cope with affects or feelings and how to communicate them. For individuals who have grown up within a dysfunctional family, to feel and express affects represents acquisition of a new developmental skill. Members also learn to develop a growing capacity for self-observation of feelings and affects as they arise within.

Within the safe environment of the support group, members can also witness role models that exhibit the ability to express affects, perform behaviors, and express nonviolent health beliefs/cognitions. Members can role play and practice interpersonal strategies for nonviolent conflict resolution. The receipt of feedback occurs, as group members metaphorically hold up a mirror and reflect back to an individual those affects, behaviors, and cognitions exhibited in group. This facilitates an increase in self-knowledge and helps cultivate the skill of self-observation, as an individual learns to compare what is metaphorically reflected in a mirror to them against their own progessively broader range of self-perceptions and self-observations. The group members' sense of self-value also increases, as other group members perform a critical function akin to a loving parent, taking the time to perceive that individual and provide important feedback about what that individual seems to feel, as well as information regarding behavior and beliefs/cognitions. Repeatedly accessing one's own internal feelings and thoughts within the group setting further leads individual group members to increased self-knowledge, self-observation, self-value, and feelings of self-efficacy. *Self-efficacy* may be defined as feelings of confidence that one can perform certain behaviors in a specific situation; feelings of self-efficacy increase with role play and practice. Group participation permits individual members to gradually approximate personal goals for behavior.

The psychoeducational support group has a therapeutic impact on individual group members who have had direct personal experiences of violence and may have gone on to engage in role reversals and to perform violent behavioral acts themselves. Here we speak of those students who have received corporal punishment at home, perhaps bordering on physical abuse, and have engaged in physical fights in school. They may take weapons to school and have already used them, or are willing to use them. Or we refer to those adolescents or adults in the community who experienced family, interpersonal, gang, or community violence and now carry handguns, may have assaulted others already, or may be at risk of using such weaponry for self-defense or in a role reversal. Such individuals would benefit from secondary prevention. Indeed, a range of individuals may need to talk about their own personal examples and experiences of personal and cultural trauma, or gay bashing, police brutality, or being a victim of a bias crime. They may also need to talk about the trauma of harming someone else through their own personal engagement in violent behavioral practices—perhaps in a role reversal. Offering a pragmatic definition, a psychoeducational support group becomes a therapeutic support group as soon as a member begins to shed tears or expresses other strong affects. The psychoeducational support group for violence prevention may become therapeutic, as group members discuss memories of traumatic violence.

This is a largely unstructured group, with group members determining the focus and content of each group. However, each session begins with increasing members' knowledge by covering several definitions, as a warmup exercise for the group. Depending on the size of the group and the length of the group session, the amount of time available for unstructured group discussion varies. Table 6.1 summarizes the content of the curriculum delivered across weeks 10 through 15, as secondary prevention against violence.

WEEK 10: TRAINING AND PREPARATION FOR A THERAPEUTIC GROUP PROCESS

The following definitions may be discussed to facilitate the experience of a therapeutic process ensuing across weeks 10 through 15.

Table 6.1
A Psychoeducational Support Group for Violence Prevention.

WEEKS 10–15	SECONDARY VIOLENCE PREVENTION CURRICULUM
WEEK:	TOPIC FOR DISCUSSION:
WEEK 10:	TRAINING AND PREPARATION FOR A THERAPEUTIC GROUP PROCESS Empathic Attunement, Hitting the Nail on the Head, Empathic Mirroring, Excavating a Chunk of Gold or Precious Pearl, Healing the Damaged Ego/Self, Ego Learning of Improved Self-Regulation
WEEK 11:	DESCRIBING THE MOVIE IN YOUR MIND "Don't Jump into the Movie!," "Tell Me What You See?," An Important Caution, Closing People Up With Use of Humor Versus Leaving Them Open
WEEKS 12–13:	EDUCATION ON DEFENSES USED BY THE EGO: DEFINITIONS AND METAPHORS
Week 12:	Definitions of Defense, Avoidance, Denial, Rationalization, Repression, Narcissism, Narcissism and the Inflated Balloon Metaphor, Inhibition, Displacement
Week 13:	Definitions of Projection, Identification, Projective-Identification, Regression, Fixation Point, A Part of Us Is Stuck on a Step of Our Stairs Metaphor, Regression in the Service of a Self-Observing Ego
WEEK 14:	UNDERSTANDING THE TENDENCY OF THE PSYCHE TO SPLIT Definition of Splitting, The Label on a Jar Metaphor (Diagnoses), A Practical Approach to Splitting, Our Parents Dropped and Broke the Glass Metaphor, the Torn and Tattered Rug Metaphor, Learning to Self-Observe Splitting, Splitting As a Role Reversal, Splitting As Resumption of the Role of Victim, Splitting and Dissociation, Definition of Dissociation
WEEK 15:	CLOSURE OR CONTINUATION? Discussion for the Purpose of Achieving Group Closure, or Making a Decision to Continue the Group Process (Or a catch up session.)

When a group member shares his or her thoughts and feelings, responses of genuine empathy and expressions of understanding from other group members are vital.

Empathic Attunement

Empathic attunement (Rowe & Mac Isaac, 1989) can be defined metaphorically as a situation when the self of the listener is used as though it is a dial for "tuning in" to a radio station. The goal is to be not too far to the left or to the right, but to be perfectly "tuned in" to the station so as to avoid hearing static. When we properly "tune in" to a radio station, we hear music clearly coming through without static. Similarly, when properly attuned to the communicator, we clearly hear the message being communicated. If I have achieved empathic attunement, then my inner self has achieved alignment with the communicator's inner self-experience and has accurately empathized with and felt the communicator's feelings.

Hitting the Nail on the Head

The listener is now in a position to hold up a mirror and reflect back to the communicator what has been expressed; this serves to validate the self experience of the communicator and enables the communicator to confirm the accuracy of the material empathically mirrored or reflected back to them.

There is now a moment of clarification or elaboration. Metaphorically, this can be thought of as finding out if the listener when providing feedback either "hit the nail on the head with the hammer" or "missed the head of the nail." The listener failed to accurately perceive, hear, and reflect back what the communicator was feeling, missing the head of the nail. The goal is to hit the nail on the head with the hammer or to be "on target."

Empathic Mirroring

Empathic mirroring (Wallace, 1991) occurs when group members, or the group moderator, gently and metaphorically holds up a mirror and reflects back to the individual (perhaps crying) what is sensed to be the affect, feeling, or meaning expressed. It is as if the listener uses the inner self to attune to the inner self experience of the one who is expressing affects. In order for one to engage in empathic mirroring, one must first have achieved successful empathic attunement with the inner self experience of the one expressing him or herself. Empathic mirroring may also be used to increase an individual's motivation to engage in behavioral change and achieve a state of readiness to take action on a problem behavior; in this case one mirrors and reflects back to the individual a discrepancy between two statements they have made, or between a statement and their behavior. For example, on the one hand I hear you saying that you don't think you have a problem with drugs, but on the other hand you say that your grades have dropped, you were fired from your job, lost your girlfriend, and are having problems with your family. Typically, this intervention re-connects the individual to their inner feelings and motivates them to change the behavior of using drugs (see Chapter 10 and Wallace, 1991).

Excavating a Chunk of Gold or Precious Pearl

It is also as if one group member digs deep within and excavates a chunk of gold or precious pearl that is tentatively displayed to other group members. Other group members tend to respond by taking seriously the moment of sharing and also digging deep within to excavate and display their own chunk of gold or precious pearl. When group members add to empathic mirroring self-disclosure of their own private feelings, they reciprocally excavate a chunk of gold or precious pearl. As other group members who identify with the feelings disclosed by the tearful individual go on to share their own formerly hidden feelings and memories, the psychoeducational support group emerges as a unique and powerful vehicle for the deep expression of affect.

Healing the Damaged Ego and Self in Groups

As individual group members undergo the experience of empathic mirroring, the self, which may have been neglected, abused, or traumatized receives not only validation but also vital stimulation that triggers growth. It is as though the interest, time, attention, and care that the listener takes in achieving empathic attunement and engaging in empathic mirroring provoke growth, just as the time and attention of the gardener watering a plant stimulate and provoke growth of the plant. Being so watered, growth may continue for a person once stunted, fixated, and stuck at a prior developmental stage when the arrest in development occurred in response to some trauma. Growing beyond the arrest in development, the interpersonal stimulation provided by empathic mirroring also serves as a kind of "re-parenting," or compensatory nurturing experience. What an alcoholic, or drug-addicted, absent, abusive, or neglectful parent could not consistently perform can be performed in a later developmental stage in the simple setting of a group or one-on-one therapeutic interaction.

The ego, which may have been fragmented and damaged from experiences of violence and trauma, becomes more whole, integrated, and cohesive. Just as a tree which will forever have distinctive rings marking several years of disease or debilitating weather patterns, an individual may forever bear internal marks from trauma and violence, or possess points of fixation. But just as a tree, in response to favorable weather patterns, may have especially good years of growth that strenghten the overall tree and permit a new level of strength as it survives into the future, so too may experiences of empathic mirroring in a group setting serve as a favorable pattern of interaction that produces a stronger individual who will carry that strength into the future.

The Ego's Development of the Capacity to Observe the Inner Self

The progressive development of a self-observing, integrated and more cohesive ego also occurs through participation in a psychoeducational support group. Hence, the ego that observed abuse, neglect and trauma—and how the self became fractured, and split—can now observe favorable interpersonal interactions in the group. From the experience of empathic mirroring, the individual's ego also learns to observe and to see his or her own self in the reflection of the mirror. Seeing this reflection also creates and stimulates the ability to observe oneself; the individual develops the ability to turn inside and to observe the feelings and thoughts that the listener has also observed emerging and has also bothered to empathically reflect back or mirror to the communicator. The communicator benefits from the process of empathic mirroring and begins also to provide some confirmation of the attempt at empathy. This confirmation involves metaphorically responding to empathic mirroring as follows: "You hit the nail on the head"; or "Move a little to the right and you will hit the nail on the head." The process of observing their own internal state and comparing it to the empathically reflected material helps individuals facilitate the development of their own self-observing ego. A part of their ego develops the capacity to better observe the inner self and what it is feeling. In this way, the ego that experienced abandonment, abuse, neglect, and trauma—and that became reliant on the use of defenses because of trauma, learns enhanced self-observation.

Ego Learning of Improved Self-Regulation

Self-observation is critical to exercising good judgment, to the ability to delay and inhibit impulses, and to decisions about overall self-care. With group participation and receipt of feedback regarding one's behavior from other members within the group, individuals develop the ability to engage in self-observation. This self-observation on the part of a much healthier ego also leads to overall improved self-regulation of (1) feelings (affects) as well as of (2) impulses, (3) self-esteem, (4) interpersonal behavior, and (5) general self-care behaviors. (See rationale for targeting these five areas for improved self-regulation in Chapters 7–9.)

Typically, an increased awareness of what is felt inside enhances the ability to regulate affects, impulses, self-esteem, and interpersonal behavior. So, enhanced self-observation is usually accompanied by an ego's improved self-regulation. The ego, in giving up overreliance on defenses, can now practice actively managing and coping with the self's emergent feelings. The door is open to learning how to actively cope with feelings, as well as learn how to better regulate feelings, impulses, self-esteem, and interpersonal behavior. What I actively observe I may better regulate.

WEEK 11: DESCRIBING THE MOVIE IN YOUR MIND

Individuals who have developed a self-observing ego can utilize this part of their egos to observe their "self" in a memory and image of the traumatic experience of violence. We refer to this image or memory in the mind as being a movie in their mind. Group members who have experienced, witnessed, or delivered violence need to integrate and work out the traumatic memory by describing the "movie in their mind" that captures their traumatic memory. In session 11, we introduce this movie metaphor as an instruction and invitation for those willing to begin to use the group for healing and working through traumatic experiences. Group members are invited to describe to the group what happened to them during traumatic experiences of violence—likened to the possession of a "movie in the mind." They can describe the feelings of aversion, desire to move away, and other powerful and intense feelings and impulses that arose within the self at the moment of trauma and overstimulation, as well as the behavioral action in the movie in the mind. The self-observing ego of group members can metaphorically describe the self in the movie in their mind and the action in that movie to others, without jumping into the movie and actually reliving the traumatic scene.

Two Critical Interventions: "Don't Jump into the Movie!" and "Tell Me What You See?"

Supportive group members actively listen to one group member, or communicator, who is telling his or her story and describing the action in the movie. Other listeners in the group, and the moderator of the group, should remind the one sharing to describe the action in the movie, and not jump in the movie and begin to relive the action. This instruction translates into members either "acting it out," if they jump into the action of the movie and relive the experience, or more effectively "working it out" by describing to others the action occurring in their movie. The goal in working it out is to use the self-observing ego to objectively describe to other group members the subjective experience of their "self in the movie." Group members may caution the communicator of their story, "Yo man, don't jump into the movie; talk about it!" Or urge the communicator to "Tell me what you see! Tell me what you see happening to you in the movie." The group leader or other members may remind the communicator in midstory to "Describe the action in your movie; don't jump in that movie now. Stay with us." We may call the communicator by name as well, prompting him repeatedly, "John, tell me what you see." We can check in with a group member and ask, "Are you with us man, did you jump in that movie?"

An Important Caution

We never urge someone to talk about a memory they are not ready to talk about. We never urge someone to go to the movies who does not want to go there, not wanting to share what is inside. Instead, we repeatedly remind group members to talk only about what they feel like talking about. We may offer, "Only use the group when you feel ready, never rush it man; talk about what you feel ready to talk about, when you feel ready to talk about it." We trust that individual group members have an inner sense of what they should do and when they should do it. Other group members respect personal decisions of when and what to share in group.

In early sessions within secondary prevention, group members learn how to function in the group in a constructive manner in order to facilitate healing and the resolution of traumatic memories of other group members who decide to share in the group. Again, sessions that may last anywhere from forty-five minutes to three hours begin with a brief discussion of the information offered in this section. Ideally, members begin to share memories of trauma. Definitions start off sessions 12 through 14, followed by open sharing by volunteers.

Closing People Up with Humor Versus Leaving Them Open

Humor is also a very functional defense with which we may try to end each group session. *Humor* when used as a defense serves to distract the ego from painful, shaming, and overwhelming material that may have come up in a session. Humor distracts the ego and forces it to focus on the positive. We do not want to "leave people open" and feeling vulnerable after material from their unconscious has just been in contact with the ego or is still near the surface. Instead, we want to "close people up" before they leave the group. In this manner, we can close the group session with a decompression period. This can last from five to fifteen minutes at the end of the group, depending on how long the session has been (forty-five minutes, one and a half hours, or three hours). We can tell a joke, be silly, talk about gross and disgusting things that are infantile, and do anything to distract the ego and re-focus it in reality.

When a group member has worked particularly hard and has processed a lot of pain, we want to skillfully distract their egos. We want the ego to suddenly realize, perhaps in the middle of a belly laugh, that we were able to distract the ego and re-focus the ego. At the end of one session in my private practice, I was able to do this with a woman who during the session had experienced a flashback to domestic violence. At the end of the session when she was sitting there smiling and laughing, she suddenly stopped and looked at me. With an intensity she said, "Thank you for closing me up. I saw all those different psychiatry residents at Bellevue and not once did they close me up. Thank you." In this manner, we need to "close people up" by re-focusing the ego in reality and distracting it from those unconscious contents that may emerge.

In another group session, a woman had successfully described a trauma in childhood, and we had "worked it out" as she described the "movie in her mind." I started directing the group to talk and laugh about something gross and stupid. We were laughing. Suddenly this woman looked up at me and smiled. She knew that whatever we had done in group had come to an end and that she was past it and had survived. She laughed at our silliness, and her ego was successfully distracted and re-focused in reality. We want to assist all of our group members who decide to share in group in becoming "closed" after having "opened up" and discussed a traumatic memory. This is an important part of psychoeducation in our groups and in any one-on-one sessions.

WEEKS 12–14: EDUCATION ON DEFENSES USED BY THE EGO: DEFINITIONS AND METAPHORS

A *defense* may be defined as the ego's use of a maneuver to block out of awareness feelings, thoughts, and behaviors (affects, behaviors, and cognitions, or our ABCs) that are associated with moments of overstimulation and trauma and cause the ego to experience anxiety and fear. Because the feelings, behaviors, and thoughts are intimately linked with an actual moment or memory of overstimulation and trauma, the ego seeks out and utilizes maneuvers designed to wipe or block out any conscious knowledge of the causes and effects of trauma. Since we naturally seek out integration and wholeness as human organisms, there is a pressure for fragments of our experience to be recognized, acknowledged, and integrated with the whole of our awareness. New and more sophisticated maneuvers are sometimes needed in the face of this healthy urge toward integration. But since the ego was overstimulated at the moment of trauma, the ego has a well-hidden phobia, or fear, of anything associated with the moment of trauma and overstimulation, and seeks to avoid contact with anything that threatens to overstimulate again (i.e., feelings, thoughts, certain behaviors), using maneuvers for the purpose of avoidance.

Definition of Avoidance

Avoidance is the most basic and common defense used by the ego. Because the ego was once overwhelmed or overstimulated during trauma, it has learned that it did not know "how to deal" or cope in that situation at that time. As a result, the ego felt anxiety and fear. But this information generalizes to other similar situations and the ego has an expectation that it will not be able to cope, so the ego uses the defense of avoidance; sometimes this is a fair and accurate judgment on the part of the ego; at other times it is a persisting and unrealistic fear that keeps us stuck or fixated in the past. Avoidance suggests that the aftermath of trauma includes the ego having a well-hidden fear or phobia of the traumatic situation. The defense of avoidance is utilized whenever anything associated with that moment of trauma arises. The ego deploys a strategy of moving away, running away, and rapidly removing one's self from a trigger associated with the trauma—as our definition of avoidance.

From the perspective of the ego, the ego "does not know how to deal, does not want to deal, and is afraid to deal" (Laurent, 1995), or try to cope. People using avoidance end up staying away or removing themselves from "people, places, and things" (Laurent, 1995), not unlike the recommendation to avoid which Alcoholics Anonymous offers to the alcoholic.

People who use the avoidance defense may be found suddenly disappearing, running away, moving away, or never entering situations that remind them, consciously or unconsciously, of the traumatic scene and moment of overstimulation. When we have suffered the trauma of alcoholism and drug addiction, we may naturally avoid triggers associated with alcohol and drug use; but we may also need to learn how to use the defense of avoidance. Sometimes the use of defenses is adaptive and critical and permits our survival in difficult or traumatic times. The problem is the overuse of defenses until they themselves become problematic and prevent us from living fully. We may need to learn how to trade in the overuse of defenses, including getting high and over-eating, for the ego overcoming its well-hidden phobia and learning how to actively cope in reality.

Definition of Denial

Another common defense is *denial,* which is the ego's maneuver to avoid a feared and painful part of reality by telling the self a "little white lie." The feared and painful entity simply does not exist or is not occurring.

Thus, "avoidance is the first step of denial" (Laurent, 1995). Whereas in avoidance the ego observes, "I don't know how to deal, I don't want to deal, and I am afraid to deal, suddenly the feared situation is right in the ego's face" and the ego will act as if it is not there (Laurent, 1995).

For example, relapsing to drugs or alcohol and fearing that one's family or spouse will discover the relapse is a painful reality. Using denial, one can tell oneself that this reality does not exist. If confronted with the facts of one's drinking or drugging behavior by a spouse or partner, denial permits one even to lie to others. The ego uses denial and acts like the feared situation that is "right in their face" does not exist. The spouse holding up the vial of crack is told "That's not mine. I'm not getting high. I don't know how it got there. Someone else must have put it there."

Unfortunately, reality may impinge on individuals even when they remain in secret isolation with the facts of their behavior and experience. Denial may not always work as a reliable and effective defense. Fearful images and painful scenarios of discovery and confrontation may flash before the ego, nonetheless, even as they revert back to a stance of denial; "It never happened, my spouse has not figured anything out; nobody knows I'm smoking crack again." Meanwhile, in the back of their mind, they keep having flashbacks and images of their spouse holding up the vial of crack and confronting them.

We can also explain this phenomenon with the following story: denial is like telling one's self a little white lie and stating to one's spouse as well as one walks out the door, "I am going to take this $20 bill and go to the cleaners and pick up my clothes." Meanwhile, in the back of my head I am thinking, "I really want to run into Johnny and purchase drugs to get high." At the same time he visualizes himself smoking crack, despite telling himself "I'm going to the cleaners." The solution to denial is to learn how to practice rigorous honesty and learn how to talk about what is in the back of one's mind, talking about those images and secret desires lurking in the back of one's mind (Wallace, 1991).

Definition of Rationalization

Rationalization, another defense, can be defined as the act of offering a long, drawn-out explanation for one's behavior, as our behavior painfully reflects either wanting to perform a behavior or avoiding the performance of a behavior. The ego observes either our compulsion to act out a pattern of behavior or our avoidance. A rationalization is verbalized aloud to others or to ourselves, as we attempt to make sense out of our compulsive patterns of behavior and avoidance. Rationalization, as a defense, protects us from feeling out of control and attempts to preserve an illusion of control. The long-drawn-out explanation of our behavior represents an attempt to suggest how we possess control, when in reality we may not.

Definition of Repression

The defense of *repression* can be defined as simply burying a feeling, thought, image, impulse, or memory associated with a moment of trauma or overstimulation. It can be likened to taking a balloon or ball and pressing it and holding it below the surface of the ocean, preferably in the ocean's depths. The balloon or ball contains the feelings, impulses, images, or memories associated with the traumatic moment of overstimulation. The act of holding the balloon below in the ocean's depths—which may take considerable energy given its tendency and disposition to rise to the surface—represents the ego's defensive maneuver of repression.

Definition of Narcissism

We also need to understand the defense of narcissism. Severe trauma, neglect, abuse, and abandonment leave the inner self full of bad feelings, or with a painfully low self-esteem. Injuries to the inner self may be thought of as narcissistic injuries (Wallace, 1991) that follow from experiences of abuse and trauma. The existence of such injuries and of a painfully low self-esteem may lead to the use of the defense of narcissism, inflation, and grandiosity. When we are narcissistic, inflated, and grandiose, we may not necessarily suffer from a personality disorder. In a narcissistic personality disorder, grandiosity is a long-standing feature stemming from an earlier developmental era and characterizing us as we mature across developmental stages. Narcissism, inflation, and grandiosity may constitute a defensive strategy used by individuals in crisis, hitting rock bottom from multiple losses, or commonly used by individuals in early recovery.

Narcissism may characterize anyone whose self-esteem may begin to plummet because of the threatened emergence of parts of the self (memories, feelings, thoughts belonging to this part of ourselves) long buried, but associated with trauma and pain. Instead of feeling the intense pain and sense of devaluation associated with the self's profoundly shaming and traumatic experience, the defense of narcissism may be used. *Narcissism* as a defense may be defined as the use of arrogance, aloofness, superiority, and grandiosity to compensate for and cover up feelings of intense shame, worthlessness, and lack of self-value.

Narcissism and the Inflated Balloon Metaphor

Narcissism is like being an inflated balloon full of hot air, floating up high in the sky. But this is a fragile state of defense and may be very temporary and unstable. All it takes is a needle, and poof, we become deflated and land on the ground, feeling empty and worthless. Here, the needle represents anything that challenges our use of defenses and can lead to a failure of the defense to keep working. We end up deflated and feeling worthless on the ground. These poles of inflation and deflation describe the sudden swings and instability in the self-value of someone who uses the narcissism defense. The therapeutic goal is to engage in neither narcissistic inflation nor rest in a deflated worthless state. Rather, the goal is to attain a balanced sense of self-worth based on assessment of our strengths and weaknesses (Wallace, 1991). This is born of empathic mirroring and the observations about us from others who effectively re-parent and nurture us, instilling compensatory feelings of value. When group members clap for an individual and state they are proud of this person for the performance of a new behavior, perhaps once feared (inside or outside of the group), the one so praised experiences an increase in self-esteem and self-efficacy. This feedback and empathic mirroring also helps cultivate a self-observing ego that can then realistically observe our strengths and weaknesses. Individuals emerge with a realistic sense of self-worth based upon a body of feedback from group members and systematic self-observation.

Definition of Inhibition

The *inhibition* defense is the ego's tendency to block the expression of an aggressive or a sexual impulse, or an affect or feeling. It is the result of the ego observing the self's feelings of wanting to move away from an object inflicting trauma, and witnessing the emergence of an accompanying aggressive or sexual impulse. Since a feeling and the accompanying aggressive or sexual impulse arose at the moment of trauma, the ego develops a fear of the feeling and impulses associated with this overwhelming and overstimulating experience. The emergence of feelings and of aggressive or sexual impulses is associated with the experience of the ego being overwhelmed and overstimulated during trauma. The ego actually develops a well-hidden fear, or phobia, of the feelings or sexual impulses that arose during trauma. This well-hidden fear or phobia leads to the ego using the defense of inhibition against the feelings and sexual or aggressive impulses. The ego inhibits or blocks the expression of feelings and sexual impulses to situations that go beyond the moment of trauma. In a variety of situations—even those in which it would be healthy and adaptive to express a feeling or an aggressive or sexual impulse—the ego tends to reflexively inhibit and block the expression of the impulse.

Inhibition is a form of overcontrol and an inappropriate failure to release impulses and feelings. It is the opposite of the kind of control loss that occurs when splitting involves the part of the self that compulsively reenacts a traumatic behavioral scenario, or what occurs in sexual acting-out, sexual promiscuity, or in aggressive acting-out behavior. For example, an adult child of a dysfunctional family who finds that people "walk all over them," and who never complain or express their dissatisfaction with the situation may represent a classic example of overinhibition or overcontrol of aggression. Persons who are afraid to express angry feelings and aggressive impulses tend to inhibit, overcontrol, or fail to release the expression of anger and aggressive impulses. They inhibit their feelings of anger and find themselves unable to verbalize these feelings. They are unable to mobilize a healthy form of self-protection because of their overuse of inhibition against aggression. The expression of a healthy sexuality may also be prevented by the inhibition of feelings of attraction and sexual impulses that are blocked or inhibited. What the ego once feared and still fears is therefore inhibited.

Individuals need to learn to observe how feelings arise within and to learn that what was once feared—because it was overwhelming and associated with trauma—may no longer require such a high level of fear. What was frightening and overwhelming for a young child may be manageable, appropriate, and enjoyable for an older adolescent or adult. As impulses are observed arising within the individual, the ego may gain new learning that replaces the prior (well-hidden) fear, or phobia.

Definition of Displacement

Displacement is a defense involving an individual who, for example, feels anger toward one person, such as his brother, and directs the affect toward a safer or more convenient object, such as a neighbor. The classic example of displacement is the man who is angry at his boss and displaces anger on his wife; the anger the wife feels toward her husband is displaced on her son; and the son displaces anger felt toward his mother upon his dog.

WEEK 13: DEFINITION OF PROJECTION

Projection is a defense that involves placing our "bad" split self, or our "bad parts," outside of ourselves by locating them in another person. Just as the ego tries to separate the good self from the bad part of the self, the ego uses the defense of projection to create distance between the good and bad part of the self by temporarily locating the bad part in another person. After projection, we may either want to fight or flee from the person in whom we now perceive something bad.

Definition of Identification

Projection is often preceded by an unconscious *identification*, that is, seeing attributes and characteristics that we have in common with someone else. In the case of toddlers, children, and adolescents, we usually think of identification as involving at first unconscious imitation and later selectively deciding to be like someone else—taking on their characteristics.

Definition of Projective-Identification

When we engage in identification and unconsciously perceive our own attributes in someone else, this may be a prelude to the use of projection. Seeing a part of ourselves within another person reminds us of our own bad part, and we then use the defense of projection and go on to locate our own bad part in this other person. This phenomenon is known as *projective-identification*; a term that correctly implies how the two processes of identification and projection may be happening simultaneously, even as an urge to fight or flee suddenly appears (see the discussion of "my mirror" in Chapter 8).

Definition of Regression

The defense of *regression* may occur in response to extreme stress. It involves an individual moving backward and returning to a prior level of developmental functioning, suggestive of a younger age. When regression is first used as a defense, it is as if the ego is facing a difficult stressor and feels a need to retreat to an earlier developmental level that was already mastered and is therefore more comfortable, being full of expected events and already tried and common behaviors. For example, a three year old's mother has a new baby; the toilet trained toddler may begin to wet himself and revert back to a bottle or earlier behavior such as thumb sucking. While distressing to the parent, it is actually comforting to the infant who can fall back on old well-known behaviors rather than try something new. Usually, the regression is temporary, and we leap forward to the appropriate developmental level and return to behaviors common to the more advanced stage. We also go on to adapt to the new stressors.

Definition of a Fixation Point

In other cases, we may regress under stress and return to fixation points. We possess fixation points because of the experience of some trauma at an earlier age. A *fixation point* is defined as a point or time in our development that is marked, if not marred, by the experience of trauma, overstimulation, or narcissistic injury during a profoundly shaming experience. As a result, we tend to regress or go back to this point in time and to perform behaviors associated with this moment. It is as though a part of us continues to be stuck, or fixated, at that moment in time. We can also speak of part of our self remaining stuck at this point in time, while other parts may go on to mature. But the part of our self that is damaged is like a flower or plant that stopped growing; it is stuck at that developmental level. This is why some speak of an arrest in self-development. The arrest is caused by the trauma, the possession of a fixation point, and a part of us that is still frozen, standing still, in a state of psychophysiological shock.

A Part of Us Is Stuck on a Step of Our Stairs Metaphor

A fixation point is akin to having tripped or been attacked while slowly and progressively climbing up the stairs of our developmental stages. One day we are attacked on step 4 of this staircase. A part of us remains lying in a state of shock on stair 4 (piece of cracked glass or torn piece of rug), even though other parts of ourself keep moving up the stairs. Under stress, or in response to certain triggers, it is as though we tumble down the staircase and automatically land on step 4; we end up connecting with the part of our self in shock. We regress to our fixation point. To recover from trauma, it is as though we need to consciously and intentionally walk down to step 4, describe what our assaulter did to us on step 4, and feel what we felt when this trauma happened on step 4. We describe our trauma in this manner, embrace that part of ourselves on step 4, and carry it up the stairs to be with us for the rest of our lives. We are obligated to pay attention to and care for this part of ourselves we have so recovered, feeling genuine empathy for its past. This constitutes the overall process of healing and integration from past trauma; we effectively heal our split or fragmentation of our self. If we have multiple pieces or "self-entities," then gradually over time we may have to recover our parts from steps 2, 3, 7, and 9, for example, since we likely experienced multiple trauma and episodes of torture.

Definition of Regression in the Service of a Self-Observing Ego

Earlier we used the metaphor of the "movie in our minds" and not "jumping into the movie" to describe regression in the service of a self-observing ego.

Regression in the service of a self-observing ego may be defined as the act of consciously observing ourselves move back in time to a fixation point, describing to others aloud what our egos can now consciously observe happening to a part of our self in a memory of a traumatic scene, and thereby consciously integrating and working out a past experience of trauma. What was unconscious, that is, a traumatic scene damaging a part of our self, is now made conscious by virtue of cognitive processing and talking by the ego.

WEEK 14: UNDERSTANDING THE TENDENCY OF THE PSYCHE TO SPLIT

Jung (1969a) has discussed splitting and the tendency of the psyche to split. Definitions and metaphors foster understanding of the tendency of the psyche to split.

Definition of Splitting

Splitting is a defense that involves the creation of a separate "self-entity" because of fragmentation of the self resulting from the sudden and shocking force of a trauma. If an individual experiences several different episodes of trauma, and splitting as a defense is used repetitively, then many different self-entities may exist. That individual may be said to have many differents parts to themselves, as a reference to several self-entities.

The Label on a Jar Metaphor (Diagnoses)

The mental health profession has a number of terms that describe splitting and how it may range in severity. Someone may merely be caught staring and not paying attention ("Where did you just go?). Another person may regularly present different or alternating self-entities and is diagnosed as a borderline personality. Yet another has a multiple personality disorder.

The problem with labels (diagnoses of mental disorders) is that when we put one on a jar and the contents of the jar change, sometimes the label remains stuck on the jar and is hard to peel off. Following a biopsychosocial approach, a continuing assessment over time reveals how diagnoses may change (Wallace, 1992).

A Practical Approach to Splitting

Professional group co-leaders refer those with extreme symptoms such as multiple personality disorder or suicidal or homicidal acting-out behavior to a psychiatrist, mental health clinic, or emergency room. But we need not feel excessive or debilitating fear. How often have we heard of Alcoholics Anonymous groups in church basements being interrupted with someone being taken to the hospital emergency room? Certainly, it may be an appropriate response, but we need not overly fear this possibility.

Instead, we need to realize that many of us are survivors of trauma and that most of us employ some degree of splitting. Because it is possible to learn how to self-observe the ego's use of splitting, we can empower readers to be able to perform this task. The subject of splitting need not cause fear or intimidate us. Metaphors make the subject much more understandable to counselors, clients, and those who over-use splitting. The weird and annoying can become manageable if we take a practical approach to the splitting phenomenon.

Our Parents Dropped and Broke the Glass Metaphor

It is as if our parents suddenly drop us, as if we are a glass, and we end up cracked, fractured, or broken. Some glasses possess hairline fractures, others have major cracks, and yet others are so broken they cannot hold water; some, scattered into multiple, separate pieces or fragments, seem almost unrecognizable as having once been a glass. This metaphor reflects the degrees of fragmentation we may possess, depending on the severity of the trauma. The question arises, "Where is my center of awareness and feeling if I am a shattered glass lying on the kitchen floor? Today, am I centered in the bottom base of the glass? Am I centered in the large right side of the glass that was holding the reflection of my mother's enraged face, spewing verbal abuse at me? Or am I centered today in the jagged, still circular left side of the glass that was facing the kitchen sink and reflecting the image of the water faucet dripping water, while also echoing the sound of that dripping water? Where is the location of what is left of my sense of a core self, even as I struggle with being broken and cracked from severe physical and verbal abuse at the hands of my alcoholic and mentally ill mother?

A particular broken-off, cracked, or fragmented "self-entity" may spontaneously appear on different days as I feel centered or located at either the base, left side, or the right side of the glass. A fragment or self-entity may spontaneously appear in response to appropriate triggers. Another fragment, or broken piece of my glass may appear and reappear, as that part of myself performs compulsive behaviors that are the exact replica of my mother hitting me and flailing her arms with a look of rage on her face. The object of this violence may be my own little girl, another student in school, or a stranger I attack on the street. The frantic and spontaneous performance of these compulsive behaviors can serve as an elaborate maneuver or defense. They prevent me from connecting with the part of my self that is located in the base of the glass that is still holding a little water—analogous to still holding the intense pain, shame, and fear of having been severely beaten by my mother. If someone in reality now triggers my feelings of shame and I go back and feel centered in the base of the glass, I may be overwhelmed with feelings of pain and shame and powerlessness. At this moment it is better to relocate my core or central sense of self in the right fragment of my glass; it is better to be located in that piece of the glass that is holding the reflection or mirror image of my raging and violent mother. At this moment, I engage in splitting as a defense and detach myself from the part of myself that feels centered or located in the broken base of the glass—holding painful and shameful feelings, as well as powerlessness. I suddenly become located in the right side of the broken glass; I become centered in the angry, raging, and verbally abusive part of myself that begins to perform a perfect imitation or replication of my mother's abusive behavior toward me. I am using the defense of splitting to deny that a part of me feels shame and powerlessness and to avoid connecting with those horrible feelings. It feels better to feel strong and to attack others in an act of violence, even if it is my own daughter. However, splitting may be automatic and out of the control of the person using the defense of splitting.

Originally, the fragmentation may have been an appropriate defense that represented the ego's best attempt to gain distance from a part of the self that was being traumatized and to preserve a part of the self that was attempting to not be destroyed. When the right side of my body, or the right side of my glass was hit with a stick by my mother, I engaged in splitting and centered my sense of self on the far left side of my glass which was reflecting the water faucet dripping. By splitting, I focused on and stared at the water faucet and concentrated on the sound of the water dripping. I did this to get as far away as possible from the pain my mother was causing me as she hit my right arm with the stick, "over and over and over again." I centered myself in the reflection of the shiny metal sink and faucet and only tried to hear the dripping of the faucet—blocking out my mother's screams and her verbal abuse of me. I did this to survive and try to preserve a part of myself, since I thought the right side of the glass might just completely shatter and be destroyed. I thought that part of me would die. I decided I could get away from the dead and dying part and just live in a corner of me, or on just one side. This was the side that would stay "good and clean," after my mother made one side "bad, dirty, and bloody" with her blows and verbal abuse.

After the moment of fragmentation and desperate attempt to keep things separate and preserved, the fragmented self, or different and separate fragments, may emerge as capable of performing elaborate behavioral scenarios in isolation from each other.

The Torn and Tattered Rug Metaphor

We may use a second metaphor to explain splitting. Our psyches are like rugs, and trauma creates tears and rips in the fabric of our rug. Thereafter, we may find ourselves standing on one part of the rug that is so torn that it is like standing on a separate island. Or, with severe trauma, we may have several separate islands and may find ourselves standing on different rug fragments, or islands, at different times. The behaviors we perform while standing on one piece of rug may be likened to being centered on one island or mobilizing and engaging into action just one fragmented part of the self. This fragment may then compulsively act out behavior, as in replicating the violence of one's mother. We may learn to observe the activity of a fragmented self, or we may learn to observe what occurs on different parts and fragments of our torn and tattered rug, island, or psyche. However, without the experience of empathic mirroring and another's observation of our compulsive behavior when a fragmented self begins to become active, and their pointing it out to us systematically, we tend to be unaware and rather unconscious of what is happening at such moments.

Learning to Self-Observe Splitting

For example, I can learn to observe how, when someone yells at me or causes me to feel shame, this triggers me to go to the left side of my glass and to reenact staring blankly into the shiny metal sink and focusing on the faucet with its dripping noise. Someone points out "You just blanked out, where did you go?" I realize I am in front of the kitchen sink, staring. I split-off from painful reality and feelings of intense shame. A few minutes later I notice that I am picking a fight and verbally abusing somebody. Suddenly, I have engaged in the defense of splitting again, and I am trying to avoid feeling pain, shame and helplessness. Someone points out to me, "Why are you looking for a fight? Why are you suddenly becoming verbally abusive? You should go look in the mirror and get a glimpse of that look of rage and hate that just came over your face. What's going on with you? Where did you go just now?" I observe myself and realize I just went to the right side of my glass and tried to feel powerful and in control by becoming my mother and imitating her behavior of physical and verbal abuse of others.

The cultivation of a self-observing ego and the receipt of empathic mirroring create the foundation for individuals ultimately coming to observe before their own eyes the process of splitting when they are transformed into assaulters. Self-observation may again lead to another transformative moment when they intervene and stop their own behavior. We can learn to stop ourselves by talking to ourselves aloud and commenting on what is happening; "Here you go again. Somebody triggered your shame and now you're looking for a fight. Get a grip, get a grip. Hold on girl. Just keep it together, keep it together. Hold your tongue. Go apologize. Take a walk and do some deep breathing in the park. That's good. Calm down. Let it go. Which affirmation should I use now? Yeah, that's a good one—I AM CALM, CENTERED AND BALANCED. Go ahead, keep repeating it."

Because of the experience of receiving empathic mirroring and developing a self-observing ego, we can replace the defense of splitting with a new level of self control. By actively talking to ourselves, we attain a new level of mental health and self-control. From our group work, the goal is to emerge capable of communicating with or talking to ourselves at the critical moment when the defense of splitting might reemerge. By talking to ourselves and stopping ourselves, we reduce or eliminate the potential for a role reversal that would lead to the assault of another person.

Splitting as a Role Reversal

The behaviors performed compulsively during moments of splitting may also reflect identification with an aggressor and may constitute that fragmented part of ourselves that experienced trauma coming to assume the behavior of the aggressor and seeking out an object to place in the role of victim. This form of splitting combines a role reversal. The defense of splitting would explain the rather unconscious and compulsive nature of a behavioral drama which appears in assaulters who may be genuinely unaware of what happens to them when they are transformed before the eyes of others into assaulters.

Splitting as Resumption of the Role of Victim

Splitting may also involve the compulsive enactment of a behavioral drama wherein we repeat the role behavior of having been a victim. In this case, we find an opportunity for unconsciously creating and expecting a situation and we thereby engender another to play the role behavior of the assaulter. We may appear, for example, to be looking for a fight or to get sexual, but we are unconsciously provoking someone else to attack us physically or sexually.

Splitting and Dissociation

Splitting may also involve what may be called a state of dissociation. When I become centered in the left side of the glass holding the reflection of the faucet dripping water, I stare blankly and intently so that I will not notice how my mother is making my right arm and side bleed from blows from her stick striking my body repeatedly. This is a state of dissociation.

Definition of Dissociation

Dissociation may be defined as an instance or state when the ego is not focused upon and does not actively perceive the behaviors that the self is performing or experiencing—for example, not focusing on my arms which are flailing in the air, being hit with a stick, and trying to block my mother's painful blows. The self may either be allowing behaviors to happen or is being subjected to certain painful and overstimulating behaviors. During moments of trauma, while the self was undergoing fragmentation and being split or broken, the ego may also have engaged in dissociation. The ego refused to fully attend to or observe the traumatic sceme. In order to avoid fully witnessing the horror transpiring to the self, the ego used the defense of dissociation. The ego instead may have placed its attention on something else—either; the ceiling, cracks in the wall, water dripping in the background from a faucet, or literally anything that could distract and hold the ego's attention from focusing on the traumatic scene involving the self. Perception of the self's negative feelings, aversion, and intense desire to move away from the object inflicting trauma—even splitting to accomplish this—may be so overwhelming to the ego that the ego seeks to avoid observation of trauma, leading to the ego's use of dissociation.

WEEK 15: CLOSURE OR A DECISION TO CONTINUE

By week 15 of a psychoeducational support group, ultimately possession of a self-observing ego has permitted substantial working through of many group members' experiences of violence and trauma, which are all too common in schoolchildren and community members. Other group members, however, may never have shared in group, having remained silent, but many have learned a tremendous amount. They may now feel ready to start to share themselves, having just developed sufficient trust in the proces by watching others actively participate. Some group members may have just figured out what the group is for and what it can accomplish. If we only had forty-five minutes in a school setting, then we could just cover the curriculum and definitions; most members never have a chance to talk in depth.

Discussion for the Purpose of Achieving Group Closure, or Making a Decision to Continue the Group Process

The decision can be made to achieve closure, have members summarize what they got of the group experience, and offer gratitude for the feedback and support they received in group. Members may feel a need to continue across weeks 16 through 30 where there is much less material to cover, just so some members can start to talk. We might even need to run into the summer and start holding longer groups so that we can start to resolve some trauma. Members may now be digesting the definitions and may be starting to have more memories and examples from their own lives. During session 15 a decison may be made to achieve closure or to continue. If the group decides to continue, a relapse prevention curriculum can be used to open group discussion in sessions 16 through 30. As members are accustomed to talking in group format at this point, some sessions might start with group sharing and not even get around to the curriculum.

In addition, some group members may have experienced so much violence in their lives that everyone knows they need to continue. Other students or community members may have engaged in a lot of violence, assaulting others, physically abusing children, and engaging in domestic violence. These individuals definitely need to continue in a group. The relapse prevention against violence is designed primarily for the most violent prone, but can benefit everyone who continues in the group across weeks 16 through 30.

WEEKS 16–30 : TERTIARY VIOLENCE PREVENTION CURRICULUM

The psychoeducational support group format may involve the exposure of a select group of students, or, ideally, all group members to a *Violence Relapse Prevention Program*;. This program may be defined as a setting in which members learn how to anticipate high-risk situations for a return to violence, triggers of their violent behavior, thoughts and cognitions that precede violent behavior, and effectively learn how to perform alternative coping behaviors instead of violent behaviors.

The Violence Relapse Prevention Program follows standard principles of relapse prevention applied to a range of problem behaviors (Dimeff & Marlatt, 1995; Gossop, 1989; Marlatt & Gordon, 1985; Wallace, 1991; Wilson, 1992). Table 6.2 summarizes the content of the tertiary or violence prevention curriculum. Assuming that every individual with a violent past has said to him or herself, "I do not want this to happen again," but it has, we can posit a history of relapsing to violence.

Everyone who has said this to him or herself has a whole body of unanalyzed personal experience that can help avoid a relapse to violence in the future. This body of experience needs to be finely and carefully analyzed in the group, "breaking down" past episodes of violence into their smallest and most detailed elements. Depending on the size of the group, several members may be able to have their past relapse episodes carefully analyzed in just one group.

Table 6.2
A Curriculum for a Violence Relapse Prevention Program.

WEEKS 16–30	TERTIARY VIOLENCE PREVENTION CURRICULUM

WEEK:	TOPIC FOR DISCUSSION:
WEEK 16:	DEFINITIONS FOR RELAPSE PREVENTION Relapse, Microanalysis of the Relapse Episode to Violence, a High-Risk Situation for Relapse, Relapse As a Process Involving Multiple Determinants, the Proper Attitude Toward Relapse, Slip Versus Fall on an Icy Pavement Metaphor, the Porcelain Vase Metaphor As Caution on Vulnerability for the First Six Months
WEEK 17:	KEY CONCEPTS TO PREPARE FOR PREVENTING RELAPSE The Abstinence Violation Effect (AVE) for a Return to Violence, Self-Talk As Active Coping, Seemingly Irrelevant Decisions (SIDS), Countering SIDS and Changing Health Beliefs on Violence,
WEEK 18:	IDENTIFICATION OF HIGH-RISK SITUATIONS AND DETERMINANTS OF RELAPSE Key Questions to Ask in a Microanalysis of a Relapse Episode, Identification of Determinants of Relapse for a Specific Problem (i.e., gang, school, domestic violence), Identifying Common and Idiosyncratic Patterns of Multiple Determinants Operating Over Time in Relapse Episodes
WEEK 19:	GROUP MEMBERS START TO TAKE TURNS DEVELOPING ALTERNATIVE BEHAVIORAL RESPONSES TO TRIGGERS IN HIGH-RISK SITUATIONS Planning the "Script" for What to Say and Do in a High-Risk Situation, Internal Cognitive Coping, Outward Cognitive Coping, Behavioral Coping
WEEK 20:	PRACTICING THE SCRIPT: REHEARSAL AND ROLE PLAY
WEEKS 21–30:	GROUP MEMBERS CONTINUE TO TAKE TURNS DEVELOPING AND PRACTICING ALTERNATIVE WAYS OF COPING TO AVOID RELAPSE TO VIOLENCE Possible Use of the S-O-A (Self-Object-Affect) Workbook (See Chapter 8)

We can spend weeks 16–30 doing such a fine analysis of past relapse episodes, also going on to practice active coping to avoid a relapse to violence. Since the length of groups may also vary—from forty-five minutes to three hours, with one and a half being good, and three hours being most helpful—we assume flexibility in how the curriculum is covered in this more open and unstructured phase of the group process. Flexibility is needed since group members are also using the group to share what is happening in their lives as it relates to continuing to change their problem behaviors revealed across sessions 10 through 15. Other group members are recalling moments of trauma and working them out in group for the first time. Nonetheless, on some schedule determined by individual groups, the process of analyzing past relapse episodes needs to occur. Covering the following curriculum material in early sessions is the first step.

WEEK 16: DEFINITIONS FOR RELAPSE PREVENTION

A *relapse* is a return to a problem behavior, after a period in which we have decided and attempted to avoid engaging in the problem behavior. *Microanalysis of the relapse episode to violence* may proceed within the group setting; it is defined as the process of carefully analyzing past incidents of violence for their multiple determinants and the process involved in becoming violent. Thus, group members take turns volunteering to discuss a past incident in which they were violent. Typically, this involves identifying high-risk situations for relapse. A *high risk situation for relapse* is a situation in which a person is likely to encounter a trigger or cue that creates a strong urge to engage in the problem behavior, requiring the "tempted" individual to actively perform coping behaviors in order to avoid a return, or relapse, to the problem behavior (Marlatt & Gordon, 1985). Group members help each other to identify the triggers, situations, and unique combination of events that lead to violent behavior; they effectively identify high-risk situations for relapse.

Relapse As a Process Involving Multiple Determinants

The majority of episodes of relapse involve multiple determinants that act together over time to help move or propel a person toward a relapse (Wallace, 1991). Relapse is a process that may occur over an extended period of time as one trigger is followed by another, and a person is gradually stressed to the point when a relapse occurs (Wallace, 1991). In other situations, it is just one special and powerful trigger that does the job and pushes us over the edge to a relapse to violence; no matter how much stress we were under, the relapse would never have occurred had it not been for the "one straw that broke the camel's back."

Sometimes in searching for the triggers of relapse, we feel that we are digging for a needle in a haystack. We search for that one needle that was used to burst our bubble and drove us to a relapse. But we also understand the possible role of multiple determinants operating over time in the relapse process.

The Proper Attitude Toward Relapse

We persevere and help each other because once we figure out the triggers to a relapse we possess powerful information that can be utilized to develop an individualized relapse prevention program—tailor-made just for the individual. Accordingly, we learn that the one good thing about our past episodes of relapse is that we can learn from them what we need to avoid or do differently in the future. Our attitude toward a possible future relapse by group members is that it is not expected in the sense that it is inevitable. However, if it does happen, we turn it into an opportunity to learn. Most importantly, the Violence Relapse Prevention Program strives to teach group members how to anticipate a high-risk situation for relapse, plan how to actively cope in that situation, and rehearse and role play active coping so that a relapse is avoided.

Slip Versus Fall on an Icy Pavement Metaphor

We also distinguish a slip from a complete fall. We can distinguish the two by thinking of the following metaphor: It is one thing to slip if you are walking down an icy pavement, but it is another to have a complete fall or relapse (Wallace, 1991). Many metaphors for relapse prevention may be taken from Wallace (1991) who offers twenty-seven such metaphors designed for a psychoeducational relapse prevention group for crack cocaine-dependent clients.

The Porcelain Vase Metaphor As Caution on Vulnerability for the First Six Months

As another example from Wallace (1991), metaphor can also help convey how the first three to six months since the last episode of the problem behavior is the period of highest risk for a return to that behavior. Consider the following: "Imagine a porcelain vase. Where can I set it down or put it? Can I put it on a ledge, the edge of the table, or some other precarious place? You are a porcelain vase. You are fragile, delicate, and vulnerable to relapse. Especially for the next ninety days and even the next six months, you must be very careful where you put yourself. Avoid high-risk situations for relapse" (Wallace, 1991).

A body of research shows that clients experience the highest rates of relapse in the three to six months after terminating a problem behavior (Marlatt & Gordon, 1985; Wallace, 1991; Wilson, 1992). Initially, the individual is encouraged to avoid high-risk situations during period. During this three to six month period, the individual learns new coping behaviors for successfully negotiating high-risk situations for relapse that cannot be forever avoided.

WEEK 17: KEY CONCEPTS TO PREPARE FOR PREVENTING RELAPSE

A number of key concepts prepare clients for the task of preventing relapse. Theory taken from Marlatt & Gordon (1985) may be extended to the problem behavior of violence, permitting developing of curriculum material.

The Abstinence Violation Effect (AVE) for a Return to Violence

In some cases, we may return to some violence, but not to the full-blown state we used to be in before we started the group. If this happens, we need to avoid the *Abstinence Violation Effect (AVE)* (Marlatt & Gordon, 1985) if we do become violent again. In the AVE for violence, we have been abstinent from violence, and then we violate that abstinence. Because of this slip, we may feel guilty and say, "Oh what the heck? What difference does it make? I slapped her so I might as well go ahead and kick her butt all the way." The effect of feeling guilty and letting go and going all the way is the AVE. We absolutely need to avoid this phenomenon by using self-talk as active coping and the skill of microanalyis of the relapse episode.

Self-Talk As Active Coping

After slapping our partner, we need to stand with our hand at our side and ask ourselves questions:"Why did I do that? Is it because they lost my check at work? Is it because I could not sleep last night because I was so angry? Did I really need to drink that 40 ounce beer—especially when I feel this way? I better sit my butt down and get a grip. Go for a walk. Apologize and tell her it won't happen again. Tell her you are going to the park to do some deep breathing and you'll be back in 1 hour. Don't worry. If you could stop kicking her butt before, you can get a grip now."

We need to respond to a slip to violence and to the AVE by using it as an opportunity to learn about the unique determinants of a relapse. At that moment of a slip we must actively cope to prevent our having a full-blown relapse to violence. We can actively deliver self-talk and self-regulate or control our violent impulses. It is highly effective to talk aloud to ourselves and have a dialogue back and forth between our self-observing ego and that part of us that tends toward the compulsive engagement in splitting and role reversal.

Seemingly Irrelevant Decisions (SIDs)

We also need to avoid making *Seemingly Irrelevant Decisions (SIDs)* that may lead to a slip or relapse to violence (Dimmett & Marlatt, 1995). When I engage in a SID, I may decide to perform a behavior that may seem innocent and harmless, but that decision actually serves to "set us up" to be violent. An example follows: "Where is my boxcutter? Let me carry it; I am getting on the subway today." The next thing you know, when someone bumps into you or is rude, you pull out your boxcutter, threaten violence, start an argument, get into a fight, and get arrested for assault.

Countering SIDs and Changing Health Beliefs on Violence

To counter all SIDs that lead us to carrying weapons again—from knives, razors, guns, or a 9 millimeter—we need to think the following: "Why buy and carry around a bus ticket to prison, if you do not want to go there?" In this way, we can stop ourselves from a setup for a slip or relapse to violence. We should discuss our personal, cultural, ethnic, or racial health beliefs on violence, or cognitions, and we also need to identify and replace all problematic health beliefs on violence. Members can take turns identifying past SIDs that may have led to a slip or relapse to violence. They can also identify their own thoughts at the moment of a slip and their own personal experience of the AVE. Questions to ask one's self when analyzing past slips, and at the moment of a slip—to prevent it from turning into a full-blown relapse—follow in the next section.

WEEK 18: IDENTIFICATION OF HIGH-RISK SITUATIONS AND DETERMINANTS OF RELAPSE

Certain high-risk situations are common to a variety of problem behaviors, such as drinking, weight gain, drug use, cigarette smoking, and gambling. Researchers (Cummings, Gordon & Marlatt, 1980; Marlatt & Gordon, 1985; Wallace, 1991) present findings on the common determinants of relapse, following from the performance of a microanalysis of relapse episodes. Drawing upon their work, typical situations for relapse can be summarized as follows:

1. **Painful or Negative Emotion** *Situations that involve the internal experience of powerful, painful, negative, and distressing emotion.*
2. **Interpersonal Stress or Conflict** *Situations that involve stressful, conflict-ridden interpersonal interactions.*
3. **Environmental Stimuli of People, Places and Things** *Encounters with things external to us like a person, place or thing, or events (parties, celebrations, reunions) that provoke us or trigger us to relapse.*
4. **Direct Social Pressure or Peer Pressure** *Direct pressure and intense persuasion from someone or a group of people who taunt, provoke, and try very hard to convince us to engage in the behavior we are trying to avoid.*

Other research suggests that for different problem behaviors there are some unique and special determinants for relapse that are specific to that problem behavior (Gossop, 1989: Wallace,1991; Wilson, 1992). In this manner, group members in different community-based settings and composed of members who share specific problem behaviors are in a unique position to conduct their own research and develop a written record of common triggers, determinants of relapse, and high-risk situations for relapse. This process begins with individuals who undergo a microanalysis of their relapse episodes in the group setting.

Key Questions to Ask in a Microanalysis of a Relapse Episode

Individuals need to learn how to identify their personal, idiosyncratic determinants of relapse. This involves conducting a microanalysis of a past or recent episode of violence. All group members need to learn the important skill of analyzing what is happening in the "here and now"and figuring out what has just triggered us to feel like being violent—even in the middle of a violent episode, or right after an episode. This task involves asking ourselves the following questions:

1. What happened just before I became violent?
2. What were the triggers for my violence?
3. What upset me?
4. What thoughts were going through my mind before I became violent?
5. Did any images flash through my mind before I became violent?
6. What feelings were arising in me before I became violent?
7. What was going on with me in general during that period of time prior to the violence?
8. Have any events in past weeks or months contributed to this act of violence?

The number and percent of relapse episodes falling into a common category can be recorded as invaluable information (Cummings, Gordon and Marlatt, 1980; Wallace, 1991). Common patterns should emerge that cut across many different individuals' microanalysis of relapse episodes.

Identification of Determinants of Relapse for a Specific Problem

A unique set of determinants of relapse may be identified in groups for specific types of violent behaviors. Group members emerge as legitimate experts who can identify determinants of relapse for their own group members with a specific problem—like gang, school, or domestic violence. An empowerment model and engaging in self-determination means that it is critical that groups discover this kind of information from their own group discussion and data collection. As a next step, "each one teaches one," or disseminates answers to the questions below:

1. "What are the high risk situations and determinants of relapse for gang violence, community-violence, drive-by shootings, turf wars, and revenge murders?"
2. "What are the high risk situations and determinants of relapse for school violence, child and adolescent fights, mob attacks, and carrying and using weapons in schools?"
3. "What are the high risk situations and determinants of relapse for physical abuse, sexual abuse, and verbal abuse within families, or among strangers who perpetrate interpersonal violence?"
4. "What are the high-risk situations and determinants of relapse for domestic violence and battering, among adolescent couples, adult couples, gay and lesbian couples?"
5. "How do media reports, movies, television shows, or newspaper reports ever trigger a relapse to sucidal behavior, school violence, interpersonal violence, gang violence, or community violence? How do they create high-risk situations for relapse, and what kind of triggers operate in this process? "

The answers to these questions can assist a group in identifying common high-risk situations and determinants of relapse that specifically relate to a problem behavior—such as school violence, for example.

Identifying Common and Idiosyncratic Patterns of Multiple Determinants Operating Over Time in Relapse Episodes

Certain unique features of relapses and slips to violence are likley to emerge in group discussion, as well as common themes. For example, a relapse to physical abuse of a child, beating up a fellow student at school, or battering one's partner may all involve being sleep deprived over several days, short of money for a week, intoxicated on the eve or day of the violent episode, and the person we assault somehow reminding us of someone we do not like. Relapse typically occurs over a period of time that involves multiple determinants acting together to provoke the final moment of relapse.

Others may be reminded of their own past physical abuse and may have a flashback. This might occur after having watched a violent movie that included a rape scene, for example, with our violent relapse transpiring hours later or a day after viewing the movie. Others may have absolutely no idea of their personal triggers and high-risk situations for relapse and may only recall vague circumstances. Observing what provokes group members to anger while they are in the group may be a starting point for acquiring data on their possible triggers for violence. Chapter 9, in a discussion of the "here and now" analysis of interpersonal behavior, clarifies this process.

WEEK 19: INDIVIDUALS START TO TAKE TURNS DEVELOPING ALTERNATIVE BEHAVIORAL RESPONSES TO TRIGGERS IN HIGH-RISK SITUATIONS

By observing the analysis of other group members' personal memories of being violent for determinants and triggers of violence, all group members learn how to engage in a microanalysis of violenct episodes. The goal is for members to analyze, retrospectively, an inventory of past situations in which they have engaged in violence. With increasing trust, members may disclose incidents associated with high levels of shame and guilt. Any slips or relapses to violence that occur during weeks 16 to 30 are also discussed and analyzed. Individuals develop knowledge of their personal, unique, and idiosyncratic high-risk situations for relapse. Knowledge of triggers, determinants, and high-risk situations for relapse provides information that is utilized as individuals are assisted in developing alternative behavioral responses to these triggers—instead of becoming violent. Hence, the purpose of pinpointing high-risk situations and determinants of relapse is to be able to carefully plan and rehearse *alternative behaviors* to becoming violent through role play. Communication, social, and coping skills, as well as conflict resolution strategies, need to be designed for each high-risk situation and actively practiced. Some high-risk situations may call for using strategies to avoid. For example, a student who does not want to relapse to drug use because it increases his chances of becoming violent may need to avoid a crack house. There are other situations, however, for which the individual needs to actively plan and rehearse alternative behaviors to their typical pattern of getting high and becoming violent. These alternative behaviors involve cognitively and behaviorally coping in the high-risk situation—without drugs or violence, for example.

Planning the Script for What to Say and Do in a High-Risk Situation

A script for what an individual should say and do in particular high-risk situations for relapse is systematically planned for each group member. This task begins in week 19 with one or two group members being able to take their turn. A logical process is followed in deciding who should take the first or second turn in this process. Quite simply, "Who has been violent recently?" or "Who is about to face a high-risk situation for relapse to violence?" In subsequent weeks (up to week 30), the goal is for all group members to have a turn being the focus of group discussion and receiving assistance in planning their script. We also learn to identify our SIDS and to think of them as health beliefs on violence which need to be changed; for example, thinking "In this neighborhood you need to carry a piece!" sets us up to be violent. We may need to arm ourselves with self-talk and a script that includes "Why purchase and carry a bus ticket to prison if you do not want to go there?" We practice aloud new health beliefs on violence ("Just walk away"). In this manner, we learn to replace health beliefs on violence that may have roots in the gang culture, or membership in an ethnic, cultural, or racial group. Cognitive self-statements and scripts for actively talking to one's self to avoid the AVE and a full-blown relapse should be designed. For example, instead of experiencing the AVE that "I already shoved this boy for disrespecting me, so I might as well go all the way and beat him up," an individual may deliver the following self-talk: "Stop! Get a grip! Don't even think about going there. You are not going to fight today! You are not getting suspended!" Scripts for what one will say and do in the presence of others are also designed. If someone is facing a crisis, in term of a high-risk situation for relapse being faced in the near future (before next week's group), the group should move directly into having that person role play how they will cope, following their script. When group members practice how to cognitively and behaviorally act in an alternative manner, they should receive feedback, suggestions, and correction, as well as praise for correct performance of good coping behaviors.

As a summary guide, the group task is to identify for each individual and rehearse within the group the following three forms of coping:

1. **Internal Cognitive Coping** *What individuals should verbally state to themselves within an inner dialogue or aloud in order to cope in a high-risk situation.*
2. **Outward Cognitive Coping** *What individuals should verbally state aloud to others with whom they interact in order to cope in a high-risk situation.*
3. **Behavioral Coping** *What individuals should actually do, or those alternative behaviors they should perform in order to cope in a high-risk situation.*

WEEK 20: PRACTICING THE SCRIPT: REHEARSAL AND ROLE PLAY

The scripts designed for the one or two group members who had a turn in week 19 planning how to cope are practiced aloud in the group in week 20. What one would cognitively think, deliver as self-talk, say aloud, and behaviorally enact are practiced in front of other group members. One or two group members volunteer to be actors in a role play designed to simulate the high-risk situation for relapse. We refine and improve our scripts based on group members' feedback and suggestions. The role play may be repeated with other group members acting out what they would say and do. The group provides feedback and suggestions regarding what they think is the most powerful way of coping. The individual for whom the role play is being performed may also take the role of those who would provoke him into violence and may talk about how it feels to be in each role. Most importantly, the individual should experience an increase in self-efficacy to be able to cope in the specific high-risk situation for which his script has been designed. Rehearsal of cognitions and the role play of coping behaviors should increase the individual's self-efficacy—along with the receipt of empathic mirroring, support and praise from group members.

WEEKS 21–30: GROUP MEMBERS CONTINUE TO TAKE TURNS DEVELOPING AND PRACTICING ALTERNATIVE WAYS OF COPING TO AVOID RELAPSE TO VIOLENCE

Throughout weeks 21–30 the group process continues, as each group member takes a turn in performing a microanalysis of their relapse episode, identifying their past experiences of the AVE, specifying their health beliefs on violence, practicing role plays for active coping, and refining their verbal scripts for self-talk and avoiding relapse. Members take turns being the focus of group discussion and receiving support designing scripts for their particular high-risk situations, moving on to actual rehearsal and role play in the group. Feedback from group members permits refining each individual's self-talk, and overall script for what to say and do in the high-risk situation, raising the self-efficacy of the group member who improves in their ability to cope and avoid relapse to violence.

This curriculum and group process will help prevent a relapse to gang violence, school assaults, fights on the subway, beating up a sibling, assaulting a girlfriend, date rape, or domestic violence. A relapse to interpersonal, family, school, and community violence may be effectively prevented for group participants. The dissemination of this critical relapse prevention for violent behavior, or tertiary prevention, may help to end the epidemic of violence that confronts our nation.

Possible Use of the S-O-A Workbook

Individuals may also chart their moments of original trauma, using the Self-Object-Affect (S-O-A) worksheets provided in Chapter 8. They may also graphically depict the transformations or permutations of the S-O-A. Possible transference dramas, role reversals, and intimacy permutations may be diagrammed and discussed. Chapter 7 provides preparation to engage in this task.

CONCLUSION

This chapter presents a curriculum in secondary (weeks 10–15) and tertiary prevention against violence (weeks 16–30). As we adapt and tailor the curriculum, groups may vary in the length of time members meet, and some may remain more educational, while others include more psychological material being shared by group members, drawing from their personal experiences of violence. The curriculum is therefore quite flexible and may find broad application when group leaders tailor it to different settings and groups. The curriculum is also suitable for groups that vary in size, just as classrooms across this nation may vary from forty-five to ten students. Flexibility and adaptability to diverse situations and settings are key features of this curriculum; creative adaptations are strongly encouraged.

Group discussion may also produce important data on high-risk situations for and determinants of relapse to violence for specific forms of violence—interpersonal, school, gang, family, and community violence. Community members are encouraged to appreciate the level of expertise they possess on topics that many professionals have little knowledge. Community and group members need to conduct their own research based on group discussions, and by simple tabulation they can produce research findings that should be used for "each one teaching one" about common determinants of relapse. Groups may also pioneer creative and culturally appropriate strategies for avoiding a relapse to violence that also need to be disseminated. Professional co-leaders should provide encouragement and direction in this process, demystifying the research process at the same time. Hence, self-determination of standards of behavior can occur among community members who benefit from an empowerment model of community outreach and are also empowered to conduct research. Progressive journals such as the *Journal of Urban Addiction*, edited by Reverend Stephen Johnson of Seattle, Washington, would likely support the publication of grassroots researchers. The time taken to review research findings across weeks 1 through 9 of the curriculum (see Chapter 5) may result in an interest in conducting one's own research within a psychoeducational group, school, or community. This results from an empowerment model.

In sum, this chapter introduces a psychoeducational violence prevention curriculum that may serve as culturally sensitive and effective secondary and tertiary prevention against homicide/violence. Future research should explore the efficacy of the proposed primary (Chapter 5), secondary, and tertiary prevention models in decreasing rates of violence in schools, families and communities.

The psychoeducation for parents and the violence prevention models presented in Part II of this book should find broad application and appeal among school, church, and community-based populations. It is hoped that the violence prevention curricula address the plight of African-American males who are dying at the highest rates from violence and homicide. We have made some progress in this part of the book in answering the questions "Where do we need to go?" and "How do we arrive there?" However, this section has provides only intermediate training that equips us to conduct psychoeducational groups. The delivery of treatment and the resolution of trauma may be further facilitated by advanced training and access to tools for use in individual and group counseling. Through advanced training and tools, Part III permits a more thorough answer to the questions of "Where do we need to go?" and "How do we arrive there?"

III

TREATMENT: ADVANCED TRAINING AND TOOLS FOR USE IN INDIVIDUAL AND GROUP COUNSELING

7

Training for Trauma Resolution in Individual and Group Counseling

This chapter presents a psychoeducational curriculum that can further prepare counselors and other outreach workers to resolve trauma. Two fundamental tenets of trauma resolution are discussed here: (1) If the counselor knows a client's trauma, that client's problematic interpersonal behavioral dramas can be deciphered, understood, anticipated, and transformed; and (2) if clients possess poor self-regulation of affects, impulses, self-esteem, and interpersonal behavior, the risk of regression, relapse, and symptom substitution remains high unless underlying problems in self-regulation are addressed. Following these two tenets, training for trauma resolution prepares counselors to remediate the underlying psychopathology by focusing on improving client self-regulation, thereby breaking the cycle of regression, relapse, and symptom substitution.

Counselors are prepared to offer clients "depth interpretations" of their symptoms and problem behaviors, although delivery of depth interpretations may be new to many counselors. An interpretation involves the counselor drawing connections between a client's childhood trauma and current symptoms and problem behaviors. These interpretations are called "depth" or "genetic" because counselors go all the way back into early developmental experiences with families and parents in making and drawing connections between past experience and present symptoms and problem behaviors.

Delivering Interpretations: The Connect the Dots Metaphor

Delivering interpretations is like playing connect the dots. A vague image begins to form in the counselor's mind, and the counselor tries to connect the dots, creating a clear picture regarding the client's problematic behavior or symptoms. The goal is to enable the client, too, to begin "seeing" a pattern or meaningful picture. By drawing these connecting lines and telling the client what may be happening, or what the larger pattern seems to be, the counselor helps the client achieve a sudden realization. At the moment of realization or insight, the client suddenly "sees" or "perceives" the pattern in his or her life. The client's sudden insight is analogous to suddenly seeing a profile or picture emerge when we play connect the dots. Interpretation is a powerful counseling technique that can produce such sudden insight and profound understanding in clients. Clients may suddenly grasp "what they do" and "why they do it" if the counselor is successful in drawing connections between past trauma and present symptoms and problematic patterns of behavior. Examples of interpretation are offered at the end of this chapter.

The Provision of Integrated Theory to Guide Our Counseling Technique

Integrated theory provides the guiding rationale for our delivery of interpretations, as well as for our use of three other counseling techniques. A second counseling technique, empathic mirroring has already been discussed (in Chapter 6), along with group members learning to identify, label, and express affects from counselor deployment of the third technique, affect labeling. A fourth counseling technique, cognitive reframing, or cognitive restructuring, has been demonstrated through the provision of psychoeducation and metaphor in Chapters 3 to 6. With this technique, we restructure and replace clients' thoughts in order to facilitate coping. The integrated theory presented in this chapter provides a rationale for when and why we utilize each counseling technique.

The Use of a Case Example: Nancy

A case example of a client, Nancy, facilitates the presentation of the model of trauma resolution and use of integrated theory. Nancy's case may resemble the life and experience of many clients who exist in reality, although the case is constructed specifically to facilitate training. Utilizing her case, this chapter seeks to answer the following question: "What modifications in assessment, theoretical conceptualization, and counseling technique are recommended to improve treatment efficacy and outcome with clients presenting histories of trauma?"

ASSESSMENT

Assessment questions are designed to ascertain central traumatic incidents, scenes, moments, and memories. The counselor accelerates the course of treatment with straightforward, focused assessment questions regarding traumatic experiences. Within psychoanalysis, a client free associates in a treatment that may span ten years with clients coming four days a week. We accelerate the course of treatment and create a model for the short-term resolution of trauma by asking clients directly about their traumatic experiences. We ask these assessment questions of clients in order to be able to readily answer the following question: "What is this particular client's repertoire of traumatic experiences, scenes, and memories?" We survey clients' childhoods and overall lives for the experience of any trauma.

Emulating the African Griot or Oral Historian of the Village

It is also at the point of assessment or initial contact with a client that we ourselves follow an important suggestion; we must listen intently and with keen interest, effectively memorizing this client's personal story or stories of trauma. We need to know the trauma so we can figure out the drama. We need "to know" the original sources of overstimulation, so that we can figure out the root causes of the symptoms and problem behaviors we observe in clients. Within the African tradition, the "griot," or oral historian, of a village could retell the story of the history of village and family life—reciting detailed facts—over the course of hours. In our groups, as we sit and listen to what has happened to children and community members in our village, we, too, should be able to sit one day—after thirty weeks running a psychoeducational violence prevention gorup—and perform like the griot, retelling the story of village life from the 1950s to 1990s as it involved trauma sustained within individual dysfunctional families. In order to be able to do so, we may suggest to ourselves, "I am an African griot; I am going to remember clients' tales of trauma." Counselors of every ethnicity may deliver this positive self-talk, experience a powerful suggestion, and emulate the African oral tradition. The goal is to listen to a client's story with keen interest so that we can "retell" it later on.

If You Know the Trauma (from Assessment) You Can
Figure Out the Drama

Assessment is the first time we hear a client's story. We must come "to know" it so that in the future we can "retell" parts of it to the client at critical points in treatment. In the future, when we see a behavioral drama being reenacted by a client before our eyes, we need to be able to recognize it, for example, as an exact replication of this client's father's behavior during a trauma. At that moment, when we see a behavioral drama being reenacted compulsively before our eyes, it is time to "retell" or deliver back to the client that part of his story about his father's behavior. In this manner, "if we know the trauma, we can figure out the drama" and we can provide this information to clients so as to assist them in stopping destructive patterns of behavior and in consciously creating new, more adaptive patterns of behavior. As we have noted, the use of interpretation draws links or connections between past trauma and present patterns of behavior and symptoms. We begin to "know the trauma," enabling us one day to interpret the drama, by asking central assessment questions.

Central Assessment Questions for Trauma Resolution

Assessment emphasizes the process of obtaining any and all evidence that suggests the experience of trauma. In all cases, when we obtain affirmative answers that there were experiences of trauma, we go on to ask clients how old they were at the time.

Ascertaining the Age and Duration of Trauma

We ask: "How old were you?" or "From what age to what age did this go on?" The first question is important in order to determine the likely impact of the trauma. Younger children may have been the most overwhelmed and overstimulated by experiences of trauma. The answer to the second question tells us about the duration of trauma and whether the trauma was chronic. For example, a client may indicate that sexual abuse occurred from the ages of seven to seventeen. Younger children (three to seven years of age) are more likley to have utilized the defense of splitting in response to trauma (Kernberg, 1976), while older children (eight years and above) may have utilized the defense of repression. If the trauma was particularly severe, then a child, regardless of age, may have also utilized the defense of splitting and also engaged in the defense of dissociation. Some children endured across years some repetitive or chronic trauma, and this suggests the habitual and deeply engrained use of defenses of splitting and dissociation.

Nine Essential Questions

The most essential questions to ask the client, in order to uncover a history of trauma, follow

1. *"What was it like growing up as a child?"*

Here we may choose to warm up the client and prepare the client for more pointed questions that follow. Sometimes this neutral question is sufficient to start individuals on the course of sharing and discussing key events in their lives that transpired within dysfunctional families.

2. "Did anything traumatic ever happen to you when you were growing up?"

This is really the critical question. If the answer is "yes," we ask clients "What happened to you?" Our interest is in hearing what spontaneously comes to mind, as well as what clients are willing to mention. In an assessment phase, we do not want to encourage detailed discussion of traumatic events. The goal is to obtain "just the facts" of what happened to clients which was traumatic. It is critical first to strengthen the client's ego and create a good self-observing ego. During an assessment phase and for the first one to three months of treatment, we emphasize the counseling techniques of cognitive restructuring with delivery of psychoeducation and metaphor which help strengthen the ego and foster good self-observation. This step is necessary before detailed discussion of traumatic memories is facilitated in later phases of treatment—perhaps three to six months into counseling. Brief spontaneous stories may emerge in response to this assessment question, but detailed description of traumatic moments is not facilitated by the counselor. When we conduct an assessment, we can remind ourselves, "I want only the facts" when I ask about trauma. We do not want to facilitate a detailed retelling of past traumatic experiences in the assessment phase.

3. "Did anything ever happen that really shocked you, or really hurt you, or really frightened you?"

Typically, we are the first person in a client's entire life to ask about trauma with keen interest and genuine empathy. Clients may respond with a willingness to share, but they may quickly answer "no" to an assessment question because they do not know what we are talking about. Many clients mis-hear the word "traumatic" as dramatic. Out of necessity we routinely rephrase the question. Some clients do not know what the word "traumatic" means. Therefore, a followup question about shocking, hurtful, and frightening experiences will provide an implicit definition of a traumatic experience. Again, if the answer to this question is "yes," we ask "What happened?" As a reminder, we also determine the age(s) at which it happened, as in all cases of an affirmative response.

4. "Were you ever molested or sexually abused as a child?"

This question needs to be a standard one in all mental health assessment. It is also frequently misunderstood if a client has not received psychoeducation on what constitutes molestation or sexual abuse. The next question helps us to discern whether there is a history of sexual abuse.

5. "How old were you when you first had sex, and with whom did you have sex?"

When the answer is "Yes, with my uncle when I was seven years old," then we usually proceed to deliver psychoeducation explaining how this was sexual abuse. Our delivery of psychoeducation serves to restructure the cognitions of clients who may have interpreted the event as "my fault," "bad," or "dirty." We may also need to alleviate possible feelings of guilt that follow from these cognitive interpretations of sexual abuse. Our task as counselors is to explain how it is always the adult's responsibility to take care of a child and to exercise self-control. We explain that nothing about a child is "sexy" or attracts and provokes an adult to engage in sexual abuse. A child is not meant to be a sexual object for an adult. It is up to children to discover their sexuality on their own timetable by either touching their genitals, private masturbation, or sexual play with a peer of similar age. However, no child is to be utilized for adult sexual gratification. Even if the child or adolescent felt pleasure during sexual abuse, the idea is that everyone is supposed to discover these feelings on their own, without the interference of an adult or older adolescent. To be stimulated sexually early and prematurely in our development is overwhelming and confusing.

To alleviate lingering feelings of guilt, one might add the following story: "I don't care if a twelve-year-old girl is tied to a tree naked with her legs spread open, an adult should not approach her sexually." Even as we engage in assessment, the immediate delivery of cognitive restructuring, through the delivery of psychoeducation and a metaphoric story, may be absolutely necessary. We also suggest that this issue needs to be discussed in a later phase of counseling, or when the client feels ready to work on this traumatic experience. Having raised an issue, we do not want merely to drop it in a fashion that might suggest that this is a dirty or shameful issue that should be swept back under the rug. We emphasize how important and significant an experience this is and how critical it is to spend time focusing on this issue as counseling proceeds. Indeed, this trauma suggests a vital need for counseling and for ensuring that feelings of shame, guilt, and any resulting symptoms and problem behaviors are worked out and eliminated.

6. "Did your parents or the people who raised you have any problems?"

If no major traumas are yet emerging, we may need to explore the environmental and family context for stressors. This question may lead to identification of extreme poverty, a parent's chronic gambling, family business problems, or parental mental illness, as well as other stressors that may have impacted children and adolescents in these families. If raised in multiple foster care homes, or left with relatives for periods of time, we need to ask about "the people who raised the client," still searching for stressors that may have introduced trauma.

7. "Did they drink alcohol? How did any chemical use or your parents' problems change their personalities or detract from their ability to be good parents?"

Asking about alcohol or chemical use can quickly lead to the identification and discussion of stressors that may have left a traumatic impact on a client as a child. However, many clients who experienced daily or weekend drinking or drug use by their parents or other caretakers were brainwashed into viewing it as "normal" or "nonproblematic." Exploration of how parents' personalities changed begins to provide evidence of how parents were inconsistent, unpredictable, or effectively abandoned their children and their needs during a binge. While a parent may have become jovial and generous, no supervision or protection of children may have been possible during states of intoxication. When we receive evidence of changes in the parents' personality, or of their failure to be good parents, we need to provide psychoeducation, explaining how this introduced dysfunction and trauma into family life. We follow the discussion presented in Chapter 3 on how stressors promote dysfunction in families and Chapter 4 on abuse, neglect, and torture.

8. "How did this kind of parental behavior affect you? Then? Now?"

We encourage self-exploration and observe whether clients perceive any symptoms or problem behaviors they may possess as in any way related to parental problems and exposure to trauma in dysfunctional families. Some clients are vague and uncertain, whereas others may quickly share their perceptions. An interpretation might be offered at this point which draws links between past trauma and present symptoms and problem behaviors. Some clients already possess insight, drawing connections themselves. Or we may need to provide psychoeducation on the possible and probable impact of parental behavior on children and adolescents, as in Chapters 3 and 4. Psychoeducation might then be followed with an interpretation. The lingering effects of trauma on adult children may also be reviewed.

9. "As an adolescent or adult, has anything traumatic, or really shocking, or hurtful happened to you?"

This question permits us to explore whether clients experienced multiple trauma that may span several developmental eras. Three eras of trauma are common in the lives of crack cocaine dependent women: (1) childhood trauma, (2) adolescent and/or adult battering and domestic violence, and (3) the trauma of abuse, violence, and rapes within the crack culture during their addiction (Wallace, 1994). It is important to ascertain whether multiple trauma has been experienced, or whether chronic trauma was experienced over many years, extending into adolescence or adulthood.

CONCEPTUALIZING TRAUMA

Trauma can be viewed as an experience of psychophysiological shock (Laurent, 1994). One way to conceptualize traumatic memories in a client's life is to use the language of psychoanalysis and self-psychology and to conceive of these events as producing fixation points toward which that client will tend to regress, or as narcissistic injuries to the self that produced a lot of shame and bad feelings about the self (Levin, 1987; Wallace, 1991). In addition, trauma represents a moment of severe overstimulation (Shengold, 1989).

A THEORETICAL FRAMEWORK FOR TRAUMA RESOLUTION

Within this model for trauma resolution, the counselor specifically focuses on improving self-regulation. A focus on self-regulation permits a shorter term psychotherapy. Integrated theory provides a rationale for counseling work focused upon improving client self-regulation.

Khantzian's Theory

Khantzian (1985) describes the regulation of affects, self-esteem, impulses, and interpersonal behavior as four areas of poor self-regulation common to the chemically dependent. The goal of improving the ability of all clients to self-regulate results from this theory. Kernberg's (1976) self-object-affect unit (S-O-A) represents an important advance in theory that can be utilized to graphically visualize and understand poor self-regulation and moments of trauma.

Kernberg's Theory

Kernberg (1976) discusses the theoretical processes of introjection, internalization, and early identification. Within this discussion, he explains that what is introjected or internalized is a unit of experience. This unit comprises an image of an interaction between the infant and/or young child's Self (S), and the image of the Object (O) of the mother or significant other. A particular emotional tone, or Affect (A), holds sway during the interaction with an impulse or drive being mobilized. The aggressive or libidinal impulse that is mobilized is also part of this unit of experience (S-O-A + Mobilized Drive).

As soon as we hear of a childhood, adolescent, or adult trauma, the therapist can utilize Kernberg's S-O-A in a manner that goes above and beyond Kernberg's intent. Kernberg's S-O-A + Mobilized Drive unit may be used to capture the moment of original trauma and to understand poor self-regulation. We may use the S-O-A to graphically visualize a client being physically beaten by his father as a small boy, feeling fear and anger with aggression also mobilized—making his small body rigid and tense, as his heart pounds and adrenaline rushes. Our attempts to memorize our client's stories of trauma are enhanced when we place a client's traumatic memory in an S-O-A + Mobilized Drive unit, effectively achieving graphic visualization of the trauma in our mind's eye. As we shall see later in this chapter, this graphic depiction and visualization of the S-O-A + Mobilized Drive unit also enables us to discern and anticipate likely contemporary behavioral dramas that the client compulsively enacts. The delivery of interpretations and psychoeducation on links between past trauma and present symptoms and problem behavior is significantly enhanced by use of the S-O-A + Mobilized Drive unit.

Jung's Theory

Jung (1969a) informs us that autonomous complexes may spontaneously reappear. These are feeling-toned complexes. We can think of a client as having a "father complex," for example, which might follow from unfavorable or traumatic interactions with the father. However, the aftermath of this trauma is that the complex may behave in an autonomous fashion. At such moments, we may think of the client as engaging in splitting. Whenever a feeling-toned or autonomous complex manifests, or splitting is occurring, Jung tells us that a "compulsiveness" suddenly appears. The individual behaves in a compulsive fashion, perhaps suddenly performing certain behaviors. Therefore, we follow Jung and seek to note any moment in our psychoeducational and therapeutic groups when a "compulsiveness" suddenly appears in a client. Does a client suddenly appear harried, rushed, driven, and somewhat removed from reality as she quickly enacts certain behaviors? In this manner, Jung's theory regarding the appearance of autonomous complexes that will seemingly follow a will and reason of their own, as they are suddenly made manifest assists us in our counseling work. We know what to look for—a sudden compulsiveness—so that we may proceed to provide interpretations and psychoeducation to the ego about this event, drawing links to past trauma with father, for example.

Moreover, Kernberg's S-O-A + Mobilized Drive unit is the exact equivalant of Jung's autonomous complex (Wallace, 1983). The S-O-A + Mobilized Drive unit gives us a graphic formula capturing the feeling-toned complex of which Jung speaks. Both Kernberg and Jung speak of splitting in their work. However, it is Jung who underscores how a certain compulsiveness appears whenever splitting is occurring and the autonomous complex has found its way from unconscious depths and invaded the realm of consciousness. The graphic model of the mind presented in Chapter 9 further elucidates the psychic processes to which Jung refers.

Pine's Recommendation

Pine (1990) recommends that at any point in therapeutic work with a client the counselor know which of psychoanalysis' four theories (drive, ego, object relations, self-psychology) explains the clinical material being observed at that moment. Ultimately, the S-O-A + Mobilized Drive unit can be utilized to integrate considerations of each of these four psychoanalytic theories, as we consider problems in self-regulation.

Following Pine's suggestion, we consider what occurs for a client in light of a drive theory that considers any conflict involving an aggressive or libidinal (sexual) drive. We consider and embrace drive theory when we emphasize the need to improve self-regulation of aggressive impulses and avoid a relapse to violence, as we did in Chapter 6. The violence epidemic and widespread sexual abuse of children only will end if we incorporate considerations of drive theory into our work.

We also need to consider ego functioning and the defenses utilized by the ego. The entire discussion of defenses and their definition in Chapter 6 can now be seen as an immersion in ego psychology—as a critical part of our training for counseling work.

When we think of object relations theory, we need to ask, "What is the most important object in the entire world to the developing infant?" The contemporary, correct answer is "the caretaker, or mother." Next, we must remember that object relations means interpersonal relationships. Object relations theory headlines as the title of Kernberg's book, and a consideration of interpersonal relationships is inherent in the S-O-A + Mobilized Drive unit; our use of object relations theory permits us to understand and therapeutically address problematic interpersonal behaviors.

An arrest in self-development, or a fixation point, occurs following trauma, with the resulting experience of emptiness in the client. The client needs empathy and mirroring from the therapist (Kohut, 1971, 1977) in order to facilitate self-development and healing. We hereby convey the essence of self-psychology. We can now see how our emphasis in Chapter 6 (and throughout this book for that matter), upon the counseling technique of empathic mirroring (Wallace, 1991) arises directly from self-psychology. Although empathic mirroring has also been utilized to resolve client ambivalence and motivate clients toward readiness to engage in behavioral change (see Chapter 10), it is the condition of an arrested self, or fixation point from trauma, that calls forth the need for the self-psychology approach advanced by Kohut (1971, 1977).

Thus, drive theory, ego psychology, object relations theory, and self-psychology are all actively considered within this approach to trauma resolution. This chapter seeks to contribute integrated theory which considers drive, ego, object relations, and self-psychology, as well as behavioral and cognitive conditioning. The application of all four schools of psychoanalytic thought by way of examination of the S-O-A + Mobilized Drive unit facilitates description of a counseling technique that improves client regulation of affects, self-esteem, impulses, and interpersonal behavior. The following case example allows presentation of the integrated theory.

THE CASE OF NANCY

Nancy is an abstinent thirty-two-year-old female who entered outpatient individual psychotherapy after completion of a month long inpatient hospitalization for multiple chemical dependence on alcohol, cocaine, and marijuana. During the referral process, the primary therapist during the inpatient stay described to the outpatient counselor not only Nancy's progress during that hospitalization, but also Nancy's behavioral problems while on the unit. These problems involved aggression and near violence directed toward female nurses, staff, and peers. In addition, there was an expressed concern about further observing Nancy for signs of abusing her own eight-year-old daughter with whom Nancy now lives.

Assessment began during the first outpatient session. In response to the assessment questions, Nancy reported the following:

I remember early in kindergarden, I was about five years old. I remember coming down the stairs one morning, having dressed myself and done my hair. When I entered the kitchen, there was no time to ask my mother how I looked. She began to yell and scream, shaking me and pulling my hair. My mother punched me and hit me out of the blue. Mother then started to throw glasses and plates against the walls. She was barefoot and her feet began to bleed and her hands were covered with blood. She just kept yelling and shaking me. I was terrified. I had never seen my mother that intoxicated and out of control. That was the beginning of her heavy drinking period and the beginning of my physical abuse.

As soon as the therapist hears about this trauma, the corresponding S-O-A can be conceptualized and graphically visualized by the clinician.

The Original Traumatic S-O-A

Capturing this moment of psychophysiological shock and severe overstimulation, Nancy's traumatic memory can be conceptualized by the use of Kernberg's S-O-A + Mobilized Drive unit, as follows:

SELF	-	OBJECT	- AFFECT	+ MOBILIZED DRIVE UNIT
S	-	O	- A	+ MOBILIZED DRIVE
NANCY at age 5	-	MOTHER is drunk	- AFFECTS OF ANGER, FEAR, ANXIETY, GUILT, SADNESS, SHAME, CONFUSION	+ AGGRESSION MOBILIZED

The S-O-A + Mobilized Drive unit is utilized beyond Kernberg's intent to visually configurate Nancy's traumatic memory of interacting with an intoxicated and abusive mother. As indicated, the biological impulse mobilized during this interaction would be the aggressive drive, naturally accompanying the anger felt during the traumatic interaction. As a guide for counselors, whenever anger is felt, aggression is the drive mobilized. Typically, during sexual abuse, both the aggressive and libidinal (sexual) drives are mobilized.

Nancy felt, in addition, fear, anxiety, confusion, terror, and sadness. She also experienced shame because she felt that she herself was "bad." When such an overwhelming feeling of shame occurs, this affect represents the precursor, origin, and root of a low self-esteem. Nancy also felt guilty, as though it were all her fault and as though she should have done something differently to prevent it all from happening. This sense of guilt and concern, and this urge "to do something to make everything alright again" is the origin of a codependency; the urgent desire to please and take care of others, such as the alcoholic mother with whom Nancy resides, soon follows. Also, as discussed in Chapter 4, as her alcoholic mother becomes more and more narcissistic and out of control, Nancy will serve as an extension of her mother, trying to care for her mother's self, as she functions as a codependent with her mother.

Considerations of Behavioral Conditioning

The same traumatic S-O-A (which for our purposes here has come to represent a memory of a client's traumatic interaction with an abusive parent) can be viewed from a behavioral perspective as capturing the moment of conditioning an anxiety, fear response, or phobia. We can recall Watson's (1930) classic experiment involving little nine-month-old Albert who through a laboratory experience conducted by Watson developed a conditioned anxiety response. Baby Albert sat and innocently and happily played with a white rat. Watson approached Albert from behind, suddenly crashing together large symbals, making a loud noise. Baby Albert was startled and frightened as he sat staring at the white rat still before him. In effect, Watson paired the presentation of a loud bang and crash with Albert's playing with the white rat. A conditioned fear or anxiety response was produced and intensely felt by Albert which was associated with the stimulus of the white rat. Albert emerged with a new fear or phobia of this and other white rats. If a white rat was placed in front of Albert after this conditioning process, he manifested fear, anxiety, and a desire to move away from or avoid the white rat. This fear or anxiety response later generalized to the presentation of a white rabbit and white piece of fur. In other words, any stimulus reminiscent of the white rat generated fear and anxiety in Albert after his trauma.

The Ego As Observer of a Traumatic Scene of Severe Overstimulation

Within this model, it is to the ego that we attribute the status of observer of the conditioning or learning process. Albert's incipient ego observed his startled response, anxiety, and fear, after hearing the loud crashing sound, and also observed the stimulus of the white rat. It is the ego that develops a conditioned anxiety or fear response to the relevant stimulus (white rat or abusive parent) abounding at the moment of trauma.

We need recall the S-O-A + Mobilized Drive unit and visualize the ego observing a traumatic scene:

```
                     * *              * * * *
         \         * * * *          * * * * * *
       E /          \ \ / /         \ \ \ / / / /
       G \        S - O - A    +    A G G R E S S I O N
       O /          / / \ \          / / / / \ \ \ \
         \         * * * *          * * * * * *
                     * *              * * * *
```

The ego observes from the position on the left, while the ego is left metaphorically "seeing stars" from the "psychic blow" of trauma. The "stars" emanating from the self's experience of intense felt affect and mobilized aggression serve to suggest severe overstimulation and a state of psychophysiological shock.

In particular, as this graphic depiction shows, the ego observes the overwhelming affects of anxiety, anger, and fear, as well as the accompanying aggression and bodily tension. What is observed may be so overwhelming that the ego may utilize an immediate defense of splitting or dissociation, as suggested by the jagged line separating the S-O-A + Mobilized Drive unit from the ego. Following our discussion and definition of splitting in Chapter 6, and the "our parents dropped and broke the glass" metaphor, the ego uses the defense of splitting to preserve and keep "good" a part of the self, while separating it from a part that suffered trauma and was made to feel "bad" when overstimualted.

The Conditioned Phobia of the Ego

From its vantage point, the ego observed, at least briefly, the stimuli of another human object and intense affects and a strong drive mobilized within the self. We say "at least briefly" because the ego may have quickly used the defenses of dissociation and splitting. If dissociation was used, then the ego focused it's attention on something else, perhaps intently observing the cracks in the ceiling instead of the traumatic scene. Typically, however, the ego observed enough, even briefly, to be able to develop a conditioned fear response to that human object—just as Albert developed a conditioned fear response to white rats and Nancy to her mother. Nancy had to obey her mother to survive and her ego used yet more defenses against her fear of her mother so that Nancy could obey her mother and avoid more beatings. In this manner, Nancy's ego utilized adaptive defenses against her fear of mother to counter her phobia of her mother. The use of adaptive defenses, such as repression of fear, made her lingering fear of her mother a well-hidden phobia. This is typical of human survivors of trauma who, as Wurmser (1992) suggests, possess extremely well-hidden phobias.

We need recall the S-O-A + Mobilized Drive unit and appreciate how the ego's conditioned phobia may be to the object ("O"), to the affects ("A"), and to the Mobilized Drive felt within the self ("S") at the moment of trauma. In addition, the fear response undergoes generalization (or spreads) to any similar stimuli or triggers, such as anything white and furry for Albert and to all women for Nancy. Hence, the ego's conditioned phobia may be to several classes of stimuli:

1. A parent, abusive human objects, or human beings in general (Os).
2. An array of emotions and affective states (As).
3. Biological states of tension in which aggression is aroused (Mobilized Drive).

In this way, the ego may develop a conditioned anxiety, phobia, or fear response to the felt experience of powerful affect and an array of emotions, to the object of a male or female object with whom one interacts, or with maximal generalization to all affects and human beings. The experience of any drive—aggressive or libidinal—being mobilized within the self may also be feared and a cause for anxiety and a phobic response.

The Phobic Response of the Ego

The ego's phobic response is typically one of avoidance. The ego will seek to avoid the experience of (1) encountering human objects reminiscent of the assaulter, (2) affects arising within the self, and (3) aggressive drives being mobilized within the self. More defenses may be utilized, in addition to the defense of avoidance, as affects are repressed and drives inhibited, for example. Indeed, an array and combination of defenses may be drawn upon as part of the ego's phobic response to feared human objects, the felt experience of affects, and drives arising within the self. Thus, we begin to explain what Wurmser (1992) has described as the well-hidden phobias common to many of the recovering chemically dependent who have survived a range of dysfunctional family types.

The Generalization of a Conditioned Anxiety Response to Human Objects as Psychoanalytic Transference

In effect, a behavioral model of conditioning of an anxiety or fear response wherein generalization of that response to similar human objects (Os) occurs is analogous to the psychoanalytic conceptualization of transference reactions. A client's ego may have a conditioned response of fear or a phobic response to women in general; the ego uses defenses and may avoid women, or the ego, following "the best defense is a good offense" philosophy may permit suddenly physically attacking a woman instead of waiting to get attacked. Such a woman may be said to be engaged in a transference reaction or may be seen as acting out a "transference drama." This integration of behavioral and psychoanalytic theory enhances the counselor's ability to understand the aftermath of moments of psychophysiological shock and subsequent problems in self-regulation of affects, impulses, self-esteem, and behavior during interpersonal interactions with feared objects.

The Overuse of Defenses Makes a Person Appear Rigid and Inflexible

A client who has suffered past trauma may routinely overuse defenses. The defenses utilized may involve the following: avoidance ("I must stay away from women, because all women are trouble"); denial ("I am not afraid of her!"); repression ("My fear and anger is buried somewhere and I don't feel it"); rationalization ("Women don't make good friends which is why I don't have or want women as friends"); and, splitting ("I am the bad little girl my mother beat and I feel full of shame," is suddenly replaced with "I can fight hard and strong just like my mother"). A person using this combination of defenses on a daily and moment-to-moment basis may be said to be engaged in the overuse of defenses. The overuse of defenses makes a person appear rigid and inflexible. For example, the adult child literature and movement refers to "black and white thinking"; this suggests a rigidity and inflexibility. People who overuse defenses are unable to engage in cognitive flexibility wherein they see things as "relative" or as involving shades of gray. When we refer to someone as being a "dry drunk," we are actually commenting on the appearance of an overuse of defenses, since they became sober, making them rigid and inflexible.

Many recovering alcoholics and chemically dependent persons who are directors of programs have often demonstrated black and white thinking when they kicked out or discharged clients from drug treatment programs for violation of the rules. No shades of gray were perceiveable, nor did an individualized assessment of clients prevail; instead, black and white thinking prevailed. The treatment we advance in this book for trauma resolution would provide an alternative to the "dry drunk" syndrome, wherein sober individuals continue to manifest subtle problems and symptoms. The symptom of cognitive inflexibility and rigidity may be targeted for change, as additional treatment and trauma resolution are pursued by individuals suffering this symptom.

Resorting to More Elaborate Defenses—Chemical Use and Compulsive Behaviors

An individual who overuses a range of defenses post-trauma may gladly resort to a state of intoxication, for a chemical defense gives the poor, tired ego a break from the regular, daily, moment-to-moment use of defenses. This may occur in adolescence or young adulthood, as experimentation with chemicals is experienced as extra-reinforcing when it actually serves to improve self-regulation of affects, impulses, self-esteem, or interpersonal behavior (Wallace, 1991). For example, cocaine use might permit affects to flow and be expressed, which are normally inhibited by the ego, as a result of its well-hidden phobia and fear of all affects arising within. Cocaine or alcohol might serve to permit sexual or aggressive impulses to flow, since the ego normally tends to overuse the defenses of inhibition. Or, cocaine produces feelings of euphoria and confidence, alleviating the need for the ego to repress or split off feelings of shame causing low self-esteem. Heroin use might sufficiently sedate so that the ego need not utilize defenses of repression or splitting against states of anger and mobilized aggression. Interpersonal behavior may seem better regulated when an intoxicated person can suddenly relate sexually, or is more confident, or is no longer avoidant.

And when a person becomes sober, he or she effectively surrenders a chemical defense and again resorts to the overuse of ego defenses. Intolerance and rigidity the day after achieving an extreme state of intoxication may not be completely attributable to withdrawal and irritability; some of this may involve an ego suddenly returning to overuse of defenses and appearing rigid, inflexible, and intolerant of shades of gray. In early sobriety, the temporary use of the narcissism defense is characteristic (Levin, 1987; Wallace, 1991). Ironically, individuals who have hit rock bottom appear inflated, grandiose, and arrogant, but, in general, there is a return to overuse of defenses, which makes the person now in recovery also appear rigid and inflexible.

Many individuals relapse or engage in symptom substitution to another compulsive behavior because the ego tires of expending energy in the daily, moment-to-moment use of defenses. Why not chemically dull, obliterate, and self-medicate all feelings and bodily tension? Or why not perform an elaborate and compulsive behavior such as compulsive working, masturbation, nail biting, or overeating to temporarily serve as an elaborate defense that gives the ego a kind of "break" from the use of simpler defenses like denial and rationalization, which are too often ineffective or fail to work for long. This eventual failure of defense especially occurs when others confront us with our problematic symptoms and behavior.

The bottom line is that an ego that (1) has a conditioned fear or anxiety response to a variety of stimuli or triggers, and (2) possesses, as a result, well-hidden phobias, will (3) overuse ego defenses. This overuse by the newly abstinent makes life with them "a drag" when they are rigid, inflexible, intolerant, "black and white" thinkers. These individuals need something more than sobriety; they need trauma resolution and access to a therapeutic counseling technique that will replace overuse of defenses with a more open stance toward interaction with human objects, toward affects, and toward their own impulses/drives. Moreover, those prone to symptom substitution—who are at one moment or another either compulsive overeaters, shoppers, workers, exercisers, or gamblers—also desperately need access to trauma resolution and a counseling technique that can free them from the cycle of either relapse or symptom substitution.

Thus, our thinking regarding learning and conditioning processes extends beyond a narrow view of behavior. In this view, the behavior of the ego may include the decision to inhibit a drive, repress an affect, or avoid a phobic human object. If the ego is now seen as engaging in behavior, then we can teach the ego new behavior. What was once learned can be unlearned and something new can be learned; fear and the use of defenses can be replaced with new responses. Our integration of psychoanalytic and behavioral theory on conditioning permits this view. However, we also integrate cognitive considerations. We can also discuss the conditioning of certain cognitions during moments of trauma.

Considerations of Cognitive Learning

Cognitions accompany the experience of some trauma. What occurs is not only the conditioning of anxiety and fear as a powerful psychophysiological response to a class of stimuli (white furry objects, female human beings), but also the conditioning of certain beliefs, expectations, or cognitively held fears (phobias). As a result of this learning during moments of trauma, conditioned cognitions will also emerge in response to certain conditioned sets of stimuli.

Following the case of Nancy, the counselor may determine through assessment what kind of thoughts or cognitions were conditioned or learned through traumatic interaction with her abusive mother. We ask the following: "How did that experience affect you?"; "What impact did that experience have upon you?"; and "What did you think when that happened to you?"

Clients' answers to these questions indicate what they cognitively learned during an experience of trauma. In the case of Nancy, her cognitive learning was that "mother could hit me out of the blue" for no clear reason. Cognitive fear and the expectation that "mother could hit me out of the blue" may have been triggered whenever Nancy saw her mother intoxicated or heard her mother call her name. Just as Albert's fear of white rats generalized or spread to white rabbits and white pieces of fur, Nancy's fear and expectation of being "hit out of the blue" may generalize or spread. An unconscious expectation might therefore involve Nancy holding the generalized form of this cognition that "*any* woman might hit or attack me out of the blue." These kinds of cognitions seem consistent with the inpatient primary therapist reporting on Nancy's behavioral problems on the hospital unit with female nurses, staff, and clients. Whether we speak of behavioral conditioning with generalization to similar stimuli (women), or of psychoanalytic transference, the resulting problem is the same. Nancy carries around an expectation of getting "hit out of the blue" by women during interpersonal interactions with females—even as Nancy becomes defensive with women.

These conditioned cognitions may emerge upon exposure to relevant conditioned cues, triggers, or discriminative stimuli (women with an air of authority) that trigger this cognition. Or the mere presence of a woman during an interpersonal interaction might be the necessary and sufficient stimulus to trigger this cognitively conditioned expectation of getting hit "out of the blue" by a woman.

When the object of fear and anxiety is a parent and such a cognitive expectation exists, defensive coping strategies become necessary. Continuing interactions with this parent might become very difficult, requiring defensive functioning to counter the phobic response or feelings of fear toward her mother. In response to the stimuli of her mother, Nancy defensively braces herself for parental interaction, while defending against emotional fear and anxiety, as well as her conditioned cognitive expectation of potentially being "hit out of the blue." At such moments when she is defensively bracing herself and trying to deny her fear subjectively, Nancy's mind might "go blank." As she utilizes adaptive defenses that permit her to obey and interact with her mother and thereby to survive, Nancy has the experience of certain cognitions and negative expectations holding sway unconsciously in her mind; "will I get hit again out of the blue?" Less internalization of good and loving interactions with the mother might follow because of the mother's new status as an object for whom a conditioned anxiety or fear response has been established. Self-development suffers by virtue of Nancy no longer seeking out and permitting empathy and mirroring from her mother—a mother who at the same time is unlikely to make such experiences available during this period of dysfunction and alcoholic drinking.

The Need for Cognitive Restructuring and Use of Thought-Stopping

Certain cognitive expectations and beliefs that may be unconscious but help to overdetermine patterns of behavior rooted in the experience of trauma exist and need to be made conscious in the course of treatment. Psychoeducation and the delivery of interpretations can make these factors conscious. It becomes critical to identify a client's idiosyncratic cognitions experienced at the moment of trauma. We may thereby target these cognitive expectations, beliefs, and fears that were also conditioned or learned at the moment of trauma for transformation, using the technique of cognitive restructuring.

We may teach the client to utilize "thought-stopping" and self-talk in response to the emergence of these cognitions, whether these cognitions emerge spontaneously or in response to a conditioned cue. In thought-stopping, clients can be instructed to pretend they are the censors on a talk show who hit a bell or buzzer whenever a guest utilizes profanity, effectively stopping the profanity from being broadcast. In a similar manner, clients are told to observe the thoughts passing across their mental space. If they note a negative thought or expectation, they are to take their hand and slam it down on the nearest table or surface, hitting the bell or buzzer as though they were the talk show censor. As a next step, the client delivers positive self-talk or engages in positive imagery.

Positive self-talk might involve repeating the statement, "I AM CALM, CENTERED, AND BALANCED"; or "I AM SAFE, PROTECTED, AND FREE FROM ALL VIOLENCE AND NEGATIVITY." The use of thought-stopping and the delivery of positive self-talk effectively restructure a client's cognitions—once dominated with the expectation "I can get hit out of the blue at any moment" and resulting in feelings of fear. Imagery may be added to the use of positive self-talk. For example, positive imagery of being surrounded by a protective white wall of light may also be used.

THREE PERMUTATIONS OF THE ORIGINAL TRAUMATIC S-O-A + MOBILIZED DRIVE

Having conceptualized the client's original memory of a trauma by way of the S-O-A + Mobilized Drive unit and considered processes of behavioral and cognitive conditioning, the therapist can proceed to identify a likely set of interpersonal patterns or dramas in which Nancy is likely to become embroiled "again and again." Three interpersonal patterns or permutations of the original traumatic S-O-A + Mobilized Drive unit follow in demonstration of a tenet of treatment: "If we know the trauma, we can figure out, anticipate, and transform the drama."

The Transference Drama

Knowing that she signed a release of information and that there were elements of her behavior while hospitalized about which she felt some shame, Nancy rather early in the second session asks the outpatient counselor if she knows about the "incidents" Nancy had while hospitalized. The outpatient counselor reports that she did speak to Nancy's inpatient primary therapist. The counselor suggests that Nancy discuss her view of what happened on the unit. Nancy describes using profanity with several female nurses, making a threat of violence against two nurses, and a near physical fight between herself and another very "bossy" female client on the unit.

The counselor attempts to bring coherence to Nancy's problematic behavior. Knowing her most shocking trauma, the outpatient practitioner may conceptualize and interpret how Nancy is prone to transferring some of the feelings and cognitive expectations that she has toward her mother to other women. It is as if Nancy reenacts with other women some of the same feelings, cognitive expectations, behaviors, and biological states of tension that she experienced with her mother during her trauma. Stimuli and cues conditioned at that time of original trauma with her mother now serve to trigger sets of responses in Nancy which are problematic.

The counselor explains the following permutation of a transference drama that unfolds with women:

SELF	-	OBJECT	-	AFFECT	+	MOBILIZED DRIVE UNIT
S	-	O	-	A	+	MOBILIZED DRIVE
NANCY at age 32	-	ANY WOMAN WITH AN AIR OF AUTHORITY ABOUT HER	-	AFFECTS OF ANGER, FEAR, ANXIETY, GUILT, SADNESS, SHAME, CONFUSION	+	AGGRESSION MOBILIZED

This version of the S-O-A + Mobilized Drive unit graphically depicts a transference drama. Using the workbook exercises presented in Chapter 8, any client and counselor can graphically depict a client's original trauma and its permutations. This transference drama suggests the way in which Nancy experiences any woman with an air of authority about her as a necessary and sufficient stimulus or trigger that evokes a conditioned response of anger, fear, anxiety, guilt, shame, confusion, terror, and sadness, along with an aggressive impulse being mobilized during the interaction. At the same time, the conditioned cognitive expectation, "This woman might attack me at any moment out of the blue," appears. This cognition and expectation primes Nancy for a defensive stance. Nancy unconsciously prepares to reenact the original traumatic S-O-A. However, in this instance, the role of the other object is to be played by "any woman with an air of authority about her." Any such woman will be unconsciously assigned the role of Nancy's threatening mother. The potential for violence exists in Nancy's mind because of her unconscious cognitive expectation of being struck, attacked, or "hit out of the blue" by a woman. Aggression is mobilized; a conditioned biological state is also triggered by the stimulus of a woman with an air of authority. Because she feels angry, her body becomes tense with aggression and she cognitively expects an attack. It is no wonder that Nancy threatened several female nurses and nearly attacked a female patient on the inpatient unit, given her tendency to respond to the trigger of a woman with a transference drama. The "best defense is a good offense" philosophy may have guided her ego in attacking others first.

The reader may begin to see the utility of Kernberg's S-O-A + Mobilized Drive unit when the intent is to conceptualize trauma and the resulting interpersonal behavioral dramas that the counselor must understand sufficiently in order to offer Nancy psychoeducation on the aftermath of trauma and interpretations that link her past trauma to current symptoms and problem behavior. While some may ask at this point in our discussion if this approach adds anything new to standard psychoanalytic views of transference, the response at this juncture might be "not necessarily." However, the concept of two specific interpersonal roles (S and O) with specific behavior being unconsciously, cognitively expected and enacted is somewhat different, as is a consideration of affective, behavioral, cognitive, and biological conditioning occurring at the moment of trauma. The concept of interpersonal roles that are repeatedly filled and played out by contemporary actors, again and again, also receives emphasis in the next configuration of the original traumatic S-O-A.

The Role Reversal

An alteration of the original traumatic S-O-A, capturing Nancy's age 5 trauma, involves a role reversal. Here, the counselor draws on the inpatient therapist's reference to unsubstantiated suspicions of child abuse directed against Nancy's daughter. While no real physical battering of Nancy's eight-year-old daughter had ever been reported, and no present cause for an investigation was deemed to exist, the inpatient therapist had been able to identify this area as one for continuing inquiry in outpatient treatment. The outpatient counselor therefore carefully listens to Nancy's stories of interacting with her daughter with an "ear" for possible signs of abuse. Within this model of trauma resolution, any practitioner being referred a client with Nancy's history of trauma would so proceed, anticipating the role reversal that would go hand in hand with Nancy's original trauma.

In the role reversal, Nancy now gets to play the part of the powerful, abusive parent or assaulter, while her daughter is assigned the role of the powerless, terrified child on whom verbal and physical abuse is delivered. This represents a reversal of roles in light of Nancy's childhood experience of trauma and abuse by her mother. This is illustrated by the following role reversal S-O-A:

SELF	-	OBJECT	-	AFFECT	+	MOBILIZED DRIVE UNIT
S	-	O	-	A	+	MOBILIZED DRIVE
NANCY at age 32	-	DAUGHTER age 8 physically abused	-	AFFECTS OF ANGER, FEAR, ANXIETY, GUILT, SADNESS, SHAME, CONFUSION	+	AGGRESSION MOBILIZED

The role reversal permits Nancy to unconsciously master her trauma by virtue of enacting the role behavior of her mother. The performance of role behavior belonging to the mother implicitly permits the experience of mastery. Nancy can now dominate and assault another (her eight-year-old daughter or some other unwitting victim assigned the role of the powerless child), in the same manner in which Nancy was once dominated and assaulted as a small, powerless little girl.

The trauma of having once felt totally helpless and powerless is thereby mastered through performance of a role reversal.

The value of understanding how a role reversal remains as a possible type of behavior for someone who has experienced a traumatic interaction should not be minimized. Clinicians must be vigilant and anticipate this possibility so that they can engage in primary prevention. Specifically, clients can be prevented from assaulting or molesting a victim by reversal of roles and assuming the role behavior of their childhood assaulter.

Failure to anticipate a role reversal can produce a major break in empathy. The counselor's empathy for a client can result in the counselor sharing strong feelings of anger toward the client's abuser. Some clients, fearful that the counselor's anger and judgment might be directed toward them, will not likely reveal evidence of being abusers themselves on occasion.

Clients may defend against memories of role reversal behavior. Strong feelings of shame and guilt also prevent disclosure of role reversal behaviors. Ultimately, the clinician is responsible for creating the therapeutic climate in which a client feels free to disclose role reversal behaviors.

Research shows that the experience of childhood abuse, or witnessing abuse and violence between parents, is related to the subsequent emergence of child abuse or spouse battering when the victims become adults and have families of their own (Milner, Robertson, & Rogers, 1990). The role reversal permutation explains how the child who was once a victim of abuse is transformed into a child bully, violent adolescent, or abusive adult.

Intimacy Permutation

The counselor must also anticipate the intimacy permutation of the original traumatic S-O-A, which might emerge as the outpatient counselor becomes familiar with Nancy's history. With regard to Nancy's past five intimate relationships over the last decade, she has experienced a series of events, beginning with mild abuse and culminating in physical battering by the men she dates who are typically alcoholics.

The intimacy configuration shows how Nancy ends up with men capable of enacting her mother's role behavior, while she falls into her childhood role behavior: a person without power in a dysfunctional household. These relationships have helped to fuel her own chemical dependency as painful interpersonal relationships with men follow one upon the other.

The following intimacy permutation captures the typical intimacy pattern that Nancy has experienced.

SELF	-	OBJECT	-	AFFECT	+	MOBILIZED DRIVE UNIT
S	-	O	-	A	+	MOBILIZED DRIVE
NANCY age of 20-32	-	MEN WHO BATTER NANCY & ARE ALCOHOLIC	-	AFFECTS OF ANGER, FEAR, ANXIETY, GUILT, SADNESS, SHAME, CONFUSION	+	AGGRESSION MOBILIZED

Once we know the nature of the trauma, we can anticipate the intimacy drama that involves repetition of the basic role behavior from the original traumatic S-O-A. In this case, the basic elements are Nancy's discovery that she is indeed getting hit "out of the blue," but in this case by a series of men she has known anywhere from two months to two years. Her cognitive expectation and fear may unconsciously extend to the object of human beings with whom one lives most intimately, such as a "live-in" boyfriend or husband. Nancy seemingly carries a template within for her earliest interactions with her intoxicated mother, as she unconsciously selects or attracts individuals capable of enacting the requisite behaviors performed by her original assaulter. Nancy may somewhow engender in her partners the reciprocal role behavior once characteristic of her mother. Nancy unconsciously performs the role behaviors of a small child who has been conditioned to expect and anticipate what is most feared—being hit of the blue for no good reason. Here, Nancy's conditioned responses generalize to human beings, whether male or female, achieving maximal generalization.

Examples of Interpretation

The three permutations of Nancy's original trauma—transference, role reversal, and intimacy—create problematic interpersonal behaviors. Examples of interpretations that metaphorically "connect the dots," or draw links between her past trauma and present problem behaviors, are as follows:

1. There seems to be a pattern in your life in which you are angry toward and dislike women. The possibility of violence exists in these relationships. Could the anger and fear you felt toward your mother have been transferred to women you encounter? You seem to act out these dramas where you feel all the feelings and aggression that you felt when interacting with your mother. Could women be a trigger for you to re-experience all of those feelings?

2. Could you be physically abusing your daughter because your own mother always beat you? You learned about physical abuse at the hands of your mother and now you are teaching your daughter about physical abuse. You seem to be reversing

roles and playing out your mother's role behavior, while your daughter takes over the role of the helpless little girl beaten by her mother.

3. Somehow you seem to end up in relationships with men who beat you and make you feel as helpless as your mother made you feel when she beat you. What do you think about that?

Frequently, interpretations are posed as questions or are offered tentatively. We give the client time to see how the connection of dots gradually gives rise to an image, as clients suddenly grasp "what they do" and "why they do it."

TOWARD AN INTEGRATED THEORY FOR TRAUMA RESOLUTION

Nancy's case permits us to appreciate the importance of considering affective, behavioral, cognitive, and biological conditioning during trauma. This represents a considerable integration of perspectives. Integration of psychoanalytic and cognitive-behavioral theory has facilitated consideration of conditioning at moments of trauma. However, we can move yet further toward integration of drive, ego, object relations, and self-psychology theory, following Pine's (1990) suggestion that in counseling work we should always know which one of these four psychoanalytic theories is applicable to the material being presented by the client. Integration of these four psychoanalytic theories may occur as we clinically observe clients' underlying psychopathology and visually configure a corresponding S-O-A. As we can see with the case of Nancy, the S-O-A configuration permits us to focus on four areas of poor self-regu-lation—affect, impulses, self-esteem, and interpersonal behavior (Khantzian, 1985), instead of diffusely pursuing the vague goal of remediation of the underlying psychopathology. The traumatic S-O-A and its three permutations enable us to consider what is happening with a client's poor self-regulation in a specific area. At the same time, we can follow Pine (1990) and learn to recognize when we are implicitly invoking a drive, ego, object relations, or self-psychology theory as the guiding rationale for deploying a counseling technique (interpretation, affect labeling, empathic mirroring, or cognitive reframing) designed to improve a specific area of poor self-regulation.

In explaining poor regulation of affect, we need only turn our attention to the "A" within Kernberg's S-O-A and to the ego's use of defenses toward the expression of affect or how affect expression is profound and exaggerated when the client enacts a drama permutation based on the original traumatic S-O-A. With regards to poor regulation of impulses, the S-O-A + Mobilized Drive unit suggests either that the ego may defend against the expression of impulses or that poor control of impulses is evidenced whenever a drama is enacted. Poor self-esteem regulation is ultimately linked to the experience of the affect of shame during the original traumatic S-O-A, while the social conditioning provided by parental verbal abuse further results in the clients themselves delivering negative self-statements. Meanwhile, interpersonal behavior appears to be poorly regulated by clients enacting a drama derived from the original traumatic S-O-A.

POOR REGULATION OF AFFECTS AND IMPULSES

We can now understand how clinically Nancy does not appear to know how to identify, label, and process feelings. This could have occurred when the ego of the five year old decided to execute a defense toward painful affect after experiencing trauma with her intoxicated mother. To defend against affect expression in general might result. On the other hand, when Nancy enacts a transference, role reversal, or intimacy permutation, she appears to poorly regulate the expression of powerful affects. Here, we largely draw on theory regarding the ego and its mechanisms of defense when paying attention to poor affect regulation.

While the S-O-A + Mobilized Drive unit can be used to conceptualize other traumas such as sexual abuse, and traumas occurring at any point across the lifespan, the concept of an original trauma permitting the clinician to predict probable dramas remains constant. In some cases, an actual ego inhibition of sexual or aggressive impulses might follow from the experience of trauma. A classic scenario involves an adult child of an alcoholic who has witnessed domestic violence, and so has not only difficulty identifying, labeling, and processing affects, but also an ego that inhibits the expression of all anger and accompanying aggressive impulses. A depressive, passive-aggressive, and avoidant interpersonal pattern may be evidence of ego inhibition of the aggressive drive.

Overgeneralization of the ego's phobia and defensive inhibition of affects may extend to anger and to the aggressive drive that normally accompanies anger. Access to that healthy aggressive drive that permits accomplishing goals and performing acitivities requiring us to go out into the world does not occur. A common complaint in such individuals is procrastination, lack of motivation, or lethargy as they observe missed goals and opportunities.

Counseling Solutions for Poor Regulation of Affects and Impulses

When offering solutions within individual or group counseling, we use a counseling technique that combines psychoeducation, cognitive reframing, affect labeling, empathic mirroring, and interpretation. Interpretation links client symptoms to past trauma and to resulting patterns of overuse of ego defenses.

The ego should also be engaged and be offered psychoeducation regarding the implications of past trauma, the legacy of well-hidden phobias and inhibitions, and the task of trading in overreliance on patterns of ego defense. A goal for the ego involves learning to engage in the expression of affects and impulses within the bounds of a healthy assertiveness. The question to pose to clients, capturing their plight of inhibition of affect and drive, is as follows: "If you were feeling your feelings, what feeling would you feel?"; or "given inhibition of affect, which affects do you need to process instead?"; and "given inhibition of an affect, what naturally accompanying biological impulse is therefore also under defensive inhibition?" If anger is repressed or inhibited, then the accompanying aggression is being inhibited. Affect labeling of the client's inner self-experience should proceed, as we also engage in empathic mirroring and reflect back to the clients the feelings of anger contained within their inner self. Cognitive reframing covers changing cognitions such as "I can't get any work done and my papers for school are late" into a new view, as follows: "Unless I feel and express my anger, instead of inhibiting it, I will not have access to that healthy aggressive drive that allows me to actively go out into the world and get my school work done." Interpretation might draw links between past experiences of being dominated and physically abused, feeling anger, splitting off scenes of the abuse, and now finding that one is removed from feelings of anger, but also not able to access a healthy aggressive drive.

Poor Impulse Regulation and Client Acting Out

Within a discussion of poor self-regulation, it becomes possible to explain the tendency to act out freely an aggressive or sexual impulse, or to explain ego inhibition of impulses. Implicit within this discussion of poor impulse regulation is dependence on a drive theory wherein we explain conflicts between the ego and the id's biological drives. The ego wants to use defenses against drives and the id wants the drives to be freely expressed or acted out. Either acting out of the impulse, or defensive ego inhibition of the drive prevails in client behavior, as the two extremes of poor impulse regulation. In the case of Nancy, she may sometimes act out freely the aggressive impulses mobilized within her when she enacts transference dramas with women with "an air of authority" or when she enacts a role reversal with her daughter. Nancy might evidence expression of an aggressive impulse when she experiences an intimacy permutation wherein she gets battered. She might also express an aggressive drive via self-defense (or as her good offense) since she is in reality an adult with more physical strength than she had as a child being beaten by her intoxicated mother. In these kinds of dramas derived from the original traumatic S-O-A, we can observe poor regulation of biological impulses, for Nancy is prone to violence whenever she enacts one of several dramas derived from the original experience of a significant trauma. In a similar fashion, sexual abuse may create dramas wherein sexual impulses are acted out or where inhibition of sexual impulses occurs.

At these moments of acting out and reenactment of a behavioral drama (transference, role reversal, intimacy permutation) the client may suddenly manifest a compulsiveness, following Jung (1969a). At this moment, we may either view Jung's (1969a) autonomous feeling-toned complex as having emerged or an S-O-A + Mobilized Drive unit activated, for these are equivalent (Wallace, 1983). We can also understand this as a moment of splitting, as discussed in Chapter 6, and as being consistent with the views of Jung (1969a) and Kernberg (1976). Kernberg would suggest interpreting and pointing out to clients how they manifest very different sets of behavior at different times, such as in two consecutive therapy sessions. Pointing this difference out to the client and asking if they are aware of this phenomenon may result in the client's admission of not noticing their discrepant behavior (Kernberg, 1976). We recommend systematically pointing out the exact moment when a subtle shift takes place and compulsiveness appears. We actively interpret all moments of subtle splitting, as well as more borderline type alternations in split parts of the self becoming manifest in counseling sessions.

We use empathic mirroring and reflect back to patients that they suddenly seem not to be there and to seem distant; or they suddenly seem angry, compulsive, and driven, showing a strange, hostile attitude and combativeness. We may ask a client, "Where did you just go" or "Where are you now?" Consistent with our torn and tattered rug metaphor (Chapter 6), we are essentially asking a client, "Upon which part of your torn and tattered rug are you now standing?" Interpretation may be used to draw links between past moments of trauma and current tendencies to move from one part of one's tattered and torn rug to another, without awareness. However, through empathic mirroring we cultivate the client's capacity to self-observe the subtle and rapid shifts and movement from one piece of the torn rug to another piece. Eventually, clients also notice their sudden splitting and compulsiveness, as it is happening. Cognitive restructuring occurs as clients who once thought "There is nothing wrong or different about me right now!" gradually come to think "Gee, you are right," asking themselves as they self-observe, "Where did I just go, and what just changed or shifted in me?" Clients can use self-talk to keep their ego focused on reality and to interrupt the spontaneous use of the defense of splitting with the emergence of a split-off self entity (S-O-A + Mobilized Drive unit, or autonomous feeling toned complex).

Empowering Clients to Break the Cycle of Regression

Clients can ask themselves, "What trigger made me start to use splitting?" The answer may be that someone yelling or raising her voice triggered a feeling of shame and they regressed to feeling like Nancy at age five—splitting with the performance of a role reversal (see Chapter 6). Creation of a new behavioral drama in which a client responds assertively and does not regress to an age five behavioral scenario may result. Clients can break the cycle of regressing to fixation points, such as Nancy's age five trauma and can find freedom in being able to stop, interrupt, and replace splitting with the creation of new, healthy, interpersonal behavioral responses.

POOR REGULATION OF SELF-ESTEEM

As suggested earlier, poor regulation of self-esteem has roots in the experience of intense shame. In addition, low self-esteem involves the social conditioning of cognitions that parents deliver during verbal abuse and that children internalize as metaphorical "tape recordings." These "tape recordings" may be played back as unconscious negative self-talk that clients repetitively deliver to themselves. The clinician can attempt to reframe these cognitions and to teach clients to use "thought-stopping" at the moment of emergence of these cognitions, as well as the use of positive self-statements or positive affirmations that can systematically come to replace the metaphorical tape recordings of parental verbal abuse. In terms of psychoanalytic theory, we ultimately draw on a self-psychology in order to provide the mirroring and empathy needed to heal the arrest in self development caused by a traumatic shame experience. But, we use an integrated theory.

The Spontaneous Emergence of States of Shame and Other Affects

The experience of intense shame and fundamentally "bad" feelings about the self during a trauma can also constitute a moment of behavioral classical conditioning. This classical conditioning may involve the pairing of the intense feeling of shame with the experience of the original traumatic S-O-A. A classical conditioning process may mean that the feeling of shame constitutes an unconditioned response or reflexive experience of affect that accompanies and is paired with the presentation of the object of mother. Just as Pavlov's (1927) dog came to salivate to the sound of a bell, a client who has survived some trauma might come to experience a conditioned response of shame at the sight and sound of certain behavioral cues. For example, Nancy may have a conditioned response to a cue reminiscent of her mother when abusing and shaming her.

Just as the spontaneous emergence of a conditioned salivation response can occur with Pavlov's dog—or in response to some vague and diffuse stimuli that were also present at the time of conditioning such as the white jacket of the laboratory worker—someone's gesturing, loud talking, and threatening behavior might be just such stimuli capable of evoking not only the conditioned response of fear, but also shame. But now it is a conditioned response of shame to certain diffuse stimuli. In this way, even affective states such as shame may spontaneoulsy emerge in a client, or emerge in response to idiosyncratic, vague, and diffuse stimuli available at the time of trauma or conditioning. Poor regulation of self-esteem appears to be intimately tied to affective responses of shame and affective conditioning at the time of trauma. This explains the key characteristic of poor regulation of self-esteem in the chemically dependent who typically experienced trauma and shaming.

The problem of self-regulation of affects can be most challenging when the emotions that a client may need to identify, label, and process spontaneously re-emerge, and at times are loosely linked to the presence of specific triggers or cues. Feelings of fear, anger, or terror might also emerge at other times. But in regard to low self-esteem, even with the teaching of cognitive restructuring, thought-stopping, and the rehearsal of positive affirmations, a client's self-loathing may not be adequately resolved until the clinician recognizes the primacy of the experience of shame at the time of trauma. The subsequent clinical task involves observing the spontaneous emergence of states of shame or the emergence of shame in response to certain cues.

Anxiety As a Signal to the Ego That Something Is about to Emerge

Typically, anxiety is first felt like a bell ringing to signal an entrance. Before shame or an autonomous complex enters and dominates in reality, anxiety may have served as a signal that something was about to emerge. A client may tell us in individual or group counseling, "I feel anxious." In response to this declaration of discomfort, we should provide the following psychoeducation: "Anxiety is a signal to the ego that something is about to emerge. Is it a thought, feeling, impulse, image or full-blown flashback from trauma? It is as though something is about to emerge from the ocean's depths and may gain entrance into our conscious daily sphere of functioning."

For the client to comment on and self-observe anxiety arising within represents a sign of growth and progress. Typically in the past, the ego has responded to the signal of anxiety by getting high, self-medicating, or performing a compulsive behavior. Literally, any compulsive behavior may be performed to block out and more actively defend against something emerging from the ocean's depths. Compulsive walking, eating, masturbation, smoking, drinking, talking, nail cleaning, or any compulsive behavior can be deployed as an elaborate defensive strategy. To be willing and ready to observe what is about to emerge, and to talk about or process the thought, feeling, image, impulse or new fragment of a memory from past trauma suggests tremendous client growth.

Counseling Solutions for a Plummet to Low Self-Esteem

Hence, the spontaneous emergence of an affect of shame—linked to a sudden plummet in self-esteem—is likely preceded by the sudden "bell toll" of anxiety "ringing" inside of us, as it signals the entrance of something from the unconscious into consciousness. This process is graphically depicted in Chapter 9 using a model of the mind. When clients manifest poor regulation of self-esteem, or a plummet in self-esteem, we counselors need to provide psychoeducation on the impact of past shaming experiences. We may need to engage in affect labeling of the shame harbored by the inner self. In addition, we can use empathic mirroring to reflect back to the clients their inner feelings of shame, as well as their positive attributes and strengths—as we also build a realistic sense of self-value. Cognitive restructuring replaces the cognition "I am bad and no good" with the following new thought: "When somebody or something triggers my feelings of shame, I tend to regress to feeling like a bad child being beaten and abused; I need to realize what is happening at that moment and actively deliver the self talk that "I AM A GOOD PERSON AND I AM GROWING EVERY DAY IN EVERY WAY." Interpretation may draw links between past experiences of trauma and feeling bad and shameful.

To resolve low self-esteem, or poor regulation of self-esteem, we must do more than have clients use thought-stopping, restructure cognitions, and deliver positive self-talk. Cients also need to resolve trauma by undergoing a therapeutically guided regression in the service of a self-observing ego to fixation points, describing to us the "movie in their mind"—as discussed in Chapter 6. This process is discussed further in Chapter 9.

POOR REGULATION OF INTERPERSONAL BEHAVIOR

The experience of an original trauma establishes the basis for experiencing multiple dramas, which are interpersonal in nature, so that a client ends up manifesting poor regulation of interpersonal behavior. Whether this is with strangers who unwittingly possess key attributes of the original abuser (merely a woman, having an air of authority, being a human being), or with one's co-workers, children, or intimate partners, interpersonal behavior appears to be poorly regulated by clients. This is because of the common experience of trauma and the resulting emergence of problematic interpersonal dramas. The psychoanalytic theory drawn upon is object relations theory, while we also conceptualize these events in terms of the affective, behavioral, cognitive, and biological conditioning transpiring during trauma. Again, we use psycho-education to inform clients about the S-O-A + Mobilized Drive unit they may manifest as a transference, role reversal, or intimacy permutation of an original trauma. Interpretation involves drawing connections between moments of original trauma and our reenactment of behavioral dramas in reality today. If we know the trauma, we can figure out the drama, offering interpretations to clients on these links between the past and the present.

CONCLUSION

This chapter conceptualizes the problems of self-regulation which are so common in survivors of trauma, moving toward integration of the four schools of psychoanalytic thought (ego, drive, object relations, and self-psychology), while also integrating cognitive-behavioral theory. A central goal of the chapter is to explain a first tenet of psychotherapy for trauma resolution: "If we know the trauma, we can anticipate, figure out, and transform the drama." We have recommended a corresponding integrated counseling technique to transform problematic symptoms and behavior. The rationale for using counseling techniques of cognitive restructuring (using psychoeducation and metaphor), affect labeling, empathic mirroring, and interpretation was grounded in integrated theory. Unless psychotherapy achieves fundamental improvement in self-regulation, the risk of regression, relapse, and symptom substitution remains high. Hence, a second fundamental tenet of psychotherapy involves the client goal of improved self-regulation. The recommended counseling technique will improve self-regulation, reduce the risk of relapse, eliminate regression to fixation points, and prevent substitution or the emergence of other compulsive behaviors. The training provided in this chapter will give counselors greater understanding of each of these unfavorable possibilities, as well as practical knowledge as to how to avoid these negative developments. The overall goal of this chapter was to give the reader a practical, tangible, and concrete approach to remediation of underlying psychopathology and to resolution of trauma. As was suggested in Chapter 6 through our description the "movie in the mind" metaphor, we may need more knowledge about the process of trauma resolution. The foundation has been laid for more detailed discussion of trauma resolution which occurs within an advanced level of training for counselors (as will follow in Chapter 9).

The graphic depiction of moments of trauma and of resulting interpersonal behavioral dramas in this chapter provides a useful training tool. Building on our use of visual and graphic tools that may assist us in our counseling work, Chapter 9 presents a graphic model of the mind, while providing even more advanced training for counselors in trauma resolution. The next chapter presents guiding principles and a workbook that prepares clients for the group model of trauma resolution described in Chapter 9.

8

Trauma Resolution in Groups: The Case of Ms. E., Guiding Principles, and S-O-A Workbook

This chapter provides training and tools for achieving therapeutic breakthrough in groups. Therapeutic breakthrough occurs when the roots of a deeply entrenched pattern of behavior are finally understood in a sudden insight and the individual also receives practical assistance in changing the pattern of behavior. Our overlapping epidemics of crack and other drug use, violence, and HIV/AIDS require that we be able to change the deeply entrenched patterns of behavior that fuel each of these epidemics. After working for three years in a residential therapeutic community, Damon House New York, Inc., I designed a practical tool that reflects what I learned. The resulting tool, the S-O-A workbook, is presented in this chapter.

This workbook was piloted in a group I began in my private practice in early 1994. It has been disseminated to select groups of paraprofessionals, recovering counselors, and professionals at intensive training workshops. The feedback received has been encouraging. The workbook codifies what I learned in therapeutic work at Damon House and practically extends the integrated theory formulated in Chapter 7.

One observer of the group I conducted at Damon House told me that what I was doing was very different from what my clinical psychology professors were doing and had taught me in training. She also commented, "Oh Barbara, you're working so hard." What I discovered working "so hard" on the front line at Damon House at the height of overlapping epidemics was born out of the conditions in the trenches. I felt like I was in a makeshift tent in the middle of a battlefield performing major surgery on soldiers brought in from battle. Their typical experience of multiple and chronic trauma across three developmental stages—childhood, adolescent/young adulthood, and adulthood in the drug culture (Wallace, 1994)—left them with large gaping wounds, dangling limbs, and massive bleeding. Few professionals or counselors were in the trenches doing this work, while others did not know how to do it. Meanwhile, I was discovering how to rapidly perform major surgery with injuries of this magnitude—something I had never encountered before. It was as if I would quickly push a group member who had just observed the reattachment of one of her own limbs to go ahead and reattach the limb of a new group arrival, even though it had only been three to six months since she had observed her own major surgery. Tired and glad to have a brief break, I would intently watch the surgical procedure being performed, marveling that what I had done in the heat of battle under a make-shift surgery tent was a teachable skill readily learned by a recovering addict with a ninth grade education.

This workbook is a handbook or guide for trauma resolution. Whether for use in the trenches or with clients in private practice, this chapter offers a codification for dissemination. The workbook is a practical tool and can serve as a prelude or accompaniment to group work; it is also a guide for participants in how to be a group member and what to observe within the group process. In terms of this group process and the guiding principles, we assume that clients are adult children of dysfunctional families. We explore the stressors that impacted their families. The seven principles presented here will empower group members, providing knowledge of basic psychological facts about human beings and defensive functioning. These principles can also guide the group work from the beginning of the process. The workbook enables group members to graphically depict the key moments of trauma in their lives, and by knowing the trauma, group members can go on to figure out other behavioral dramas in their lives and discover the roots of established behavior patterns. By knowing the trauma, they also come to figure out their personal behavioral dramas. The workbook exercises and worksheets empower group members to replace behavior patterns with new, more adaptive patterns. Counselors and community members can also benefit from the exercises in this workbook, similarly figuring out their personal behavioral dramas and replacing them with new, healthier behavior patterns.

THE CASE OF MS. E.

A celebrated case of successful resolution of trauma that occurred in the women's group at Damon House is told in a poem. The poem documents the treatment of Ms. E. who is considered a "miracle"; appropriately, Ms. E. refers to herself as a miracle. On the continuum of family types presented in Chapter 4, Ms. E.'s family type falls at the far right end described as involving extreme forms of abuse, neglect, and torture. Ms. E. utilized the therapeutic group at

Damon House to resolve the following traumas: parental alcoholism; parental heroin addiction; severe neglect and hunger; chronic sexual abuse by her father which crossed the line into torture; witness of the physical beating and torture of her brother; her own physical abuse; witness of some of the worst domestic violence imaginable; intermittent parental abandonment; life as an orphan on the streets; adolescent incest and sexual abuse; adolescent rape; violent murder of her daughter's father; separation from a second partner because of his incarceration; her own incarceration for a violent assault with a boxcutter; and the trauma of hitting rock bottom from crack cocaine addiction, including the loss of custody of her two children. As Ms. E. offers, having been abstinent from crack cocaine since December 1990 and having regained child custody in November 1992, "I am a miracle!"

Her entire life is a miracle, for the the one little girl who knew of Ms. E.'s lengthy weekend rapes by her father was found in an alley dead with her uterus on her chest. This little girl had also shared her secret of sexual abuse by her father with Ms. E. During that same period of time, Ms. E. was taken to the emergency room two weekends in a row. After being raped, Ms. E. required stitches in her genital areas: a week later, her father persisted in raping her nonetheless, and so she was taken to the emergency room again, after he reopened her stitches. The threat of death if she told the truth seemed ever so real, as embodied in the death of the little girl, the only person to whom Ms. E. (as a little girl) had disclosed her own secret of sexual abuse. And so it was that she faithfully mumbled the lies her father instructed her to tell in the emergency room.

By the time Ms. E. joined the women's group at Damon House, the recovering women and I had been performing field surgery and reattaching bloody limbs for about a year. We had figured out what we were doing. We were prepared for any bloody mess laid before us in the trenches of Damon House, but in Ms. E. we were facing a case of extreme, multiple, and chronic trauma. My partners in surgery told Ms. E. to follow instructions and submit to the surgery we were to perform. Ms. E. worked so hard in seeking a therapeutic breakthrough that she came to typify what the process of healing was all about. Her second grade education and Ph.D. in street life and hard times permitted her to understand everything we explained to her about trauma. Consistent with Ms. E. being a miracle, she survived the difficult and prolonged series of surgeries the women of Damon House and I performed on her.

Ms. E. left after 14 months at Damon House, after which she came to see me in my private practice. The day I called Damon House to inquire about her sudden discharge, having just had the news passed on to me by another resident, Ms. E. called Damon House on another telephone line. The counselor at Damon House had just told me that they had no idea where Ms. E. was or how to contact her. But she called at that precise moment on another line, inquiring about picking up her belongings. The counselor followed my instructions and gave her my telephone number so she could make an appointment to see me. She received free individual psychotherapy, thereafter. Ms. E. was in the group in my private practice which I started a year later, paying $3 per group. Again, she served as role model for trauma resolution and serves living proof that the group technique seemed to work. She was consistently clean and sober.

Ms. E. had been kicked out of fourteen outpatient treatment programs for urine toxicology results positive for cocaine before her parole officer mandated her to Damon House in December 1990 for nine months of treatment. She stayed at Damon House five months beyond the mandated period, until her sudden discharge. Ms. E. discontinued regular psychotherapy in my private practice in June 1994, after coming twice a month, once a month, or as needed. She left because she no longer needed therapy, after having also experienced a period of family therapy and psychotherapy for one of her children. As of this writing she maintains abstinence from crack cocaine and retains custody of her two children. Her daughter graduated from junior high school, and just last year her son's school gave her a special certificate for being one of their best and most involved parents. She is continuing to pursue her basic education and has recently been placed in the advanced class. The school newsletter published a short article she wrote about her life in June 1994; the brief article ended with: "I look back and tell myself that I am special and a miracle child." Ms. E. stands as a symbol for the hope of therapeutic breakthrough. A poem was written by the author as a tribute to Ms. E. and for delivery as a speech at a Damon House graduation. Although she was not formally graduating from Damon House at that time, a judge had recently decided that Ms. E. could regain child custody, and her departure from the facility was anticipated. This poem serves as introduction to the group process, conveys the process of trauma resolution, and embodies the hope of therapeutic breakthrough. The poem suggests that if others follow the path Ms. E. took when she "thoroughly processed her pain" and her "tears fell like rain," then they, too, might achieve a therapeutic breakthrough. The following workbook is a tool for the task of achieving therapeutic breakthrough.

OUR S-O-A WORKBOOK FOR RECOVERY FROM THE TRAUMA OF ABUSE, VIOLENCE, AND ADDICTION: A PSYCHOEDUCATIONAL GUIDE

This workbook is dedicated to the women of Damon House who created a circle in which we worked very hard and I learned a great deal. It is in memory of our work together and what we shared from January 1990 to December 1992 that I dedicate this attempt to create a practical source of help for women and men in recovery.

The following poem serves as introduction to our group work together. It should be read and discussed in our first group meeting.

Our Pride and Love for Ms. E.

It is with pride and love that we behold Ms. E., our dear friend,
as her time in women's group is about to come to an end.

For, according to the judge's dictate,
she and her children will be reunited under a new drug free state.

She is here before us about to take a stand,
embodying all that is the beautiful, drug free, Black woman.

A magnificent love and such depth to her soul
she does emanate in ways both so soft and so bold.

Her hands embrace her sisters with such love,
even when she must confront them with or without "kid gloves."

Ms. E. worries if with her children she will again resort to abuse
for her whole life experience is a lesson in its overuse.

From rape at her father's hand, to a witness of physical torture,
from mother's addiction and abandonment to intense food hunger.

She went to school just so she and her brother could get food,
fearing weekends when there would be no meals and nothing good—

just domestic violence, more rapes, and intense fear
that if she told of her secret torture death would come near.

How many times can a soul suffer every conceivable abuse?
Why does violence as a solution emerge for common daily use?

Can a tortured and injured soul hope that she can turn her life around?
Can we replace the doomsday prophecy to which such souls are bound?;

That mental space where low and negative expectations are found—
along with scripts for repeating dramas of family dysfunction—

we speak of an internalized set of fateful instruction.
Directions for each new generation to feel pain at that junction

where we either chose a path of the old, familiar, and same;
or choose another path with directions for a new transcendent game.

This new game and script of which I speak
permits free expression of a creativity which we must all seek.

This creative energy permits expression of a God potential within.
And our place in the kingdom of heaven on earth we finally win.

In this state of grace we break cycles of pain with ease.
And surrender violence, compulsions, and chemical disease.

Ms. E. has sat with us in group and fully processed her pain.
She cried so intensely her tears fell like rain.

Her body sobbed and shook with such somber force
that the depths of her pain became for her group a great resource.

'Cause her sisters watched and felt this powerful healing process.
And her sisters began to sense that in this role of witness

they learned about the path to their own healing inside.
And, though frightened, tried to open themselves up more wide

So they, too, could cleanse and heal the injuries to their soul
and dream of that wonderful family reunification goal.

Looking forward to the day when they, too, can speak with pride
of school, aftercare treatment, and home with children inside.

Ms. E., it is with love and an outpouring of faith
that we see you off to join your family and start a drug free race.

Remember your feelings, inner voice, and gut should be your guide.
Remember the lessons of the "house" which you learned here, inside.

Remember how you were strength, direction, and gentle correction
to your peers with whom you will always have a connection.

As we witness your climb up a set of golden stairs,
remember any mistakes or errors can always be repaired.

Just reach out for support and learn how to pass the *next* test,
'cause there will always be another one, after just a brief rest—

opportunities to grow and learn even more
so we can finally make it to that great shore.

I speak of a place where we will get that ultimate gift
of being rocked in the arms of God and feeling the ultimate uplift

when reunited with the one who always loved us so dear,
even when lying raped, battered, and abandoned with death near.

So, Ms. E. go out into the world replacing new faith for old fear.
And never forget the magic therapeutic group process we did share.

But, as we say a soulful goodbye remember one thing.
Our intense pride and love for you, Ms. E., makes our hearts sing!

> A poem for Ms. E. who is Everyone who both dreams of and dreads
> the reunification goal with their children. Written by
> Barbara Wallace 9/28/91.

Group members express their feelings, thoughts and reactions to the poem.

THE RELEVANCE OF THE POEM ABOUT MS. E FOR OUR WORK

The poem makes several key points that guide us in our work:

1. When we have been physically, verbally, or sexually abused, we have to admit our own risk of becoming a physical, verbal, or sexual abuser of others. This is shocking and may cause us fear.

2. When we have experienced violence and abuse, because of what we have learned, we think that violence and abuse is a normal way of solving problems.

3. Because of our trauma, we may have negative thoughts about ourselves and what we can do. Our thoughts are like a doomsday prophecy or negative expectation which we may unconsciously try to meet or fulfill. We may unconsciously try to show that we are nothing and can do nothing. We do this because we have been treated like we are nothing and came to think we are nothing.

4. We have family scripts for repeating dramas of family dysfunction inside of us. We follow these scripts unconsciously and repeat the exact words and actions of our abusers. Our children and each family generation that follows can experience the same abuse.

5. We have hope because we can break old patterns, and create new dramas, new scripts, new behaviors, new thoughts, and new expectations for ourselves.

6. As we create new behaviors and new patterns of relating to our partners and children, and create new patterns of relating to each other in the group, we are moving closer to our highest potential or God potential.

7. We reach our highest potential by following Ms. E.'s example from the poem. We may need to fully process our pain. We may find that by moving through that pain we end up traveling a path that leads to healing.

How can trauma resolution in group therapy help us to break our family patterns of abuse and violence, reach our potential, empower us, and improve our ability to cope?

As a partial answer to this question, the following seven principles are offered as a guide to our group work.

SEVEN PRINCIPLES TO GUIDE OUR GROUP WORK

Principle 1 *Whenever we dislike something in another, it is really our own problem.*

Feelings of "dislike" serve to reveal a part of ourselves which we need to work on and do not like. The presence in our lives of someone we dislike provides a rare opportunity to see in this "mirror" of the "other person" a part of ourselves we do not like; beyond the moment of shocking recognition is the hard work of self-examination, self-acceptance, and decisions regarding behavioral change. We can call someone we don't like, or who gets on our nerves, our "mirror." We may state to them "You are my mirror." This prepares the other person who annoys us for our inevitable reactions of not liking them; this helps them not to take it personally. Sometimes, and quite often two people are each other's mirror. Neither one of them likes the part of themselves that is loud, has a nasty attitude, and curses people out; it reminds both of them of the abusive mother each of them went on to imitate. We may also remind a group member who is upset with someone "That person is your mirror." We may gently add, "You should be grateful God put them in your life. Look at yourself and change what you don't like. If she was not here to be your mirror you might not see what you need to change. Go ahead and work on it girl. Get yourself together."

Principle 2 *Our anger (and willingness to confront the disliked other, sometimes with resulting violence) is a defense against our pain.*

This principle produces the goal of our letting go of the defensive use of anger and merely feeling our pain and moving on. Or, to put it metaphorically, we must be transformed from "rocks with loud speakers." Metaphorically, we may find ourselves being transformed from "rocks with loud speakers" into human beings. At first we feel like we are drowning in a pond of water, or pool of pain; but we discover the ability to swim to shore. Identification with our abusers helps to make us like rocks with loud speakers. We can shout and gesture in a state of anger just the way our parents or abusers shouted at us.

We need to admit that when we are angry we are really in a state of defense against our pain (Bailey, 1991) from our abuse. It is easier to feel powerful and strong by being angry, instead of feeling weak and powerless if we feel our pain. It is easier to do a role reversal and act like our abuser. Now we feel powerful and strong, instead of helpless, weak, and out of control—like the times when we were abused. But to grow we must feel our pain and move on, traveling down the road to our healing and our true Real Self. We frequently remind ourselves, "My anger is a defense against my pain." We then ask ourselves, "What hurt me? What is my pain?"

This principle reminds us that whenever a person becomes really angry and keeps harping on a small, minor point, just tell them "Your anger is a defense against your pain." We may then ask them, "Who hurt you? What is your pain?"

Principle 3 *If we learn to be sexual early, and prematurely, and with people with whom it is inappropriate (through molestation, incest, and sexual abuse), for the rest of our lives our behavior may reveal what we learned as a child. We may as adolescents and adults "get sexual" early, prematurely, and with people with whom it is inappropriate.*

This third principle produces the goal of consciously observing how we become sexual early, and prematurely, and with people with whom it is inappropriate because of the power of childhood learning. We must learn to allow feelings to come up without the learned response of acting out sexually. An opportunity exists to observe how our inappropriate sexual feelings go away with time. We must draw upon this principle in knowing that for the rest of our lives "sexual feelings may come up in us early, prematurely, and with people with whom it is inappropriate." We can now understand how sexual feelings can come up quite early on when we meet strangers. We can wait for sexual feelings to go away, accepting that these feelings are our problem from our past learning. We can remind ourselves "This too shall pass," as we observe the sexual feelings decrease in intensity and eventually pass away. This is not too different from how we can watch a craving for a drug or alcohol decrease in intensity and pass away. We learn to stop sexual feelings from leading to our engaging in sexual behavior—early, prematurely, and with people with whom it is inappropriate.

Sometimes other people experience inhibition of sexuality after sexual abuse. This produces the goal of freeing the ego of its overuse of defenses and any well-hidden phobia or fear around feeling sexual impulses. This will permit the ego to discover some free expression of sexual impulses.

A version of this therapeutic principle follows with respect to aggression:

A Version of Principle 3 *If we have learned to be violent and aggressive, then for the rest of our lives our behavior may reveal what we have learned. As adolescents and adults, we are aggressive and violent with others.*

We must replace old learning that violence is normal behavior for solving problems with new learning. The new learning and rule is as follows: "*For the rest of your life, violence is not an option.*" For clients who have past records of incarceration for assaults and for whom a moment of loss of control, or even behavioral reenactment of a flashback, or a role reversal could lead to violence, this new learning and rule is very important. We can stop ourselves from performing violence by stopping ourselves and reminding ourselves of this new rule. This is the stopping of a violent impulse or violent behavior. We remember how we only choose to be violent because we have been taught to be violent. We can learn that aggressive impulses also pass. We remind ourselves "This too shall pass." We can learn new behaviors and think: "Violence is not an option." "Walk away and let it go." "It's not worth a violent confrontation, another jail term, a school suspension, or getting kicked out of my program or housing."

For some people, another possibility involves a response of overinhibition, overcontrol, or suppression of the aggressive impulse. The ego has a well-hidden phobia of aggressive impulses and angry feelings. In this situation, we must experience our own feared feelings of anger and rage, and observe the emergence of powerful aggressive impulses within ourselves. We need to learn to let anger and aggression flow through us and watch it go away. We can let it flow without doing violence to others as we talk about our anger. We can learn to let anger and aggressive impulses flow when we have suffered from keeping them inside and inhibiting or stopping them. We don't want to be rugs people just walk all over and we never say anything. Depending on the situation, we are able to become appropriately angry and can speak up for ourselves. If it is the right situation, then this represents good self-care behavior.

Principle 4 *The projection of our own "bad" parts onto a "different other" constitutes an act of violence against another and ourselves.*

To even project our own "bad" parts, our shadow side, our disliked parts, or a negative and low expectation (Who does she think she is! She is nothing!) can now be fully appreciated as an act of violence against the different "other." Violence and anger directed toward others reveals unconscious dislike for parts of ourselves. Unconsciously we may believe "I really feel like I am nothing deep inside." Meanwhile, she is serving as my mirror and we don't like the "bad parts" of ourselves we see reflected in our mirror. By disliking others and parts of ourselves we see in others, we actually commit some violence against ourselves. A person engaging in the projection of their bad parts (the part that feels like nothing) on to others is revealing some self-dislike, self-hatred, and is actually engaging in violence against one's self. To think that one is nothing is to do violence against one's self. We can stop all of this violence. We can learn to accept parts of ourselves we do not like and stop doing violence to our "mirror" and ourselves.

We should utilize thought-stopping to eliminate negative self-statements or self-talk, for example "I'm no good." When we notice ourselves thinking "I'm no good, I'm nothing" we shout aloud "STOP!" and slam our hand down on the nearest table. This is called thought-stopping. Following the stopping of negative thoughts about the self, we then deliver to ourselves positive self-statements or affirmations—thereby raising self-esteem. For example, we repeat "I AM A GOOD PERSON. I AM GROWING EVERY DAY IN EVERY WAY." Or, "I AM CALM, CENTERED AND BALANCED." We close our eyes and repeat these affirmations for 3 or 5 mintues over and over again. At first we repeat them aloud, and then silently within. To raise our self-esteem we can put ourselves on a formal program and repeat positive affirmations 3 times a day for 3 to 15 minutes each time. We can combine this with deep breathing and perform a kind of "mini-meditation," as we replace old "tape-recordings" that may be left over from parental verbal abuse with new thoughts about ourselves. It is as though we re-program our computers, or minds, with new positive thoughts and self-talk.

Principle 5 *If you know the trauma, you can figure out the drama.*

Our task is to observe how current behavior repeats elements of our past trauma(s). We were hit as children, so we hit our children. We were yelled at by our parents, so we yell at other people. We can learn to stop repeating old behavioral dramas based on our past trauma. In this case, we do "behavior stopping." We must also learn to change our thoughts and expectations (I am nothing, and I can do nothing right). We can use thought-stopping and the delivery of positive affirmations to change our thoughts and expectations. We can replace old thoughts, expectations, and our doomsday prophecy with dreams, goals, hopes, and plans for positive creative action. Our homework will focus on breaking old patterns and creating new patterns of behavior. We will learn to not yell, not hit, and not beat up others, for example.

Principle 6 *I AM BECAUSE WE ARE. WE ARE, THEREFORE I AM.*

Survival in an era of multiple epidemics (crack, drugs, violence, AIDS) and coping in a group therapy situation where we face our trauma and abuse experiences means that we need each other. We must work as a group to heal each other and form bonds of trust. We need models of counseling that are not based on an authoritarian power relationship between client and therapist. The therapist is not in the powerful "one up" position and the client is not in the powerless "one down" position. Instead, we work together toward our goals of mutual healing and empowerment. We seek to empower each other to be better human beings. We create in the circle of our group work a powerful support system with each other. We identify with each other, empathize with each other, and even reenact old behavioral patterns with each other. But we learn to see these old patterns and to create new interpersonal behavioral patterns. Together, we learn the role of cooperation and about mutual support and trust.

Following Parker (1992), the principle that "I AM BECAUSE WE ARE. WE ARE, THEREFORE I AM" fosters appreciation for one's family and our connection to our family. An awareness begins to develop that we are connected with our ancestral and family past. Following this principle, we may need to develop a sense of gratitude, connection to, and caring about one's ancestors, family, community members, group therapy members, children, and future generations. We find that survival also involves learning to cooperate with family and community members, as well as learning to think about the collective or group. The group also becomes like a family, or extended family, in the African tradition. We are no longer self-centered or selfish. We replace competition with our sisters with cooperation.

Principle 7 *I AM THAT I AM. I AM ONE WITH MY HIGHER POWER.*

As a possible positive affirmation, we might meditate or think about this statement. We may utilize it as a mantra or self-statement for purposes of centering, balancing, and calming ourselves as we encounter any stress. The use of this seventh principle fosters strength through developing our spirituality. We use this positive affirmation, or involvement in twelve step groups, or some other spiritual activity to connect with one's higher power. That connection with one's higher power gives us more self-acceptance so that one feels "I AM THAT I AM." We then strive to be at "ONE" with our higher power and to follow a higher will.

PREPARING FOR THE WORK OF TRAUMA RESOLUTION

How do we begin our group work and work on ourselves?

We begin our group work, remembering to follow our seven principles, by learning about our experiences of trauma.

What is trauma? How do we define or understand trauma?

Think of each moment of *trauma* as a point in time when an ego of a child was overwhelmed. It can be a moment of overstimulation when we felt more anger, rage, fear, confusion, terror, shame, guilt than we were ever meant to experience as children or human beings. It is a moment of shock in which we feel more hurt, pain, fear, and shame than we were ever meant to experience for our age and developmental stage. We may have become overstimulated by sexual and aggressive impulses which we were never meant to experience at such intense levels for our age.

How do we explore our history to find out if we experienced trauma?

Within this model of group therapy, nine essential assessment questions help us to uncover experiences of trauma in our past. We ask ourselves the following questions:

1. What was it like growing up as a child?
2. Did anything traumatic ever happen to you when you were growing up?
3. Did anything ever happen that really shocked you, or really hurt you, or really freightened you?
4. Were you ever molested or sexually abused as a child?
5. How old were you when you first had sex, and with whom did you have sex?
6. Did your parents or the people who raised you have any problems?
7. Did they drink alcohol? How did any chemical use or your parents' problems change their personalities or detract from their ability to be good parents?
8. How did this kind of parental behavior affect you? Then? Now?
9. As an adolescent or adult, has anything traumatic, or really shocking or hurtful happened to you?

What are my traumatic experiences, scenes, and memories?

The purpose of asking the nine assessment questions is to identify key traumatic incidents, scenes, moments, and memories. Answer the nine assessment questions. If you know you have experienced trauma—or multiple trauma—identify your traumatic scenes in the space below (or in your journal, or on separate pieces of paper):

1._____

_____

_____

_____

2._____

_____

_____

_____

3._____

_____

_____

4._____

_____

_____

5._____

_____

_____

6._____

_____

_____

7._____

_____

_____

8._____

_____

_____

9._____

_____

_____

OTHER KEY DEFINITIONS WE NEED TO KNOW

What other definitions do I need to know to pursue trauma resolution?

- *Affect* means feeling.

- *Avoidance* is a defense that involves moving away, running away, and keeping distance from something that causes us fear and anxiety. After a trauma we typically experience a fear of certain things and desperately try to avoid them.

- *Conditioning* means learning. Powerful learning or conditioning occurs at the moment of trauma. Thoughts and patterns of behavior, or ways of responding can be conditioned or learned at the moment of trauma.

- *Cognition* means thought.

- A *defense* is a strategy the ego uses to block out of awareness feelings, thoughts, and behaviors that are associated with a moment of trauma. If the ego feels like it cannot deal with something, a defense is used.

- *Dissociation* is a defense which the ego uses to not watch or see what is happening to that part of the self that is being damaged by trauma. The ego focuses on something other than the traumatic scene—like the ceiling, floor, or a noise in the background (for example, water dripping).

- *Drive* and *impulse* mean the same thing and refer to an aggressive or sexual feeling. An aggressive or sexual impulse may be said to be *mobilized* when it is felt inside of us.

- The *ego* is the part of us that is focused in reality and observes what is happening in reality.

- *Generalization* means our learning spreads to apply in other situations.

- *Inhibition* is a defense the ego uses to block a feeling or impulse from being expressed. We hold back the feeling or impulse and do not express it.

- *Permutation* refers to an altered or changed form of an original pattern of behavior.

- *Phobia* means fear. Whenever we experience a trauma we end up having a well-hidden fear of anything associated with that moment in time when we were overwhelmed. We may have a well-hidden phobia or fear of strong feelings arising inside, impulses being mobilized within our body, women, or men, for example.

- *Repression* is a defense the ego uses to bury the memory of something bad. It is like pushing something under water, or digging a whole and putting it in the ground. It's still there, but the ego can't see it.

- *Splitting* is a defense the ego uses to crack off, fragment off, or separate a part of the self that is experiencing a lot of pain and trauma. By splitting or fragmenting or breaking off a part of the self, the ego tries to preserve and keep safe another part of the self that is still good, safe, and undamaged.

THE CASE AND EXAMPLE OF NANCY

Will a case example help us to see the connection between our past experiences of trauma, current problems with violence, and other symptoms and problem behaviors?

If we use a case example, then we can figure out how to proceed in working on our own trauma.

Nancy is a 32-year-old female who was addicted to alcohol, cocaine, and marijuana. We ask Nancy, "Did anything traumatic ever happen to you?" Nancy tells us the following memory of a trauma. It is the first traumatic memory that pops into her head, or the one she feels comfortable telling us:

I remember early in kindergarden, I was about five years old. I remember coming down the stairs one morning, having dressed myself and done my hair. When I entered the kitchen, there was no time to ask my mother how I looked. She began to yell and scream, shaking me and pulling my hair. My mother punched me and hit me out of the blue. Mother then started to throw glasses and plates against the walls. She was barefoot and her feet began to bleed and her hands were covered with blood. She just kept yelling and shaking me. I was terrified. I had never seen my mother that intoxicated and out of control. That was the beginning of her heavy drinking period and the beginning of my physical abuse.

How should we understand Nancy's original trauma?

As soon as we hear about such an event, a traumatic S-O-A can be identified. Nancy's traumatic memory can be understood via the use of an S-O-A + mobilized drive unit:

SELF	-	OBJECT	-	AFFECT	+	MOBILIZED DRIVE UNIT
S	-	O	-	A	+	MOBILIZED DRIVE

"S" stands for self. "O" stands for object or the person with whom we interact during our original, or first experience of trauma. The "A" is for the affects or feelings that arose inside of us at that moment. The mobilized drive is the aggressive or sexual impulse we felt. Altogether, the "S-O-A + Mobilized drive" makes up the unit. This explains the title: "Our S-O-A Workbook for Recovery from the Trauma of Abuse, Violence, and Addiction." The S-O-A is our guide to figuring out the symptoms and problem behaviors that follow from our experience of trauma.

How does the S-O-A help us to figure out the symptoms and problem behaviors that follow from a trauma?

The case example of Nancy will help us to see the utility of the S-O-A in figuring out the root cause of many different symptoms and problem behaviors, including substance abuse and being violent, for example. We can use the S-O-A + Mobilized drive unit to capture Nancy's moment of original trauma at age 5 when she was physically abused by her intoxicated mother in the kitchen:

SELF	-	OBJECT	- AFFECT	+	MOBILIZED DRIVE UNIT
S	-	O	- A	+	MOBILIZED DRIVE
NANCY at age 5	-	MOTHER is drunk	- AFFECTS OF ANGER, FEAR, ANXIETY, GUILT, SADNESS, SHAME, CONFUSION	+	AGGRESSION MOBILIZED

What is my original, or first memory of trauma? Which memories come to mind?

What are the first memories that come to mind? Select the first memory that comes to mind, your original trauma, or one that you feel most comfortable working on at this time. (You may use other sheets of paper or a journal.)

_____

_____

_____

_____

_____

_____

Do any fears or feelings come up as you think about this trauma or other traumas? (You may use other sheets of paper or a journal.)

_____

_____

_____

Do you feel ready to work on this trauma and talk about it in individual or group counseling? (You may use other sheets of paper or a journal.)

_____

_____

_____

Before we do more extensive homework and concentrate on our own personal trauma(s), there is more to learn. To further understand our future homework, we can follow Nancy's case and see what kind of cycles, symptoms, and behavior problems follow for Nancy from her original trauma. We will identify three *permutations* (or changed forms of the original pattern of behavior) of her original trauma, as shown on the next page. But first, can we guess what kind of problems Nancy has as an adult woman?

What are Nancy's symptoms and problem behaviors?

_____

_____

_____

Table 8.1
Predicting the Three Permutations of the Original Traumatic S-O-A: "If You Know the Trauma, You Can Figure Out the Drama."

---

1. The Transference Drama*

SELF	-	OBJECT	-	AFFECT	+	MOBILIZED DRIVE UNIT
S	-	O	-	A	+	MOBILIZED DRIVE
NANCY at age 32	-	ANY WOMAN WITH AN AIR OF AUTHORITY ABOUT HER	-	AFFECTS OF ANGER, FEAR, ANXIETY, GUILT, SADNESS, SHAME, CONFUSION	+	AGGRESSION MOBILIZED

* Problem 1: Nancy transfers her feelings toward her mother to similar women.

---

2. The Role Reversal**

SELF	-	OBJECT	-	AFFECT	+	MOBILIZED DRIVE UNIT
S	-	O	-	A	+	MOBILIZED DRIVE
NANCY at age 32	-	DAUGHTER age 8 physically abused	-	AFFECTS OF ANGER, FEAR, ANXIETY, GUILT, SADNESS, SHAME, CONFUSION	+	AGGRESSION MOBILIZED

** Problem 2: Nancy reverses roles and takes the role of the powerful abuser, placing her daughter in the role of victim of abuse.

---

3. The Intimacy Permutation***

SELF	-	OBJECT	-	AFFECT	+	MOBILIZED DRIVE UNIT
S	-	O	-	A	+	MOBILIZED DRIVE
NANCY age of 20–32	-	MEN WHO BATTER NANCY & ARE ALCOHOLIC	-	AFFECTS OF ANGER, FEAR, ANXIETY, GUILT, SADNESS, SHAME, CONFUSION	+	AGGRESSION MOBILIZED

*** Problem 3: Nancy somehow, almost magically selects men who play out the same role behavior as her mother, abusing Nancy in domestic violence.

UNDERSTANDING WHAT WE LEARN FROM THE EXPERIENCE OF TRAUMA: THE CASE OF NANCY

It is because of Nancy's learning or conditioning at the moment of trauma that she develops several symptoms and problem behaviors. Her symptoms and problem behaviors include using a lot of defenses, trading in the use of defenses for chemical defenses (getting high/substance abuse), not being able to handle intense feelings, and having well-hidden phobias and inhibitions. See Figure 8.1 for a summary of Nancy's conditioning and a graphic depiction of the moment of trauma.

Figure 8.1
Graphic Depiction of Conditioning at the Moment of Trauma.

```
                            * *              * * * *
        \                 * * * *          * * * * * *
   E /                     \ \ / /          \ \ \ / / / /
   G \        S - O - A    +   A G G R E S S I O N
   O /                     / / \ \          / / / / \ \ \ \
        \                 * * * *          * * * * * *
                            * *              * * * *
```

- The *ego* is the part of Nancy that stood in the kitchen and saw what happened to her small self at the hands of her alcoholic and violent mother. Nancy's ego executes the *defense* of *splitting* at the moment of trauma. When the defense of splitting is used, we just cut ourselves off from a painful scene and no longer have awareness of what is happening to a part of us during the painful scene. Our ego attempts to split off from overwhelming, overstimulating and extremely high levels of anger, shame, anxiety, fear, and aggression.

- Nancy may be said to have *dissociated* at the moment of trauma—no longer focusing on what is happening to her small body. Because of dissociation Nancy only remembers "The kitchen tiles were black and white and very cool against my cheek; I heard the kitchen faucet dripping water." Or after the trauma we can repress or bury the memory, using the defense of *repression*.

- Nancy's ego, having been overwhelmed and overstimulated, learns rather early in our childhood to become overreliant on the use of defenses. Later in life Nancy begins to use drugs/alcohol as a defense, or way of coping.

- The ego observes the moment of trauma and the "self" being overwhelmed with intense affects (feelings) and impulses.

- The ego acquires well-hidden *phobias* (fears) and *inhibitions* (holding back feelings and impulses.)

UNDERSTANDING WHAT HAPPENS TO OUR ABILITY TO HANDLE FEELINGS AS A RESULT OF TRAUMA: THE CASE OF NANCY

As a result of her trauma, Nancy has many problems with her affects, or feelings. For example, she has a well-hidden phobia or fear of feelings arising inside of her. Her symptoms from the original trauma include Nancy getting high to avoid feelings, not expressing feelings, and occasionally losing control and unleashing anger. Figure 8.2 suggests the nature of her affective conditioning.

Nancy needs to learn how to affectively cope. In order to cope with her affects, Nancy will need to learn how to identify, label, and process, or talk about her feelings. She also must learn how to interrupt, stop, and control the explosive expression of feelings as a part of affective coping. Nancy also needs to learn how to be assertive and verbally express any feelings of irritation, annoyance, and anger, before she becomes enraged and explodes, losing control.

Figure 8.2
Affective Conditioning at the Moment of Trauma.

```
                         * *               * * * *
         \               * * * *           * * * * * *
     E /                 \ \ / /           \ \ \ \ / / / /
     G \       S - O - A     +    A G G R E S S I O N
     O /                 / / \ \           / / / / \ \ \ \
         \               * * * *           * * * * * *
                         * *               * * * *
```

Affective Conditioning

- Nancy emerges with a well-hidden *phobia* of the experience of *affects* and aggressive impulses being mobilized (or built up) within her.

- After trauma, Nancy's ego continues to be over-reliant upon defenses (or drugs and alcohol) and defends against the experience of any feelings or affects that may arise inside of her. And, Nancy inhibits (or holds back) the expression of aggressive impulses.

- Nancy admits to an inability to identify, label, and process affects, feelings.

- Nancy admits that she is unable to express feelings of anger or aggression by being assertive. People can walk all over Nancy because she never gets angry or protests.

- But Nancy also admits to instances of near loss of control of her feelings of anger (and aggression) as captured in the role reversal, for example, with her daughter.

UNDERSTANDING WHAT HAPPENS TO OUR BEHAVIOR AS A RESULT OF TRAUMA: THE CASE OF NANCY

Powerful learning occurs at the moment of trauma, impacting Nancy's behavior. For the rest of her life Nancy's behavior reflects the learning that women (and perhaps all people) cannot be trusted. We observe in Nancy the behavior of moving away from women, avoiding women, and excluding women as friends. Figure 8.3 summarizes what is learned behaviorally by Nancy.

Nancy needs to learn how to cope behaviorally, no longer avoiding feared objects. She needs to overcome her well-hidden phobias from past trauma.

Figure 8.3
Behavioral Conditioning at the Moment of Trauma.

```
                            * *              * * * *
        \                 * * * *          * * * * * *
    E /                    \ \ / /          \ \ \ \ / / / /
    G \         S - O -  A     +   A G G R E S S I O N
    O /                    / / \ \          / / / / \ \ \ \
        \                 * * * *          * * * * * *
                            * *              * * * *
```

Behavioral Conditioning

• Nancy's ego ends up with a learned anxiety or fear response (*phobia*).

• Watson (1930) demonstrates with 9-month little Albert how we can learn an anxiety or fear response to a white rat.

• The phobia (fear) generalizes (or spreads) to things that look and feel similar to a white rat. Little Albert is now afraid of a white rabbit and even a white piece of fur.

• In the same way, Nancy's ego ends up with a *conditioned* (learned) anxiety or fear response to her mother (even if she also learns to hide her fear and act as if she is not afraid of her mother).

• As a result of *generalization* (spreading of her fear to similar objects), Nancy responds with a conditioned anxiety or fear response to women in authority even when she grows up. She uses the defense of *avoidance* and stays away from women, not becoming friends with or getting close to women, as a result.

• With maximal generalization (or spreading of her fear) Nancy might appear to be afraid of all human beings and will trust no human. She may find it difficult to become friends or get close to anyone. Nancy may lack feelings of trust and avoidcloseness with all human beings.

UNDERSTANDING WHAT HAPPENS TO OUR THINKING AS A RESULT OF TRAUMA: THE CASE OF NANCY

Trauma also impacts Nancy's thinking, resulting in negative expectations. She expects violence to erupt with women, and possibly with any human being (see Figure 8.4). Nancy needs to learn how to cope cognitively. She must learn thought-stopping, or how to stop old, conditioned thoughts and expectations. In addition, Nancy must replace old negative thoughts and expectations with new, more positive thoughts. For example, she may deliver to herself the affirmation "I AM GROWING IN MY ABILITY TO TRUST AND LOVE EACH AND EVERY DAY." Survivors of trauma often expect bad things to happen out of the blue, even when things are going well. A recommended affirmation ("LIFE IS GOOD AND IT KEEPS GETTING BETTER AND BETTER!") may change past conditioning to expect something bad to happen out of the blue.

Figure 8.4
Cognitive Conditioning at the Moment of Trauma.

```
                          * *              * * * *
            \             * * * *          * * * * * *
    E /                   \ \ / /          \ \ \ \ / / / /
    G \         S - O - A     +     A G G R E S S I O N
    O /                   / / \ \          / / / / \ \ \ \
            \             * * * *          * * * * * *
                          * *              * * * *
```

Cognitive Conditioning

- Nancy learned or experienced a *cognition* (thought) at the moment of trauma which capturing the ego's attempt to understand and make sense out of her experience:

    *"I can get hit out of the blue at any moment by **mommy**."*

- Nancy also came to possess the generalized form of this conditioned cognition:

    *"I can get hit our of the blue at any moment by **a woman**."*

- Nancy may experience maximal *generalization* of this conditioned cognition:

    *"I can get hit out of the blue at any moment by **any human being**."*

- Conditioned cognitions represent powerful expectations that may help to create or trigger violent behavior on the part of men who fit into Nancy's S-O-A. Magically, she selects or attracts men who fit into the "O" of her S-O-A. These men hit Nancy, just as she expects. Her prophecy becomes reality when she does get hit by men.

OUR HOMEWORK: A WORKSHEET FOR GRAPHIC DEPICTION OF OUR ORIGINAL TRAUMA FOLLOWING FIGURE 8.1

What traumas do I want to work on, using the S-O-A? What is the first trauma to come to mind? We can refer to Figure 8.1 to start our homework and map out a trauma.   Or start with the trauma with which you feel most comfortable.

Draw and write out one of your own traumas, using the S-O-A + Mobilized Drive unit:

SELF	-	OBJECT	-	AFFECT	+ MOBILIZED DRIVE UNIT
S	-	O	-	A	+ MOBILIZED DRIVE

(Use the space below to write out your **(S)** name and age; the **(O)** object or person with whom you interacted during the trauma; the **(A)** affects or feelings you felt or witnessed in the other person; and the impulse (Mobilized Drive) that you felt or witnessed in the other person:)

(You may use other sheets of paper or a journal.)

WORKSHEET TO DETERMINE MY AFFECTIVE CONDITIONING:
FOLLOW FIGURE 8.2

What was my affective learning or conditioning from my trauma? What kind of feelings did I experience as overwhelming? What kind of feelings or affects did I escape with drugs and alcohol, or escape with other behaviors (compulsive shopping, eating, sex, working)? For example, did I learn to feel powerless, feel helpless, or to have trouble with feelings of fear, anxiety, anger, terror, or shame, etc.? Did I turn to drugs or compulsive behaviors to avoid, cope with, or to finally feel certain affects?

My affective conditioning or learning was
(You may use other sheets of paper or a journal.)

_____

_____

_____

_____

_____

_____

_____

_____

What did I learn from other traumas? (You may use other sheets of paper or a journal.)

_____

_____

_____

WORKSHEET TO DETERMINE MY BEHAVIORAL CONDITIONING: FOLLOW FIGURE 8.3

What was my behavioral learning or conditioning from my trauma? For example, did I learn to be avoidant, withdrawn, and to isolate?

My behavioral conditioning or learning was
(You may use other sheets of paper or a journal.)

_____

_____

_____

_____

_____

_____

_____

_____

What did I learn from other traumas?
(You may use other sheets of paper or a journal.)

_____

_____

_____

_____

_____

WORKSHEET TO DETERMINE MY COGNITIVE CONDITIONING:
FOLLOW FIGURE 8.4

What was my cognitive learning or conditioning? How was my thinking impacted? What kind of thoughts or expectations do I have for myself and my behavior? How do I expect others to treat me ? For example, did I learn to think "I am nothing," or "People betray me," or "Nobody likes me"?

My cognitive learning or conditioning was
(You may use other sheets of paper or a journal.)

_____

_____

_____

_____

_____

_____

_____

_____

What did I learn from other traumas?
(You may use other sheets of paper or a journal.)

_____

_____

_____

_____

CONCLUSION TO WORKBOOK: CREATING CIRCLES OF SUPPORT

The workbook prepares us and guides us to begin our group work. We may have done our homework and are not sure when and what we will share about our past trauma. Hopefully, we will take turns in group, sharing what we have learned about our trauma, or we can sit with the counselor and share what we worked out in the workbook. Others may share with selected group members. As the group process continues and we follow our seven group principles and begin to talk more openly about what we learned during moments of trauma, we need to use each other for support both inside and outside the group. So, let's form support networks, or circles of support within our larger supportive circle of the group, exchanging relevant information below:

NAME   TELEPHONE NUMBER   OKAY TIME TO CALL

(You may use other sheets of paper or a journal.)

_____   _____   _____

_____   _____   _____

_____   _____   _____

NAME   TELEPHONE NUMBER   OKAY TIME TO CALL

_____   _____   _____

_____   _____   _____

_____   _____   _____

NAME   TELEPHONE NUMBER   OKAY TIME TO CALL

_____   _____   _____

_____   _____   _____

_____   _____   _____

Daily Homework: State a brief prayer for the two other sisters/brothers in your support circle. My chosen prayer:

(You may use other sheets of paper or a journal.)

_____

CONCLUSION

Other women and men may benefit from the seven principles that guided our group work. Ms. E. could probably pass an oral quiz on these seven principles. She could also answer the questions on the impact of her traumas and what she learned from them in terms of her behavior, feelings, and thoughts. We may work with clients individually or in groups following these principles and the guide for graphically depicting S-O-As, coming to understand the impact of past learning during moments of trauma. This chapter makes available the training and tools for others to seek a therapeutic breakthrough and change deeply ingrained behaviors. We may not need the workbook for use by group members; nor does the homework necessarily need to be performed by clients. As an alternative, we, as counselors, may be the ones who need this guide to graphically depict and visualize moments of trauma for our clients. We may need to figure out on a piece of paper after a group or a one-on-one counseling session a client's transference, role reversal, and intimacy permutations. Or we can figure it out in our head, using the graphic image of the S-O-A for this purpose. It is also up to us to listen carefully and observe intently a client's affective, behavioral, and cognitive conditioning. Ultimately, it is we, as counselors, who in knowing our client's traumas can help decipher and give them feedback on the behavioral dramas they keep reenacting or are at risk of enacting—as in a role reversal and the risk of child abuse.

As a self-help manual, the workbook may be an invaluable tool for those counselors and clients who want to increase their understanding of their own behavior independently. Another snap-shot piece of education we can provide clients to guide them in the process of trauma resolution was shared in a group one day by a woman who had "prior concept"—or prior education from a former treatment facility:

> Trace it!
> Face it!
> Erase it!
> Replace it!

In this manner, we offer little that is new or original in the statement "If you know the trauma, you can figure out the drama." Nor is it necessarily novel to create an elaborate workbook in order to trace the roots of our problem behaviors, face the facts of those roots in past experiences, erase the impact or memory of past trauma, and replace it with new adaptive behavior.

Nonetheless, in this chapter we have striven to codify in a handbook what one naturally learns in the trenches doing surgery with wounded soldiers of the crack, violence, and AIDS war. What is codified may assist others in accomplishing therapeutic breakthrough in groups. With this workbook in hand, clients and counselors should emerge prepared to engage in a specific four-phase model of group counseling described in the next chapter.

9

Four-Phase Group Therapy: Utilizing a Graphic Model of the Mind for Training

In this chapter, clinicians and practitioners who want to advertise and start group therapy either in their private practice or in an outpatient clinic will find a viable approach to group work with adult children of alcoholic and other dysfunctional families. Many adults with insurance or the means to pay for group psychotherapy have become interested in the adult children of dysfunctional families movement, have heard the message to augment twelve-step group involvement with professional psychotherapy, and are seeking out either professionally led groups or individual counseling—and frequently both. A market exists for practitioners who want to advertise and become engaged in this important and exciting work. Marketing strategies might also focus on survivors of trauma.

Some counselors in residential therapeutic communities and other diverse inpatient, residential, and outpatient facilities need a model for conducting group counseling. A confrontation or encounter group within a therapeutic community might be replaced with the four-phase model of group work. Any counselor in any setting—prison, corrections facility, group home, school, community clinic—who is in the work of resolving client trauma, or who addresses a range of symptoms and problem behaviors, may seek to initiate a four-phase counseling group. Problem behaviors and symptoms, the phenomenon of symptom substitution, and interpersonal conflict may prevent many clients from reaching their potential. Nor may they achieve the goal of successfully pursuing "love and work."

For clients with a range of adult child, codependent, or trauma survivor symptoms and problem behaviors, this chapter describes a four-phase model of group counseling that is highly recommended. I have successfully implemented the model and have adapted elements of it to individual counseling work.

The four phases of the group may be identified as (1) psychoeducation; (2) articulation of trauma; (3) "here and now" analysis of permutations of the original traumatic S-O-A (transference, role reversal, and intimacy); and (4) working through and integration of traumatic memories. A graphic model of the mind is offered next to facilitate the demonstration of counseling techniques.

A FOUR-PHASE MODEL OF GROUP WORK WITH ADULT CHILDREN OF DYSFUNCTIONAL FAMILIES: THERAPEUTIC BREAKTHROUGH

The case of Ms. E. (see Chapter 8) indicates that the four-phase model of group work may help us achieve therapeutic breakthrough with individuals who have been "treatment failures" and experienced multiple relapses. Hopelessness and resignation might easily prevail for many counselors told of Ms. E.'s history and then asked to engage in the task of counseling her. However, this chapter seeks to offer a description of what has seemed "to work" with her and many others as a therapeutic breakthrough is achieved. I am reminded of hostile and skeptical group members who eventually became caught up in the group process, experienced a therapeutic breakthrough, and became better co-therapists than the masters level counseling psychologists who sat with us. They not only were converted to the position that the counseling model "works," but they also learned "how to work it"—being able to assist other group members in achieving therapeutic breakthroughs. What I learned to do that seemed "to work" in the Damon House counseling group I also used in individual and group counseling in my private practice with a range of clients. The model permitted the achievement of therapeutic breakthrough involving successful prevention of relapse, avoidance of symptom substitution, and resolution of trauma in relatively short-term work—spanning three, six, nine, twelve, or eighteen months—depending on individual client needs.

PHASE I: PSYCHOEDUCATION

Table 9.1 summarizes the four phases of group work and shows how psychoeducation is essential preparation for engaging in counseling. Psychoeducation occurs in the first phase of group work, which may span the first session or several of the initial sessions, depending on a variety of counselor and client factors.

Table 9.1
A Four-Phase Group Counseling Model.

TIMING	FOUR PHASES	GOALS OF COUNSELING IN PHASE
Phase I work of delivering psychoeducation occurs heavily in months 1 to 3, but also at any point in counseling.	I. Psychoeducation	• Introduction to and preparation for later phases of counseling. • Education on childhood development, impact of trauma, and defenses assumed. • Education on task of remediating underlying psychopathology, improving self-regulation, and trauma resolution. • Create strengthened ego and cultivation of capacity for self-observation by ego.
Phase II work of articulating trauma occurs at any point.	II. Articulation of Trauma	• Briefly verbalize memories of trauma.
Phase III work of "here and now" analysis of permutations occurs as soon as the counselor observes them, but most heavily in months 4 to 6. This work further strengthens the ego and fosters greater capacity for self-observation of responses to triggers.	III."Here and Now" Analysis of Permutations	• Utilize knowledge of trauma to figure out, decipher, and transform permutations of original S-O-A in "here and now." • Stop, interrupt, and teach ego to observe moments of being triggered, regression, projection, and splitting. • Reframe contemporary behavioral problems, symptoms, and poor self-regulation as reflection of the aftermath of trauma. • Facilitate increase in self-esteem and self-efficacy through the ability to perceive, stop, and replace regression, projection, and splitting with new behavior.
Phase IV working through of memories occurs in months 7 onward, or earlier based on individual assessment findings.	IV. Working Through and Integration of Traumatic Memories	• Support client's ego in a therapeutic regression in the service of the self-observing ego with expression of painful affect and description of the "movie in the mind."

Clients may or may not be able to read and do the workbook exercises at home, or counselors may not have control over client attendance and may keep repeating certain elements of psychoeducation across many weeks. A high-functioning group that completes the S-O-A workbook in advance of the group beginning may focus on psychoeducation over a briefer period within the group.

The reality, however, is that even beyond a formal introductory phase of the group, the need for psychoeducation arises again and again. Psychoeducation covers childhood development, the impact of trauma, and the defenses assumed after traumatic experiences. Much of this psychoeducation is contained in Chapters 5, 6, 7, and 8, with the S-O-A workbook powerfully conveying information. Indeed, an important feature of the group model is the group process's constant movement back and forth across phases I to IV. At any given moment in a single group session, we may be doing phase I, then phase II, then phase I, then phase III, then phase I group work. At any point in time, we may need to provide psychoeducation, or stop and listen to a member articulate some new traumatic memory that has just arisen. Then, in response to that moment of sharing, we may need to provide more psychoeducation to that client. After a client engages in phase II work and articulates a memory of a trauma that spontaneously emerges in group, or that emerged in a dream at night, it may be time to provide psychoeducation again on what constitutes sexual abuse, or parental alcoholism—being tailorred to meet this particular client's need. For example, after a new group member joins a group, older group members may be asked to offer and explain a piece of psychoeducation on a selected topic; this format powerfully demonstrates the efficacy of the oral teaching of psycho-education and clients' ability to accurately recite psychoeducational facts.

Rationale for Heavy Use of Cognitive Techniques in the Early Phases of Counseling

The repeated delivery of psychoeducation constitutes heavy reliance on the counseling technique of cognitive reframing. Cognitive techniques are largely utilized in the early phases of counseling in order to strengthen the ego and systematically cultivate in clients a self-observing ego. Phase I work and cultivation of a self-observing ego prepare the client over the first few months (months 1 to 3) of group counseling for the task of phase III work. Phase III work involves clients learning over the next several months (months 4 to 6) how to stop, interrupt, and observe regression, projection, and splitting—reenactment of a permutation of an original traumatic S-O-A which just occurred in the reality of the "here and now." Phase I and III work with the resulting creation of a considerably strengthened ego that can engage in self-observation also permits phase IV work (months 7 onward, based on individual assessment findings) addressing integration of traumatic memories. By month 7, the ego's capacity to self-observe permits a regression in the service of that self-observing ego to the fixation point and original moment of trauma. This is the essence of trauma resolution in phase IV work. Table 9.1 summarizes the suggested timing for the delivery of interventions within Phase I, II, III, and IV work. Individual assessment findings dictate when and if a client needs to work through and integrate traumatic memories in an earlier Phase—perhaps as early as the first month in counseling. A client with a strong ego and good capacity for self-observation may be ready much earlier in counseling. Or working within a residential therapeutic community setting may permit more intensive work earlier in counseling than is advisable in an outpatient setting.

PHASE II: ARTICULATION OF TRAUMA

Articulation of trauma may occur at any time in the group process when a client spontaneously recalls a traumatic memory, or has a memory somehow evoked. More formally, we may move our group after a psychoeducational phase (I) into a systematic and brief disclosure of trauma by each group member (II)—perhaps moving around the group circle in one group session. Clients answer our assessment questions presented in Chapter 7 within a group session, taking turns in one session, or across several weeks. Ideally, individual counseling first permits an assessment of trauma, and clients share what they feel comfortable disclosing in the group. Flexibility and adaptations to various settings, client populations, and counselor preferences is the rule.

PHASE III: "HERE AND NOW" ANALYSIS OF PERMUTATIONS

Phase III work involves the analysis within the "here and now" setting of the group of permutations of the original traumatic S-O-A. Transference dramas, role reversals, or intimacy permutations may appear, as clients respond to triggers, undergo regression, engage in projection, and thereby present states of splitting. This analysis involves use of counseling techniques of interpretation, as links are drawn between past trauma and current behavioral problems, symptoms, poor self-regulation, and problems with regression to fixation points, symptom substitution, and relapse. Client cognitions may be immediately restructured with psychoeducation delivered. In phase III work, "if we know the trauma, we can figure out the drama," and the S-O-A workbook and worksheets on permutations of the original traumatic S-O-A may prove invaluable in this work of "here and now" analysis. Again, without use of the workbook, as in the case of Damon House, effective discussion of role reversal, transference, and the concept of repetition of patterns may still occur.

Strengthening the ego and cultivation of the capacity to self-observe occur with the counseling techniques of affect labeling and empathic mirroring. By self-observing their internal state and affects arising within, clients may compare what they self-observe to the affects labeled and empathic mirroring offered by the counselor. Following the metaphor presented in Chapter 6, clients tell us if we have "hit the nail on the head," achieving accuracy. They should begin to be able to stop, interrupt, and observe moments of splitting in the "here and now." In addition, emergence of the ability to stop, interrupt, observe and replace problematic patterns of behavior increases the clients' self-esteem and sense of self-efficacy. As group members practice new alternative patterns of behavior, within and outside of the group, replacing the repetitive, unconscious acting out of permutation dramas, they receive praise and reinforcement in the group. Group members may even clap in unison for one who returns to report that they made a female friend, after years of only transference dramas with women that resulted in threats of violence and actual violence. The goal of analysis of permutation dramas in the "here and now" of the group setting is to replace client regression in response to triggers, projection, and splitting with new, more adaptive patterns of behavior.

PHASE IV: WORKING THROUGH AND INTEGRATION OF TRAUMATIC MEMORIES

The counseling work in phase IV focuses on the task of working through and integrating traumatic memories. We follow the classic Freudian dictum that resolution of trauma involves clients articulating what happened at the moment of the trauma and also feeling what was felt at the moment of trauma. The psychoanalytic instruction for there to be a regression in the service of a self-observing ego is made crystal clear, when we utilize the graphic model of the mind to visualize this process, as well as creatively deploy multiple metaphors. An elusive and heretofore vague concept that has been hard to grasp for many professional clinicians is translated into practical steps that seem easy to follow for any newly trained or experienced counselor.

We find practical guidance for the task of working through and integrating traumatic memories in several metaphors from Chapter 6. Clients are instructed to describe the "movie in their mind," and to avoid "jumping into the movie" and acting out the action in the movie. The counselor is urged to be verbally active and to use their voice as though it is a glue keeping client egos focused on reality. The counselor repeatedly directs the client to "tell me what you see, tell me what you see," also calling out the client's name, as the client describes the "movie in their mind." In addition, we receive more metaphoric instruction to "close clients up" with the use of humor, versus leaving them open—refocusing and distracting the client's ego after the work of trauma resolution. Clients are also metaphorically guided down their stairway to, for example, step 4, where they possess a fixation point or have left a part of themselves on a step where original trauma occurred. Yet another metaphor elaborated in this chapter suggests a walk down a spiral staircase under the surface of the ocean, as the counselor's voice serves as glue keeping the feet and hands of the client fixed on the stairs and handrail during the client's descent into dark, murky ocean waters. A scene of original trauma is then described, via the self-observing ego, to those left sitting at the top of the spiral staircase in the circle of group counseling in reality.

Meanwhile, client egos are supported in the conscious processing of powerful affects in the "here and now" of the group—affects which were experienced at the moment of the original trauma. The poem in Chapter 8 describes how "Ms. E. sat with us in group and fully processed her pain. She cried so intensely her tears fell like rain. Her body sobbed and shook with such somber force." This is an accurate description of the classic experience of many clients at the moment of working through and integration of trauma, as they engage in the "full body sob," emerging fatigued and drained after the experience. Body memories, as in pain of the uterus, for a woman raped, may also emerge at such a moment; we may need to immediately provide psychoeducation on body memories, as they tend to be triggered and bodily remembered at the very second that we consciously recall what happened to us during moments of trauma. During the actual group process when Ms. E. was working through and integrating memories of traumatic rape by her father, experiencing a body memory pain in her uterus, another group member had body memories triggered wherein she felt the hands of several men on her body—holding her down and groping her, as in the original gang rape. The psychoeducation immediately offered in the group benefited both women.

Body memories and affects of what we felt at the moment of original trauma may also linger for a period after the group session—perhaps for days. We continue to talk about them and integrate them into conscious awareness.

Trauma resolution is important because we can thereby retrieve the split-off and damaged part of our self that was left fixated at the moment of the original trauma. We now possess a vulnerable part of ourselves that we have to take care of, love, nurture, and assist in catching up with other parts of ourselves developmentally. We have to give that part of ourselves tremendous empathy and not reenact harsh treatment, judgmental attitudes, or abuse. If we are successful in getting guidance and support in this process within group or individual sessions, then we may realize the steps mentioned at the end of Chapter 7: trace it, face it, erase it, and replace it. It is one thing to know the trauma, and another to figure out, transform, and replace a drama. A critical step is to erase or resolve the fixation point, by integrating the part of our self that was split off, injured, or damaged during trauma.

TRAINING USING A GRAPHIC MODEL OF THE MIND:
TRIGGERS, REGRESSION, SPLITTING

The graphic model of the mind permits graphic visualization of how triggers in the environment can provoke a regression. This regression is typically to fixation points, which are graphically shown as located within the unconscious. The aftermath of the experience of personal trauma is captured in our possession of a fixation point. The fixation point is the location of an image of the original trauma stored in the unconscious; here we speak of that "movie in the mind" which is also captured as a Self-Object-Affect Unit, or S-O-A. The graphic model also permits us to visualize how after we regress to a fixation point and activate the images captured within an S-O-A—as the old, original "footage" of our "movie in the mind" begins to run—we seek a "screen" for "projection" of our "movie." Typically, the object in reality who may happen to be around, or who possessed those triggers that led to our regression, becomes the "screen" in reality on which we project our movie. A new, mutant, or slightly varied version of our original "movie in the mind" may be played out in reality with the new actor/object in reality. We may also play a different role than we did in the original "movie in the mind," perhaps reversing roles and taking on the behavior of an assaulter. Meanwhile, a new object in reality is forced into the role we had to play as a child and is now a victim of our assault. At such a moment, when we enact a scene or version of a scene from our "movie in our mind," we may be said to be engaged in splitting. Quite often, we are also unaware of what is happening to us, even as others may observe us to have manifested a sudden compulsiveness. In sum, the graphic model of the mind trains us further so that we thoroughly understand how triggers provoke regression to fixation points and projection of the content of the "movies in our mind" upon the screen of contemporary reality and actors/objects with whom we interact.

INTRODUCTION TO THE GRAPHIC MODEL: FIGURE 9.1

Figure 9.1 introduces the graphic model of the mind. In the spirit of the work of Jung (1969a, b), the model depicts two intersecting continuums—a space-time and a consciousness-unconscious continuum. The continuums intersect and permit diagramming of how psychic contents may engage in regressive or progressive movement within a dynamic system. All events occur in space and time, and at different points in time we possess a state of being that may be said to reflect one of many levels or states of consciousness or unconscious awareness. Depending on whether we are an infant, dreaming, in a state of reverie, or engaged in fantasy, we may be said to reflect a particular level of unconscious awareness.

Figure 9.1
Introduction to a Graphic Model of the Mind for Training.

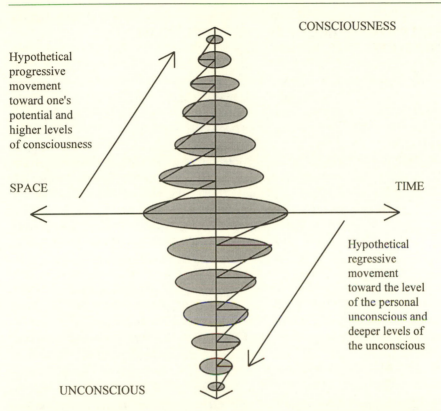

This figure introduces a graphic model of the mind. The basic model involves two intersecting continuums: a space-time continuum and a consciousness-unconscious continuum. The model suggests the dynamic nature of the psyche and the manner in which psychic contents, through regression and progression, may move from an unconscious realm and invade consciousness; or how cognitive restructuring and self-observation permit a progressive expansion in consciousness and achievement of higher levels of consciousness dominated by balanced states of awareness. The spiral suggests both regressive and progressive movement within our dynamic psyches.

Or, if we are engaged in meditation, chanting, decreeing, deep breathing, prayer, exercise, talking, reading, or conversation, we may be said to reflect a particular level of consciousness. The spiral is widest at the center of Figure 9.1, as the central circle suggests the existence of an ego complex (discussed in the next figure). The hypothetical progressive and regressive spiralling activity is meant to suggest we may move toward and achieve one of many different levels of either consciousness or unconscious awareness.

THE EGO COMPLEX AS AN ISLAND LOCATED IN THE MIDDLE OF AN OCEAN: FIGURE 9.2

The shaded area in Figure 9.2 depicts the location of the ego. Following Jung (1969a), this is an ego complex, suggesting that it is a structure within the psyche. Here, the ego complex is depicted as an island in the middle of a vast ocean. Developmentally, the ego of the infant exists largely in space, feeling connected to the mother and a part of her body. But, as the infant begins to observe events in reality, images of interacting with human objects are stored. The infant learns to anticipate the next feeding and the arrival of the caretaker; awareness of time also begins to form. This marks the birth of an incipient ego. As fleeting moments of awareness and anticipation of events emerge, it is as though an island mass begins to emerge out of the ocean. The ego arises out of the unconscious, or the id. The incipient ego of the infant continually develops and expands. The ego of the toddler is like a small island that continues to grow yet further in mass and size. Eventually, the adult ego is like a large island with a mountain peak—perhaps with an active volcano—that sits in the middle of a vast ocean expanse. The unconscious is symbolized as a vast ocean with varied depths. We are able to look right below the surface of the ocean and glimpse the contents of the preconscious of which Freud (1917) spoke.

The next level of the unconscious is the personal unconscious which contains our original traumatic S-O-As, as well as our earliest unconscious identifications with our caretakers, or those with whom we interacted as infants, toddlers, and young children. In this regard, Kernberg (1976) speaks of internalization and introjection as occurring when we create psychic images of interactions between the object of the caretaker and our self—as an affect or feeling tone holds sway during the interaction, and, a corresponding libidinal or aggressive drive is mobilized. In this manner, our ego and self structure is hypothesized as actually being built from images of interacting with caretakers. The development of our self structure also involves a process whereby we separate "good" and "bad" feeling-toned interactions (Kernberg, 1976). The bad feeling-toned interactions may begin to constitute memories of trauma, which we may not be able to recall as coherent memories if they occurred very early in life (infancy, toddlerhood, young childhood).

Returning to our metaphor, the ego is like an island with a part that is submerged under the ocean surface, because it reflects our very earliest unconscious internalizations, introjections, and identifications based on interacting with other human objects.

Figure 9.2
The Ego Complex, Levels of the Unconscious, and the Realm of Consciousness.

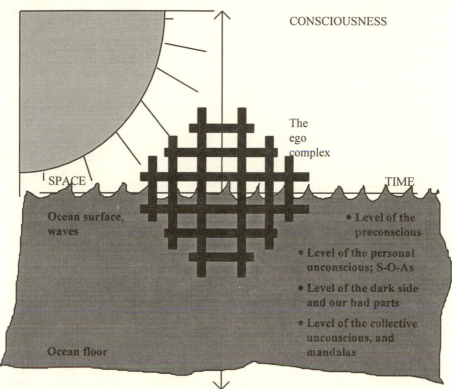

The figure depicts the structure of the ego, or ego complex, as a cross-hatched area, or island in the middle of an ocean. The area below the ocean surface contains the levels of the unconscious: preconscious, personal, dark side, and collective. The area above the waves of the ocean is the realm of consciousness, characterized by access to fresh air and sunshine. Part of the ego, or island, includes our earliest internalized images of interactions with caretakers, which are part of the personal unconscious. Part of the ego above the ocean surface is composed of conscious identifications.

The part of the ego that is above the ocean surface and waves is built from our conscious identifications. Following Kernberg (1976), these occur later in childhood and are more selective identifications, as we consciously choose to be like the adults and role models to whom we are exposed. Everything above the surface of the ocean involves contact with fresh air and sunshine—which is symbolic of the realm of consciousness.

On the other hand, the depths of the ocean are removed from the light and sunshine. We enter the dark, murky waters of the personal unconscious. The personal unconscious contains images that were originally overstimulating, overwhelming, frightening, and therefore relegated via defense to the ocean depths. We even encounter a deeper level of the unconscious which contains our dark side and our "bad parts." This is akin to Jung's (1969b) shadow side.

As the self separated into "good" and "bad" feeling-toned parts, the "bad parts" may be thought of as having been relegated to as deep a level of the unconscious as possible. Primitive responses of rage and aggression characterize our bad parts, as we became too frustrated as infants and toddlers, waiting to be fed or being left unattended far too long.

Part of this dark side may also contain inherited patterns conditioned across generations and passed on as genetic material reflecting the survival responses of anger and a willingness to engage in self-defense. Let us imagine how, long ago, nomadic tribes in the desert may have encountered a "different other" in the form of a group of strangers passing by. "Fight or flight" responses to the "different other" may be instinctive, or deeply conditioned, for purposes of survival. When a tribe "stayed put" in one locale, fight or flight responses may have been activated when strangers appeared. However, we can now appreciate on a deeper level the stress that arises with the development of patterns of immigration and migration—for both those remaining in one locale and those passing by or arriving to the new location. The stress of immigration and migration may have involved greater activation of patterns of "fight or flight" response to the perception of the "different other." When the "different other" was perceived, it also provided an opportunity for the projection of our "bad parts" upon the "screen" of the new arrival or stranger. We then perceived with fear and suspicion the bad, dark, and shadowy behavior of the "different other," whose customs, ways, and language we could not understand, facilitating the projection of our bad parts; fear and suspicion reigned. We can now see how easy it was for violent attacks to ensue, or how efforts were made either to flee or to get the new arrival to depart. Just as we bury and "repress" our bad parts, so we typically try to "oppress" the bad stranger.

Below the level of the personal unconscious and the level of our bad parts, or shadow side, we find the deepest level of the unconscious—the collective unconscious. The level of the collective unconscious reflects genetic patterns or inherited material; this includes, for example, instinctive patterns of relating between an infant and a mother. All human beings possess the collective unconscious. According to Jung (1969a, b), we may think of these patterns as archetypes of the collective unconscious that may also appear in dreams, imagination, literature, and art work. Material from the collective unconscious may arise—along our continuum of consciousness-unconscious—and enter the realm of ego functioning. We may become consciously aware of the material from the collective unconscious which tends to attract our attention and is particularly fascinating. It is as though contents from the deepest level of the ocean floor may arise and wash up on the beach or island of the ego complex. Similarly, we possess a deep excitement and fascination when we pick up on the beach, or pluck from the ocean, an object that has traveled a long distance and appears on the ocean surface or is washed on the beach or shore. We are similarly fascinated with contents of the collective unconscious when they make contact with consciousness. The storm conditions of a midlife crisis (Jung, 1969a) require that we weather a depression—as contents from the personal unconscious wash upon the shore of the ego complex, or our island. However, after this period of making contact with material from the personal unconscious during the midlife crisis and rectifying the imbalance created by these contents relegated to the personal unconscious, we may pursue further psychic development.

Perhaps we have a "really big dream" which contains the gift of a symbol of our having made progress toward healing and wholeness. We may awaken with the dream image of a mandala which washed upon our shore or beach one morning. A *mandala* is a symbol of healing and wholeness composed of a quadrant or circle shape, perhaps akin to a cross (Jung, 1969a). This mandala may signal the integration of the self and the achievement of a new balance and centeredness within the psyche. Mandalas may also spontaneously appear in artwork and in creative productions as outward symbols of an internal process and movement toward integration of the self and achievement of wholeness and healing.

A THREE DIMENSIONAL MODEL AND FANTASTIC VOYAGE IN A DYSFUNCTIONAL FAMILY BOAT: FIGURE 9.3

Figure 9.3, just as the ocean and island image, suggests how the model is actually three dimensional. The figure also depicts the circumstances in which a family finds itself when an adult parent is dysfunctional. There may be a period when parental dysfunction is exacerbated or further intensified when that parent goes through a mid-life crisis (Jung, 1969a). The family is stuck in the dysfunctional family boat, as children are forced to grow up in turbulent waters. A depressed female parent around age 35 or a male parent around age 40 may create upheaval in family life when alcoholic or drug-taking behavior accelerates to cope with depression, or other symptoms. Family members may feel that a tidal wave appeared out of nowhere during a sudden and unexpected storm—that is, the parents' midlife crisis. Parents who are adult children and experienced abuse and trauma in their own childhood or across the developmental stages of their lives are most likely to suffer a psychic imbalance from years of overusing defenses.

Figure 9.3
The Model as Three Dimensional: Negotiating within the Dysfunctional Family Boat.

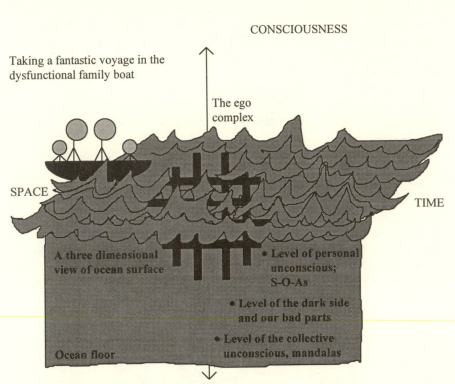

CONSCIOUSNESS

Taking a fantastic voyage in the dysfunctional family boat

The ego complex

SPACE

TIME

A three dimensional view of ocean surface

• Level of personal unconscious; S-O-As

• Level of the dark side and our bad parts

• Level of the collective unconscious, mandalas

Ocean floor

UNCONSCIOUS

The model is meant to suggest a three dimensionsal experience in reality, as the ego (conscious part of ego complex) orients us to events in reality and permits social interaction. Too often, we are tossed by waves and rough waters, as the unconscious contents from one or several family members violently wash over the ego complex, create chaos, and take family members on a fantastic voyage in the dysfunctional family boat. Instead of children being centered on the island of their ego complex, they are forced into rough waters as a codependent within the dysfunctional family boat.

What was relegated to ocean depths by the ego's use of defense after trauma is now emerging as metaphoric tidal waves and other debris that wash upon the shore of their ego complex. But family life depends on the functioning of this adult ego. The island of the parental ego is partly shared by family members, especially young children. The tidal wave washes over the adult's ego complex and life for children now seems to be occurring in an atmosphere of especially rough tidal and ocean waters, instead of upon a safe and dry island mass of an intact parental ego complex. This creates a crisis and severe storm conditions within the family. Thus, children and family members dependent on this dominant parental figure who is experiencing a midlife crisis are also overwhelmed and touched by the emergence of contents from the personal unconscious of this parent. All family members may find themselves being washed out to sea, discovering a new period of family life is being spent taking a fantastic voyage in the dysfunctional family boat.

Ironically, these storm conditions facilitate the achievement of a new psychic balance for the parent who has past trauma, split parts of the self, and has overutilized ego defenses throughout life. Following Jung (1969a), unconscious contents become active and demand attention, having been too long ignored. This is actually an opportunity to achieve psychic balance, but the ego merely feels usurped from its role of rigidly reigning and controlling conscious life. Family life that was already dysfunctional because of chronic parental alcohol or drug use—or other dysfunctional dynamic—may become even more chaotic during these storm conditions. During the midlife crisis, the worst period of parental drinking, drug use, domestic violence, or physical abuse of children may occur. The worst period of dysfunctional family life may involve parents at the age of 35 to 45.

Spouse and children may develop prominent codependent patterns during these storm conditions. The most dysfunctional parent loses control, and emergency strategies to reestablish control are frantically enacted or further amplified by other family members. During this period of profound dysfunctionality within family life, codependents must work harder than ever. Knowledge of one's parents' trauma during their own childhood and adolescence may help to explain the degree of upheaval that occurred when that parent had to negotiate the midlife crisis and rectify psychic imbalance from years of overuse of ego defenses. When we view a dysfunctional parent as having "mellowed out" or "gotten better," we frequently refer to their maturation in age beyond the period of the midlife crisis and some rectification of psychic imbalance, or coming to terms with the facts of their traumatic past.

The Beach Metaphor: Therapy

Therapy is akin to sitting on the beach. Counselor and client sitting across from each other or members of a group seated in a circle may ask, "What has arisen from the unconscious today, or what has washed upon the shore or the beach from the unconscious depths?" Frequently, we find that a dream or memory has emerged from ocean depths. Or a trigger has provoked regression, projection, and splitting, as two individuals on the beach find that a sudden storm has blown in from sea and one or both individuals are compulsively caught up in a tense interpersonal pattern of relating.

THE AFTERMATH OF PERSONAL TRAUMA: FIGURE 9.4

The aftermath of personal trauma, which may have been sustained by a child during a dysfunctional parent's midlife crisis, is captured in Figure 9.4. Personal trauma results in fixation points. This personal trauma may range from physical, sexual, or verbal abuse, to exposure to domestic violence, or it may include the forms of neglect, abuse and torture discussed in Chapter 4. The figure shows how fixation points from personal trauma leave clients with a potential for regression, projection, and unconscious acting out of behavioral dramas. Triggers in reality may operate as conditioned cues and evoke sudden regression to a level of the personal unconscious. On the level of the personal unconscious, we find stored the original "footage" of our "movie in the mind," documenting the traumatic scene. Images from this movie are activated when we encounter a trigger and regress to a fixation point. We then project the content of our "movie in the mind" upon the "screen" in reality and try to engender an object in reality, or actor, to play out a drama that is a version of our original traumatic S-O-A. At other times, we may consciously decide to describe the content of our "movie in the mind." Or another group member discussing traumatic memory serves as a trigger that makes us regress to our own fixation point and automatically view our own "movie in the mind."

For example, Figure 9.4 shows how we as counselors may be sitting across from a client, perhaps in an individual or group session, and we may remind a client such as Nancy of her mother. Or, as is common in groups, we will observe how one client reminds another client of their mother. Let's say the client on the right in Figure 9.4 possesses the stimuli of talking loud, being bossy, and having a bad attitude. As a female with an "air of authority about her" the client seated on the right may serve as a trigger who evokes in Nancy, seated in the left chair, a regression. Following the arrow, regression is symbolized by downward movement, or spiraling. Metaphorically, we descend down a spiral staircase to a fixation point. The level of Nancy's personal unconscious is activated as it contains the images captured in the original traumatic S-O-A of a kitchen scene wherein Nancy is beaten by her intoxicated mother (see Chapters 7 and 8).

A transference drama, as a permutation of her original traumatic S-O-A, is reenacted in reality with the female client sitting across from Nancy in group counseling (or with the counselor in an individual or group counseling session). Unconsciously, Nancy may begin to feel the fear, anger, and confusion she felt as a child, and may cognitively expect to "get hit out of the blue." She transfers the feelings she felt toward her mother upon a new female object in reality.

Figure 9.4
The Aftermath of Personal Trauma: Triggers, Regression, Projection, and Splitting.

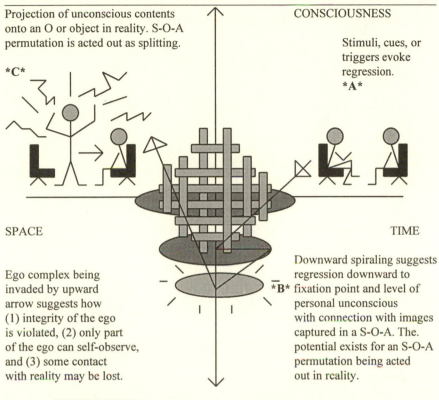

Projection of unconscious contents onto an O or object in reality. S-O-A permutation is acted out as splitting.

C

CONSCIOUSNESS

Stimuli, cues, or triggers evoke regression.
A

SPACE

TIME

Ego complex being invaded by upward arrow suggests how (1) integrity of the ego is violated, (2) only part of the ego can self-observe, and (3) some contact with reality may be lost.

Downward spiraling suggests regression downward to *B* fixation point and level of personal unconscious with connection with images captured in a S-O-A. The. potential exists for an S-O-A permutation being acted out in reality.

UNCONSCIOUS

The figure shows triggers (*A*) in reality evoking regression (downward spiraling to fixation points (*B*), as connection is made with images ("movie in our mind") of an S-O-A. Projection of S-O-A from the personal unconscious occurs on the "movie screen" of current reality and, in particular, involves reenactment of the S-O-A "movie" action with a new actor/object in reality (*C*); this is splitting. A compulsivenes appears as an S-O-A permutation (some variation of scene from movie) is acted out with a new actor/object in reality, based on the original traumatic scene.

As an adult with more strength now, Nancy may defend against her feelings of fear with anger and may decide to attack first, instead of waiting to be attacked or "hit out of the blue." She acts upon "the best defense is a good offense" philosophy. This is one version of her "movie in the mind" which she may project on to the "screen" of reality and reenact with the object/actor in reality, as a drama compulsively enfolds. Nancy may be said to be engaged in splitting, as she compulsively reenacts a behavioral drama derived from the kitchen scene of her physical abuse at the hands of an intoxicated mother.

After having just engaged in a transference drama, a role reversal drama may also unfold. Nancy, having sat for a brief moment looking full of fear and shock, may suddenly rise from her chair and engage in splitting again. Now she enacts a role reversal. In the role reversal permutation of her original trauamtic S-O-A, or in this version of her "movie in the mind" being projected on the "screen" of reality, Nancy now takes the role of her mother—as played in the original "movie," or original traumatic scene. Now, Nancy places the object/actor in reality in the role of victim which she played at age five in the kitchen. Nancy is primed to violently attack the female client sitting across from her in group, as a compulsiveness holds sway in her demeanor.

COMBINING THE INTRODUCTORY, INTERMEDIATE, AND ADVANCED TRAINING WITH THE GRAPHIC MODEL: WHAT DO WE SAY AND DO AS COUNSELORS?

Given this tense moment in group therapy, what do we say and do as counselors? Following the Chapter 4 guidelines for limit setting and managing aggression in groups, I may rise, sit next to Nancy, and firmly hold her wrist. In a clear tone, I give her the psychoeducation she needs to sit down, and violence is not an option. Once Nancy is sitting down, the question is raised, "What just happened here?" Nancy's ego is actively engaged and asked to perform self-observation in the "here and now." This creates an opportunity for Nancy's ego to grow and gain knowledge of Nancy's behavior and to begin to observe splitting. Nancy may be unaware of what just happened in group, perhaps as she now feels fatigued after having been upset, tense, compulsive, and has had her entire body primed to engage in violence. Nancy is informed about what just happened, and psychoeducation is delivered on transference and role reversal dramas. The expectation is created that she needs to observe herself carefully whenever she encounters the trigger of a loud, bossy female, and she is told what to watch out for—compulsiveness, fear, expectation of getting hit, and a willingness to engage in violence.

For purposes of our training as counselors and our clear understanding of the psychoeducation we must deliver to clients such as Nancy, Figure 9.4 shows how the projection (upward spiral and arrow) of unconscious contents violates the integrity and functioning of Nancy's ego. The arrow moving through the ego complex symbolizes how ego functioning is disrupted by the projection of contents from the personal unconscious. We can understand how the ego's judgment of events in reality is temporarily disrupted as an irrational client suddenly becomes angry and aggressive. However, as counselors we also cultivate a part of that ego complex that increasingly gains in the ability to self-observe what happens when the client encounters a trigger. To accomplish this, we as counselors continually point out to clients what we observe happening to them when they encounter a trigger. Eventually, a carefully and systematically cultivated self-observing ego within the client may be able to observe along with us, as counselors, what happens in the presence of a trigger—that is, regression to a fixation point, projection, and splitting with compulsive enactment of a tense interpersonal drama.

THE VOLCANIC ERUPTION METAPHOR AS INTERFERENCE OF EGO FUNCTIONING

We can further clarify this process through a volcanic eruption metaphor. It is as though Nancy's ego with its mountain peak had just had a volcanic eruption of molten lava and ash which just spewed out into reality, making a tense interpersonal mess. Her entire island has shaken violently, and parts of her firmament may have been cracked in the process. During the volcanic eruption, Nancy's ego was interrupted in its functioning of (1) staying focused on reality, (2) observing reality, (3) testing the conditions of reality, and (4) making judgements about what is going on in reality and how to respond. If the ego is akin to a cap on a mountain top, this cap "blew off" or flew to the side during the volcanic eruption. In sum, the ego was not centered, balanced, and intact during the projection of unconscious contents upon a "screen" and object in reality. As a result, the moment of splitting does not typically involve the ego staying focused on reality, observing reality, testing reality, and making judgments in reality. Poor reality testing may lead to an assault that results in an arrest and imprisonment, for example.

After the volcanic eruption and things have calmed down, we engage the shaken, surprised, and fatigued ego, asking "Do you know what just happened?" Nancy may respond, "I exploded, I'm sorry; I don't know what came over me. I just don't like her." In other cases of severe splitting and experiences of severe, multiple trauma, a client may have no memory of what happened. However, in Nancy's case, we may proceed from what she remembers. In other cases, we may have to literally reconstruct what happened for the client.

INVOKING PSYCHOEDUCATION BASED ON GUIDING PRINCIPLES IN THE WORKBOOK

We may ask Nancy, "What is it about her you don't like?" Nancy may respond, "She's bossy and has a nasty attitude!" A few group members may suppress a giggle, as they think that, ironically, this is a perfect description of

Nancy. The counselor asks Nancy, "Does she remind you of anybody?" Nancy answers, "Yeah, my mother! I can't stand that attitude!" And she glares again at the female sitting across from her. I remind Nancy to look at me. As the counselor, I ask Nancy, "Do you remember our very first principle of psychology? Do you remember Principle 1?" Psychoeducation proceeds as we remind Nancy of Principle 1 from the workbook (Chapter 8): "Whenever we dislike something in another, it is really our own problem." Expanding on this principle, I also give Nancy the psychoeducation that "She is your mirror." Other group members may help explain that both women, Nancy and the group member she wanted to attack, are bossy and have bad attitudes. They join in to convince Nancy that this other female client is her "mirror."

Psychoeducation offered by the counselor or preferably by other group members might go on to cover Principle 2 from the workbook (Chapter 8). A group member or the counselor initiates exploration of what both Nancy and the woman she wanted to attack have in common—a bad attitude.

Anger As Crystallized Defense: Combining Psychoeducation and Interpretation

The counselor may explain how an angry, mean, or nasty attitude may be a crystallized defense that becomes a part of our personality style; whenever people see us or interact with us, we have a mean and nasty attitude. A client may be asked about the period when she first became really angry. I am reminded of a client, Ms. F., whose father left home when she was sixteen. Ms. F. became angry and started to present a mean and nasty attitude to the world, shortly thereafter initiating heavy sniffing of cocaine. Ms. F. was offered the interpretation that her "anger was a defense against her pain"; being habitually used, it turned into a personality style.

In this manner, we invoke Principle 2 from our workbook and offer it as psychoeducation: "Our anger (and willingness to confront the disliked other, sometimes with resulting violence) is a defense against our pain." In this vein, Nancy would be offered this principle. An interpretation may be made linking Nancy's anger at having to take care of her mother and sacrifice her childhood to her current personality style of having an angry and nasty attitude.

Turning to our second client who also has a bad attitude, we can offer similar intepretations to her, based on her personal history of trauma. Perhaps she is emulating the mean, nasty attitude of the grandmother who raised her. Similarly, the interpretation may be offered that Nancy also engaged in "identification with the aggressor," taking on the behavior and attitude of her violent and intoxicated mother. Our interpretation is actually combined with the delivery of psychoeducation as we go on to deliver a version of Principle 3 to Nancy, or that part of this principle which applies to learning about violence from physical abuse (versus the first part of Principle 3 covering learning about sex from sexual abuse). Principle 3 follows: "If we have learned to be violent and aggressive, then for the rest of our lives our behavior may reveal what we have learned. As adolescents and adults, we are aggressive and violent with others."

This psychoeducation is directed toward both Nancy and the woman in group she was about to attack. Not surprisingly, both women were physically abused as children, and both learned to be violent and aggressive from women who beat them severely—a mother and a grandmother, respectively. Grimacing, angry faces and nasty provocative verbal abuse characterizes both women, as a common "nasty, mean, and bad attitude" which is the natural accompaniment to their "learning to be violent for the rest of their lives." This psychoeducation may actually serve as a stimulus that begins to trigger regression to each woman's memories of child abuse. The woman who looks the most contemplative, Nancy, is asked, "What are you thinking about?" Nancy states, "How much I hate my mother for what she did to me."

Sleep As the Last Line of Defense: When Is It Time to Work in Group?

Perhaps the second woman begins to compulsively clean her finger nails, or falls asleep; the group material is too much for her at this time, and this second woman self-regulates by using the last line of defense—sleep—which permits the ego to totally tune out and avoid that with which it feels ill-prepared to cope. Sleep protects the client against our provocative group discussion, which could trigger the emergence of her own memories. For months in our work at Damon House, the group leader and master's level counseling students struggled in supervision sessions to understand the meaning of sleep. Was it a sign we had created a holding environment and members felt safe enough to sleep? At what point do we awaken someone? If we view sleep as a defense and view clients as self-regulating through a desensitization hierarchy, then we may properly understand sleeping behavior in group. We must also decide in individual cases when sleep is a habitual defense to which clients resort. At what point do we interpret to clients that they need not utilize sleep as a defense and can now actively cope with triggers in the group?

We may need to convince a client, such as a Ms. P. whom I recall, that she needs to stay awake in group and begin to work on her own issues. Within weeks, Ms. P. was engaged in a full body sob and was working through and integrating the traumatic memories involving the death of two infants and the pending anniversary of the birthday of one infant who died within six months of her birth. Trauma reolution proceeded to address emergent feelings of guilt and unworthiness to nurture a surviving six-year-old daughter.

Compulsive Nail Cleaning in Group as a Defense

At other times we may interpret compulsive nail cleaning as a defense to the client. The reality is that conversation and the comments individuals make in group may serve as triggers for a regression to fixation points. While within a group, the ego may actively defend against a regression. I recall one day in group at Damon House when I asked the group as a whole, "Which two group members are trying harder than anybody else to not pay attention?' After a quick survey they all announced "Ms. K. and Ms. B." I exclaimed, "Don't you know that compulsive nail cleaning is a way to resolve trauma." This joke served to interpret the use of nail cleaning as defensive avoidance, while it was no coincidence that our group discussion was focused on a female who shared in common with our two compulsive nail cleaners three vital attributes: (1) childhood physical abuse, (2) adolescent physical abuse, and (3) adult battering in domestic violence. The woman talking that day provided a group process that was replete with powerful triggers for the two other women who sought refuge in the defense of compulsive nail cleaning.

USING A COMBINATION OF SEVERAL COUNSELING TECHNIQUES AND MOVING FROM PHASE TO PHASE IN GROUP WORK

A combination of several counseling techniques may be deployed in rapid succession within groups. For example, returning to the case of Nancy, the counselor first briefly reiterates the psychoeducation that "Anger is a defense against our pain." An interpretation is then offered that "Although you are feeling anger and hate for your mother, could it be that a part of your self is really in a lot of pain? I think both of you have little girls inside who are terrified and full of hurt and pain." The question is asked, "What do you think about that?" With eyes averted, both women may mumble "Yes, that's true."

Demonstration of Empathic Mirroring and Affect Labeling

Empathic mirroring may be used as the counselor or other group members hold up a mirror and reflect back to each woman, (or the one working the hardest, experiencing the most inside, or the one awake), stating as follows: "I can feel the pain you have inside. There is some shame and a lot of fear. The little girl inside is terrifed and feeling really bad about herself." Through the delivery of empathic mirroring, affect labeling has been implicit. Affects of pain and shame have been labeled. Checking to see if this affect labeling and empathic mirroring constitute "hitting the nail on the head" (see Chapter 6), the counselor asks, "Is that true, do you feel some shame? What are you feeling inside?" The counselor has used the averted eyes as a cue that shame was triggered within Nancy. In response, Nancy offers: "Yes. My mother made me feel like I could never do anything right, like I was the worse thing on the planet. She made me feel horrible about myself. She took away all my self-esteem. I used to be such a happy little girl. My father always told me I was pretty; then she drove him away and I was stuck with a drunk."

The client begins to engage in observation of her inner self experience, self-observing and comparing it to the material empathically mirrored to her. In addition, she enters into phase II work, moving from the phase I work of psychoeducation, and articulates in phase II some part of her trauma. This movement from phase I to phase II work and back to phase I again is very common in the group process. The ego grows stronger from psychoeducation on Principles 1–3; the ego gains knowledge about its own functioning, and the seeds are sown for the ego acquiring better self-regulation of affects, impulses, self-esteem, and interpersonal behavior.

Returning to the Use of Psychoeducation for Cognitive Restructuring

The counselor may also reiterate psychoeducation on how no child should have to survive the conditions Nancy was thrust into. The part of herself full of feelings of shame is told, "You are special and deserve to be treated like you are special. You deserve to be loved and made to feel the way your father did." This is an attempt to repair the self and replace some of the bad feelings about the self with positive feelings. Cognitive restructuring is also implicit in replacing the cognition,"I am bad and deserved to be treated badly by my mother," with the cognition that "I am good and special and deserve to be treated well by others." Counseling work involves deployment of a combination of counseling techniques in rapid succession and sometimes in merged combinations, as just illustrated. In addition, group work moves back and forth from phase I to phase II, for example, as well as from phase III or IV back to phase I. It may be critical to deliver phase I psychoeducation at any point in the group process within the four-phase model.

HOW DOES FOUR-PHASE GROUP THERAPY IMPROVE SELF-REGULATION, REMEDIATE UNDERLYING PSYCHOPATHOLOGY, AND BREAK THE CYCLE OF RELAPSE/REGRESSION?

Chapter 7 suggested that training in the model of trauma resolution permits counselors to remediate underlying psychopathology by focusing on improving client self-regulation, thereby breaking the cycle of regression, relapse, and symptom substitution. This section answers the question as to how four-phase group therapy permits counselors to accomplish this goal.

ACCOMPLISHING ENHANCED SELF-REGULATION OF AFFECTS

To promote better regulation of affects, the counselor and group members have helped, and will continue to help, Nancy label her affects whenever she has a moment of sudden emergence of anger, shame, or sadness. Group members and the counselor will use empathic mirroring and reflect back to Nancy what they have—through empathic attunement—sensed to be Nancy's inner self-experience of felt affect. As a result, Nancy will gain in the ability to identify, label, and process affects, improving her overall affect regulation. Self-observation of inner states of feeling will improve for Nancy. Group members receive feedback from Nancy as to whether they "have hit the nail on the head" with their attempts at affect labeling and empathic mirroring. Nancy goes on to elaborate on her feelings. This serves to increase the chance that Nancy will verbally process affects and better regulate affects outside of the group.

ACCOMPLISHING ENHANCED SELF-REGULATION OF IMPULSES

Improved self-regulation of impulses follows from Nancy's experience of being stopped, or interrupted, when she is in the middle of splitting. The acting out of aggressive impulses would be characteristic of a moment of splitting. Nancy is primed for attack by others, or she engages in a role reversal and seeks to attack violently. When the counselor rises, crosses the room, sits next to Nancy, and places her hand firmly on Nancy's wrist, calls her name, tells her to sit down, and reminds her that violence is not an option, splitting is being interrupted. When the counselor thereby "grabs the attention of Nancy's ego" and forces it to observe what "just happened," new learning is occurring for the ego. What was in the past a routine, automatic, unconscious conditioned response to a trigger—followed by regression to a fixation point with resultant projection and splitting—is now a newly observed "happening" worthy of close attention and future observation by Nancy's ego. Psychoeducation serves to strengthen the ego, as the ego is given a blueprint and guide for the future negotiation of this "happening" or moment of splitting. The ego is given psychoeducation on triggers of regression (women generally, and loud, bossy women with bad attitudes).

Whenever such stimuli are encountered, the ego is given psychoeducation on what to do. Within this blueprint and guide for effective coping, thought-stopping may be taught to the ego, as the ego learns to interrupt thoughts of "I can't stand her attitude." The following positive self-talk may then be delivered by the ego as cognitive coping with triggers that threaten to provoke regression, projection, and splitting: "Walk away. Violence is not an option. She is just a trigger for me because she reminds me of my mother. She is my mirror, reminding me of what I need to work on. Don't let her provoke you to violence. Just walk away." If Nancy repeats these thoughts to herself, this may constitute effective cognitive coping that enhances her self-regulation of aggressive impulses. This cognitive coping improves the self-regulation of impulses, for violence is no longer enacted with the unleashing of aggressive impulses during splitting and reenactment of permutations of the original traumatic S-O-A.

ACCOMPLISHING ENHANCED REGULATION OF SELF-ESTEEM

Self-esteem regulation is also improved as Nancy learns about moments when her inner self is full of feelings of shame—as during moments when affect labeling and empathic mirroring by group members and the counselor occur in group. Nancy can now generalize this new learning and ability to self-observe feelings of shame arising within her self to situations outside of the group.

She may learn about the kind of triggers that evoke feelings of shame or a plummet in self-esteem. Such triggers may involve receipt of criticism from a woman or someone merely talking to her in a loud voice. Feelings of shame may trigger the defensive use of anger and splitting in which she performs a role reversal permutation of her original traumatic S-O-A.

Nancy may learn to deliver self-talk to cope at such moments of being triggered by a stimulus or cue that leads to a plummet in self-esteem and the emergence of states of shame. She may then generalize the delivery of positive self-talk to all situations when she is triggered. This generalization may be based on the role modeled use in group of the counselor's statement to her, now delivered in this form to herself: "I am special and deserve to be treated well by others." Nancy may also use thought-stopping if cognitions arise that "I am bad and deserve to be treated badly," again using some form of positive self-talk, such as the following examples: "I AM A GOOD PERSON, I AM GROWING EVERY DAY IN EVERY WAY;" or, using Principle 7 (see Chapter 8), "I AM THAT I AM, I AM ONE WITH MY HIGHER POWER."

Ultimately, however, shame as a source of low self-esteem may only be thoroughly resolved, and self-regulation of self-esteem completely improved, through trauma resolution work in phase IV.

ACCOMPLISHING ENHANCED SELF-REGULATION OF INTERPERSONAL BEHAVIOR

Enhanced regulation of interpersonal behavior follows from enhanced control of impulses. The ego gains in the ability to observe and stop moments of splitting, and self-talk is used to guide the ego to perform new alternative behaviors to violence, such as walking away. The "here and now" analysis of permutations of the original traumatic S-O-A and of moments of splitting considerably improves self-regulation of interpersonal behavior within the group. This new ability is generalized outside of group to other interpersonal interactions.

Fixation points for regression and the potential for projection and splitting still exist, however. Trauma resolution can "erase the fixation point." This trauma resolution involves the working through and integration of traumatic memories. Although Nancy started to talk briefly about hating her mother for what her mother did to Nancy and for driving the father away, group work has involved mostly psychoeducation thus far in phase I, with brief articulation of trauma in phase II. The entire group membership needs to move on to phase II and to engage in articulation of trauma. Group members also need to gain more practice systematically observing and interrupting members' enactment of S-O-A permutations in the "here and now" within phase III work. This is necessary before movement can be made toward working through and integrating traumatic memories in phase IV. As group members receive psychoeducation in phase I work, hear each other take turns articulating memories of trauma in phase II work, and watch the group process repeatedly invaded in the "here and now" with dramas that are permutations of original traumatic S-O-As in phase III work, every group member is developing a stronger ego. A strengthened ego is capable of good self-observation. Several months of moving back and forth between the delivery of some new psychoeducation or reiteration of previously delivered material faciliate the strengthening of the ego and it's capacity to self observe. Gradually, clients are becoming more and more proficient with self-regulation of affects, impulses, self-esteem, and interpersonal behavior through delivery of counseling interventions of affect labeling, empathic mirroring, cognitive reframing, and interpretation. The groundwork is being laid for an effective working through and integration of traumatic memories.

ACCOMPLISHING TRAUMA RESOLUTION: DESCENT DOWN THE SPIRAL STAIRS METAPHOR

Because of the group work accomplished in the early months of counseling, the group can begin the phase IV task of working through and integrating traumatic memories after month seven—with the "timing of this work" varying by individual and within different groups. After all, some group members have been sleeping, compulsively cleaning nails, and responding at different rates to invitations to surrender these defenses for more active group participation. However, we recall our caution in Chapter 6 that no one be urged to "go to the movies" before they feel ready to engage in trauma resolution work. Other group members experience constant invasion of the "movie in their mind" into consciousness and engage in this work before month seven arrives, following the clarification provided by Young (1990, 1995). Table 9.2 suggests the correct timing of trauma resolution work, recognizing individual variability in readiness for this task, and considering the phases of recovery for the chemically dependent described by Wallace (1991, 1992).

Thus far, Nancy is working hard in group and may emerge with a sufficiently strengthened ego and capacity for self-observation that she becomes a candidate for trauma resolution by month seven in group. Her improved self-regulation of affects, impulses, self-esteem, and interpersonal behavior also support moving on to this next phase of work. Once engaged in the work of trauma resolution, this involves a therapeutically guided regression to the level of the fixation point in the personal unconscious. We need to descend down a spiral flight of stairs, and go to the step where a part of us is stuck or fixated—still lying crumpled and beaten down on step 4, for example.

Clients are also assisted in expressing the powerful and painful affects felt at the moment of trauma, while their egos are supported and the ego of an individual remains focused in reality. After the successful integration and working through of a traumatic memory, the client is also helped to "close up," as we use humor (see Chapter 6) to close up clients, instead of leaving them open. This involves effectively redirecting the ego to refocus on something else in reality that is silly, gross, or ridiculous. This diversion creates a gentle transition away from the serious and fatiguing work of trauma resolution.

USE OF AN INTEGRATED, MULTIFACETED COUNSELING TECHNIQUE: THE KEY TO ACCOMPLISHING TREATMENT GOALS

Some counselors would question whether a client like Nancy could handle the work of trauma resolution by month seven in group therapy. Is her self-regulation really that improved? Is she really ready for insight-oriented work? What about provoking a relapse to substance abuse? Why not leave that material alone, letting it stay in the unconscious? As a partial answer, we can only engage in a therapeutically guided regression in the service of Nancy's self-observing ego because of the treatment systematically delivered (see Table 9.2) across the phases of recovery Nancy has negotiated; regression to her fixation point is actually "well-timed."

Table 9.2
Guidelines for the Delivery of Treatment Interventions across Phases of Recovery.

PHASE OF RECOVERY	TIME IN TREATMENT	TREATMENT DELIVERED
PHASE I: WITHDRAWAL from chemicals, or early initial efforts to change a problem behavior. First contact with treatment is made. Engagement into treatment process occurs.	WEEKS ONE TO TWO	• Begin to use psychoedu- cation to strengthen ego, to teach self-observation, and prepare to cope with cues, triggers (stimuli at *A* in Figure 9.4) that could evoke regression (to*B* in Figure 9.4) or a relapse. • Assess client for traumas in order to identify likely triggers and S-O-A permu- tions to be projected and enacted (*C* in Figure 9.4).
PHASE II: PROLONGING ABSTINENCE from chemicals, or period for learning how to change and sustain behavioral change.	WEEK THREE TO MONTH SIX	• Ego should learn, practice, and master self-observation during this period. Client is assisted in interrupting the process of being triggered in group and reality by cues and stimuli (*A*) that lead to regression (to *B*) and relapse. • Client achieves ability to stop their conditioned re- sponses to cues for re- gression and relapse. • Client learns and practices alternative coping re- sponses (behavioral, affective, and cognitive).
PHASE III: PURSUING LIFETIME RECOVERY from chemical dependency, and other problem behaviors. Period for learning how to maintain behavioral change.	MONTH SEVEN ONWARD (Greatest support needed in the first twenty-four months.) Some may begin trauma resolution work as early as month three or before.	• Establishment of a strong self-observing ego permits a therapeutically guided re- gression to fixation points (*C*) and resolution of trauma. • Clients describe the "movie in their mind" and process affects without jumping in the movie or "acting it out."

In addition, an integrated, multifaceted counseling technique (Wallace, 1991) helps to accelerate the course of treatment. This permits improved coping skills and rapid stabilization of recovering chemically dependent and other clients presenting a range of symptoms and problem behaviors.

This counseling technique combines the use of psychoeducation, psychoanalytic, cognitive-behavioral, and metaphorical interventions. A primary purpose of treatment utilizing such a counseling technique is to teach clients to better regulate their affects, impulses, self-esteem, and interpersonal behavior. Fixation points are removed, and the risk of regression, relapse, and symptom substitution is diminished or eliminated.

The Use of Psychoanalytic and Behavioral Counseling Techniques

The forging of integrated theory results in the use of integrated counseling techniques that include elements of the psychoanalytic and behavioral. Meanwhile, many moments in which the counselor achieves empathy with a client's inner self-experience and mirrors back to the client the nature of that affective or other experience systematically improves a client's affect regulation and improves self-observation of internal states. The use of empathy and mirroring facilitates the growth and development of the client's self from that point of arrest or fixation that has existed ever since the moment of significant trauma.

Empathy Produces New Conditioning to Counter the Ego's Phobia

Empathic mirroring of the client's inner self-experience helps the counselor become an object of the client's positive feeling. A kind of new behavioral conditioning can also be seen as occurring. Through the counselor's genuine empathy, the client learns that indeed some human interactions can be free of anger, fear, and anxiety and that it is possible to relate to a human object without a phobic response. A new response to human objects becomes possible, which may replace past conditioning of a phobic, anxious response to the class of stimuli of human male or female objects. The extinction of past phobic responses may thereby occur. Such moments of empathy and mirroring, as conceptualized psychoanalytically, become important counseling tools in a model of trauma resolution. The ego may thereby overcome its conditioned phobias from the experience of observing events at the moment of trauma.

Treatment As Moving Clients through a Desensitization Hierarchy

Using behavioral theory, we can also conceptualize moments of interaction with a counselor, or with members of a therapy group within a desensitization hierarchy. A client may move from initial flooding with a phobic human object as the client sits in sessions, to gradual desensitization to phobic human objects. The use of ego defenses may protect clients from overwhelming emotions and impulses triggered in response to a phobic human object. The selective use of ego defenses may permit clients to move through a desensitization hierarchy as they gradually feel affects, or impulses, or permit interpersonal interaction with which they feel comfortable. Eventually, clients interact interpersonally with the counselor and with other group members without the use of ego defenses, thereby acquiring new learning within a therapeutic milieu regarding human objects, affects, and impulses. Clients resort to neither sleep nor compulsive nail cleaning.

Ironically, clients with characteristically poor self-regulation are able to utilize defenses selectively and automatically in group psychotherapy to self-regulate through a desensitization hierarchy. Clients either fall asleep, split off, compulsively clean their finger nails as a distraction, or otherwise "tune out" when stimuli might trigger an affect, impulse, or interpersonal behavioral reaction with which they are not as yet prepared to deal. Consistent with a desensitization hierarchy, the ego gradually tolerates exposure to less toxic stimuli of affects, impulses, or interpersonal interaction, progressing systematically to exposure to more and more difficult stimuli. When no trauma occurs with a human object of the counselor or another group member, and the ego successfully copes with affects, impulses, and phobic objects, this interpersonal experience provides opportunities for moving through a desensitization hierarchy. Again, moments of flooding may still occur when the ego is caught off guard and defenses are not deployed, providing other opportunities for new learning with once feared human objects. Herein lies the power and utility of both empathic and interpersonal interactions as they occur in individual and group sessions.

Using a Cognitive-Psychoanalytic Technique: Interpretation and Psychoeducation

Interpretation and psychoeducation may permit clients to understand the power of their cognitive expectations and the power of learning and conditioning at the moment of trauma. The combined use of these two tools goes even further than the use of either one alone. Interpretation can produce sudden insight in the ego which sees in the "here and now" something pointed out as occurring by the counselor. However, with the use of psychoeducation we tell the ego why it occurred, what it means or signifies, how it is related to past trauma, and we give the ego a sense of control. We do not foster dependency in clients because we empower the clients' ego to engage in self-observation and self-analysis and to be able to eventually interpret their own behavior.

Psychoeducation essentially gives clients' egos a blueprint so that they can figure out their own psychological and behavioral functioning. The seven Principles in the workbook (see Chapter 8) may permit self-help and self-analysis consistent with an empowerment model.

With psychoeducation and increased knowledge, the ego gains a sense of control. We can think of the ego as a "control freak." We give the ego a sense of control by giving it a map and teaching it how to get around the territory of reality. The ego is delighted to be given information that increases its sense of control and takes away fear. The ego uses the map to feel that it knows "where it is, where it has been, what is going on in the present, and where it is going." The ego gets stronger and stronger and achieves more self-control, as a result of psychoeducation exponentially increasing the benefits of psychoanalytic interpretation. Compared to traditional psychoanalytic or psychodynamic treatment, this may produce a shorter treatment because of the extensive provision of psychoeducation that empowers clients' egos.

Producing a More Comfortable Treatment Experience for Clients

How many professionals can recall their own therapy where they had been gently encouraged one day to "talk about what happened"? The next thing they knew they had regressed to a traumatic scene, were sobbing, talking about the trauma, and then "time was up"; they felt drained and left the session thinking, "Boy, I had no idea that would happen today, or would ever happen. What did just happen?" As they left the session, the psychoanalyst silently nodded her head. How much better if the ego had the following kind of information in advance:

We are preparing for the day that you describe that movie in your mind of your trauma. You will describe it when you are ready. I will use my voice and ask you what you see. I will remind you to tell me what you see in the "movie in your mind." The goal is to "work it out" and integrate the memory, and not to "act it out." This means don't jump in the movie and become an actor reliving the scene in the movie. Instead, just describe what you see in the movie and allow youself to feel what you felt at the moment of trauma. Okay?"

The ego has a guide that enables it to retain a sense of control. The ego is given assurances that it will be assisted in maintaining a sense of safety and control when it tries to look at what is feared and dreaded—the movie of their trauma. The map tells the ego "where they have been, where they are, and where the are going" in terms of trauma resolution. To use a cognitive-psychoanalytic technique that relies heavily on the use of psychoeducation has advantages. But, again, it is truly a technique based in the integration of cognitive, psycho-analytic, and behavioral theory, because we are preparing clients to go through another step of their desensitization hierarchy when they watch and describe their feared movie in the mind.

Short-Term Treatment for Trauma Resolution: Therapeutic Breakthrough

Because of the use of a multifaceted counseling technique, it may not be necessary for clients to work through and integrate literally every major trauma they have experienced. Many clients have experienced multiple and chronic trauma, as in the case of Ms. E. A substantially strengthened ego may find that even with the working through and integration of just one or two major traumas, substantial improvements in overall functioning are occurring so that a goal of working through and integrating perhaps every major traumatic experience may be modified. Resolution of trauma and a therapeutic regression to fixation points reduce the risk of acting out behavior with splitting—as an undesirable regression to fixation points. Substantial stabilization of client functioning results. Evidence of substantial improvements in self-regulation and overall functioning within as short a period of time as just three to six months may justify use of an integrated counseling technique, combining cognitive, behavioral, psychoanalytic, psychoeducational, and metaphorical elements. This short-term model of treatment for trauma resolution and improved client self-regulation may permit a therapeutic breakthrough, in work with challenging clients presenting past histories of multiple and chronic trauma.

MICROANALYSIS OF SLIPS/RELAPSES: BREAKING THE CYCLE OF RELAPSE, REGRESSION, AND SYMPTOM SUBSTITUTION

The chemically dependent and diverse adult children with a range of symptoms and problem behaviors present a common cycle of regression, relapse and symptom substitution which counselors seek to break. A slip or relapse to literally any problem behavior, including a defensive stance, should be viewed as an opportunity to learn. This learning covers determinants of that relapse and permits structuring active coping strategies for that high-risk situation (see Chapter 6). The graphic model permits us to visualize triggers of a regression or relapse, enhancing our training as we extend relapse prevention to a consideration of idiosyncratic triggers of a regression to acting out behavior of role reversals and transference dramas. Coping strategies for encounters with idiosyncratic triggers can be developed. A microanalysis of slips and relapses (see Chapter 10) is deployed to discover determinants of the slip or relapse (Marlatt & Gordon, 1985; Wallace, 1991). Clients who learn from past relapses and can identify the triggers and cues that may lead to a relapse or regression to a fixation point, or enactment of dramas rooted in past trauma, possess knowledge of idiosyncratic triggers for which a plan of action is also developed for future coping with such triggers in order to avoid a negative outcome. The graphic model permits us to analyze cues, stimuli and triggers (our point *A* in Figure 9.4) that lead to a regression to fixation points (our point *B* in Figure 9.4). Mobilizing an internal state of shame may make one vulnerable to the defense of splitting or performance of some other compulsive behavior as symptom substitution. The model permits us to bring a fresh perspective to relapse, regression, and compulsive symptom substitution, for external triggers may provoke activation of internal contents that then call for the use of defensive strategies such as projection (our point *C* in Figure 9.4) and splitting.

Relapse to chemical use remains likely when clients with substantial histories of trauma do not learn how to improve self-regulation and resort to chemicals for defensive purposes. An external trigger that activates an S-O-A and attached state of shame may now involve an internal trigger (shame) that needs to be addressed to prevent relapse. Given this analysis, resolving the trauma and addressing the cause of states of shame emerge as necessary forms of relapse prevention.

In other words, without remediation of the underlying psychopathology or improvement in self-regulation, past traumas that may have a relationship to the development and maintenance of an addiction or any compulsive and destructive problem behavior can continue to determine chemical use, relapse, regression, and symptom substitution. Instead, resolution of trauma can end cyclic regression, relapse, and symptom substitution.

ENSURING DEPLOYMENT OF A CULTURALLY SENSITIVE COUNSELING TECHNIQUE

The graphic model introduced in this chapter also permits us to expand on the basic training for cultural competence presented in Chapter 3. Figure 9.5 depicts the process of responding to stimuli, cues, and triggers (skin color, a last name, physical traits) that evoke a sudden regression to our performance of culturally learned patterns of behavior. Our possession of conditioned cognitions, health beliefs on violence, myths, stereotypes, and misinformation permits us to have conditioned responses to overt stimuli. We in effect emerge as nativistic and xenophobic, as discussed in Chapter 3.

Using the graphic model of our dynamic psyches, we can also visualize a hypothetical regression to a level of the unconscious containing Jung's (1969b) shadow, or our "bad parts." Our "bad parts" represent what we do not like about ourselves or have separated during acts of splitting from the "good" aspects of ourselves.

Figure 9.5
The Aftermath of Cultural Conditioning: Triggers, Regression, Projection of Stereotypes, and Tense Dramas.

Projection of unconscious contents and bad parts onto a "different other" in reality. Conditioned stereotypes and negative and low expectations create a tense interaction, as a culturally learned S-O-A is enacted.
C

CONSCIOUSNESS

Stimuli, cues, and triggers may evoke a sudden regression.
A

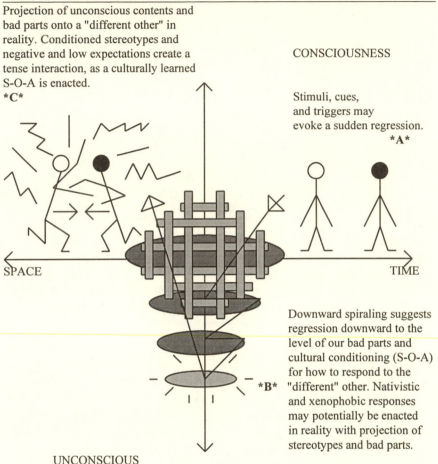

SPACE

TIME

Downward spiraling suggests regression downward to the level of our bad parts and cultural conditioning (S-O-A) for how to respond to the "different" other. Nativistic and xenophobic responses may potentially be enacted in reality with projection of stereotypes and bad parts.

B

UNCONSCIOUS

The figure suggests how cultural conditioning by parents, the media, and throughout our culture of violence conditions our selves (S) to act, project images and expectations upon the "different other" (O), and feel fear and hate (A)—comprising a cultural S-O-A. Triggers (at point *A*—skin color, etc.) cause us to regress to the level of our bad parts (point *B*) and cultural conditioning for how to respond to a "different other." We project stereotypes upon an O in reality (at point *C*), as a tense drama unfolds with potential violence. The arrows emanating from each actor (at point *C*) suggests how each projects a mythic image upon the other when a cultural S-O-A is enacted.

When we project our "bad parts" upon a "different other," we also reveal our history of social conditioning in nativistic and xenophobic responses within this country. Objects in reality may receive our projection of our "bad parts," and we may compulsively enact tense interpersonal dramas. The compulsiveness suggests that we are engaging in splitting, in which our "bad parts," once split off, now spuriously appear as an autonomous feeling-toned complex. The autonomous complex has a feeling tone of hate, while aggression may also be mobilized. Or a culturally learned S-O-A may be said to have been mobilized, which is characterized by affects of hate and the direction of aggression against a disdained "different other."

As counselors, our ethical standard requires that we do not engage in projection of our "bad parts" or reveal our social conditioning within the United States into nativist and xenophobic traditions. Instead of committing covert violence and doing harm to clients, we must ensure that we use thought-stopping and self-observation to avoid being triggered in such a manner that processes of regression and projection transpire with clients. The graphic model of the mind enhances our training by permitting visualization of processes discussed in Chapter 3.

IMPLICATIONS OF THE MODEL FOR HUMAN DEVELOPMENT

The model can also be used to depict progressive development in consciousness, as suggested earlier in Figure 9.1. We can positively depict how our collective counseling interventions produce an ego that is fundamentaly strengthened and can engage in self-observation, as ego functions have come to include good judgment, reality testing, delay of impulses, and the ability to stop problematic affects, behaviors, and cognitions. As a fundamentally strengthened ego, we have systematically built up a larger ego mass which has formed into a large solid island with a strong mountain, as suggested in Figure 9.6.

In addition, the graphic model of the mind also illustrates potentially higher levels of consciousness which may be reached. Metaphorically, it is as if individuals ascend a crystal set of stairs through active pursuit of their higher human potential. Reaching one's highest potential in human development follows as the result of practicing active connection with one's higher power through twelve-step group (Alcoholics Anonymous, etc.) participation or rigorously following the twelve steps. Or, the active practice of prayer, meditation, deep breathing, repeating positive affirmations, decreeing, and chanting may result in the achievment of higher levels of consciousness.

We may also follow Jung (1969a) and consider the process of *individuation* and establishment of a "*Self*" which becomes the center of the psyche. The process of individuation involves achieving healing, wholeness, and balance.

Figure 9.6
Movement Toward Unity with Our Higher Power: Progressive Development in Human Consciousness.

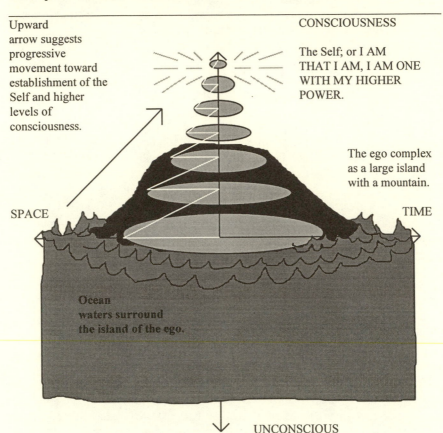

Upward arrow suggests progressive movement toward establishment of the Self and higher levels of consciousness.

CONSCIOUSNESS

The Self; or I AM THAT I AM, I AM ONE WITH MY HIGHER POWER.

The ego complex as a large island with a mountain.

SPACE

TIME

Ocean waters surround the island of the ego.

UNCONSCIOUS

The figure suggests how our counseling interventions produce a strengthened ego with good self-observation and ability to perform ego functions of reality testing, judgement, delay of impulses, and ability to stop affects, behaviors and conditions. This is akin to the first three steps of the upward spiral which produce a large island mass with a mountain surrounded by the waters of the unconscious. The next four steps steps of the upward spiral are potentially higher levels of consciousness which we may apsire to reach. The upward arrow suggests movement toward these higher levels. In this manner, the figure depicts progressive development in consciousness toward achievement of our highest human potential. The Self is established as the center of the psyche, as Jung's (1969a) process of individuation produces a new centered, balanced, whole, non-narcissistic center of the personality. Following a central twelve-step program dictum, the Self permits following the will of a higher power.

Individuation follows from the hard work of integrating unconscious contents into consciousness and developing a Self which is free from the imbalance and one-sidedness characteristic of the ego—with its preoccupation with control. Unlike the false narcissism and one-sidedness characteristic of the ego which has a need to rule supreme, the Self is a creation reflecting a genuine expansion in consciousness and attainment of a state of being centered, balanced, and whole. The Self rests at the center of the psyche, and permits attaining the twelve-step program goal of following the will of a higher power, versus the narcissistic schemes of the ego. The Self may come to replace the narcissistic ego as our guide to action in reality. See Figure 9.6.

CONCLUSION

This chapter answers the following question: "What modifications in assessment, theoretical conceptualization, and counseling technique are recommended in group counseling in order to improve treatment efficacy and outcome with clients who present histories of trauma?" The four-phase group model permits the achievement of goals of client stabilization and effective coping in the real world wherein clients can successfully pursue "love and work"—without regression to fixation points, relapse, or symptom substitution with other compulsive and destructive behaviors.

The goal of remediation of psychopathology focused on the specific areas of poor self-regulation of affects, impulses, self-esteem, and interpersonal behavior, as four phases of group work were pursued. The four phases of group work covered are (1) psychoeducation, (2) articulation of trauma, (3) "here and now" analysis of S-O-A permutations, and (4) working through and integration of trauma. A focus on specific areas of poor self-regulation and on trauma resolution may enable counselors to expedite improvements in functioning within a short-term model of psychotherapy, even with once a week group meetings. Key modifications of a psychoanalytic technique, and in particular the use of the recommended multifaceted counseling technique, may produce improvements in self-regulation within six to nine months. Improvements in functioning and the quality of life continue when treatment extends into a longer period. Clearly, individual differences and needs must be acknowledged, which may alter the nature and course of trauma resolution work.

Only a long-term investigation and follow up of clients can determine whether or not this model provides for more effective recovery, fewer relapses, and less evidence of symptom substitution than is found with a control group and comparison to other group counseling models. In terms of addressing the trauma rampant in the lives of our clients, we have gained greater clarity regarding the question, "Where do we need to go, and how do we get there?"

10

Trauma of Domestic Violence: A Treatment Model for the Battered, the Couple, and the Batterer

Carden (1994) asserts that violence is a culturally transmitted "disease" of epidemic proportions in our nation and that domestic violence is one of its most insidious expressions (p. 539). In addition, Carden presents summary statistics suggesting that violent crimes occur more frequently within families than among strangers, cutting across every race, religion, social class, and educational level. A figure published in 1988 is likely an underestimate, but it suggested that 1.8 million were victims of spousal abuse annually. The FBI estimates that every 15 to 18 seconds in this country a woman is beaten; consistent with this statistic, Worcester (1992) reports that many women identify violence and fear of violence as the number one health issue they face. A wide range of chronic health problems result from domestic violence, including headaches, backaches, sleep disorders, anxiety, abdominal complaints, eating disorders, depression, and chronic pain. This list suggests how both physical and psychological injuries result from violence (Worcester, 1992). Other statistics show that a woman is more likely to be physically assaulted, raped, or murdered by a current or former male partner than by any other assailant, and over 50 percent of all female murders are perpetrated by a spouse compared to 12 percent of male murders being spouse perpetrated. Wife abuse may lead to miscarriage, abortion, drug and alcohol abuse, attempted suicide, physical disfigurement or disability, cognitive distortions, chronic depression, anxiety, and low self-esteem. Many women meet the criteria for post-traumatic stress disorder (Carden, 1994). In effect, the domestic violence epidemic means that women are being subjected to a physical and psychological health crisis. This chapter responds to the crisis with a model of treatment for the battered, the couple, and the batterer.

HISTORICAL AND CONTEMPORARY APPROACHES TO THE CRISIS OF DOMESTIC VIOLENCE

The battered women's movement began in England in 1972 with the establishment of the first shelter for abused wives, Chiswick Women's Aid. A second shelter opened in Holland in 1974. Moving beyond Europe, a grassroots movement sprang up in the United States with demands for shelters and substantial change in the treatment of abused wives. The Women's Advocates in Minnesota opened in 1972, followed by Transition House in Boston in 1974 and Women Together in Cleveland in 1976 (Carden, 1994; Pagelow, 1992). There are approximately 2,000 shelters, transitional houses, and community programs for battered women and their children in the 3,200 counties of the United States (Carden, 1994, p. 546). Meanwhile, seventeen states have passed mandatory arrest laws for spousal abuse, and many other states have enacted pro-arrest or preferred arrest guidelines for police intervention in domestic violence incidents (Carden, 1994).

As this short history suggests, programs for abused women are a relatively new addition to the social services arena; advocates for women, and local, statewide, and national coalitions have played a key role in lobbying for legal protections and public funds to support the network of services for abused women (Davis, Hagen, & Early, 1994). Abused-women coalitions exist in all fifty states, with two in California and one in the District of Columbia. These coalitions exist to empower abused women and were surveyed in July 1989, with thirty-eight state agencies and twenty-one state coalitions responding. The survey identified (1) major service inadequacies in shelter services for abused women in rural areas, (2) inadequacies in services to nonsheltered abused women, and (3) inadequacies in shelter services for abused women in general (p. 700).

UNDERSTANDING THE MULTIFACETED AND DYNAMIC NATURE OF DOMESTIC VIOLENCE

Carden (1994) states that seventeen "years after the founding of the first program designed to eliminate wife abuse by working with the wife abuser, we have only the most primitive notions about what works, why and how it works, or whether, in the long run, it does work" (p. 573). Carden (1994) summarizes what we do know about the multifaceted problem of wife abuse.

Types of Wife Abuse

Wife abuse may include physical violence, sexual violence, property violence (destroying objects, walls, doors, or throwing objects), and psychological violence (isolation, humiliation, demeaning, controlling). Carden (1994) also cites the contributions of Pence and Paymar (1986) who describe violence in an educational curriculum as involving the use of the following: intimidation (fear created by looks, gestures, displaying weapons); emotional abuse (putdowns, name calling, making her think she is crazy, humiliating her, making her feel guilty); isolation (control what she does, who she sees, what she reads, where she goes, using jealousy to justify the control); minimizing, denial, and blaming (make light of the abuse, don't take her concerns seriously, saying the abuse did not happen, saying she caused the abuse); using children (making her feel guilty about the children, using children to relay messages, using visitation to harass her, threatening to take the children away; using male privilege (treating her like a servant, making all the big decisions, acting like the master of the castle, being the one to define men and women's roles): using economic abuse (preventing her from getting or keeping a job, making her ask for money, giving her an allowance, taking her money, not letting her know about or have access to family income); and using coercion and threats (making or carrying out threats to hurt her, threatening to leave her, threatening to commit suicide, threatening to report her to welfare, making her drop charges, making her do illegal drugs).

The Cycle of Violence

Vital to a dynamic understanding of violence is the work of Walker (1979) on the cycle of violence, which Carden (1994) also recognizes. This cycle begins with a Tension Building Phase in which the woman denies the impending violence. During this first phase, the male increases his threats of violence, pushing and shoving may start, and the wife tries to increasingly please and calm down the abuser—useless efforts that only postpone the violence. The second phase involves the Act of Violence. In this phase, acutal violence erupts, involving hits, slaps, choking, beatings with fists, sexual abuse, and use of weapons (guns, knives, belts) and the woman denies her partner's responsibility for what is happening. In the third phase, the Honeymoon, the abuser apologizes, perhaps excessively, expresses guilt and shame, promises the violence will not happen again, often buys her gifts, minimizes the violence or blames it on the woman, and suggests the violence never would have happened had she not made a comment or done something that made him angry. The woman now denies the severity of the abuse she suffered and denies the reality of future abuse.

Following Shengold (1989), we can also see how denial of this type involves serious cognitive distortions and reveals a powerful brainwashing process that occurs. Carden (1994) points out that Walker's (1979) work has been educationally and clinically useful over the past fifteen years, but that we must remember that many different patterns may appear.

In recognition of a cycle or phases that may be decipherable, Worcester (1992) explains that the battering incident seldom comes from "nowhere," but is the expected "explosion" from a protracted period of increasing tensions. Some women report that "waiting for the straw which will provoke the battering, as so awful that some women remember when even a severe battering was a welcome 'release' from the unbearable tension" (p. 285). Worcester (1992) notes that in the early years of an abusive relationship the battering is almost always followed immediately by the "honeymoon" stage wherein abusers and the women think the abuser means it when he says it will never happen again. Worcester (1992) identifies the emergency service provider as being able to intervene immediately after the battering and before the honeymoon stage. This "is a key time to make sure the woman knows her options and resources, because she may be the most open to exploring alternatives to staying in a violent relationship" (p. 285). Unfortunately, once the honeymoon stage begins, "the woman may be locked into another cycle, convinced that if only she tries harder the violence will end" (p. 285). Continuing with a longitudinal perspective, Worcester (1992) suggests that unless "there is intervention and a sincere commitment from the abuser to learn entirely new ways of communicating in the relationship, battering relationships tend to escalate over time" (p. 285). In this manner, the incidents of violence become more frequent and more severe, even as economic pressures serve to keep women from leaving home.

Most importantly, while encouraging health care workers to assess women for injuries that might be due to violence, Worcester (1992) offers a critical caution:

Battered women must be empowered to make their own decisions at their own pace. Outside intervention, certain behaviors, or attempts to leave at the wrong time can escalate the violence. Thirty percent of women murdered in this country are killed by the men they had loved. Most of these murders occur when women are trying to get out of a relationship. Understanding the complexities of leaving battering relationships is central to serving battered women's needs.

Health care workers seldom know the effects of their responses to battered women. Saying "You don't deserve to be treated like this" or "Here is a list of community resources" may be the medical advice that saves more lives and does more for the mental health of patients than many more medical skills. (p. 286)

The Power of a Brief Intervention: Advice on Departure

The "clean break" and "total transplant to a new community" are two survival strategies that may avoid the tragic outcome of murder of a woman who thought she had gotten away, only to be stalked and murdered. No job is that precious, no town that important, and no persuasion to stay near extended family is worth it, in retrospect, if it means the battered woman's funeral and orphaned children.

Again, it is important to keep reminding ourselves of tailor-made interventions to meet women's unique sets of circumstances. However, more of us within the community need to realize how the very briefest of interventions—verbal encouragement to leave, empathic reflection of her value, or a referral to a shelter—may set in motion a process that begins to save a woman's life. Following the work of Hester and Miller (1995), brief interventions that involve one contact with a professional or paraprofessional are increasingly being documented as effective for a range of problem behaviors. Members of the community need to feel empowered to deliver brief interventions.

SURVEY OF RECENT RESEARCH

Some data suggest that a woman's witnessing of domestic violence as a child is a more reliable predictor of battering than having experienced child abuse. In contrast, for men, abuse in the family of origin is neither a sufficient nor a necessary condition for battering his partner (Carden, 1994). Carden points out that while 20 percent to 80 percent of domestic violence cases may suggest that alcohol use and battering co-occur, the remaining 80% to 20% where there is no alcohol use with battering must be accounted for as well. Cantos, Neidig, and O'Leary (1993) investigated attributions of blame for the first and latest episodes of violence. Couples had low rates of agreement, and both men and women tended to blame the other partner at a high rate. Men were significantly more likely to blame themselves for the latest episode of violence than for the first episode of violence. Husbands who were drinking at the time of the latest episode of violence were also more likely to accept sole blame for the violence. Wives who reported having been physically abused in childhood blamed themselves more frequently for the first episode of violence than wives who had not been abused in childhood.

Is it only women who suffer from violence in the home? Cantos, Neidig, and O'Leary (1994) report that men and women may engage in similar aggressive acts and may also receive injuries. Women's injuries were related to slaps, kicks, being hit with fists, and beatings. Men's injuries, on the other hand, tended to be from thrown objects, bites, hits with fists, and threats with knives or guns. Most importantly, women live in greater fear, and a woman is more likely to receive injuries. Moreover, being hit has different physical and psychological consequences for women than for men. Women victims suffer more psychological injury in terms of psychosomatic symptoms, stress, and possibly more depressive symptomatology.

For women who had committed homicide, killing their abusive male spouses, both the woman and her murdered spouse had higher levels of alcohol consumption than did women in a shelter for battered women who had not murdered their batterers (Blount et al., 1994). These authors therefore conclude that alcohol counseling should be a significant part of programs for both battered women and for men who batter, adding to a body of literature on the role of alcohol and drugs as contribtors to homicide. Blount et al. acknowledge that women may use alcohol to nullify the pain, but it makes them more vulnerable to abuse. In addition, many factors contribute to whether or not a woman resorts to homicide, other than alcohol, such as religion, a childhood growing up with spousal abuse, and a possible cultural bias concerning shelter use—as a greater proportion of White women use shelters, according to these authors. In this manner, multiple factors operate in the development and escalation of domestic violence.

Bennett and Lawson (1994) acknowledge that research on the relationship between substance abuse and the abuse of women is a public health research priority and go on to make contributions in this area. They found that in a survey of seventy-four chemical dependency and domestic violence programs some 46 percent of male substance abusers in care were batterers, whereas 60 percent of female substance abusers were victims and 42 percent of women in domestic violence programs were found to be substance abusers. Bennett and Lawson (1994) accuse both chemical dependency treatment programs and domestic violence programs for being irresponsible in neglecting to address the issues of battering among men, and substance abuse among women, respectively. Improved assessment of clients for cross-problems is also identified as needed, while assessment and provision of interventions for cross-problems should be considered a quality-assurance issue (p. 285). Chemical dependency and domestic violence programs need to work together, for there is a need for interagency linkage, referral, and cross-programming.

Pagelow (1992) uses a large body of research evidence to debunk several myths about domestic violence. First, these are not sadistic men and masochistic women. Stereotypes of mental disturbance do not apply to the majority of abusers and victims (p. 108). Second, it is a myth that police officers who answer these calls face the greatest danger, risk of injury, and risk of death by responding to domestic violence. Actually, robberies are the most dangerous calls. Belknap and McCall (1994) provide evidence that police officers have moved beyond fear in their attitudes toward domestic violence; a full 94 percent of police officers report referring battered women to a shelter at least occasionally.

It is also a myth that women are more violent than men and that there are more male than female victims. According to Pagelow (1992), there is a preponderance of evidence showing that the vast majority of victims of spousal abuse are females, and the vast majority of abusers are male (p. 109). It is also a myth that domestic violence involves "mutual combat," since evidence shows that it is women who are typically battered; judges' use of mutual restraining orders perpetuates this myth (p. 110). A final myth that Pagelow debunks is the family "cycle of violence" that includes children. Only 25 percent to 35 percent or one out of three previously abused adults will maltreat their children, while two out of three will not abuse their children—since a history of abuse is only one risk factor out of many (Pagelow, 1992, p. 110).

Problems with Self-Report Data: Why Not Lie about Shameful Behavior?

In analyzing research findings, we must recall problems with self-reported information about drug use behavior, alcohol consumption, and sexual behavior. People often misrepresent the truth. This is likely the case with self-reports about both engaging in violent behavior and being a victim of violence. Quite simply, people are ashamed about being assaulters and victims. Who wants to admit that their partner is physically abusing them? Who wants to admit they are abusing their spouse? It is much easier to engage in denial, misrepresentation, and outright lying to avoid feelings of shame.

The Need to "Talk Around a Subject" and Build Trust

Counselors must still perform an individualized and thorough assessment, often re-asking key questions after trust has been developed. Sometimes we assume that something may be true, even when the person has outrightly answered "no" to a question. Sometimes it is culturally appropriate and better to "talk around something" and to arrive at the topic slowly and indirectly—only eliciting in this manner the disclosure of details about a behavior that causes much shame. A direct question on the same topic might result in a direct denial, while "talking around it" is tolerated as the individual "feels you out" and "warms up" to talking about a forbidden or taboo subject. The counselor's advantage in a one-on-one individualized assessment is that with increasing trust, perhaps acquired over the course of a forty-five minute interview, we may get increasingly honest responses if we respond with unconditional and consistent displays of genuine empathy (Wallace, 1991).

When Is the Delivery of Prevention Actually a Vital Intervention?

The problem of not always receiving accurate histories regarding current problem behaviors justifies why we talk about the options of delivering prevention, intervention, and treatment. Sometimes we simply do not know the answers to the following questions: What problem is already manifest and requires an active intervention or treatment? What problem is potential and requires prevention? When is the delivery of prevention actually the delivery of a vitally needed intervention? When does someone who agrees to receive primary prevention really need secondary or tertiary prevention, but is too ashamed even to admit to having the problem? And if people do not answer survey questions honestly about highly shameful issues, or answer all assessment questions in interviews honestly, then we may need to deliver the kind of prevention that serves purposes of intervention.

Finding a Significant Correlation: The Difficulty of Determining Causation

Sometimes research subjects apparently answer our survey questions honestly, but we still lack definitive answers to the problem or question under investigation. An interesting study by Wilson et al. (1992) investigated the relationships between help-seeking, learned helplessness, and severity of abuse in a sample of four groups of women. The researchers found that abused women seeking help evidenced higher levels of self-reported abuse and learned helplessness. For women who were seeking help by virtue of either residing in a shelter or attending a support group, when compared to women who were not seeking help or to a group of women not being abused, the women seeking help had higher levels of self-reported abuse and learned helplessness. Their hypothesis of increasing learned helplessness with increasing levels of abuse was supported (p. 61). Higher help-seeking groups evidenced higher levels of abuse. Shelter women reported the highest incidence of abusive behavior on the part of their spouses that resulted in medical treatment needs. Threats with weapons were also highest among shelter and support group women. Another interesting finding was that spousal abuse was not related to socioeconomic or sociocultural factors with victims in all demographic groups being victims. However, help-seeking was highly associated with minority status (and educational level, income source), since abused women from the university setting may have had other resources besides shelters and support groups. This contradicts the earlier report that more White women used shelters (Blount et al., 1994), suggesting the common problem of different research results being found with different populations and samples. Wilson et al. (1992) conclude that their correlational study may be interpreted in two ways:

The fact that levels of abuse rose with levels of learned helplessness could suggest two things. First, it is possible that women who feel less helpless are less likely to become victims of the same severity of abuse as women who feel more helpless. Second, increasingly severe abuse may result in increasing levels of helplessness. It is impossible to decide which is true given the correlational nature of the data obtained for this study. However, it appears extremely important to investigate the cause and effect direction of this relationship further, as it may lead to important and greatly differing prevention paradigms. In the meantime, it would be prudent to help women feel less helpless in general. Such an intervention would prove beneficial regardless of whether help-seeking increases the likelihood of abuse or whether abuse increases the likelihood of learned helplessness. In either scenario, decreasing women's helplessness will help them extract themselves from abusive situations. (p. 65)

Wilson et al. (1992) discuss the possibility that women who have become passive and submissive in abusive relationships and have given up on being able to help themselves may believe that escape is possible only with help from others. The women who have sought help in shelters and support groups might be seeking external help, while still feeling helpless if left to their own devices and resources (p. 66). Wilson et al. (1992) go on to speculate that women who are not seeking help may not feel helpless and may believe that they can rely upon themselves to manage or alter their abusive home situation (p. 66). What women who are seeking help from shelters and support groups may need to realize—even as they need the help they are seeking—is that they can rely on themselves "once they have removed themselves from the high-risk abusive relationship" (p. 66).

Moreover, Wilson et al. go on to explain that "it would probably be unrealistic to encourage these women to function independently of the shelter or support group prematurely, as they may first need to recover a sense of self-efficacy" (p. 66). The authors identify a noteworthy possibility below:

[I]t cannot be ruled out that seeking more help results in increased feelings of learned helplessness, in other words, that level of abuse has nothing to do with the increase in learned helplessness, but rather that both variables, i.e., *helplessness and severity of abuse both happen to increase with increased help-seeking* [italics added]. (p. 66)

MOTIVATING WOMEN THROUGH STAGES OF CHANGE, PHASES OF RECOVERY, AND RELAPSE PREVENTION: A NEW APPROACH TO DOMESTIC VIOLENCE

This section is based on my treatment of numerous individual women, couples, and abusers over the course of several years in private practice. References to "she as the abused" and "he as the abuser" are used for convenience, but sensitivity to the realities of diversity in what constitutes a "couple" is maintained. Domestic violence and the battering relationship is viewed as a problem behavior.

A recommended new approach to domestic violence involves motivating women through stages of change so they take action to change their problem behavior (DiClemente, 1991; Miller & Rollnick, 1991; Prochaska, DiClemente, & Norcross, 1992). Counselors also seek to assist women in moving through phases of recovery (Wallace, 1992) from domestic violence, as well as provide psychoeduation on how to avoid slips and relapses (Marlatt & Gordon, 1985; Wallace, 1991). In this manner, we integrate three contemporary approaches to problem behaviors and apply the emergent model to the health crisis of domestic violence.

THE STAGES OF CHANGE MODEL

Within the transtheoretical model of Prochaska and DiClemente (1982; Rollnick & Morgan, 1995; Prochaska, DiClemente, & Norcross, 1992), stages of change have been identified and research has shown how individuals may cycle through these stages several times before changing a problem behavior.

The following stages of change have been identified by these researchers:

1. **Precontemplation** *The individual is not even thinking about engaging in behavioral change.*
2. **Contemplation** *The individual is thinking about changing a problem behavior.*
3. **Determination/Preparation** *The individual has made a determination to make a behavioral change. Sometimes we also consider this stage as preparation wherein the person is preparing to make a change.*
4. **Action** *The person has actually taken the first steps and is in the process of acting to change behavior.*
5. **Maintenance** *The individual has made a change in their behavior and is trying to maintain the change.*
6. **Relapse** *The individual had changed their behavior, but has returned or had a relapse to the problem behavior.*

We can apply the Stages of Change model to the problem behavior of domestic violence and battering from the perspective of the woman being abused, the couple, or the batterer. What stage of change is she in, or are they in, or is he negotiating? How do we begin to use empathic mirroring to motivate either the woman, couple, or abuser through the stages of change?

Creating Readiness and Motivation to Change: Empathic Mirroring

Empathic mirroring (Wallace, 1991; see Chapters 4, 6) can be used to motivate someone who is not even thinking about leaving a domestic violence situation to actually prepare and take action to leave. Relapse prevention can be utilized to insure that she maintains the behavior of having left the batterer and the home. If the woman does relapse and return home, empathic mirroring or motivational enhancement may be used to move her toward thinking about leaving home again, restoring hope and instilling a sense of empowerment for this possible next step. Wallace (1991) refers to empathic mirroring, while Miller and Rollnick (1991) speak of motivational interviewing, for both works suggest an identical technique.

Four principles for creating readiness to change a problem behavior (or motivation enhancement) follow:

1. **Empathy** *Be empathic and not confrontational.*
2. **Cognitive Dissonance** *Point out discrepancies in the client's thinking or between thoughts and behavior.*
3. **Mirroring** *Reflect or mirror back to the client, after intensive listening, what she or he is saying and feeling.*
4. **Self-Determination** *Finally, ask the client what they think they should do about the problem behavior.*

Quite simply, with highly ambivalent clients who have problem behaviors but are not quite taking action on them, these techniques seem to "get people moving in the right direction—toward taking action and changing their problem behavior. This discussion also considers the difficulty of assessing which stage of change a person is actually negotiating when the trauma of abuse has split an individual into separate self-entities, as discussed in Chapter 6. Different self-entities may be in different stages of change—even as we seemingly sit and talk to just one human being.

Practical Methods of Creating Readiness to Escape Abuse or Change

The provision of basic psychoeducation and simple advice is also important. Common practical advice given to women involves making long-term plans such as accumulating a secret savings account or storing a secret set of keys to the house, and a packed bag of clothing, in case they have to run out of the house to avoid violence. A long-term plan to leave the house may involve beginning to receive education and job training in order to prepare for economic independence. Several months of rent may need to be saved, or family members lined up who will forward a loan. A woman may go through a series of practical steps to prepare to leave the home, even as she performs behaviors to avoid violent attacks while she is still in the home. The woman must surrender the use of any verbal provocation that might trigger the Act of Violence phase; she may tolerate the tension within the home by taking refuge in her practical fantasy of escape.

With secret savings and a hidden packed bag, a woman may one day suddenly run out of the house, never to return. Even though the actual day of departure may be provoked by the prospect of a beating, the woman can progressively prepare to leave over a long period of time—perhaps over three to twenty-four months.

A woman may secretly be in the preparation or action stage, even though she is still sleeping at home at night. Through psychoeducation and the delivery of simple advice, we may assist a woman in deciding to leave, preparing to leave, taking a series of action steps to leave, and struggling against urges to relapse and cancel plans (or spend secret savings). A helpful intervention is to have the woman visualize living alone and even to allow herself to walk around grieving the loss of the good things about the relationship. She should begin to go to movies alone, even secretly, in order to prepare for a loneliness she may fear.

It may also be a good idea for a woman to undergo "withdrawal" from sexual intimacy, as she prepares for a period when she will live without intimate contact with her abuser. Having prepared mentally and practically, one day she just leaves. Receiving assistance in developing a plan to leave, coping with grief reactions while still living in the home, and rehearsing separation in imagination can all be beneficial exercises. These are all highly practical methods of creating readiness to change and may be delivered by anyone as simple advice to a battered woman.

PHASES OF RECOVERY: WITHDRAWAL, PROLONGING ABSTINENCE, AND PURSUING LIFETIME RECOVERY

Consistent with both the recognition of a cycle of violence, and the different patterns of abuse that may appear, we follow a biopsychosocial approach that suggests a thorough individualized assessment across phases of recovery and treatment (Wallace, 1991, 1992). The concept of Phases of Recovery (Wallace, 1992) may be extended to the problem behavior of domestic violence. While working with a battered woman, or a couple caught up in domestic violence, or the abuser, we need to assess and observe the intricacies of their idiosyncratic pattern of abuse over time. Perhaps we observe a woman or couple in one of the following phases:

Phase I: Withdrawal Phase *The first two weeks since the last episode of violence.*
Phase II: Prolonging Abstinence *This phase spans week three up to month six, since the last episode of violence. This is a high risk period for a slip or relapse to domestic violence, and a time for acquiring new learning regarding alternative behaviors and ways of coping.*
Phase III: Pursuing Lifetime Recovery *This period covers from month seven onward. In order to continue to maintain behavior change, clients may require treatment and support for the first and second year of their recovery from domestic violence.*

Working with a Couple in a Withdrawal from Violence Phase

In a first phase of recovery and treatment, we focus on stopping the behavior of violence and ensuring the biological safety of human beings. This may be akin to a two- or several week "Withdrawal Phase" which may be full of anxiety and uncertainty. The biological healing of bruises and wounds from the last episode of violence which occurred before the treatment began may characterize this phase. The use of separation, avoidance, and "time out" are presented wherein the couple merely stops talking and each goes to separate rooms. Either member of the couple gives the "T" signal with their hands and they automatically "stop" and retreat to separate rooms. No communication about the incident is allowed until the next weekly couples session. Only basic communication is permitted—such as "goodbye, excuse me, the telephone is for you, and I need to use the bathroom to take a shower now"—in order to maintain civility in the home. This is the nature of the anxiety and tension characterizing the withdrawal phase. As soon as we start working with a couple, even in the withdrawal phase, we begin to help the couple learn and practice listening and communication skills (see Chapter 6 discussion on empathic mirroring), identifying high-risk situations for relapse, and coping effectively with these situations.

Couples Work in the "High Risk for Relapse" Phase: Prolonging Abstinence

The second phase, "Prolonging Abstinence from Violence," spans the next six months and is recognized as the highest risk period for relapse, consistent with research findings on a range of problem behaviors. The main goal is to prevent a relapse by continuing to improve the couple's communication skills and successful negotiation of high-risk situations for relapse. Whenever tension and verbal abuse or arguments begin, the "T" signal is given, time out is taken, and the incident is discussed in the next weekly counseling session. During this phase, the counselor and couple may work together in identifying a new determinant of relapse, or high-risk situation for relapse. A coping strategy is determined for this high risk situation, or communication is facilitated to resolve the argument or dispute. In this three- to six-month period where the goal is to prolong the period of abstinence from violence, communication, social, self-regulation, and self-control skills all gradually improve. Moments of good feeling in the relationship increase. Shared pleasurable activities are attempted, while some of the highest risk situations for relapse that may be idiosyncratic for that couple are still avoided, such as the couple being around her family members or the wife calling his job by telephone.

During this high-risk period for relapse, the first six months of attempting abstinence from violence, any slips or relapses are used as an opportunity to learn about idiosyncratic triggers for relapse. They are discussed in weekly counseling sessions, and coping strategies are designed, rehearsed, and implemented. Coping improves considerably during this six month period of treatment. Phone calls to the counselor may be utilized for coping during high-risk situations encountered between weekly sessions.

Couples Work in Phase Three: Pursuing Lifetime Recovery

By the time six months have passed, the couple generally experiences persistent fears of relapse to violence, as they enter the third phase of "Pursuing Lifetime Recovery from Violence." The first two years of this lifetime pursuit are the most difficult and the risk of relapse persists, although it may be somewhat diminished. The reality is that certain triggers or cues could still lead to a relapse to violence. But at this point couples may also possess renewed hope that they may be able to stay together. The woman may still have secret keys stored, a packed bag, secret funds, and an emergency departure plan. Or both may be saving money separately in case they decide things will not work out and one or the other has to move.

The couple may honestly live each day wondering whether the relationship will work out, while they both have come to accept the idea that a violent relationship is not worth having. The couple tentatively begins to discuss mutual dreams as a year passes and there have been no serious relapses to violence. Weekly counseling may stop after six months or one year, as the couple no longer is in denial and vigilantly observes their interaction—using those self-observing egos cultivated over months of counseling (see Chapters 6, 9)—to monitor how they are doing as a couple. Or a need to stay in treatment and pursue more "insurance" against relapse may prevail.

A NEW APPROACH TO RELAPSE PREVENTION: TRAUMA RESOLUTION USING THE S-O-A WORKBOOK

What if a little girl "watched on" when Daddy came home from work late and noted that he reeked from another woman's perfume, was intoxicated, her mother was enraged, and a violent fight ensued? How does this little girl react when years later her own husband comes home late, but nothing else is relevant? Could this one trigger lead her to have all sorts of expectations and fantasies that provoke arguments and violence? What if the husband were physically and verbally abused as a little boy by an alcoholic father? What if this little boy, now become a grown man, has a low tolerance for being yelled at and falsely accused of things he did not do, because that is what his father used to do? Could this grown man now become defensive, undergo a role reversal to avoid feeling small and powerless again, and attack the woman who is yelling at him?

This scenario suggests that sometimes relapse prevention against domestic violence needs to include some resolution of past trauma. It is hard to regulate your affects and impulses if your partner's behavior (arriving home late) or voice (yelling behavior) triggers you and reminds you of a past abuser from childhood. This trigger causes a regression to fixation points and projection follows, along with splitting and the performance of an intimacy permutation (see Chapters 6, 7, and 9). When a woman has been exposed as a young child to domestic violence between her parents, or when a man has been exposed to physical abuse by his father, each may have powerful cognitive expectations about violence in interpersonal interactions. Chapters 6 through 9 demonstrate how to identify, work through, and transform these cognitive expectations and to resolve the trauma of childhood abuse and overstimulation. This step may be necessary to further reduce the risk of relapse to domestic violence. Remediation of the underlying psychopathology and trauma resolution work with each member of the couple may be an important step in relapse prevention against domestic violence. This can be done in couples counseling, in individual sessions, or in group counseling.

Working with the Batterer

If just the batterer is coming to sessions, this work can be done with him (or her) as preparation for a future relationship that will be free of the violence that characterized the past relationship. Even if a woman left him, this work can permit him to have self-control and avoid a relapse to battering behavior in his next relationship. When a batterer can state to his wife that he has had six months to a year of this kind of treatment, then it may be safe for her to consider returning to the home or resuming the relationship. Ideally, couples counseling for a couple reuniting ensures avoidance of relapse to violence. For example, a man who was physically abused, choked, and punched by his father can learn that he tends to perform role reversals and places his girlfriend or wife in the position of the little boy being beaten, while he takes on the behavior of his assaultive father. It may also help to know that he tends to select women who are never pleased and for whom nothing he does is ever good enough; just as with father, his attempts to please were never good enough. This man may wisely consider a relationship with someone whom he is able to please. In retrospect, he comes to understand that he only expects bad treatment (like Daddy delivered). He tends to "link up" (enact an intimacy S-O-A permutation) with people who are going to treat him the way Daddy did, in an unsatisfactory relationship. As he undergoes trauma resolution and remediation of underlying psychopathology, he begins to prefer a woman who is not like his father, can be pleased, and finds him to be good enough. This improvement in his functioning reduces the chances of a role reversal and abuse in future interactions with women.

Working with a Lesbian Batterer and Couple

Following the same pattern, a lesbian batterer physically abused and tortured in childhood by a heroin addicted older brother, and a witness of domestic violence between alcoholic parents may tend to engage in splitting and a role reversal (see Chapter 6). A female lover may find herself suddenly being beaten, tortured, and humiliated by an abuser who is caught up in treating a new object in the manner in which the abuser was treated as a child. A moment of feeling criticized, or the affect of shame arising within, may trigger a regression to a fixation point, projection, and splitting wherein a role reversal is enacted. Meanwhile, the female lover being beaten may have an adolescent history of being physically abused by her stepfather. This female lover may suddenly find herself reenacting an intimacy permutation of her original traumatic S-O-A. Someone new, her lesbian partner, is now beating her in adulthood, just as she was in adolescence. But this violence occurs in adulthood with much more severe consequences, as the line is crossed into torturous domestic violence—with interpersonal behavioral dramas reenated that are reminiscent of the torture delivered by a heroin addict in withdrawal upon his little sister.

The Goal of Adequate Resolution of Personal Trauma

The couple learns to work out their traumatic S-O-As, discovering how their individual S-O-As set them up to enact behavioral dramas with each other. Resolution of trauma using the S-O-A workbook as a guide for individual or group counseling may serve as a powerful form of relapse prevention. If one or both partners do not work out their traumatic S-O-As and there is an overwhelming amount of past conditioning to be violent, then relapse to violence may be overdetermined and separation may be best. However, with hard work and intense and persistent resolution of trauma, an intimate relationship may not turn into a repetititon of old behavioral dramas from the past. If clients do not receive this kind of treatment (Chapters 5, 6, 8, 9), a life lived in a separate household of one's own may be preferable to a cycle of violence, possible homicide, repeated incarceration, or suicide. However, as this book seeks to make the means of producing enduring behavioral change more widely accessible, hope prevails.

Some people have egos that are sufficiently strong and intact that they may effectively "swear" that what they saw or had happen to them in childhood will never occur again in their lives; or that violence in an adolescent or adult relationship will never happen again—and, it does not. Others, however, may have egos that are heavily burdened with defenses (splitting, avoidance, denial, rationalization; see Chapter 6), and somehow just get caught up in unconsciously reenacting different versions of the traumatic S-O-As. Some lives are characterized by chronic, repetitive patterns of regression, projection, and splitting which people cannot merely "decide" to change. A decision of this kind is soon followed by repetition of the cycle of regression, projection, and splitting, again and again.

Psychoeducation of the type provided in Chapters 5, 6, and 8, as well as in this chapter, can systematically educate and strengthen the ego so that it becomes capable of behavioral change and avoidance of violence. Psychoeducation alone may be a powerful intervention that can effectively change problem behavior, especially in those with relatively strong and intact ego functioning, as Tuchfeld (1986) has also suggested. On the other hand, much more systematic psychoeducation, using the S-O-A workbook in addition to the four-phase model of group counseling (Chapter 9) or kind of counseling suggested in this chapter, may be needed by clients more prone to a relapse to violence. For those who need help in counseling and in stopping domestic violence and battering behavior, to work on their S-O-As may reduce the risk of relapse to domestic violence and battering. Couples who use the S-O-A workbook may be able to further reduce their risk of relapse by engaging in the recommended resolution of trauma, during the phase of pursuing lifetime recovery in months 6 to 12 of counseling. Or those clients with severe cases of childhood trauma may utilize the S-O-A workbook within individual counseling, working perhaps up to one, two, or three years in counseling. Not everyone who batters or is a victim of domestic violence has a traumatic childhood past. However, for those with such histories, a relapse to domestic violence may be more likely—just as relapse to chemical use is more likely for those with a traumatic childhood history within an alcoholic home (Wanck, 1985). Counseling work using the S-O-A workbook accomplishes remediation of the underlying psychopathology for those who do have histories of childhood trauma; this represents a vital form of relapse prevention.

RELAPSE PREVENTION AGAINST DOMESTIC VIOLENCE: UTILIZING THE STANDARD APPROACH

If we need not consider past childhood or family violence, we may take a more straightforward and standard approach to relapse prevention. Those with violent childhood histories also follow this standard approach to relapse prevention.

Microanalysis of Past Slips and Relapse Episodes for Determinants

Looking back on both past episodes of violence and recent slips, we engage in a microanalysis of the slip or relapse episode to learn about idiosyncratic triggers that led to a relapse or violence episode. The goal is to identify high-risk situations for relapse and determinants of relapse, many of which may be quite idiosyncratic (Marlattt & Gordon, 1985). This may proceed even if we have the woman in treatment alone, or the couple, or the male abuser. As shown in Chapter 6, classic determinants of relapse involve *painful or negative emotional states* (frustration, anger), *interpersonal conflicts or stress* (arguments over money), *environmental stimuli of people, places and things* (sitting at the dinner table), and *direct social pressure or peer pressure* to engage in a behavior (provocation such as "Hit me!" or "Don't let her disrespect you like that, man!"). Even though we utilize the standard approach to relapse prevention of a problem behavior, we may still integrate recognition of the Tension Building, Act of Violence, and Honeymoon phases, as well as Withdrawal, Prolonging Abstinence, and Pursuing Lifetime Recovery phases.

Relapse involves the role of multiple determinants that exert their influence over time (Wallace, 1991). We may think of the Tension Building Phase as a time in which multiple determinants of relapse operate. For example, the batterer may have had an especially stressful week at work—being harassed by his supervisor. On Friday evening he returns from work and sits down at the family dinner table. While trying hard to please, the wife first burns the dinner, spills a beer while opening it for her spouse, and says the wrong thing, such as "Relax," making the abuser angry. The final trigger that leads to relapse to the Act of Violence phase may be the abuser becoming intoxicated, polishing off a ninth can of beer, and deciding to rape and beat up his wife—after a week of interpersonal stress at work, feeling anger toward his wife, and six hours of drinking beer at the dinner table. In this manner, relapse to violence occurs over time and involves multiple determinants. Following Wallace (1991), a microanalysis of this relapse would identify the following determinants: interpersonal conflict, a painful emotional state, and disinhibition from alcohol intoxication. As a result, counseling may need to focus on communication skills to avoid interpersonal conflict, on helping the abuser learn to cope with anger and frustration (at home and work), and on assessing the abuser's drinking and teaching him to become a moderate drinker (Hester & Miller, 1995) or completely abstain from alcohol—depending on assessment findings.

There may be idiosyncratic triggers of relapse to violence that may be discovered in work with an individual woman, a couple, or the abuser. Identifying high-risk situations for relapse, improving communication skills, teaching coping skills so alternative behaviors may be deployed in high-risk situations, and increasing self-efficacy to cope in these situations are all important parts of relapse prevention.

Cognitive Distortions: Defenses, Seemingly Irrelevant Decisions (SIDs), and the Abstinence Violation Effect (AVE)

A woman who is in the early stages of deciding to leave or trying to leave may suffer so many cognitive distortions and symptoms of post-traumatic stress disorder that she has difficulty making good decisions. Cognitive distortions may follow from the use of denial—as just one ego defense. The abused woman somehow does not perceive danger, engages in provocation, or "sets herself up" for abuse. Or from the trauma of battering she may use other defenses, such as denial, avoidance, dissociation and splitting; she appears to have poor judgement. Self-medication with alcohol and drugs, as well as falling into states of dissociation where she just stares into space, combine to cause poor cognitive functioning and poor judgment. Her cognitive functioning can contribute to a relapse to violence.

We can also speak of her use of Seemingly Irrelevant Decisions (SIDs) that lead to her setting herself up for a relapse (Dimeff & Marlatt, 1995) to violence. For example, after going to a safe house she thinks "I will go and get my clothes," running into the batterer in the house and being held hostage and beaten some more. Or if she gets slapped, she may engage in the Abstinence Violation Effect (AVE) and provoke a full-blown relapse (Dimeff & Marlatt, 1995; Marlatt & Gordon, 1985) to violence. After the period of abstinence from violence has been violated with a slap in the face, she thinks the following: "I'm gonna break the television set. So what if he tries to beat me up, I already have my face marked up. " A slip to some violence (slap in face) can lead to a full-blown relapse to severe abuse and a horrific beating because of the AVE. (For an example of an AVE for a violent batterer, see Chapter 6.)

SIDs may operate across phases of recovery and treatment. For example, while in a withdrawal phase of the first few weeks away from the abuser and unconsciously feeling totally helpless to escape, the abused woman may think: "Why not let him know where I am and get it over with? He will show up here, drag me off, and take me home, where I know what will happen. I can't get away from him anyway. At least I know what to expect if I let him take me home. I have no idea what will happen if I leave him forever. Will I just run into another abuser? At least this one has a job." SIDs may reflect her feelings of learned helplessness. The next thing we know the abuser has the address or phone number of the safe place we created for her. She may offer a SID to which she consciously admits: "He was upset and just wanted to talk; I don't want him to kill himself and leave the kids fatherless." Meanwhile, the safe place to which the abused woman could escape for her life is no longer safe. Now the best friend, her apartment, and her safety are in jeopardy—all because the woman set herself up for relapse and re-contact with her abuser, after a SID.

In an early withdrawal phase, a second six-month phase of prolonging abstinence, or a phase of pursuing lifetime recovery—spanning one or several years—a SID may operate in setting up a relapse. A woman must learn to check out her "spontaneous good ideas" with others who can screen them for potentially being a SID that could lead to relapse. A counselor, buddy, or sponsor needs to be accessible by telephone for this process of screening.

Powerful Cues from Classical Conditioning Trigger a Relapse

The experience of being beaten, dominated, and ordered around during domestic violence is repeatedly associated with and paired with what become conditioned stimuli of the physical presence of his voice, face, and gestures. When dominated and ordered about, the woman being abused merely becomes passive and follows orders in order to survive. This is what we mean by becoming an "automaton."

Even if cognitively she has started to think about leaving, if she is exposed to a trigger of the abuser's physical presence, voice, face, and gestures she may have a conditioned response and relapse to being passive and following orders (see Figure 9.4 and point *A* in Chapter 9). The abused woman is automatically in a high-risk situation for relapse if exposed to such powerful cues. Her assaulter's voice is a powerful trigger to which the woman can experience an automatic conditioned response of behaving like a robot or an automaton.

The General and Soldier Metaphor: Conditioned Obedience

Useful psychoeducation that fosters self-observation on the part of the ego of the "automaton" or the conditioned part of her self is the General and Soldier metaphor. The abuser is the General, and she is the sturdy little soldier who is always ready to follow orders. If knocked down or nearly blown up, she gets up and is ready to follow orders again and again, marching behind him back into the bloody war zone. Like a sturdy little soldier, she keeps returning to battle, following the General's orders. She may die in battle as a result of following his orders and receiving his abuse. She is like a soldier—who is conditioned into having a functional denial of the possibilities of death—and will follow the General's order to charge up the hill into gunfire, facing death.

She may effectively be seen as relapsing to the mentality and behavior of an abused wife who is like a soldier whenever exposed to certain triggers or cues. There is both a behavioral component and a cognitive component to this relapse. If she had been thinking about and planning to leave and was coping through use of alternative behaviors to protect herself, with this kind of relapse she is an automaton (soldier) again who is locked into the cycle of violence. If in the Tension Building phase, she relapses and resumes her cognitive denial of the impending violence and performs old conditioned behaviors of pleasing, calming, and following his (the General's) orders. If she is impacted by an Act of Violence and relapses into being a conditioned automaton (soldier), she will deny her partner's responsibility for what is happening or just happened; she follows orders and is violently raped, or otherwise told what to do during the height of violence. If she is in a relapse during the Honeymoon phase she denies the severity of past abuse and the reality of future abuse while trying to be careful not to say or do the wrong thing to preserve the honeymoon. To be in a relapse is to be locked into the pattern of being an automaton who is both cognitively and behaviorally conditioned to obey the General. Denying the reality of the danger of death, as does any sturdy little soldier, she follows the General's orders no matter what.

THE TRAUMA OF DOMESTIC VIOLENCE CREATES A SPLIT SELF

There are cases where persons had no trauma in childhood that left them vulnerable for the experience of domestic violence. There are cases, too, where even if childhood and adolescent physical abuse did occur, the experience of adult battering created trauma and overstimulation in its own right. Battering by a partner is new trauma, whether or not layered on top of old trauma.

The Metaphor of a Vase Cracked or Split into Two Parts

A battered woman is like a porcelain vase cracked or split down the middle by trauma. Accordingly, the trauma of battering may be seen as cracking or splitting her into two pieces. One piece is the part of the vase getting beaten and conditioned to obey (the soldier). The second piece is being kept or preserved in a "good," rational, and sane condition—as the ego separates it through the defense of splitting from the part of the vase being hit by the abuser. The "bad" part being hit is the soldier sustaining injuries in battle, while following the General's orders. A "bad" irrational part conditioned to obey no matter what (soldier) and a "good" sane rational part result, for the woman is like a vase cracked or split down the middle. As discussed in Chapter 6, the ego may use the defense of splitting to permit survival of violence and trauma. Perhaps an adult woman does not typically fragment totally into multiple pieces the way a more vulnerable young child might. Although this is possible. A woman once reported to me that she felt herself starting to fragment during severe domestic violence, but she did not totally fragment. Typically, there is at least a split into two parts—the rational, good, valued self versus the conditioned "bad" soldier who gets muddied and bloodied in war with the General.

Opportunities to Observe the Defense of Splitting in Abused Women

After the trauma of battering, a woman may end up evidencing the defense of splitting, or after having been split she may spontaneously go from one state (soldier) to another (rational self). The woman's ego may also be able to describe how she can observe the actions and behavior of each part of her split self. One part may want to call the abuser and have dinner with him (soldier), while the other part thinks that is a crazy idea and never wants to see him again (rational self).

A trigger may lead to splitting as a defense. For example, the General calls by phone and delivers an order: "Meet me across the street from work for dinner at 5:30 p.m." This cue or trigger of his voice and order leads to splitting; the soldier suddenly appears and takes the order and verbally promises to follow it. This is a defense that permits survival because, at this point, only the soldier knows how to cope and deal with the General, that is, by taking orders and sustaining abuse. The soldier survives and so does the entire woman. To not follow an order (i.e., if her rational self came to the fore and said "You are crazy, I don't want to see you again!") might constitute poor and risky coping behavior with the General and create a real state of endangerment, unless she is in a safe and secret place. Oddly, splitting and the appearance of the "bad" part that has always suffered abuse represents a strange adaptation that we need to understand and respect as a strategy for survival.

There Is Hope for Active Coping As Survival

Instead of the woman eternally following orders like a conditioned soldier and ending up abused again and again in the cycle of violence, there is hope. We must teach the rational self how to cope, accepting support and guidance from the ego. However, the ego has a phobia and just wants to avoid and engage in denial. We must also teach the ego how to cope instead of just using the defenses of denial, avoidance, and splitting. If we teach the ego to actively cope, it can join in alliance with the rational self and help the woman avoid abuse—escaping the cycle of violence. Sometimes a woman is so conditioned and the cycle of violence has been so pernicious that it is time to just help the rational self and the ego escape.

Counselors Must Not Be Confused by Splitting Phenomena

People who reach out to an abused woman or try to help her escape the cycle of violence must be prepared to observe her suddenly transformed into a robot and an automaton (soldier). The part of her that is conditioned to respond to the abuser's voice or physical stature with an automatic obedient stance (the soldier) can relapse before our eyes in what was supposed to be "the goodbye phone call." The next thing we know plans have been made to meet the abuser—automatically responding to an order when the automaton side (soldier) is triggered by the abuser's (General's) voice. We are witnessing splitting. Counselors must not become confused, frustrated, or angry with a woman for splitting. We must appeal to her rational part and the ego. We must decrease her disillusionment with herself by explaining through psychoeducation processes of splitting, perhaps using the General and Soldier metaphor and the Split or Cracked Vase metaphor.

She may begin to observe herself being transformed into a robot (soldier). She may become disgusted with her loss of control and strict obedience when the soldier is triggered to come to the fore by contact with the abuser. The rational part of the woman is the side of her that keeps her coming to counseling and seeking help; it knows that she is in danger for her life. This is the part of her that can experientially feel and recall what the ego observed happening when she was choked, kicked, suffocated, hit, slapped, raped, tortured, and humiliated. The rational part of her self and her ego feel the danger and the need to get out of the situation to save her life. Not suprisingly, such a woman may ask herself, "Why can't I make up my mind? Why do I keep changing up?" She may not know how to interpret splitting phenomena. She may not know why she seems unable to make up her mind and stick to a decision to leave. She needs to be taught how she is transformed into an automoton or soldier when exposed to triggers associated with the General. She must understand her two parts or her two split self-entities (soldier and rational self), receiving an explanation of how she is like a cracked or split vase. She must be taught the importance of avoiding triggers of his physical person, voice, face, and gestures if she is to avoid a relapse to obedient soldier behavior.

Going back to the Wilson et al. (1992) study, if such a woman tests as high in helplessness it could be because she tried to leave, and then observed herself splitting and becoming transformed into the soldier who is conditioned to obey the General. She is totally disillusioned with herself and feels helpless, knowing more than ever that somebody had better help her because the soldier is totally out of control, responding to the triggers associated with the General. However, as counselors, *we* must not be disillusioned. We must understand just how common splitting phenomena are in this and any abused population.

Splitting As a Defense to Permit Survival

When experiencing the trauma of battering, it was an act of survival for her ego to use the defense of splitting and to split off just one part that took the abuse—like some good little, sturdy soldier. The split-off soldier obeyed, submitted, became passive, and obeyed some more. "Stand still! Get in that bed! Take off your clothes! Stop crying!" The soldier obeys and they survive, even being ordered into the honeymoon period, where they will wait and observe the tension building until the next violent episode.

A Survival Defense Gone Awry

The defense that permitted a rational part to remain safe, "good," separate, and full of good feelings, while the "bad" soldier volunteered to go on a violent mission and risk death, has now gone awry. Instead of continuing to survive by obeying the General, the escalation of violence in the home now means that to return home and follow an order could lead to real death. Instead of permitting the overall woman to survive moments of abuse, the soldier may now march the entire self into a deadly domestic violence scenario—merely by following an order delivered by the General. This is a defense now gone awry.

THE COMMON FANTASY OF THE HELPLESS AND HOPELESS: SUICIDE, HOMICIDE, AND SUICIDE/HOMICIDE

The counselor's task is to empathize with and fully appreciate the depth and extent of helplessness and hopelessness felt by the woman. Many women in domestic violence situations possess a common fantasy of ending the cycle of violence by homicide or suicide. Batterers who also are conditioned to behave as Generals may similarly sense the lack of freedom to act other than in the conditioned manner and also possess a complementary fantasy of ending it all by homicide or suicide—or as is common for some, by committing both. Couples frequently talk openly about joint suicide in an attempt to end the cycle they feel completely helpless to stop or escape. Not all homicide and suicide fantasies are acted upon, but most batterers, abused women, and couples possess these fantasies. The counselor must assess the abuser, abused, and couple for a fantasy, plan to bring about the fantasy, evaluate the probability of acting out the fantasy or plan, and ascertain whether the situation is urgent enough to warrant emergency intervention by a psychiatrist and police. Assessment findings may indicate that we are obligated to involve these personnel.

Challenging the Cognitive Distortion that There Is No Escape

We must work hard to convince the couple, abuser, or abused that there is another option, which is to leave each other and escape. The couple suffers the cognitive distortion that they cannot escape or end the cycle because they are both overconditioned to respond to each other in certain familiar ways. They may need support and assistance when one of them is removed and rescued from the situation and the cycle of violence finally ends. Sometimes a "clean break" is recommended as an escape phase is carefully planned for the battered woman who finally takes action to change.

THE ESCAPE PHASE

When we plan an escape phase, we must recognize the real threat and possibility of death, given the couple's fantasies and even plans for suicide and homicide. But if we begin to separate her from the abuser, we need to prevent the split part of her that responds like an automaton (soldier) from being exposed to triggers of the abuser's (General's) voice and physical person.

Fostering Avoidance of Triggers in the Escape Phase

Many advocate a "clean break" and not even any final phone calls. Any phone call could trigger the automaton (the soldier) and lead to a relapse to reconnection—during any phase of recovery or treatment. This is why we recommend the clean break for so many women. An escape may be the only way to prevent another abuse episode and save her life. Triggers may lead to the soldier's conditioned response of following orders and marching back to the General at home. The cycle of violence starts all over again, and there is a resumption of the tension building cycle. Cognitively, the automaton (soldier) is in denial of the impending violence, and behaviorally, she marches along following orders in an effort to please. In an escape phase from domestic violence, total avoidance of triggers associated with the abuser is essential.

Empathic Mirroring, Psychoeducation, and Active Reminders: Our Hope for Motivating Her to Escape and Recover

We may need to catch the abused woman after a battering incident, or the Act of Violence phase, as Worcester (1992) suggests. However, the therapeutic breakthrough tool of empathic mirroring is a powerful motivational technique. And psychoeducation can cultivate a self-observing ego. The use of active reminders breaks through the ego's use of denial of impending violence and the severity of past violence. With these and other tools, herein lies our hope of being able to intervene with battered women.

Use of Empathic Mirroring to Motivate

We can motivate her to enter the stage of contemplation regarding a decision to leave, to the stage of making preparations to leave, to taking action to leave, to maintaining and sticking with the behavior change of having left, or we can motivate her out of relapse and to think about leaving again. Too many women who leave a ninety-day battered women's shelter relapse and decide to go back home. They may become resigned precontemplators (DiClemente, 1991) and not even think about leaving again, feeling especially helpless after seeking help resulted in no fundamental or real change, just a three-month vacation. These women will require special efforts to motivate them to consider leaving again. We have to be able to instill a sense of hope in a group of women documented to have profound levels of helplessness and, likely, an associated hopelessness. They may lack faith in themselves and trust in what they say because they have observed how they are triggered into automaton behavior when they are near their abuser.

We can use empathic mirroring or motivational interviewing to appeal to the battered woman at any point in the cycle of violence (Tension Building, Act Of Violence, Honeymoon) or at any point in the stages of change (Precontemplation, Contemplation, Determination/Preparation, Action, Maintenance, Relapse). During any part of the cycle, or when in any stage of change, we can appeal to the part of her that is her "rational self" and is in alliance with her ego. With empathic mirroring we can move beyond her denial of (1) the impending violence; (2) her partner's responsibility for the violence; and (3) the severity of the abuse and the reality of future abuse. We gently reflect back to her the facts of her past bruises, current bruises, and likelihood of future bruises and even death. The counselor or outreach worker gently reflects back to her the fantasy of suicide/homicide and contrasts this with her knowledge of other options. We use this empathic mirroring to reflect back her genuine worth and potential to take good care of herself and her children again. We gently "plug her back in emotionally" (Wallace, 1991) so that she can feel her own pain and become motivated to do something about ending this pain through constructive acts of good self-care—of which we convince her she is quite capable.

If empathic mirroring works with ambivalent crack dependent clients who are denying the pain associated with their addiction (Wallace, 1991), we can use it to achieve empathy with women in pain from abuse, battering, feelings of helplessness, fear, and fantasies of death, homicide, or suicide. We can ever so gently reflect back to her that part of herself that is in severe pain over the abuse and maltreatment. We can gently hold up a mirror and reflect back to her the pain and facts of her abuse, and contrast it with her beauty, intelligence, and competence. We can create cognitive dissonance by pointing out the discrepancy between her feelings of helplessness, being trapped, and cognitions that "I can't leave, or I am not ready to leave," with the facts that she is competent, can take care of her self and her children, and has already taken steps to change. As women see these loving reflections of their inner pain and their actual strengths held up to them and reflected back to them in a mirror, their motivation to change increases. They move beyond denial toward either thinking about leaving, determining or preparing to leave, taking action to leave, and strengthening their motivation to maintain the behavior of leaving/having left. Or if they have relapsed/returned, they begin thinking about leaving again. We accomplish these changes, depending on the stage where the woman is when we greet her and begin to engage in outreach to her, and, depending on her unique situation with requirements for an individualized and tailored approach.

Cultivation of a Self-Observing Ego with Empathic Mirroring and Psychoeducation

The ego develops the ability to self-observe through empathic mirroring and psychoeducation. We strengthen the ego and encourage the ego to observe what they both feel inside and the facts of their competence. We use psychoeducation to systematically educate the part of herself (the ego) that engages in self-observation. By means of psychoeducation, empathic mirroring, and active reminders of the past history of her violent relationship, we get the rational part of her self and the part of her ego that has seen and witnessed the abuse to grow stronger. She feels empathy for the soldier who is bloody and tired of war. She embraces and loves this part, beginning the process of healing the split down her middle.

The Use of Active Reminders As Flooding and Desensitization

The ego wants to take the easy way out and just deny the possibility of abuse. The ego never wants to face anything it is afraid of in reality; the ego has a well-hidden phobia, or fear, of anything associated with past trauma and wants to avoid. The ego is afraid of abuse and violence. Classic treatment techniques for adults suffering from a phobia may be utilized—behavioral flooding and systematic desensitization. We want the ego to surrender the use of denial and avoidance, and to be able to tolerate our delivering active reminders and descriptions of what their own ego saw in past abuse, using her exact words and descriptions. We do not intend to be confrontational, but desire to enhance her motivation to enter into taking action on her problem. However, we matter of factly refer to her own descriptions of what she has in reality experienced within the trauma of domestic violence. This serves as both an active reminder of why she should not return and it initiates the work of trauma resolution—work that technically should begin in later months of recovery for survivors of past childhood trauma. However, because domestic violence is typically adult trauma, a woman's ego can tolerate much earlier in recovery—even in an escape phase—graphic descriptions and active reminders of her past injuries and beatings. The ego prefers denial and avoidance of these "facts," but counselors should use active reminders to flood the ego into feeling anxiety, forcing the ego to make contact with the freightening "facts" of past violence.

Usually anxiety causes the ego to use the defense of avoidance and denial—effectively ending any conversation with her about leaving her spouse. Cognitive distortion reigns and the woman might try to convince us that there is no problem with violence at home. Our repeated use of active reminders prevents the ego from engaging in cognitive distortion, serves to deliver many trials of flooding which place the ego in contact with feared scenes of past violence, and effectively desensitizes the ego. Consistent with the principles of flooding, the counselor, neighbor, or best friend selects the most horrific epidoses of violence and most severe injuries as the material covered when delivering active reminders—facts previously described by the woman and delivered to her using her exact words. As a result of the process of flooding and desensitization, using active reminders, the woman can no longer engage in the denial of past violence, severity of violence, and reality of impending violence. We also create cognitive dissonance by pointing out the discrepancy between her present behavior of acting as if there is no severe problem and prior statements regarding her battering and injuries. Consistent with our principles for creating readiness to change or enhancing motivation, we may be able to assist the woman in moving toward taking action on her problem of domestic violence.

A Psychoeducational Metaphor: Why Duck Plates When You Can Move into a Safe Fort?

The counselor may still strategically play into the ego's need for control and avoidance, as we seek to enhance her motivation to leave. We want the ego to become aware of more effective and elaborate strategies to avoid, no longer splitting or sending the soldier off to suffer more abuse in war. We tell the ego through psychoeducation about defensive strategies that are much more elaborate and more likely to afford protection to the part of the self that is still rational and good and that it seeks to protect. We tell the ego: "don't just duck and pretend like a plate did not just fly by your head, instead, let's move into a fort and make sure getting hit in the head by a flying plate is no longer an option."

We empower the ego to avoid relapse by telling it to watch out for the other part of the self that is still in precontemplation and overconditioned to obey. We tell the ego the following: "Now, if you don't want to have to duck from plates anymore, and like the plan for moving into a fort where no more plates will ever be thrown, please do this: watch the part of the self that is the robotic, automaton, sturdy little soldier like a hawk. When that soldier part starts trying to manipulate the rest of you and wants to call or go visit the General (abuser), cut them off at every twist and turn." These kinds of elaborate metaphorical instructions to the ego may empower the ego to utilize its predilection for defense in battle. The side of her that is irrational, stuck in precontemplation, and conditioned to respond like an automaton or soldier must be watched closely for relapse.

CONCLUSION

This chapter provides advanced training for counselors who may work with the battered, the couple caught up in domestic violence, or the batterer. In this work, we must recognize that we use empathic mirroring at different times with different parts of the split self in order to motivate each part through the stages of change. We go beyond starting where the client is, and we start where each part of the split self is to be found. One part (the rational self) is in preparation, or action, or relapse, and another part is in precontemplation (soldier). We work to move the rational part of the self into the action stage, help it stay in maintenance, and prevent it from falling into relapse. We do this by helping the ego to recognize sabotage attempts on the part of the soldier and by teaching the ego active coping with triggers to relapse. Next, we use empathic mirroring with the soldier part of the self to move it to the action stage. Eventually, the soldier merges with the rational self and is glad to be taken care of by the protective ego. The soldier self is now relieved that the ego is starting to use good judgment and good self-care, instead of splitting and pushing forward the soldier to cope with abuse. The soldier self is thereby eventually joined with the rational self in the action or maintenance stage. But at first we are exasperated when the soldier self seems hopelessly stuck in the precontemplation stage.

Having used psychoeducation to explain the batterer (General) as a trigger, splitting as a defense (appearance of soldier), and ways to avoid this trigger (no phone calls, or visual contact), we increase her self-efficacy and assist her in realizing that there is hope she can change and get free of her abuser. The counselor assists the woman in appreciating that there are other options besides being trapped, and homicide and suicide. Her sense of helplessness decreases.

Hence, we must recognize a high-risk period for relapse that may span several months or a year, consistent with other problem behaviors (Marlatt & Gordon, 1985; Wallace, 1991). The ego and counselor must remain vigilant for attempts by the irrational self (soldier) to set up an opportunity to relapse as the General orders: "Come home, I need you. I'm sorry. It will never happen again." If the soldier hears this promise and order from the General, she may obey and go home. Counseling and sources of support for the ego are therefore needed for a prolonged period of recovery from battering, perhaps spanning one year or more.

Other people must be used for support and assistance in all decision making during the high-risk period for relapse during the first year or so away from the batterer. Other auxiliary egos (counselors, neighbors, friends) can help her ego realize that a plan to visit her mother-in-law on Christmas day is a sure "set-up." The woman states, "But we have exchanged gifts like that for years!" The battered woman in recovery may need help discerning this and other idiosyncratic high-risk situations that may put her in contact, accidentally or coincidentally, with the General where she may hear an order and be vulnerable to relapse. The next thing you know they are spending New Year's Eve togther and moving back in together. This is an example of a Seemingly Irrelevant Decision (SID) playing a role in relapse (Dimeff & Marlatt, 1995). Even after a period of separation when all seems to be going smoothly, a woman may have a relapse to a SID, and to dangerous behavior as well.

We help her make decisions, monitor her decisions, and cut her off at the pass, again and again. Her ego begins to help us, and we feel relief and increasing hope of enduring behavioral change. Certainly, an empowerment model is called for, and her self-efficacy must rise as she comes to believe she can take care of herself—replacing any past feelings of helplessness. However, in early stages of recovery from battering, there is a high-risk period for relapse, including the rescue and escape period. Just as with other problem behaviors, this spans the first six months.

If the ego is supported by counselors and others, then it can get help and direction: "What typically happens when you see him? What does he tend to trigger in you when you see him? Did you remember stating that you need to stay away from him in order to stay alive? What do you think will happen if you go by the house to pick up the rest of your things and he is there?" We need to be available by telephone as counselors, friends, sponsors, and members of her support network to ask questions that permit the woman to verbally remind herself of the process that occurs within her experience of being battered. Our questions guide her into a state of cognitive dissonance, as she sees the contradiction between her cognitions: "I want to go by the house, but I know there is a chance he will trigger me into acting like a soldier, and that I may be beaten to death." Next, we ask her the critical question that permits her to engage in self-determination and increase in her sense of self-efficacy, while her sense of helplessnes decreases: "What do you think you should do?" The ego that was about to set her up to experience the abuser's voice as a trigger for reenactment of compulsive obedience (splitting, appearance of the soldier) is therefore "cut off at the pass" and prevented from making a SID that would have led to relapse. We question her judgment continually because it is the judgment of a person suffering from the aftermath of trauma and cognitive distortions. However, we do this by asking her questions that permit her to hear aloud her very own words which contradict her distorted view of the high-risk situation. We use our egos and deploy empathic mirroring to strengthen her ego as she engages in self-determination and feels empowered in making good decisons to keep her safe.

11

Conclusion: Two Case Histories, a Description of Group Process, and Future Directions in Research

This chapter presents the case of Mr. O. and Ms. L. to illustrate the process of a drug and alcohol recovery discussion group held in a nursing home serving end-stage AIDS clients. Finally, future directions in research within the area of community mental health promotion are recommended.

TWO CASE HISTORIES AND DESCRIPTION OF A GROUP PROCESS

The room was still as Mr. O. sat in his wheelchair facing the wall on his side of the room. He was just sitting, not particularly looking at anything. As I approached him from behind I thought to myself how he was only dressed in an open-back hospital gown, a diaper, and socks. I asked, "Mr. O. do you want to go to group today?" He responded, "Yeah, I want to go." Moving in front of him and bending down, I said "Let me put your feet on the foot rest," knowing he lacked the strength to lift them off the floor himself. As I grabbed his frail, thin-as-a-rail legs, I thought how they had diminished in size since, as an already thin ambulatory man, Mr. O. had arrived at the nursing home exactly three months ago at age 44. Bony knees rounded out the legs I lifted, as I turned and manipulated the wheelchair foot rest and leg support into place. As I reached for his left leg and foot it seemed that his gray and day-glow-orange trimmed sweat socks swallowed his feet that no longer filled them. I wondered what the brownish stain on the top of his left sock might be, as I gently placed his foot on the foot rest and moved his leg against the leg support. Slowly and gently, I lifted the wheelchair and turned it toward the door of his nursing home room, and we proceeded down the long hallway to the group room. I was so glad Mr. O. was able to go to group today.

My thoughts wandered back to the Friday before when Mr. O. was so weak and disoriented that he could neither speak coherently nor seemed to know where he was. The mental status examination questions I asked seemed so silly. He did not answer when I asked him where he was. I decided to discontinue the assessment, while at that exact moment he called to another resident, Ms. L., in a voice that was weak and barely audible. He tried to tell her that someone was trying to get her attention. Still being helpful to others, Mr. O. knew what was going on.

Today he was having a good day, and although I knew there would be more bad days, I did not know just how many before his last day. As I traveled to work this day, Mr. O. was the only resident I thought of when I asked myself, "Who will have died when I arrive?" But Mr. O. was alive and coming to group. This was my pleasure for the day.

Toward the end of our group session, a resident mentioned that he was just trying to get used to not being incarcerated. So many come to us from prison with AIDS. He also explained that while he was in prison some of his relatives had died and he did not get to attend their funerals.

Mr O. free associated and offered, "I feel like I am dying. And, it is a very serious matter. There is nothing funny about it." The group fell silent, and an awkward moment prevailed. For nine members of a nursing home admitted for end-stage AIDS to discuss death in a drug and alcohol recovery group was too raw, too close to home. But Ms. L. could always be relied upon to respond. When Ms. L. was actively using crack cocaine and constantly hustled and engaged in the exchange of sex for money and drugs, she was not talkative at all. She announced this fact in a different recovery group last week. I wonder if her two children, living somewhere in foster care, perhaps by now adopted, were talked to by this mother before they were separated. I wonder what words they would like to hear fall from their mother's mouth if they were reunited in time, for a time? But here on the unit, this sober woman seems to be making up for the years she did not talk much when high, as her conversation and joking manner continue on a non-stop basis. I wonder if Ms. L. is taking it personally when Mr. O. says that there is "nothing funny about it"? What will she say?

Ms. L. proceeds to agree that it is a very serious matter, as she typically agrees. It is hard for me to imagine a little girl living with an alcoholic, physically abusive mother, being sexually abused by a stepfather and older cousin, and not agreeing, if agreeing means she will survive—somehow. Like so many within the drug culture she would be called a "people pleaser," but this is too simple a description of the adaptations she has made to life in order to survive. As I look at her beautiful, bright, shiny eyes, looking out from her twisted body, I wonder about the little girl who survived into an adult who could tell my fellow psychologist just three weeks ago two painful views on her life, when asked of her response to her traumatic history; Ms. L. replied, I am told, "If I had it all to do over again I would choose different parents. Or maybe I would not want to have been born at all." My mind moves from her traumatic past up to the present. I think of what else she said as this session with my colleague came to a close, "Yes, I have used humor as a defense in order to survive."

Mr. O. is sitting at full attention. His bony knees point skyward, as his balding head is diminished by his large circular eyes, staring out from a thin skeletal frame. He sits with such majesty and commands attention, as he seems to pursue a direct confrontation with the lady who laughs every hour she still breathes in life. Mr. O. repeats that it is not a laughing matter. He remarks how children make him feel so good. I know he is thinking about his own fifteen-year-old daughter and nine-year-old son, and I wonder if his ex-wife will bring them up to see him. Does anyone know how close he hovers to death? Does anyone want to say goodbye to this man before he departs this life? These are my secret thoughts, as I watch Ms. L. and wait for her rebuttal.

I offer, "You miss your children." Simple affect labeling.

"Yeah," he moans, seemingly trying to cover up regret with quiet dignity and acceptance.

Removing his hand from his mouth and betraying his slumped position with eyes closed, Mr. B. abruptly joins in. Mr B. offers, "I can't afford to look back on the past and think about what I have done, getting high and everything. I have to look forward. Every day when I can get out of bed, feed myself, and dress myself I know I am doing good. It makes me feel good when I can do for myself." I am surprised by his boldness, and I worry how Mr. O. is being made to feel by these comments since he can no longer do any of these things—at least not consistently every day. Not these days, anyway. My mind visualizes the day last Friday when I briefly fed Mr. O. and was not sure if he could even swallow. When I gave up and asked Mr. O. what was on his mind, he said he wanted to go to bed and he needed to be changed; upon my inquiry he clarified "a number two." Rolling toward the nurse's aide, shocked by the fundamentalness of his answer, the aide heard me quietly reiterate his two requests, and she began to take charge of her patient, preparing to meet the basic needs of Mr. O. Yes, this man, what was he feeling at this moment of indirect confrontation by Mr. B.?

Mr. O. sits straight as a rod, surveying each member of the group with his bright, fully open eyes. He states, "I just want somebody to talk to, that's all. I know that what I did got me in this situation."

Ms. L. quickly adds, amazing us with a few moments passing with no use of humor, "That's right, what we did got us here. Nobody told us to go out there and do what we did. If it weren't for this disease I'd be dead. Getting shot woke me up." This constant repeating of her story and decrees of gratitude serve to indirectly inform the new group member of how Ms. L.'s body got twisted and why she needs to use a walker. She is among the grateful walking wounded, having survived years of prostitution and a gunshot wound to the head. Half of her body is "dead meat," Ms. L. typically explains, but she holds back this joke today.

I think of Ms. L.'s last proclamation that "what I did got me in this situation," contrasting it with her traumatic childhood history. What is it like leaving an alcoholic physically abusive mother and sexually abusive stepfather and going to live with an aunt at age nine? What of the thought process of a child who decides to be silent about sexual abuse in that new household because she perceives that she has no place else to go? I try to visualize a little eleven-year-old girl finally just walking up to a police officer on the street and telling him she can't take the sexual abuse anymore. What was it like in the group home, being reunited with a brother already living there? As my mind lands upon a thought of parents abusing and neglecting children who are left vulnerable to addiction, I have an urge to disagree with Ms. L., but I control it. There is no time, nor is the timing right for delivery of psychoeducation on this topic. I am reminded of how I also always decide to hold back psychoeducation on what constitutes physical abuse when Ms. L. goes into her speech on how she is glad her mother beat her and how children today need discipline; the timing is never right.

Our time for group is running out. The moment has come, and I offer an interpretation with implicit affect labeling and empathic mirroring contained in the intervention. I say to Mr. O, "So you take responsibility for your past actions with dignity." He responds, "Yes, I do. That's all I can do. I have no choice."

Ms. L. quickly adds, "I really respect you for that, cause we all put ourselves here. Nobody else did it."

I add a final closing comment that is both psychoeducation and interpretation: "Well, I think we have to understand that Ms. L. had a very painful childhood and she started using humor a long time ago in order to survive it. I think we have to respect how humor has permitted her to survive with dignity."

Mr. O. gets it, for he too can recall a mean and angry mother and a father who terrorized him with physical and verbal abuse. When the high school to which he was transferred wanted him to skip a grade, his father refused this option. Mr. O. was devastated. In our assessment interview Mr. O. posed the critical question so central to his life: "How can you go from algebra back to fractions?" With a simple-minded act his father established the equation for the rest of Mr. O.'s life, as he would only reach half of his potential. That was the beginning of the end, leading directly to this day—as heroin use, then crack use, unemployment, boredom, negative expectations and accusations of relapse by his wife, actual relapse, and then loss of access to his wife and children followed. This was his trail of tears, and there are none left for this day.

Taking responsibility with dignity; the use of humor permitting one to survive with dignity.

The sound of a hammer hitting and driving the head of a nail resounds in the room. There is no more conflict or tension between Mr. O. and Ms. L.

Ms. L. exclaims, "Dr. Wallace, Your eyes are red!" She seems shocked. Why did she have to announce it so loudly? I am so relieved that the group is over and that my eyes are simply red and swollen with tears held back. What a tremendous personal victory in the heat of battle did I just win, as the tears did not fall. My state of empathy with Mr. O.'s pain was so genuine, and so real, as I felt his inner self longing for and missing his children. I heard the secret message that because of all that he had done he had to accept that no one would be by his bedside in the last days before death when family members enact the traditional gathering ritual. In this ritual, all of the people who regularly visited and those too scared or too busy to come to the nursing home surround that frail figure, typically wearing oxygen mask with chin pointed north, as chest heaves up and down, gasping for the last breaths—sometimes for days or hours. Death then knocks at the door, sometimes with family still around, or with the lonely figure enclosed behind four walls. Eyes wide open, staring blankly, signal the patient's standing at the portal to death. Can they hear me? Are they coherent? Are they hallucinating? How would Mr. O. be at that moment? Would he hear my voice? Will I be able to talk to him and soothe his soul before his spirit takes flight out of a broken body?

I felt profound respect for this 44-year-old man sitting in a diaper who was able to accept the idea like a noble and brave soldier in battle both that death was coming and that he had to take responsibility for every decison he ever made up to this point in time. He had to take responsibility for all that resulted in his ex-wife's refusal to allow his children to be by his side when he died. I knew he would pay any price to hold his daughter and son one last time in physical reality, while his imagination lingered over the image of their smiles. Through empathic mirroring, I chose to reflect back and point out with interpretation the affect of respect he also felt for his life path, refusing to linger over feelings of regret. Mr. B. had felt this too, when he spoke of how he could not look back to his own past with regret.

Somehow as I wheeled this man out of the group room, asking him where he wanted to go, I knew that I would be the one to talk to him, going in his room every once in a while. Mr. O. decided he wanted to go to the day room, as I wheeled him up to a table near the television set and his peers. Departing to get a clean white sheet, I folded it, standing by his side. As I placed the sheet over his legs and feet, Mr. O. stared ahead with dignity and a sense of expectation. I thought of what he had said to me last Friday when I struggled to place his feet on the wheelchair foot rest: "It's your job." At that time I wondered if he was cognizant enough to realize I was not a nurse, but Dr. Wallace, his psychologist. Today he was aware and accepted the sheet placement without a thank you being offered. This was not narcissism; or was it? To me it seemed a purple heart for courage in battle dangled from his breast, as I gladly performed a simple gesture—an act of kindness—to make him comfortable.

It had been an exceptionally good group. And, for Mr. O., it was a good day.

STORY AS METAPHOR AND THE INTENT OF THE BOOK

Story is metaphor, and it seems appropriate to end this book with this tale of an actual group process on an end-stage AIDS unit. This book has attempted to prepare a volunteer army corps willing to engage in outreach to individuals such as Mr. O. and Ms. L., for they represent the masses of children, adolescents, and adults possessing critical needs at this time of overlapping crack and other drug, violence, and HIV/AIDS epidemics—that metaphorically create our contemporary war. At a poignant moment, we witness poised and dignified characters awaiting the end of long and painful roads marked by a lifetime of trauma. Whether childhood abuse and neglect, adolescent abuse, adult trauma in the violent crack culture, or the trauma of hitting rock bottom as children are lost to foster care, and families are lost because of personal loss of control, trauma is conveyed in this tale. However, both Mr. O. and Ms. L. needed interventions during childhood, adolescence, and young adulthood. At age 44 and 35, respectively, this group is "too little, too late."

All too often on the end-stage AIDS unit, I cannot engage in thorough individualized assessments. Sensitivity demands that I tread lightly when short- and long-term memory begin to fail. Are the cognitive deficits clients possess from the years of intense substance abuse or from an HIV disease-related-dementia (Gillen et al., 1991; Kovner et al., 1992)? So many thin faces twist and become contorted, as clients wonder inside, "Why ask me this? What difference does it make? I am tired."

But a multitude of questions flood my mind. What are the answers to the questions I cannot ask? Are these end-stage AIDS patients just like a former inpatient crack cocaine dependent population where nine out of ten were from dysfunctional families and a third experienced immigration or migration trauma involving separation from and feelings of abandonment by parents (Wallace, 1991)? Were their parents migrants from the South or immigrants from a foreign shore? Or were their grandparents, great-grandparents, or ancestors also migrants and immigrants? Have historical stressors impacted their families' lives so that in their parents' generation a rationale existed for alcoholism and child abuse? Will children being raised in foster care away from a crack cocaine dependent prostitute and children kept away from a polydrug dependent father with AIDS serve to break generational cycles of family dysfunction? Do the children of Mr. O. and Ms. L. have any idea of the trauma suffered by their drug dependent parents in childhood within dysfunctional families? Do these children know that Mr. O. and Ms. L. recreated dysfunctional family dynamics, unintentionally harming their own children in this generation? Are Ms. L.'s children or Mr. O.'s child and adolescent receiving any interventions to address their at-risk status? Are any of us willing and trained to deliver services to their children and adolescents, as well as to the multitudes like them who will be survivors of deceased soldiers who wore invisible purple hearts on an end-stage AIDS unit before they died?

OFFERING HOPE IN A HANDBOOK

This book provides a handbook and training for those engaged in counseling and outreach. While the group process depicted in this metaphoric tale involves those who will soon die, the handbook prepares a volunteer army corps to enter the heat of battle and work in the trenches with children, adolescents, and adults for whom the hope of behavioral change means breaking generational cycles of family dysfunction well into the twenty-first century. Psychoeducational curricula train counselors and our overall specialized army corps, while they may also be delivered in group settings to parents, community members, students, professionals and paraprofessionals. A model of trauma resolution in groups has been conveyed in practical terms, having also provided integrated theory and graphic and visual training models as preparation for this sacred work. It is sacred work when we realize that we are responding as a volunteer army corps at a time when few are willing to engage in outreach to a forgotten and disdained population, but it is work that urgently needs to be done. At-risk youth and adults left ill-equipped to cope need access to culturally competent counselors and outreach workers who can both perceive and build upon their inherent strengths as survivors of trauma. They need to be empowered to engage in self-determination of their own behavior and may benefit from assistance in changing deeply engrained patterns of action.

The proposed use of the Self-Object-Affect + Mobilized Drive unit and graphic model of the mind provide innovative tools for training counselors. While the training offered in this book is intended for a diverse audience, the creative use of metaphor has permitted making complex theory and a sophisticated counseling technique accessible to an audience who may feel sufficiently empowered to engage in the work of prevention, intervention, and treatment for community mental health promotion. The hope is that many of us will enter the trenches, perhaps using this handbook as a guide and finding that it offers some assistance in the process of outreach to community members in need of mental health promotion. Paraprofessionals and professionals exposed to this training may overall emerge as more competent in assessing the impact of trauma and violence, and in managing their aftermath, meeting a vital training need—as this book provides the training and tools for this task.

FUTURE RESEARCH DIRECTIONS IN COMMUNITY MENTAL HEALTH PROMOTION

The psychoeducation and group counseling models described in this book to accomplish fundamental affective, cognitive, and behavioral change have not been evalauted in formal outcome evaluation research. However, a variety of recommendations may be offered for future research in the area of community mental health promotion. Alliances between schools of public health, academics, researchers, professionals, and community-based agencies may permit evaluation of programs impelmented for prevention, intervention, and treatment of a range of problem behaviors (Lashof, 1994; Thomas et al., 1994).

IMPLEMENTATION AND EVALUATION OF VIOLENCE AND TRAUMA PREVENTION MODELS

If the violence prevention models were to be implemented in a school or community, and partnerships were formed throughout that community to ensure a widespread response to the public health crisis of violence, impact on a community might be assessed by examining the rates of homicides, assaults, and episodes of school violence in that community for any pattern of decline, following the work of Davidson et al. (1994). These researchers examined the period 1988 through 1991 and sought to assess the impact of an injury prevention program in Harlem. Similarly, a widespread response and psychoeducational campaign for the promotion of mental health might target sexual, physical abuse, and domestic violence; this would constitute prevention against trauma. Media campaigns, along with schools and churches offering psychoeducational interventions in groups, might effectively result in a decline of reported cases, perhaps after an initial increase, as awareness among community members translates into higher reporting rates when the program is introduced. Higher referrals to and rates of utilization of a range of community mental health services might also result. There is a need to facilitate greater utilization of mental health services (Padgett et al., 1994) and communitywide outreach and mental health promotion might impact utilization rates.

If we seek to address the needs of children, adolescents, and adults from dysfunctional families who have been injured by trauma, violence, and overlapping epidemics, then we may implement communitywide interventions. Research that assesses the impact of a communitywide intervention, perhaps including the use of focused media campaigns targeted to the community, may justify continuation, replication, and expansion of community mental health promotion efforts. Given the relationship between mental health status and morbidity and mortality (Vogt et al., 1994), it becomes important to facilitate greater use of mental health services, perhaps utilizing media campaigns and communitywide approaches.

Other more focused research might compare longitudinally child and adolescent outcomes among a cohort who receive school-based prevention, intervention, and treatment through the academic year-long violence prevention curriculum, meeting once per week in the school setting (Chapters 5 and 6). Compared to a control group, do children and adolescents exposed to the curriculum have fewer suspensions, expulsions, physical fights, and incidents of weapon carrying during subsequent academic years? Perhaps a sixth grade cohort is compared to a control group upon followup throughout the high school years. Over the long term, is there a lower incidence of assault, arrests, or self-reported interpersonal, gang, and community violence?

EVALUATING THE RELAPSE PREVENTION MODELS AGAINST VIOLENCE

The relapse prevention models for violence and domestic violence presented in Chapters 6 and 10 could also be implemented and empirically evaluated. However, research design would have to be sufficiently sophisticated in measuring any slips or relapses to violence that are followed by a return to stable functioning. For example, dichotomous responses of "yes" or "no" in terms of the presence of the violent behavior during a followup period might be too simplistic in research that appreciates the complexity of the process of behavioral change as it occurs over time and typically includes slips. State-of-the-art approaches to research in the field of relapse prevention would need to be followed (Donovan and Marlatt, 1988; Wilson, 1992), permitting investigation of the multideterminants of relapse, process of relapse as it occurs over time, and the emergence of learning curves over time that illustrate increased self-efficacy in exhibiting a new pattern of behavior.

Tailoring and Evaluating Relapse Prevention Models for Adolescent and Adult Sexuality and HIV/AIDS Transmission

The model of relapse prevention against violent behavior pesented in Chapter 6 may also be extended to adolescent sexual behavior. Group models of primary, secondary, and tertiary prevention may follow Chapters 5 and 6, delivering tailor-made programs for specific age groups and for problems such as inconsistent use of birth control, teenage pregnancy, combined alcohol/drug use and risky sexual practices, sexually transmitted diseases, and HIV/AIDS among adolescents (Flanigan et al., 1990; Joyce & Mocan, 1990; Kearon, 1990; Lowry et al., 1994; Minter, 1990; Phinney et al., 1990; Romer et al., 1994;

Wattleson, 1990; Weinman, 1990). Adolescent and adult women need to be empowered to assert the need for use of condoms and to engage in sexual decision making, despite a variety of pressures (Fullilove et al, 1990; Pete & Desantis, 1990); and group models that use microanalysis of relapse episodes to noncondom use and permit the rehearsal of cognitive and behavioral coping strategies may be modeled after Chapter 6, merely changing the focus to other problem behaviors such as high-risk sexual practices. After tailoring and designing the program for a specific problem behavior, research may explore program efficacy, examining within the research sample rates of pregnancy, abortion, sexually transmitted diseases, and HIV/AIDS.

Children and adolescents who have lost parents to AIDS, such as those of Mr. O., are among the large ranks of schoolchildren and community members who need to be empowered to protect themselves against the acquisition of HIV/AIDS. While school boards across the nation wrestle with the ethics of more or less explicit sexuality and HIV/AIDS education, generational cycles involving death from HIV/AIDS need to be prevented. This book has attempted to make the methods and means of behavioral change available through psychoeducation to school, church, and community-based populations. For even younger children and older adults, we may seek to tailor appropriate primary, secondary, and tertiary HIV/AIDS prevention, following Chapters 5 and 6. Most importantly, models of relapse prevention against a return to noncondom use or risky sexual practices may be designed for younger children or adults.

The tremendous diversity to be found among those who need tailor-made prevention programs must also be appreciated. For example, adults and adolescents who are HIV positive and gay or lesbian have specific needs. In addition, we cannot deny the needs of those who continue to intermittently engage in injection drug use and require tailor-made harm reduction and relapse prevention programs that are community-based and provide culturally sensitive interventions; just as relapse prevention is utilized with moderate drinking goals (Marlatt & Gordon, 1985), harm reduction approaches need to be augmented with relapse prevention. Indeed, a range of community members who have seen the devastating impact of HIV/AIDS may nonetheless require access to empowerment models that permit them to determine their own standards of behavior. For example, consider the following dilemmas: As I am determined to use injection drugs, how do I properly clean a needle if I am forced by circumstances to share injection equipment? If I am HIV positive and determined to engage in anal intercourse, how can I protect my sexual partners and avoid a relapse to noncondom use? If we face reality, then we may engage in community outreach to diverse members of our community and provide access to tailor-made empowerment models that assist community members in engaging in self-determination of standards of behavior. A vital need exists for innovative means of protecting communities from the spread of HIV/AIDS (Abdul-Quadar et al., 1992; Mandell et al., 1994; Pivnick et al., 1994; Tortu et al., 1994; Vlahov et al., 1994). Researchers will have to evaluate emergent models so that the effective models are disseminated in the literature and replicated by others, enabling a larger community to benefit from findings.

RESEARCH EVALUATING THE MODEL OF PSYCHOEDUCATION ON HEALTHY PARENTING BEHAVIOR

Might a cohort of parents exposed to the psychoeducational curriculum on healthy parenting behavior and how to avoid abuse and neglect be followed over a period of time and compared to a control group for rates of involvement with agencies addressing child abuse/neglect complaints and also for self-reported patterns of abuse and neglect? Does exposure to the psychoeducational curriculum effectively assist parents in realizing a new standard of childcare? A school might make the curriculum available to a group of parents permitting comparison to a control group of parents not exposed, with followup of each group.

Or a smaller, more focused study might randomly select a sample from those engaged in family preservation projects (Chamberlain et al., 1992; Cimmarusti, 1992; Pecora, Fraser, & Haapala, 1992) and augment interventions by social workers with exposure to the psychoeducational curriculum on healthy parenting behavior. Would comparison to a control group not exposed to the curriculum reveal children in the experimental group manifesting more signs of resiliency upon followup? Can parents actually change parenting behavior "midstream," as suggested in Chapter 4, and emerge as capable of producing a more resilient or invulnerable child, despite some prior at-risk status? The psychoeducational curriculum on healthy parenting behavior might find a role in longitudinal research within the area of resiliency and invulnerability (Anthony & Cohler, 1987; Herrenkohl, Herrenkohl, & Egolf, 1994). Elements of healthy parenting behavior identified in Chapter 4 might also assist in selecting variables for investigation in this area when trying to discern factors contributing to the emergence of the resilient or invulnerable child.

EVALUATING THE FOUR-PHASE MODEL OF GROUP COUNSELING

Within other research, a therapeutic community might implement the four-phase model of group counseling and compare it to a standard group treatment and an additional control group, in an effort to assess the efficacy of the proposed model for trauma resolution. Or, in any outpatient or residential setting we might compare this model of trauma resolution and implementation of the four-phase model to a standard treatment or control group. Does the group exposed to the four-phase model achieve greater success in maintaining relationships, regaining child custody, avoiding reports of child abuse/neglect, experiencing fewer arrests, having fewer relapses to problem behaviors, or present less symptom substitution to a range of compulsive or destructive behaviors?

GRASSROOTS RESEARCHERS EMPOWERED TO CONDUCT INVESTIGATIONS

Suggestions have also been offered throughout this book for future research, touching upon the need to value quantitative and qualitative methods. For example, consistent with an empowerment model, groups may engage in their own research which is based on the microanalysis of determinants of relapse and high-risk situations for a particular problem behavior such as a relapse to school or gang violence. Dissemination of findings and of creative interventions to prevent relapse to a particular problem behavior may follow, as "each one teaches one" within the community. In this manner, this book has embodied the goal of empowering community members who have suffered trauma within dysfunctional families and within school and communities plagued by violence. The research process may be demystified sufficiently that community members feel empowered to engage in grassroots research.

Qualitative Research and the Collection of Focus Group Data

As we encourage group members to discuss their beliefs regarding violent behavioral practices, qualitative focus group data may also be obtained that may augment the existing literature. The concept of health beliefs on violence has been introduced. Focus group data may permit us to acquire knowledge of cultural and ethnic patterns of health beliefs, following Pappas (1994), while health beliefs on violence may specifically be explored. I have collected pilot-study data from focus groups and more structured surveys, revealing the personal possession and attribution to others of a range of health beliefs, with many identifying health beliefs on violence rooted in family, religious, and ethnic group experiences. Further pursuit of this kind of research may stimulate growth and maturation in the field of violence, as it is needed, following the view of Christoffel (1994). Group discussions following the curriculum in Chapter 5 may also produce invaluable focus group data on prevalent health beliefs on violence held by different populations—whether school students, gang members, or community members of various ages. A range of future research investigations may therefore arise from the psychoeducational and therapeutic group models presented in this book.

CONCLUSION

With the dawning of the twenty-first century, and the setting of the sun in the lives of individuals such as Mr. O. who embodies the reality of overlapping epidemics of crack and other drugs, violence, and HIV/AIDS, we offer hope. When we work with the dying or their progeny, perhaps we will perceive the invisible purple hearts dangling from their breasts. We must remember that each client and his or her descendants deserve to be ministered to with cultural competence and compassion. Ideally, clients interact with one also competent in delivering the recommended interventions of affect labeling, empathic mirroring, cognitive restructuring, and interpretation. Most importantly, all interventions should be delivered with genuine empathy and deep respect for clients who have survived war conditions. Given lifetimes of multiple and chronic trauma, beginning with childhood development within dysfunctional families, this is what they deserve and this is what this handbook has sought to compel a specialized volunteer army corps to deliver.

References

Abdul-Quadar, A. S., Des Jarlais, D. C., Tross, S., McCoy, E., Morales, G., & Velez, I. (1992). "Outreach to Injecting Drug Users and Female Sexual Partners of Drug Users on the Lower East Side of New York City. " *British Journal of Addiction* 87: 681–688.

Ackerman, R. J. (1987). *Same House Different Homes: Why Adult Children of Alcoholics Are Not All The Same*. Pompano Beach, Fla.: Health Publications.

———(1986). "Alcoholism and the Family." In R. J. Ackerman, ed., *Growing in the Shadow: Children of Alcoholics*, Pompano Beach, Fla,: Health Publications.

Anthony, E. J., & Cohler, B. J., eds. (1987). *The Invulnerable Child*. New York: Guilford Press.

Astemborski, J., Vlahov, D., Warren, D., Solomon, L., & Nelson, K. E., (1994). "The Trading of Sex for Drugs or Money and HIV Seropositivity among Female Intraveous Drug Users." *American Journal of Public Health* 84, No. 3: 382–387.

Baker, A., & Dixon, J. (1991). "Motivational Interviewing for HIV Risk Reduction," In W. R. Miller and S. Rollnick, eds., *Motivational Interviewing: Preparing People To Change Addictive Behavior*. New York: Guilford.

Bailey, C. (1991). September, Personal Communication. New York.

Belknap, J., & McCall, K. D. (1994). "Woman Battering And Police Referrals." *Journal of Criminal Justice* 22, No. 3: 223–236.

Bennett, L., & Lawson, M. (1994). "Barriers to Cooperation Between Domestic-Violence and Substance-Abuse Programs." *Journal of Contemporary Human Services* 75, No. 5: 277–286.

Berger, D. M. (1987). *Clinical Empathy*, New York: Jason Aronson.

Berman, C. (1991). *Adult Children of Divorce Speak Out About Growing Up with and Moving Beyond Parental Divorce*. New York: Simon & Schuster.

Billingsley, A. (1968). *Black Families in White America*. Englewood Cliffs, N.J.: Prentice Hall.

Black, C. (1990). *Double Duty.* New York: Ballantine.

———(1985). *Repeat After Me.* Denver, Colo: M.A.C.

———(1981). *It Will Never Happen to Me: Children of Alcoholics As Youngsters, Adolescents, Adults.* Denver, Colo.: M.A.C.

Blount, W. R., Silverman, I. J., Sellers, C. S., & Seese, R. A. (1994). "Alcohol And Drug Use Among Women Who Kill, Abused Women Who Don't, And Their Abusers." *Journal of Drug Issues* 24 No. 2: 165–177.

Blume, E. S. (1990). *Secret Survivors: Uncovering Incest and Its Aftereffects in Women.* New York: John Wiley & Sons.

Blumenthal, R. (1992). "Bystanders Increasingly in Crossfire: Turf Battles Endanger Residents, Police Say." *New York Times* August 31, B1, 3.

Blumstein, A. (1994, June). "Youth Violence, Firearms, and Illicit Drug Markets." Pittsburgh: Carnegie Mellon University, The Heinz School.

Bollerud, K. (1990). "A Model for the Treatment of Trauma-Related Syndromes among Chemically Dependent Inpatient Women." *Journal of Substance Abuse Treatment* 7: 83–87.

Bonacich, E. (1987). "A Theory of Ethnic Antagonism: The Split Labor Market" In R. Takaki, ed., *From Different Shores: Perspectives on Race and Ethnicity in America.* New York: Oxford University Press.

Boyd-Franklin, N. (1989). *Black Families In Therapy: A Multisystems Approach.* New York: Guilford Press.

Bradshaw, J. (1995). *Family Secrets: What You Don't Know Can Hurt You.* New York: Bantum Books.

——— (1990). *Homecoming.* New York: Bantam Books.

———(1988). *Healing the Shame That Binds You.* Pompano Beach, Fls.: Health Communications.

Brown, R. I. F., (1989). "Relapses from a Gambling Perspective." In M. Gossop, ed., *Relapse and Addictive Behaviour.* New York: Tavistock/Routledge.

Brown, S. (1991). "Children of Chemically Dependent Parents: A Theoretical Crossroads." In T. M. Rivinus, ed., *Children of Chemically Dependent Parents: Multiperspectives from the Cutting Edge.* New York: Brunner/Mazel.

———(1988). *Treating Adult Children of Alcoholics: A Developmental Perspective.* New York: Wiley & Sons.

Brown, S. & Beletsis, S. (1986). "The development of family transference in groups for the adult children of alcoholics." *International Journal of Group Psychotherapy* 36, No.1: 97–114.

Cantos, A. L., Neidig, P. H., & O'Leary, K. D. (1994). "Injuries of Women and Men in a Treatment Program for Domestic Violence." *Journal of Family Violence* 9, No. 2: 113–124.

———(1993). "Men and Women's Attributions of Blame for Domestic Violence." *Journal of Family Violence* 8, No. 4: 289–302.

Carden, A. D. (1994). "Wife Abuse and the Wife Abuser: Review and Recommendations." *The Counseling Psychologist* 22, No 4.: 539–582.

Carlson, R. G. & Siegal, H. A. (1991). "The Crack Life: An Ethnographic Overview of Crack Use and Sexual Behavior among African-Americans in a Mid-West Metropolitan City." *Journal of Psychoactive Drugs* 23, No. 1: 11–20.

Carnes, P. (1991). *Don't Call It Love: Recovery from Sexual Addiction.* New York: Bantam Books.

Centers For Disease Control (1994a). "Homicides Among 15–19-Year-Old Males—United States, 1963–1991." *MMWR* 43, No. 40: 725–727.

———(1994b). "Adolescent Homicide—Fulton County, Georgia, 1988–1992." *MWR* 43, No. 40: 728–730.

———(1992). "Health Objectives for the Nation: Behaviors Related to Unintentional and Intentional Injuries among High School Students—United States, 1991." *MMWR* 41: 760–772.

Cermak, T. (1988). *A Time to Heal: The Road to Recovery for Adult Children of Alcoholics.* J. P. Tarcher.

Chamberlain, P., Moreland, S., & Reid, K. (1992). "Enhanced Services and Stipends for Foster Parents: Effects on Retention Rates and Outcomes for Children." *Child Welfare* No 5: 387–401.

Children of Alcoholics Foundation. (1986). *Report of the Conference on Research Needs and Opportunities for Children of Alcoholics.* New York: Children of Alcoholics Foundation.

Christoffel, K. K. (1994). "Editorial: Reducing Violence—How Do We Proceed?" *American Journal of Public Health* 84, No. 4: 539–541.

Cimmarusti, R. A. (1992). "Family Preservation Practice Based upon a MultiSystems Approach." *Child Welfare* No. 3: 214–256.

Clark, M. & Jette, N. (1991) "Short-Term Psychoeducational Group for Adult Children of Alcoholics: Catalyst for Change." In T. M. Rivinus, ed., *Children of Chemically Dependent Parents: Multiperspectives from the Cutting Edge.* New York: Brunner/Mazel.

Comer, J. P. (1980). *School Power: Implications of an Intervention Project.* New York: The Free Press.

Cooper, C. S., Dunst, C. J., & Vance, S. D. (1990). "The Effect of Social Support on Adolescenct Mothers' Styles of Parent-Child Interaction As Measured on Three Separate Occasions." *Adolescence* No. 97: 49–57.

Corbin, R. M. (1986). *1,999 Facts about Blacks: A Sourcebook of African-American Accomplishment.* Beckham House Publishers.

Cork, M. (1969). *The Forgotten Children.* Toronto: Addiction Research Foundation.

Cotten, N. U., Resnick, J., Browne, D. C., Martin, S. L., McCarrager, D. R., & Woods, J. (1994). "Aggression and Fighting Behavior among African-American Adolescents: Individual and Family Factors." *American Journal of Public Health* 84, No. 4: 618–622.

Cummings, C., Gordon, J., & Marlatt, G. A. (1980). "Strategies of Prevention and Prediction." In W. R. Miller, ed., *The Addictive Behaviors.* Oxford: Pergamon Press.

Curtis, P. A. (1990). "The Consequences of Acculturation to Service Delivery and Research with Hispanic Families." *Child and Adolescent Social Work* 7, No. 2: 147–159.

Davidson, L. L., Durkin, M. S., Kuhn, L., O'Connor, P., Barlow, B., & Heagarty, M. C. (1994). "The Impact of the Safe Kids/Healthy Neighborhoods Injury Prevention Program in Harlem, 1988 through 1991." *American Journal of Public Health* 84, No. 5: 580–586.

Davis, L. V., Hagen, J. L., Early, T. J. (1994). "Social Services for Battered Women: Are They Adequate, Accessible, and Appropriate?" *Social Work* 39, No. 6: 695–704.

Derby, K. (1992)."Some Difficulties in the Treatment of Character Disordered Addicts," In B. C. Wallace, ed., *The Chemically Dependent: Phases of Treatment and Recovery.* New York: Brunner/Mazel.

Des Jarlais D. C. (1992). "The First and Second Decades of AIDS among Injecting Drug Users." *British Journal of Addiction* 87: 347–353.

DiClemente, C. C. (1991). "Motivational Interviewing and the Stages of Change." In W. R. Miller and S. Rollnick, eds., *Motivational Interviewing: Preparing People to Change Addictive Behavior.*" New York: Guilford Press. pp. 187–201.

Dimeff, L. A., & Marlatt, G. A. (1995). "Relapse Prevention," In R. K. Hester & W. R. Miller, eds., *Handbook of Alcoholism Treatment Approaches: Effective Alternatives,* 2nd ed. Needham Heights, Mass.: Allyn & Bacon.

Dinnerstein, L., Nichols, R. L., Reimers, D. M. (1990). *Natives and Strangers: Blacks, Indians, and Immigrants in America.* New York: Oxford University Press.

Donovan, D. M., & Marlatt, G. A., eds. (1988). *Assessment of Addictive Behaviors.* New York: Guilford Press.

Drake, G. (1991). "Chair's Dinner Address." First Annual Summit on Crack Cocaine, September 20. Riverside General Hospital, Houston, Tex.

Durant, R. H., Cadedhead, C., Pendergrast, R. A., Slavens, G., & Linder, C. W. (1994). "Factors Associated with the Use of Violence among Urban Black Adolescents." *American Journal of Public Health* 84, No. 4: 612–617.

Fanon, F. (1967). *Black Skin, White Masks.* New York: Grove Press.

Flanigan, B., McLean, A., Hall C., & Propp, V. (1990). "Alcohol Use As a Situational Influence on Young Women's Pregnancy Risk-Taking Behaviors." *Adolescence* No. 97: 205–214.

Freud, S. (1917). *Introductory Lectures on Psychoanalysis.* James Strachey, Trans. and ed., 1966. New York: W. W. Norton.

Fullilove, M., Fullilove, R., Haynes, K., & Gross, S. (1990). "Black Women and AIDS Prevention: A View Towards Understanding the Gender Rules." *Journal of Sex Research* 27: 47–64.

Garcia, M. T. (1987). "Americanization and the Mexican Immigrant, 1880–1930." In R. Takaki, ed., *From Different Shores: Perspectives on Race and Ethnicity in America.* New York: Oxford University Press.

Gillen, R. W., Kranzler, H. R., Kadden, R. M., & Weidenman, M. A. (1991). "Utility of a Brief Cognitive Screening Instrument in Substance Abuse Patients: Initial Investigation." *Journal of Substance Abuse Treatment* 8: 247–251.

Gladstein, J., & Slater, E. J. (1988). "Inner City Teenagers' Exposure to Violence: A Prevalence Study." *Md Medical Journal* 37: 951–954.

Glanz, K. Lewis, F. M. & Rimer, B. K., eds. (1990). *Health Behavior and Health Education: Theory, Research and Practice.* San Francisco: Jossey-Bass.

Goedert, J. J., & Cote, T. R. (1994). "Editorial: Public Health Interventions to Reduce Pediatric AIDS." *American Journal of Public Health* 84, No. 7. 1065–1067.

Gossop, M., ed. (1989). *Relapse and Addictive Behaviour.* New York: Tavistock/Routledge.

Grier, W. H. & Cobbs, P. M. (1968). *Black Rage.* New York: Basic Books.

Grove, D. J. & Panzer, B. I. (1991). *Resolving Traumatic Memories: Metaphors and Symbols in Psychotherapy*. New York: Irvington Publishers.

Guinta, M. A., & Allegrante, J. P. (1992). "The President's Committee on Health Education: A 20-Year Retrospective on Its Policies and Policy Impact." *American Journal of Public Health* 82, No. 7.: 1033–1041.

Halfon, N. (1989). "Intervention, Treatment, & Policy." A Presentation at the Drug-Free Pregnancy Conference, December 8, San Mateo, Calif.

Hamilton, N. G. (1988). *Self and Others: Object Relations Theory in Practice*. New York: Jason Aronson.

Harris-Offutt, R. (1992). "Cultural Factors in the Assessment and Treatment of African-American Addicts: Africentric Considerations." In B. C. Wallace, ed., *The Chemically Dependent: Phases of Treatment and Recovery*, New York: Brunner/Mazel. pp. 289–297.

Hawkins, D. F. (1990a). "Black Homicide—A Public Health Crisis." *Journal of Interpersonal Violence* 5, No 2: 147–150.

———(1990b). "Explaining the Black Homicide Rate." *Journal of Interpersonal Violence* 5, No. 2: 151–163.

Haugaard, J. J., & Repucci, N. D. (1988). *The Sexual Abuse of Children*. San Francisco: Jossey-Bass.

Heather, N. (1995). "Brief Intervention Strategies." In R. K. Hester & W. R. Miller, eds. *Handbook of Alcoholism Treatment Approaches Effective Alternatives*, 2nd ed. Needham Heights, Mass.: Allyn & Bacon.

Herman, J. L. (1992). *Trauma and Recovery: The Aftermath of Violence—From Domestic Abuse to Political Terror*. New York: Basic Books.

Herrenkohl, E. C., Herrenkohl, R. C., & Egolf, B. (1994). "Resilient Early School-Age Children from Maltreating Homes: Outcomes in Late Adolescence." *American Journal of Public Health* 84, No. 4: 301–309.

Hester, R. K. & Bien, T. (1995). "Brief Treatment." In A. M. Washton, ed., *Pscyhotherapy and Substance Abuse: A Practitioners' Handbook*. New York: Guilford Press.

Hester, R. K., & Miller, W. R., eds. (1995). *Handbook of Alcoholism Treatment Approaches: Effective Alternatives*, 2nd ed. Needham, Mass.: Allyn & Bacon.

Higham, J. (1987). "Strangers in the Land: Nativism and Nationalism." In R. Takaki, ed., *From Different Shores: Perspectives on Race and Ethnicity in America*. New York: Oxford University Press.

Hill, R. (1972). *The Strengths of Black Families*. New York: Emerson-Hall.

Hunter, M. (1990). *The Sexually Abused Male. Volume 1: Prevalence, Impact and Treatment*. Lexington, Mass.: Lexington Books.

Ifill, G. (1992). "Tenacity and Change In a Son of the South: William Jefferson Clinton." *New York Times,* July 16, pp. A1, A16.

Inciardi, J., Lockwood, D., & Pottieger, A. E. (1993). *Women and Crack Cocaine*. New York: Macmillan.

Johnson, K. (1989). *Trauma in the Lives of Children: Crisis and Stress Management Techniques for Counselors and Other Professionals*. Claremont, Calif.: Hunter House.

Jones, C. (1994). "An Act of Youthful Savagery Stuns a Suburb." *New York Times,* pp. 1, 9.

Jordan, W. (1987). "First Impressions: Libidinous Blacks." In R. Takaki, ed., *From Different Shores: Perspectives on Race and Ethnicity in America*. New York: Oxford University Press.

Joyce, T. J., Mocan, N. H. (1990). "The Impact of Legalized Abortion on Adolescent Childbearing in New York City." *American Journal of Public Health* 80, No. 3: 273–278.

Jung, C. G. (1969a). *The Structure & Dynamics of the Psyche*. 2nd ed. Princeton, N.J.: Princeton University Press.

———(1969b). *The Archetype and the Collective Unconscious*. 2nd ed. Princeton, N.J.: Princeton University Press.

Kaye, E. (1991, August). "The End of the Line: From Dallas to Los Angeles to Chappaquiddick to Palm Beach, It's Been a Tumultuous and Tragic Ride for a Nation and It's Royal Family." *Esquire*, pp. 92–96, 98, 100, 102, 126.

Kearon, W. G. (1990). "Deinstitutionalization, Street Children, and the Coming AIDS Epidemic in the Adolescent Population." *Juvenile and Family Court Journal,* pp. 9–18.

Kernberg, O. (1976). *Object Relations Theory and Clinical Psychoanalysis*. New York: Jason Aronson.

Khantzian, E. J. (1985). "On the Psychological Predisposition for Opiate and Stimulant Dependence." *Psychiatry Letter*, III, 1.

Kitchens, J. A. (1991). *Understanding and Treating Codependence*. Englewood Cliffs, New Jersey: Prentice Hall.

Klein, M. W., Maxson, C. L., & Cunningham, L. C. (1991). "Crack, Street Gangs, and Violence." *Criminology* 29, No 4: 623–650.

Kochanek, K. D., Maurer, J. D., & Rosenberg, H. M., (1994). "Why Did Black Life Expectancy Decline from 1984 through 1989 in the United States?" *American Journal of Public Health* 84, No. 6: 938–944.

Kohut, H. (1977). *The Restoration of the Self*. New York: International Universities Press.

———(1971). *The Analysis of the Self: A Systematic Approach to the Psychoanalytic Treatment of Narcissistic Personality Disturbance*. New York: International Universities Press.

Kovner, R., Lazar, J. W., Lesser, M., Perecman, E., Kaplan, M. H., Hainline, B., & Napolitano, B. (1992). "Use of the Dementia Rating Scale as a Test for Neuropsychological Dysfunction in HIV-Positive IV Drug Abusers." *Journal of Substance Abuse Treatment* 9: 133–137.

Landry, D. (1994, December). "A Novel Peptide: Research on Antibody-Catalyzed Degradation of Cocaine." *Monograph of the Chemical Dependency Research Working Group* No. 1: 21–22.

Lashof, J. C. (1994). "Editorial: Building Partnerships for Healthy Communities—The Role of the Academic Health Center." *American Journal of Public Health* 84, No. 7: 1070–1076.

Laurent, M. (1995, June). Personal Communication. New York.

———(1994, September). Personal Communication. New York.

Levine, H. B. (1990). *Adult Analysis and Childhood Sexual Abuse*. Hillsdale, N.J.: Analytic Press.

Levin, J. D. (1987). *Treatment of Alcoholism and Other Addictions: A Self-Psychology Approach.* New York: Jason Aronson.

Lewin, T. (1995). "Creating Fathers Out of Men with Children." *New York Times,* pp. A1–A20.

Light, I. (1987). "Ethnic Enterprise in America: Japanese, Chinese, and Blacks." In R. Takaki, ed., *From Different Shores: Perspectives on Race and Ethnicity in America.* New York: Oxford University Press.

Loo, C. & Ong, P. (1987). "Slaying Demons with a Sewing Needle: Feminist Issues for Chinatown's Women." In R. Takaki, ed., *From Different Shores: Perspectives on Race and Ethnicity in America.* New York: Oxford University Press.

Lowry, R., Holtzman, D., Truman, B., Kann, L., Collins, J. L., & Kolbe, L. J. (1994). "Substance Use and HIV-Related Sexual Behaviors among U.S. High School Students: Are They Related?" *American Journal of Public Health* 84, No. 7: 1116–1120.

Mandell, W., Vlahov, D., Latkin, C., Oziemkowska, M., & Cohn, S. (1994). "Correlates of Needle Sharing among Injection Drug Users." *American Journal of Public Health* 84, No. 6: 920–923.

Marlatt, G. A., & Gordon, J. R. (1985). *Relapse Prevention.* New York: Guilford Press.

Masson, J. M. (1984). *The Assault On Truth.* New York: Farrar, Strauss, Giroux.

McAdoo, H. P. ed. (1981). *Black Families.* Beverly Hills, Calif.: Sage.

McGrady, B. S. & Delaney, S. I. (1995) "Self-Help Groups." In R. K. Hester & W. R. Miller, ed., *Handbook of Alcoholism Treatment Approaches: Effective Alternatives.* 2nd ed. Needham Heights, Mass.: Allyn & Bacon.

Miller, W. R. & Rollnick S., eds. (1991). *Motivational Interviewing: Preparing People To Change Addictive Behavior.* New York: Guilford Press.

Miller, W. R. (1995). "Increasing Motivation for Change." In R. K. Hester & W. R. Miller, ed., *Handbook of Alcoholism Treatment Approaches:Effective Alternatives,* 2nd ed. Needham Heights, Mass.: Allyn & Bacon.

Milner, J. S., Robertson, K. R., & Rogers, D. L. (1990). "Childhood History of Abuse and Adult Child Abuse Potential." *Journal of Family Violence.* 5, No. 1: 15–34.

Minkler, M., Roe, K. R., & Robertson-Beckley, R. (1994). "Raising Grandchildren from Crack-Cocaine Households: Effects on Family and Friendship Ties of African-American Women." *American Journal of Orthopsychiatry* 64, No. 1: 20–29.

Minter, P. (1990). "Teen Talk: Peer Groups Addressing Teen Pregnancy."*American Journal of Public Health* 80, No. 3: 349–350.

Moss, A. R., & Vranizan, K. (1992). "Charting the Epidemic: The Case Study of HIV Screening of Injecting Drug Users in San Francisco, 1985–1990." *British Journal of Addiction* 87: 467–471.

Moynihan, D. P. (1965). *The Negro Family: The case for National Action.* Washington, D.C.: U. S. Department of Labor.

Padgett, D. K., Patrick, C., Burns, B. J., & Schlesinger, H. J. (1994). "Ethnicity and the Use of Outpatient Mental Health Services in a National Insured Population." *American Journal of Public Health* 84, No. 2: 222–226.

Pagelow, M. D. (1992). "Adult Victims of Domestic Violence." *Journal of Interpersonal Violence* 7, No. 1: 87–120.

Pappas, G. (1994). "Elucidating the Relationship Between Race, Socioeconomic Status and Health." *American Journal of Public Health* 84, No. 6: 892–893.

Pavlov, I. P. (1927). *Conditioned Reflexes*. G. V. Anrep, Trans. London: Oxford University Press.

Pecora, P. J., Fraser, M. W., & Haapala, D. A. (1992). "Intensive Home-Based Family Preservation Services: An Update from the FIT Project." *Child Welfare* No. 2: 177–188.

Pence, E. & Paymar, M. (1986). "Power and Control: Tactics of Men Who Batter: An Educational Curriculum." Available from the Minnesota Program Development, 206 West Fourth St., Duluth, Minn. 55806.

Perez-Stable, E., Marin, G., Marin, B. V. (1994). "Behavioral Risk Factors: A Comparison of Latinos and Non-Latinos in San Francisco." *American Journal of Public Health* 84, No. 6: 971–976.

Pete, J. M., & Desantis, L. (1990) "Sexual Decision Making in Young Black Adolescent Females." *Adolescence* No. 97: 145-154.

Phinney, V. G., Jensen, L. C., Olsen, J. A., & Cundick, B. (1990). "The Relationship Between Early Development and Psychosexual Behaviors in Adolescent Females." *Adolescence* No. 98: 321–332.

Pine, F. (1990). *Drive, Ego, Object, and Self: A Synthesis for Clinical Work*. New York: Basic Books.

Pivnick, A., Jacobson, A., Eric, K., Doll, L., & Drucker, E. (1994). "AIDS, HIV Infection, and Illicit Drug Use within Inner-City Families and Social Networks." *American Journal of Public Health* 84, No. 2: 271–273.

Prochaska, J. O., & DiClemente, C. C. (1982). "Transtheoretical Therapy: Toward a More Integrative Model of Change." *Psychotherapy: Theory, Research, and Practice* 19: 276–288.

Prochaska, J. O., DiClemente, C. C., & Norcross, J. C. (1992), "In Search of How People Change: Applications to Addictive Behaviors." *American Psychologist* 47: 1102–1114.

Prothrow-Stith, D., & Weissman, M. (1991). *Deadly Consequences*. New York: Harper Collins.

Ratner, M., ed. (1993). *Crack Pipe As Pimp: An Ethnographic Investigation of Sex-For-Crack Exchanges*. Lexington, Mass.: Lexington Books.

Rivera, B., & Widom, C. S. (1990). "Childhood Victimization and Violent Offending." *Violence and Victims* 5, No. 1: 19–35.

Rivinus, T., ed. (1991). *Children of Chemically Dependent Parents: Multiperspectives from the Cutting Edge*. New York: Brunner/Mazel.

Roane, T. H. (1992). "Male Victims of Sexual Abuse: A Case Review within a Child Protective Team." *Child Welfare*, No. 3: 231–239.

Rodriguez, C. E. (1987). "Puerto Ricans and The Political Economy of New York." In R. Takaki, ed., *From Different Shores:Perspectives on Race and Ethnicity in America*. New York: Oxford University Press.

Rohsenow, D. J., Corbett, R., & Devine, D. (1988). "Molested As Children: A Hidden Contribution to Substance Abuse?" *Journal of Substance Abuse Treatment* 5: 13–18.

Rollnick, S., & Bell, A. (1991). "Brief Motivational Interviewing for Use by the Nonspecialist." In W. R. Miller and S. Rollnick, eds., *Motivational Interviewing: Preparing People To Change Addictive Behavior*. New York: Guilford Press, pp. 203–213.

Rollnick, S., & Morgan, M. (1995). "Motivational Interviewing: Increasing Readiness for Change." In A. M. Washton, ed., *Pscyhotherapy and Substance Abuse: A Practitioners' Handbook*. New York: Guilford Press.

Romer, D., Black, M., Ricardo, I., Feigelman, S., Kaljee, L., Galbraith, J., Nesbit, R., Homik, R. C., & Stanton, B. (1994). "Social Influences on the Sexual Behavior of Youth at Risk For HIV Exposure." *American Journal of Public Health* 84, No. 6: 977–985.

Rowe, C. E. & Mac Isaac, D. S. (1989). *Empathic Attunement: The Technique of Psychoanalytic Self Psychology*. New York: Jason Aronson.

Schiffer, F. (1988). "Psychotherapy of Nine Successfully Treated Cocaine Abusers: Techniques and Dynamics." *Journal of Substance Abuse Treatment* 5: 131–137.

Shakoor, B. H., & Chalmers, D. (1991). "Co-victimization of African-Ameircan Children Who Witness Violence: Effects on Cognitive, Emotional, and Behavioral Development." *Journal of the National Medical Association* 83: 233–238.

Sheline, J. L., Skipper, B. J., & Broadhead, W. E. (1994). "Risk Factors for Violent Behavior in Elementary School Boys: Have You Hugged Your Child Today?" *American Journal of Public Health* 84, No. 4: 661–663.

Shelov, S. P. (1994). "Editorial: The Children's Agenda for the 1990s and Beyond." *American Journal of Public Health* 84, No. 7: 1066–1067.

Shengold, L. (1989). *Soul Murder: The Effects of Childhood Abuse and Deprivation*. New Haven, Conn.: Yale University Press.

Sorenson, S. B., Peterson, J. G. (1994). "Traumatic Child Death and Documented Maltreatment History, Los Angeles." *American Journal of Public Health* 84, No. 4: 623–627.

Stallard, A., & Heather, N. (1989). "Relapse Prevention and AIDS Among Intravenous Drug Users." In M. Gossop, ed., *Relapse and Addictive Behaviour*. New York: Tavistock/Routledge.

Stevenson, H. C. & Abdul-Kabir, S. (1995). "Reflections of Hope from the 'Bottom': Cultural Strengths Among African American Mothers." A symposia presented at the Twelfth Annual Winter Roundtable on Cross-Cultural Psychology and Education. February 17. New York: Teachers College, Columbia University.

Sutherland, E. H. & Cressey, D. R. (1978). *Criminology*, 10th ed. Philadelphia: Lippincott.

Tabor, M.B.W. (1992). "Where the Drug Culture Rules: Neighborhoods Symbolizing City, State and National Failure." *New York Times*, October 2, pp. B1–B2.

Takaki, R., (1990). *Iron Cages: Race and Culture in 19th Century America*. New York: Oxford University Press.

————, ed. (1987). *From Different Shores: Perspectives on Race and Ethnicity in America*. New York: Oxford University Press.

Thomas, S. B., Quinn, S. C., Billingsley, A., & Caldwell, C. (1994). "The Characteristics of Northern Black Churches with Community Health Outreach Programs." *American Journal of Public Health* 84, No. 4: 575–579.

Tilden, V. P., Schmidt, T. A., Limandri, B. J., Chiodo, G. T., Garland, M. J., & Loveless, P. A. (1994). "Factors that Influence Clinicians' Assessment and Management of Family Violence." *American Journal of Public Health* 84, No. 4: 628–633.

Tortu, S., Beardsley, M., Deren, S., & Davis., W. R. (1994). "The Risk of HIV Infection in a National Sample of Women with Injection Drug-Using Partners." *American Journal of Public Health* 84, No. 8: 1243–1249.

Tuchfeld, B. S. (1986). "Adult Children of Alcoholics." *Hospital & Community Psychiatry.* No. 3: 235–236.

Vannicelli, M. (1989). *Group Psychotherapy with Adult Children of Alcoholics: Treatment Techniques and Countertransference Considerations.* New York: Guilford Press.

Vlahov, D., Ryan, C., Solomon, L., Cohn, A. S., Holt, M. R., & Akhter, M. N. (1994). "A Pilot Syringe Exchange Program in Washington D.C.." *American Journal of Public Health* 84, No. 2: 303–304.

Vogt, T., Pope, C., Mullooly, J., & Hollis, J. (1994). "Mental Health Status as a Predictor of Morbidity and Mortality." *American Journal of Public Health* 84, No. 2: 227–231.

Walker, L. E. (1979). *The Battered Woman.* New York: Harper & Row.

Wallace, B. C. (1995). "Women and Minorities in Treatment," In A. M. Washton, ed., *Psychotherapy and Substance Abuse: A Practitioners' Handbook.* New York: Guilford Press.

———(1994). "Drugs, Alcohol, and the Dysfunctional Family: Male/Female Differences," In R. R. Watson, ed., *Addictive Behaviors in Women.* Clifton, N.J.: The Humana Press.

———(1993). "Cross-Cultural Counseling with the Chemically Dependent: Preparing for Service Delivery within Our Culture of Violence." *Journal of Psychoactive Drugs* 24, No. 3:. 9–20.

———, ed. (1992). *The Chemically Dependent: Phases of Treatment and Recovery.* New York: Brunner/Mazel Inc.

———(1991). *Crack Cocaine: A Practical Treatment Approach for the Chemically Dependent.* New York: Bruner/Mazel Inc.

———(1983). "A Jungian Conceptual Framework for Adult Developmental Research and Adult Psychotherapeutic Technique." Master's Thesis. City College of the City University of New York, New York.

Wanck, B. (1985) "Treatment of Adult Children of Alcoholics." *Carrier Foundation Letter* 109: 6.

Washton, A. M. (1989). "Cocaine Abuse and Compulsive Sexuality." *Medical Aspects of Human Sexuality:* 32–39.

Watson, J. B. (1930). *Behaviorism* (rev. ed.). New York: W. W. Norton.

Wattleson, F. (1990). "Teenage Pregnancies and the Recriminalization of Abortions."*American Journal of Public Health* 80, No. 3: 269–270.

Wegscheider, S. (1981). *Another Chance: Hope and Health for the Alcoholic Family.* Palo Alto, Calif.: Science Behavior Books.

Wegscheider-Cruse, S. (1986). "From 'Reconstruction" to 'Restoration'." In R. J. Ackerman, ed., *Growing in the Shadow: Children of Alcoholics.* Pompano Beach, Fla.: Health Communications.

Weiner, L., Theut, S., Steinberg, S. M., Riekert, K. A., & Pizzo, P. A. (1994). "The HIV-Infected Child: Parental Responses and Psychosocial Implications." *American Journal of Orthopsychiatry* 64, No. 3: 485–492.

Weinman, M. L. (1990). "Sociodemographic and Maternal Behaviors In Younger and Older Pregnant Adolescents." *Child and Adolescent Social Work.* 7, No. 1: 43–51.

White, J. (1984). *The Psychology of Blacks: An Afro-American Perspective*. Englewood, Cliffs, NJ: Prentice Hall.

Widom, C. S. (1989a). "Does Violence Beget Violence? A Critical Review of the Literature." *Psychological Bulletin* 106: 3–28.

———(1989b). "The Cycle of Violence." *Science,* 244: 160–65.

Wilson, K., Vercella, R., Brems, C., Benning, D., & Renfro, N. (1992). "Levels of Learned Helplessness In Abused Women." *Women and Therapy* 13, No. 4: 53–67.

Wilson, P. H., ed. (1992). *Principles and Practice of Relapse Prevention*. New York: Guilford Press.

Winiarski, M. G. (1995). "HIV and AIDS," In A. M. Washton, ed., *Pscyhotherapy and Substance Abuse: A Practitioners' Handbook*. New York: Guilford Press.

Woititz, J. G. (1985). *Struggle for Intimacy: Dedicated to Adult Children of Alcoholics*. Pompano Beach, Fla.: Health Communications.

———(1983). *Adult Children of Alcoholics*. Pompano Beach, Fla.: Health Communications.

Worcester, N. (1992). "The Role of Health Care Workers in Responding to Battered Women." *Wisconsin Medical Journal* : 284–286.

Wood, N. P. (1990). "Black Homicide—A Public Health Crisis." *Journal of Interpersonal Violence* 5, No. 2: 147–150.

Wurmser, L. (1992). "Psychology of Compulsive Drug Use." In B. C. Wallace, ed., *The Chemically Dependent: Phases of Treatment and Recovery*. New York: Brunner/Mazel Inc.

Yates, A. (1991). *Compulsive Exercise and the Eating Disorders: Toward an Integrated Theory of Activity*. New York: Brunner/Mazel.

Young, E. B. (1995). "The Role of Incest Issues in Relapse and Recovery." In A. M. Washton, ed., *Pscyhotherapy and Substance Abuse: A Practitioner's Handbook*. New York: Guilford Press.

———(1990). "The Role of Incest Issues in Relapse." *Journal of Psychoactive Drugs* 22, No. 2: 249–258.

Zraly, K., & Swift, D. (1990). *Anorexia, Bulimia, and Compulsive Overeating: A Practical Guide for Counselors and Families*. New York: Continuum.

Index

Abdul-Kabir, S., 95
Abington Township,
    Pennsylvania, 91–92
Ackerman, R. J., 21
adult children of alcoholics
    movement, 19–20
adult children of dysfunctional
    families. *See* dysfunc-
    tional families (adult
    children of)
African-Americans: crack
    cocaine epidemic and,
    84; criminal stereotypes
    and, 90–91; family
    strengths of, 39, 40;
    flexible roles and,
    43–44; mortality rates
    and, 83–84; parenting
    behavior and, 65, 95;
    past cultural trauma and,
    36; post-slavery abuse
    of, 31; poverty and, 42;
    religious faith and, 46;
    slave trade and, 30–31;
    violence epidemic and,
    83, 84–85, 95–96, 142
AIDS/HIV. *See* epidemics,
    overlapping
Alanon, 19
Alateen, 19
Albuquerque, New Mexico, 93
Alcoholics Anonymous, 8, 12,
    19, 117
Atlanta, Georgia, 85

Barr, Roseanne, 24
Belknap, J., 252
Bennett, L., 252
Black, Claudia, 21, 22
Blount, W. R., 252
Blume, E. S., 20, 21–22
Boston, Massachusetts, 248
Boyd-Franklin, N., 39
Bradshaw, J., 22-23
Broadhead, 93
Brown, Stephanie, 21

About the Author

BARBARA C. WALLACE is Associate Professor in the Department of Health and Nutrition Education at Teachers College, Columbia University. Dr. Wallace is the author of *Crack Cocaine: A Practical Treatment Approach for the Chemically Dependent* (1991) and editor of *The Chemically Dependent: Phases of Treatment and Recovery* (1992).

ISBN 0-275-94475-1

90000>

EAN

9 780275 944759

HARDCOVER BAR CODE